01341 1152123 0

Trials of Reason

Trials of Reason

Plato and the Crafting of Philosophy

DAVID WOLFSDORF

OXFORD
UNIVERSITY PRESS

2008

OXFORD
UNIVERSITY PRESS

Oxford University Press, Inc., publishes works that further
Oxford University's objective of excellence
in research, scholarship, and education.

Oxford   New York
Auckland   Cape Town   Dar es Salaam   Hong Kong   Karachi
Kuala Lumpur   Madrid   Melbourne   Mexico City   Nairobi
New Delhi   Shanghai   Taipei   Toronto

With offices in
Argentina   Austria   Brazil   Chile   Czech Republic   France   Greece
Guatemala   Hungary   Italy   Japan   Poland   Portugal   Singapore
South Korea   Switzerland   Thailand   Turkey   Ukraine   Vietnam

Published by Oxford University Press, Inc.
198 Madison Avenue, New York, New York 10016

www.oup.com

Oxford is a registered trademark of Oxford University Press

Library of Congress Cataloging-in-Publication Data
Wolfsdorf, David, 1969–
Trials of reason : Plato and the crafting of philosophy / David Wolfsdorf.
p. cm.
Includes bibliographical references and index.
ISBN 978-0-19-532732-8
1. Plato.   2. Philosophy, Ancient.   I. Title.
B395.W8155 2007
184—dc22   2007003713

2 4 6 8 9 7 5 3 1

Printed in the United States of America
on acid-free paper

οὐ μὴν ἔστι καλλίων ὁδὸς οὐδ' ἂν γένοιτο ἧς
ἐγὼ ἐραστὴς μέν εἰμι ἀεί, πολλάκις δέ με ἤδη
διαφυγοῦσα ἔρημον καὶ ἄπορον κατέστησεν

ACKNOWLEDGMENTS

I thank the University Professors Program at Boston University; C. A. P. Ruck of the Classics Department at Boston University, who first instructed me in Latin and Greek, and K. Haynes, then a graduate student, who first oriented me in the Western humanities tradition; R. Foster, *magistro optimo* of the Università Gregoriana and the Vatican; the British School in Athens; the Herder Institut at the Universität Leipzig; the Leibnizleute and the Seminar für klassische Philologie at the Universität Heidelberg, especially G. W. Most for demonstrating the importance of and facilitating my research in the history of scholarship and *das Nachleben der Antike*; the Classics Department at the University of Chicago for allowing me the freedom to pursue philosophical studies outside of classics; M. Nussbaum, R. Kraut, E. Asmis, and the late A. W. H. Adkins; the Philosophy Department at Fairfield University, T. Regan, J. Gordon, C. Naser, K. Schwab, J. Thiel, M. Patton, and V. Rosivach, for their humanity and collegiality; the Writing Program and the Philosophy Department at Boston University, especially M. Prince, J. Walsh, K. Halil, C. Griswold, and D. Roochnik; the Philosophy Department at Temple University, and C. Dyke for encouraging my interest in Greek mathematics; the Philadelphia *philoplatonikoi*, especially A. Payne and C. Kahn; the editors of the classics and ancient philosophy journals who have published my papers; the many scholars of Plato's early dialogues from whom I have learned so much, above all G. Santas, N. Smith and T. Brickhouse, H. Benson, T. Penner, and the late G. Vlastos; and Oxford University Press, for giving this project a chance.

A number of people have sustained and inspired me at various points since I began to study Plato in earnest. I am deeply grateful to B. K. Fowler, F. Whiting, B. Gründler, A. Mori, L. Nalencz, R. E. Harder, M. Haley, R. Islam, M. Mello, M. Schuder, J. Lorenz, my brothers Ronan and Adam, and my parents Joseph Isidore and Gail Anne Wolfsdorf to whom this labor of love is dedicated.

CONTENTS

Trials of Reason

I

INTERPRETATION

1. Introduction

Trials of Reason is a study of Plato's *Apology*, *Charmides*, *Crito*, *Euthydemus*, *Euthyphro*, *Gorgias*, *Hippias Major*, *Hippias Minor*, *Ion*, *Laches*, *Lysis*, *Meno*, *Protagoras*, and *Republic* 1. These texts are widely believed to constitute Plato's early writings. It is debatable whether *Hippias Major* is spurious, as well as whether *Republic* 1 was composed independently of and significantly prior to the rest of *Republic*. It is also debatable whether other texts should be included among the early works, for instance, *Alcibiades I* and *Theages*. However, it is not crucial to this study that the whole set of early dialogues be treated. In fact, it is not crucial that the set be early. I will continue to speak of the dialogues under examination as early merely for convenience.

My justification for treating the early dialogues as a unity is not chronological, but thematic. The subject that unifies these texts is philosophy itself. Philosophy, as Plato conceives it, is a kind of motivation, the desire for knowledge, specifically for ethical knowledge, knowledge of the good. This motivation gives rise to a practice, the pursuit of ethical knowledge. How ethical knowledge is pursued depends upon how this object of desire qua form of knowledge is conceived. Plato's conception of knowledge entails that one who knows understands and that understanding requires explanation.

Plato conceives of knowledge, understanding, and explanation as things that occur in and through language, in short, as discursive. Consequently, the practice of pursuing ethical knowledge assumes the form of a kind of discourse. One attempts through discourse to achieve ethical knowledge by formulating and proposing putatively true ethical propositions and then examining and testing these to determine whether and how they are true, in other words, giving reasons for and against them. Finally, the practice of pursuing ethical knowledge itself yields particular consequences. Ideally, it yields the ethical knowledge sought;

3

however, in the early dialogues, this ideal is never achieved. Instead, all of the pursuits end in some psychological condition weaker than knowledge: in the most successful instances, well-reasoned belief; in the least successful, perplexity.

In sum, philosophy, as Plato conceived it, can be understood in three ways: primarily, as a type of motivation; secondarily, as a practice arising from this motivation; and thirdly, as the result of the practice. One's philosophy or philosophical beliefs are those with which one is left in the wake of inquiry. A glance at the table of contents will now reveal that the study is structured according to this conception of philosophy. It begins with desire, moves to knowledge, which is the object of desire, examines method, or the practice of pursuing ethical knowledge, and concludes, as the early dialogues do, with aporia.

The idea that philosophy itself is the subject that unifies the early dialogues has not been adequately understood. The most striking symptom of this misunderstanding today is the divide among scholars between treatments of these texts that focus either on the philosophical and argumentative or on the literary and dramatic dimensions of the dialogues. For example, the jacket copy introducing R. M. Dancy's recent study of Plato's early theory of Forms runs: "Scholars of Plato are divided between those who emphasize the literature of the dialogues and those who emphasize the arguments of the dialogues... [this book] focuses on the arguments."[1]

This divide is an artifact of misunderstanding, which can be transcended by appreciating that philosophy itself is dramatized in these texts. This means that Plato's early dialogues also encompass metaphilosophy. They do not merely express the results of the practice of philosophy, as most canonical philosophical texts do. They portray the need for philosophy as motivation and practice, the identity of philosophy as motivation and practice, and the difficulties of realizing philosophy with respect to motivation, practice, and goal. This first chapter is devoted to articulating a framework for interpreting the early dialogues that identifies the various kinds of dramatic elements within them and explains how Plato integrates these elements in his introduction, demonstration, and examination of philosophy.

2. Interpreting Plato

The history of the reception of Plato has been described as oscillating between two poles, doctrinal and skeptical.[2] The distinction is vague and imprecise; nonetheless, in attempting to summarize such a vast body of information, it is heuristic and convenient. Doctrinal interpretations maintain that Plato conceived of the dialogues as containing and conveying knowledge. Accordingly, such interpretations focus on the positive doctrines and conclusions that emerge from discussions in the texts. Skeptical interpretations understand Plato to be an epistemological

---

1. Dancy (2004).
2. See Press (1996).

skeptic of some kind. Accordingly, they focus on aporiai and inconclusiveness in the discussions in the texts.

Aristotle treats Plato doctrinally, as apparently did Plato's immediate successors in the Old Academy, Speusippus (347–339) and Xenocrates (339–314).[3] Skeptical interpretations arose with Arcesilaus (ca. 266–240)[4] and his successors. For example, Cicero relates that "Arcesilaus was the first who from various of Plato's books and from Socratic discourses seized with the greatest force the moral that nothing which the mind or the senses can grasp is certain."[5] Under Carneades (167–137) and his successors, the Academy maintained the impossibility of knowledge, but admitted so-called probabilism, a form of rationally justifiable positive belief. By around 90, Antiochus of Ascalon and his successors had reestablished a doctrinal interpretation against the skepticisms of the Middle Academy. Likewise, during the Roman Empire Neoplatonists such as Plotinus and Proclus treated Plato doctrinally.

During the Western Middle Ages the only widely circulating Platonic dialogue was *Timaeus*, a text that especially lends itself to doctrinal interpretation. During this period doctrinal neoplatonic interpretation reigned. Mere traces of skeptical Platonism survived through Cicero's *Academica* (composed in 45 BCE), itself informed by the Middle Academic tradition, and Augustine's *Contra Academicos* (composed in 386 CE), informed by the former. With the reintroduction of the rest of the corpus through Byzantine scholars into the West in the Quattrocento, Italian Renaissance Platonism remained doctrinal, specifically neoplatonic; and neoplatonic interpretation dominated through the sixteenth century.

In the early modern period, a range of alternative conceptions emerged. Skeptical interpretations of Plato in particular were compatible with several currents of thought: the rediscovery of Pyrrhonism and the rise of early modern skepticism, as well as fideism with its emphasis on the irrationality of divine truth. Additionally, independent thinkers such as Philipp Melanchthon (1497–1560) and Claude Fleury (1640–1723) appreciated the difficulties that the dialogues presented for establishing Platonic doctrines.

By the mid-eighteenth century, the neoplatonic interpretation of Plato was moribund. Still, doctrinal interpretation, albeit of a non-neoplatonic kind, prevailed. This period witnessed the birth of the modern historiography of philosophy with such works as Jacob Brucker's *Historia critica philosophiae* (1742–44) and Dietrich Tiedemman's *Geist der spekulativen Philosophie* (1791–97), as well as the first modern monographs on Platonic philosophy. Through the influence of rationalism, the interpretation of Plato's corpus came to be governed by the view that any philosopher worthy of the name had a system, and in the nineteenth

---

3. Note that these are the dates during which these philosophers occupied the scholarchy, that is, leadership of the Academy. All dates in the classical period are BCE unless otherwise noted.
4. During these dates Arcesilaus was scholarch.
5. *De orat.* 3.67, cited from Schofield in Algra et al. (1999) 327.

century there followed systematizations of the corpus, largely according to Kantian and Hegelian categories.[6]

With the rise of academic philology and historicism, evidence was increasingly generated in the later nineteenth and twentieth centuries to determine a more historically accurate conception of the corpus. In the nineteenth century, Germanophone scholarship in particular was preoccupied with two interpretive problems: the authenticity of the dialogues and their chronological order. Through the first three quarters of the nineteenth century, the corpus was subjected to some extreme, highly idiosyncratic athetization.[7] But especially with the rise of stylometry in the last quarter of the century,[8] the authenticated set assumed more or less the shape widely accepted today.

The rise of stylometry also corroborated the growing developmentalist conception of the organization of the corpus into early, middle, and late periods. In other words, correctly organized and understood, the dialogues bear witness to a process of intellectual development over the course of Plato's philosophical career. Developmentalism, first influentially formulated in Karl Friedrich Hermann's *Geschichte und System der platonischen Philosophie* (1839), became ascendant in the nineteenth century.

In the twentieth century, the principal debate was between developmentalists and unitarians. Unitarianism is the view that Plato's philosophical ideas essentially remained consistent throughout his life.[9] In the second half of the twentieth century, esotericism, a doctrinal interpretation first introduced in the late eighteenth century, reemerged with some force in continental Europe, especially in Germany. Esotericism is the view that Plato was committed to a mathematico-metaphysical system to which the contents of the dialogues merely allude. Accordingly, the dialogues are exoteric works, that is, they were intended as introductory or propaedeutic for an uninitiated public. In contrast, the esoteric system was reserved for the community of philosophers within the Academy. Anglophones, however, largely remained focused on the dialogues; their reception of esotericism was cool. In the last decades of the twentieth century, Anglophone Platonic scholarship was principally conducted within a developmentalist and relatively doctrinal framework.

At the beginning of the twenty-first century, among Anglophones, unitarianism is regaining adherents. The shift away from developmentalism relates to growing emphasis on Plato's artistry. It is increasingly considered naïve to assume that the contents of a given text represent Plato's views, or at least Plato's complete views on the matters discussed there. Plato could have composed individual dialogues as well as sets of dialogues, for pedagogical or didactic purposes.

---

6. My account of the early modern reception of Plato is heavily influenced by Tigerstedt (1974), (1977).
7. That is, rejection of texts as spurious.
8. Stylometry is the quantitative study of stylistic and linguistic features of the texts.
9. Observe that in principle both developmentalist and unitarian interpretations may be doctrinal or skeptical interpretations.

The present development of interest in the dramaturgical and literary dimensions of the dialogues is explicable as a response to a principal mode of exegesis to which the texts were subjected in the second half of the twentieth century. The spread of analytic philosophy, particularly within Anglophone universities during this period, to a significant degree repudiated or at least challenged the study of the history of philosophy. Overturning Whitehead's famous dictum that Western philosophy could most safely be read as a series of footnotes to Plato, early analytic papers endeavored to dispense with footnotes, on the grounds that the contributions of canonical predecessors were confused, insufficiently clear, logically or analytically wanting, and in short had been superseded by Frege, Russell, and their heirs. Plato scholars responded with heavy emphasis on the analysis of arguments in the dialogues, examining these according to standards of logic in its current state, as well as through the application of contemporary conceptual categories. The effect was either to expose the shortcomings of Plato's thought or to reveal greater subtlety in his arguments, however sound they were.

Positively, this exegetical tendency brought welcome rigor and clarity to the arguments in the dialogues. But the defect of this approach, especially in the hands of historically insensitive scholars, has been anachronism, in two respects. On the one hand, there has been misconception of the form and meaning of the arguments through importing into them logical and conceptual material foreign to the author and his times. On the other, there has been misconception of the function of the arguments and the dialogues more generally through treatment of them as though they were treatises or journal articles intended to be conclusive expressions of their author's settled opinions. Increasing attention to the dramaturgical or literary dimensions of the texts variously serves to check both tendencies. It encourages examination of arguments in relation to their dramatic contexts. For instance, arguments may be deployed ad hominem, instrumentally, or for any number of reasons other than to defend the author's thesis on a specific topic. More generally, appreciation of the very fact that Plato deploys arguments in such ways enhances understanding of the dialogues as sui generis philosophical works.

This is the state of contemporary Anglophone scholarship on Plato's dialogues. Argumentation is central to Plato's texts and the conception of philosophy in them. However, arguments are embedded in dramatic dialogues and developed through complex, largely informal dialogic exchanges between literary characters. Understanding the philosophical content of Plato's dialogues, therefore, requires understanding the relation between the dramatic and argumentative dimensions of the texts.

3. The Political Culture of Plato's Early Dialogues

Each of the early dialogues is a well-integrated drama whose centerpiece is a discussion, examination, or inquiry into a particular topic or set of interrelated topics. One topic central to several texts is the identity of excellence or a part of it. The discussions in dialogues that pursue this question are governed by a question of the form "What is F?" Hereafter, this question will be referred to as the WF question. The symbol F ranges over excellence or a part of it. For example, the question "What is holiness?" governs the discussion in *Euthyphro*. There are seven such early dialogues: *Charmides*, *Euthyphro*, *Hippias Major*, *Laches*, *Lysis*, *Meno*, and *Republic* 1. In these dialogues, F stands for sound-mindedness, holiness, fineness, courage, friendship, excellence itself, and justice, respectively.

Protagoras is also largely concerned with the identity of excellence. However, it approaches this question by considering the relation between the parts of excellence: justice, holiness, sound-mindedness, knowledge, and courage. Moreover, the examination of the relationship between the parts of excellence occurs in response to the question whether excellence is teachable, for it is assumed that determining whether excellence is teachable depends on understanding what excellence is.

The dramas of *Apology* and *Crito* more intimately depend on particular historical events than those of the other early dialogues, namely Socrates' trial and condemnation. *Apology* is concerned to defend Socrates against the accusations of impiety and corruption of the youth. In the process of making his defense, Socrates articulates his conception of the pious and socially beneficial philosophical activity that has constituted his life's work. *Crito* discusses the question whether Socrates should escape from prison before his execution and engages the broader question of the individual's relation to the state and the law.

Euthydemus contrasts the eristic style of argumentation of the brothers Dionysodorus and Euthydemus with genuinely philosophical argumentation.[10] In the process, Socrates develops protreptic arguments concerning the value of philosophy.[11] *Gorgias*, which focuses on the subject of rhetoric, also juxtaposes two kinds of discourse. The dialogue begins with a question akin to the WF question, "What is rhetoric?" It then turns to the question of the value of rhetoric. In the process, the ethical question is examined whether it is better to suffer or to do injustice; and in the process of examining this question, goodness is distinguished from pleasure. These topics are unified by the suggestion that rhetoric, as widely practiced, involves a false commitment to ethical hedonism (the identification of goodness with pleasure).

Hippias Minor examines the relationship between honesty and dishonesty, and whether it is better voluntarily or involuntarily to do wrong. Finally, *Ion* examines whether the rhapsode Ion's ability to perform Homer's epics and comment on them is a kind of knowledge.

The early dialogues treat a range of topics, and it is an important question to what extent these topics are related, because the answer implies a certain conception of the unity of the dialogues. Here the anachronisms of certain of our predecessors are heuristic. In the previous section, it was mentioned that a number of interpreters in the eighteenth and nineteenth centuries sought to systematize the corpus according to Kantian and Hegelian categories. For instance, Gottlieb

---

10. "Eristic" means "contentious." Euthydemus and Dionysodorus deliberately deploy sophistical arguments in an effort to refute their interlocutors.
11. "Protreptic," which means "serving to exhort or encourage," is often used in the context of Platonic scholarship to refer to dialogues that introduce and encourage the practice of philosophy.

Wilhelm Tenneman divides Plato's thought into epistemology, theoretical philosophy, and practical philosophy; Eduard Zeller into dialectics, physics, and ethics. More recently, Thomas Brickhouse and Nicholas Smith organize the philosophical content of the early dialogues according to subdisciples of late-twentieth-century Anglophone academic philosophy: method, epistemology, ethics, psychology, political philosophy, and theology.

Division of philosophy into subdisciplines by the Greeks postdates Plato and perhaps Aristotle. In *Topics*, Aristotle distinguishes dialectical or logical, physical, and ethical propositions, but the Stoics establish these as parts of philosophy.

Granted, there may be a number of pedagogical or expository reasons for distinguishing aspects of Plato's thought according to modern philosophical categories. But it is anachronistic to suggest that Plato conceived of his various early writings as contributions to various subdisciplines of philosophy. In other words, it is anachronistic to think that from within the conceptual horizon of the early dialogues, there are grounds for divisions of the philosophical content according to modern philosophical subdisciplines.

The early writings focus on what we now call ethical problems and problems in the epistemology of ethics. More precisely, they focus on *aretê* and its acquisition. *Aretê* is typically translated as "virtue" or "excellence." The disadvantage of "virtue" is that it specifically identifies a psychological state or condition. Excellence, like *aretê*, may be a property of animals and even inanimate objects. For instance, in *Republic* 1 Socrates speaks of the *aretê* of dogs and of horses.[12] Thus, the phrases *aretê andros* (the excellence of a man) and *anthrôpeia aretê* (human excellence) are not redundant.[13] *Aretê* is often used in the texts without qualification to refer to human excellence. But it is questionable whether human excellence is to be identified with a psychological condition. Consequently, I will translate *aretê* as "excellence" throughout.[14]

In the fifth and fourth centuries *aretê* had particular class and status connotations. For example, in *Politics* Aristotle divides the free population in a city-state (*polis*) into the ordinary citizens and the elite.[15] He distinguishes the elite according to four characteristics: wealth, nobility or good birth, education, and *aretê*.[16] Of these, *aretê* is the least concrete. It refers to the paradigmatic values and conduct of the culture of the leisure class. In the fifth and fourth centuries, out of an average citizen body of twenty to thirty thousand males over the age of eighteen both of whose parents were Athenians, the leisure class consisted of approximately twelve hundred to two thousand men whose family fortune was at

---

12. *R.* 1, 335b.
13. The phrase *andros aretê* occurs at *Prt.* 325a2; the phrase *anthrôpeia aretê* occurs at *R.* 1, 335c4.
14. Note that throughout the study the first instance of a Greek word will be followed by a translation. A list of commonly used Greek words with translations is also provided in appendix 1.
15. *Polis* is standardly translated as "city-state" on the grounds that these political bodies were as small as modern cities, but politically autonomous like states. Throughout I will use both "polis" and "city-state."
16. *Pol.* 1291b14–30.

least a talent (= 6,000 drachmas).[17] The possession of such wealth enabled these citizens to preoccupy themselves with activities such as symposia (drinking parties), homoerotic affairs, hunting, horsemanship, and frequenting gymnasia (athletic campuses) and wrestling schools, and to provide their sons with the most elaborate educations available.

Prior to the emergence of its particular form of democracy, Athens was, like most Greek city-states, oligarchic. The formal and informal exercise of political power had been a distinct privilege of the upper classes. During the democracy, this changed, but the pursuit and exercise of political power remained a central ideal of the leisure class, and the most politically influential citizens of the fourth century were, to a large extent, members of this class.[18]

In *Protagoras* Socrates identifies *aretê* as *politikê technê* (the specialized knowledge of being a citizen). Throughout, the early dialogues focus on courage, sound-mindedness, holiness, and justice as principal constituents of *aretê*. Civic and personal excellence are largely coextensive. This is because the distinctions of private and public, and so of the personal and the political, existed to a relatively limited great degree. There are several reasons for this: the Mediterranean climate and the fact that the lives of males were for the most part conducted outdoors, the relatively small size of the citizenry, and the extent to which citizens were directly involved in formal political institutions. Josiah Ober, drawing on the work of Niklas Luhmann, describes this as a relatively small degree of role differentiation between ordinary citizens and political leaders. Accordingly, the political leader tends to be judged by ordinary social values; indeed it was believed that the condition of the city-state corresponded to the character of its citizens, including its leaders.[19]

The Athenian democracy had an elaborate system of political offices. But most of these were held for only a year at a time, and aside from the role of military general, political influence did not reside in the occupation of any such office. The "politicians" of Athens were rather those individuals whose talents, education, and specifically rhetorical ability enabled them to persuade the people, above all within the city-state's sovereign political body, the Assembly (*ekklêsia*). In principle, any citizen could address the Assembly on matters of policy. But in practice only a few dozen regularly did, and, as I have noted, these leaders of the people (*dêmagôges*) were largely derived from the leisure class.

Philosophy is an intellectual and discursive discipline, competence in which requires considerable effort and time. Such time is available only to the leisure

---

17. Davies (1971).
18. Hansen (1987); Ober (1989) 112–18.
19. "The recognition that Athenian political roles were rather less differentiated from the social role of the average citizen than has often been the case in modern societies helps to explain the relative lack of interest shown by the Athenians in separating policy proposals from the individual character and behavior of the proposer, legal culpability from immoral behavior, or abstract political principles from popular ideology" (Ober, 1989, 126; Luhmann, 1982, 139–46).

class; for example, Isocrates says that its members traditionally engaged in "athletics, hunting, and philosophy."[20] Alternatively, nonwealthy practitioners of philosophy, as Socrates is portrayed, must be willing to abandon their livelihoods and live in poverty or dependence on patronage. Plato and the audience to whom the early dialogues were addressed belonged to the leisure class, and the texts are conceived in terms of its culture, particularly its political activity.

Most of the early dialogues are situated in distinctly upper-class milieus. *Charmides, Euthydemus, Laches,* and *Lysis* are set at the wrestling school of Taureas, the gymnasium of the Lyceum, an unidentified gymnasium, and the wrestling school of Miccus, respectively. The leisure class could afford the time to enjoy these social and athletic arenas as well as the expenses for the military and athletic trials and competitions related to them. *Gorgias, Hippias Minor, Protagoras,* and *Republic* 1 are set at the homes of wealthy Athenians or metics (resident aliens); Cephalus, at whose house most of *Republic* 1 is set, was one of the wealthiest metics of the fifth century, and in *Protagoras* Callias' house is described as one of the most opulent in the city. The settings of *Ion, Hippias Major,* and *Meno* are not precisely defined. But Meno is visiting Athens in the distinguished political role of an ambassador from Thessaly, and the historical Meno came from one of the wealthiest Thessalian families. Hippias is a celebrated itinerant wise man who seeks students and patrons from among wealthy Athenians. And the fact that Ion is a rhapsode from Ephesus who performs throughout the Greek city-states indicates that he belonged to a network of foreign relationships that imply an aristocratic milieu.[21] Indeed, this is true of all the itinerant *sophoi* (wise men) in the texts.

In contrast, *Apology, Crito,* and *Euthyphro* are situated in public spaces: a law-court, a prison, and the Basileic Stoa in the agora. There are, of course, good historical and dramatic reasons for these settings, but it should also be noted that Socrates' presence in these democratic locations is highly unusual. This is not simply because Socrates' trial and condemnation were unique experiences in his life. It is customary to think of the historical Socrates as engaging in philosophy principally in the agora, the geographical center of the democracy, and with whoever was willing to speak with him. But, in fact, in the early dialogues philosophy is for the most part practiced among the members of the upper class, outside of demotic spaces.

Plato conceives of philosophy as a political activity, precisely in opposition to the democratic political process as that process actually operates in the city-state.[22] Throughout the early dialogues it is argued that *aretê* is the knowledge

---

20. 7.45.

21. I am grateful to M. D. Usher for this point.

22. In principle, Socrates and Plato admire the free speech (*parrhêsia*) and open-ness to debate of the Athenian constitution. But as Socrates emphasizes in *Apology,* there is little genuine free speech or openness to debate in the city-state's political arenas. In fact, Socrates claims that if he had attempted to enter politics in a conventional way early in his life, he would have been destroyed.

that a political leader needs. Such knowledge is conceived as a *technê* (craft or expertise), which is to say, knowledge unavailable to the many and hence unavailable to the mass of ordinary citizens that constitute the *dêmos* (populus). Accordingly, the *dêmos* should not be a politically influential body. Rather, they should follow the governance of the elite, that is, the excellent ones (*aristoi*), who possess *aretê*.

In democratic Athens most of the political leaders were members of the leisure class; however, they were beholden to the will of the people. Their prominence and influence depended upon the satisfaction of the *dêmos*. As such—and this is Plato's central criticism of democracy—political leadership was dominated by rather than in control over the people. Political leaders catered to rather than cultivated the *dêmos*. As Socrates puts it in *Gorgias*, politics as practiced in Athens is a form of flattery. In contrast, Plato envisions a political system where the leader possesses a *technê* akin to an athletic trainer or horse-breeder whose guidance and care benefit his wards.

Central to the early dialogues, then, is education (*paideia*), for philosophy, as a pursuit of knowledge that constitutes *aretê*, is a form of education or cultivation of the citizen who will become a political leader. As such, the dialogues are principally populated by three kinds of character: fathers interested in the education of their sons (Lysimachus, Melesias, and Crito), male youth interested in their education and specifically in education that will enable them to become prominent citizens (Hippocrates, Charmides, Lysis, Menexenus, Ctesippus, Hippothales), and sophists who allege that they are able to educate youth to attain *aretê* (Protagoras, Gorgias, Hippias, Thrasymachus, Euthydemus, and Dionysodorus).

Philosophy (*philosophia*) as Plato conceives it in the early dialogues, then, emerges as the love, desire for, and pursuit of (*philia*) the particular kind of knowledge or wisdom (*sophia*) that the political leader or politically influential citizen ideally should possess. *Apology* develops this conception of philosophy and its value. *Protagoras* criticizes democracy and emphasizes the important of a specialized knowledge of politics. *Ion* clarifies the distinction between knowledge and the most salient traditionally conceived form of wisdom, that of the divinely inspired poet. The dialogue suggests that Ion does not in fact possess knowledge. Through investigation of the definition of excellence and its putative parts, *Charmides*, *Euthyphro*, *Hippias Major*, *Laches*, *Meno*, and *Republic* 1 pursue the knowledge that the philosopher seeks and the statesman requires. *Euthydemus* distinguishes the philosophical reasoning such investigation requires with a form of pseudophilosophy, eristic argumentation. Similarly, *Gorgias* contrasts the respective values of rhetoric and philosophy, denigrating the former and extolling the latter as a worthy political enterprise. *Hippias Minor*'s puzzle concerning voluntary wrongdoing and injustice pertains to the conceptualization of the wisdom or knowledge sought by the philosopher, specifically to the relation of this *sophia* to other forms of professional knowledge and how this relates to the psychology of action. Finally, *Crito* examines the problem of civil obedience.

This account oversimplifies the contents of the early dialogues. Nonetheless, the conception of philosophy as the desire for and pursuit of ethical knowledge, which is conceived as political knowledge, the knowledge that befits a political leader, unifies the texts.

4. Dialogue

The preceding section explains the interrelation and unity of the various early dialogues. Yet, arguably, it does so in a way that is compatible with Plato's having written philosophical treatises criticizing democracy, explaining the value of philosophy as a political activity, defining excellence, and so on. However, Plato did not write monologic treatises, but dialogues, and the question is often put why he did. In examining this question, it is important to qualify that it should not depend upon the assumption that Plato was the first to write philosophical dialogues. There is reason to believe that he wasn't. There were a number of other Socratics, that is, immediate philosophical heirs of Socrates, who wrote what Aristotle calls *sokratikoi logoi* (Socratic discourses). Some Socratics were older than Plato, and some had schools or students of their own, including schools in Athens during the time that Plato was active in the Academy. Antisthenes is a good example. He was perhaps twenty years Plato's senior, and the list of his writings extant in Diogenes Laertius' life of him is compendious. Consequently, the question why Plato wrote dialogues should not be conceived as the question why Plato invented the form of philosophical dialogue. More appropriate is the question how Plato uses the dialogue form.

A common theme pervades the early dialogues: the conflict between philosophy, as Plato conceived this, and antiphilosophy, its antithesis. Plato's conception of philosophy was defined earlier as the love, desire for, and pursuit of the kind of knowledge that the political leader needs. Since that knowledge is *aretê*, philosophy can be redescribed as the pursuit of excellence. As such, Plato's conception of philosophy is consistent with traditional Greek aristocratic values. On the other hand, Plato's conception of excellence, as well as the means to it, is distinctive. In traditional Greek aristocratic culture, *sophia* was also prized, but as one among many constituents of excellence. The early dialogues, however, argue that the value of *sophia* is distinct from and superior to all other conventionally conceived goods such as health, wealth, physical beauty, military prowess, fame, and pleasure.

Furthermore, in traditional Greek culture wisdom was valued for its practical efficacy. In contrast, the early dialogues place strong emphasis on the theoretical dimension of wisdom. As I will discuss in chapter 4, this emphasis relates to the way ethical knowledge is conceptualized as a form of understanding. Understanding entails the ability to explain what one knows, and the relevant sort of explanatory capability, in turn, justifies claims to possess that knowledge.

In accordance with the distinct epistemic conception of excellence in the early dialogues, the pursuit of excellence involves distinct means—what may vaguely be called logical reasoning or argumentation. Compare this, for example, with training in arms, which the fathers Lysimachus and Melesias consider obtaining for their sons in order to make them *aristoi*. Such training is intended to prepare the boys for military experience so that they will achieve fame and glory on the battlefield.

Antiphilosophy encompasses all that is antithetical to philosophy and includes much that is conventionally and traditionally valued in Greek culture and specifically Greek aristocratic culture. For instance, in all the early dialogues, popular values are criticized. More precisely, in the definitional dialogues and in *Protagoras*, popular conceptions of excellence and its putative parts are criticized. In *Apology* and sections of *Euthyphro* and *Gorgias*, critical remarks are made about forensic rhetoric. *Gorgias* is, on the whole, an attack on conventional political rhetoric. Epideictic rhetoric is criticized in *Protagoras* as well as *Hippias Minor* and *Gorgias*. And in *Ion* as well as *Protagoras* the poetic tradition is criticized.

Much in the early dialogues is also devoted to criticizing sophistry or pseudo-philosophy. This critique has two principal aspects. The first is the distinction of sophistry from philosophy, which constitutes Plato's well-known attempt to distinguish and legitimate the form that his particular discipline assumes in contrast to that with which the public identified it. The distinction of eristic argumentation from philosophical argumentation in *Euthydemus* is a good example. The second aspect is the association of sophistry with certain political or popular values, in particular, the pursuit of pleasure and power as conventionally conceived. Evidence for this is found especially in *Gorgias*.

In sum, all the early dialogues, albeit in various ways and by focusing on various aspects, dramatize the conflict between philosophy and antiphilosophy. The dramatization of this conflict is fundamental to their dialogicity in the sense that the texts incorporate and engage two or more distinct perspectives, systems of value, modes of discourse, and forms of life.

Ostensibly, this dialogic engagement does not occur wholly within the sphere of philosophical discourse. Rather, the physical, psychological, and, broadly, cultural settings and contexts in which the practice of philosophical inquiry occurs are the settings and contexts of conventional aristocratic, and occasionally, more broadly, demotic Greek life. For instance, in *Lysis* Socrates arrives at Miccus' wrestling school during a festival in honor of Hermes; in *Laches* Lysimachus and Melesias are judging Stesilaus' course in training in arms; in *Apology* Socrates defends himself in court against Meletus' accusations.

Philosophy emerges out of these nonphilosophical contexts, and this is significant in two respects. The first pertains to the conflict between philosophy and antiphilosophy. The emergence of philosophy within the dialogues is coupled with critique of conventional and traditional values; and it is precisely the conditions of the settings and contexts of the dialogues in which philosophy emerges that philosophy criticizes. In *Gorgias* Socrates and Chaerephon arrive at Callicles' house immediately after Gorgias' rhetorical exhibition, and Socrates proceeds to criticize rhetoric. In *Protagoras* Hippocrates seeks Socrates' help in gaining access to Protagoras' instruction, and Socrates proceeds to examine Protagoras' pedagogical competence. In *Lysis*, Socrates counters Hippothales' erotic interest in Lysis with a demonstration of how to treat boys and then with an investigation into the nature of friendship.

The second respect pertains to what may loosely be described as the philosophical-pedagogical function of the dialogues. Within the conceptual horizon of the interlocutors, philosophy has not already defined, legitimated, or established itself. The dialogues are not addressed to individuals already committed to the philosophical enterprise. Rather, a crucial part of the work of the texts is this definition, legitimization, and establishment of philosophy. Not only does the practice of philosophy within the dialogues serve to introduce this practice and to clarify its form and function, the dialogues also explicitly distinguish the discursive form of philosophical practice from others. In *Protagoras* Socrates urges Protagoras to refrain from lengthy speeches and to stick to the mode of succinct question and answer. In *Gorgias*, Socrates repeatedly distinguishes Polus' rhetorical competence from his dialectical incompetence.

The dialogues' embedding of philosophy within a more conventional cultural framework serves precisely to engage the intended audience in a familiar condition and to guide them from there into philosophy. As such, all the early dialogues are propaedeutic and protreptic. This particular pedagogical function of the dialogues is manifest in a dramaturgical feature that I call α-structure, a dramatic or discursive structure constituted by a linear sequence or progression of beliefs and values, at one pole of which lie conventional and traditional (antiphilosophical) views and values and at the other pole of which lie Platonic (philosophical) views and values. α-structures in the dialogues serve to engage the intended audience at points of conventional belief and, through critique of this, to lead the audience to novel Platonic beliefs, regardless of whether the discussions and examinations in the dialogues conclude aporetically. For instance, the investigation of courage in *Laches* begins with a conventional conception of courage as paradigmatic hoplite conduct; it advances toward an unconventional Platonic conception of courage as a state of knowledge. Similarly, the investigation of the parts of excellence in *Protagoras* begins with a conventional conception of the partition of excellence and gradually leads to the position that these putative parts are identical. More generally, *Protagoras* begins with a view of Protagoras as wise and gradually undermines this view. Likewise, *Euthydemus* and *Hippias Major* begin with views of the brothers and Hippias as wise and then undermine these. Indeed, many of the dialogues introduce authoritative figures only to undermine their authority in the course of the dialogue. In such cases, α-structures order the dramatic sequence of whole dialogues. But α-structures of more limited extent operate within the texts as well. For instance, in *Gorgias* Polus begins with the view that effective orators have great power, but as a result of his argument with Socrates it is concluded that the orators may have no power at all. Laches and Meno begin with the view that they know what courage and excellence is and that this is easy to say, but they soon realize the contrary.

The contrast between conventional or traditional opinions and unconventional Platonic views about which the dialogues are organized according to α-structure may concern specific propositions debated in the course of the investigation, but, importantly, it may also concern the grounds of or justifications for belief of those propositions. That is to say, the value of the rational justification of beliefs about excellence and its means of acquisition are often implicitly or explicitly contrasted with the following alternative grounds of belief. It is not epistemologically adequate to maintain a belief merely because the belief is common, held by the majority, traditional, or advanced by an allegedly wise person, or because it has been expressed in a rhetorically compelling manner. In other words, the early dialogues criticize conventional and traditional beliefs, but also the conventional and traditional grounds upon which beliefs are held.

In sum, Plato composed the early dialogues according to a-structure for protreptic reasons, to encourage his readers to abandon the antiphilosophical life for the philosophical life. He addressed his intended audience in the doxastic position in which they stood,[23] committed to conventional and traditional beliefs and values and modes of life. In the course of the discussions, these views are scrutinized, undermined, and rejected. Meanwhile, novel, unconventional Platonic views are introduced and developed—the latter often in the process of criticizing the former. Thus, ideally, the reader is led through a critique of his own views; he is impressed by the problems of the grounds of his belief; and he is shown superior beliefs or a superior manner of grounding his beliefs and, more generally, of orienting his life.

5. Character and History

This description of the conflict of philosophy and antiphilosophy as the early dialogues' pervasive theme and of a-structure as their pervasive pedagogical structure to a large extent explains the form of the texts. More specifically, it explains the relationship between the argumentative content and the literary form. This point is also relevant to the characterology and historicity of the texts.

Both the characterology and historicity of the texts contribute to the texts' realism. The characters represent historical individuals, the dramatic settings represent historical places, and the characters are represented as saying and doing things that real people would. In fact, Plato's dialogues are more realistic than any other Athenian literature of the fourth century. Yet realism has been a deceptive form of literary presentation, for scholars have often viewed the dramatic aspects of the dialogues merely as instrumental to engaging the reader in the texts' philosophical substance. Such a conception oversimplifies and neglects large dimensions of the texts, for Plato employs character and history, as well as philosophical inquiry and argumentation, in dramatizing the conflict of philosophy and antiphilosophy and in advocating the value of the former over the latter.

The characters' conduct as well as their utterances reflects the conditions of their souls, specifically their beliefs and values. Lysimachus and Melesias are concerned with the well-being of their sons; they want their sons to become excellent, but they believe that training in arms may be the right course of training to this end. Hippocrates would like to become an outstanding citizen, but he believes that association with Protagoras is the right means to this end. Protagoras has the company at Callias' house discuss Simonides' ode because he believes that the study of poetry is the most important part of a man's education.

---

23. "Doxastic" means "relating to belief."

Euthyphro prosecutes his father for murder because he believes that doing so is holy and that he knows what holiness is.

The characters' values and beliefs are revealed not merely in the theses and premises they contribute in the philosophical discussions, but also in their attitudes toward the discussions. Critias initially resists joining the investigation of sound-mindedness; Protagoras twice stubbornly falls into silence; and Callicles is ultimately unwilling to continue the investigation. Such instances expose the characters' fear of humiliation and desire to safeguard their reputations. Such attitudes suggest a distinct prioritization of values.

Related is the character who is willing to engage in discussion, but for antiphilosophical reasons. His contributions aim to outdo or defeat his interlocutor rather than to foster a cooperative pursuit of truth. Euthydemus and Dionysodorus' sophisms are a good example. In *Laches*, once Nicias supplants Laches as Socrates' principal interlocutor, Laches becomes contentious, eager to see his colleague refuted as he was. Thrasymachus' violent and abusive manner shows flagrant disregard for his company's well-being. In short, the characters' topically nonphilosophical as well as philosophical claims manifest their values. Generally, their motives for speech or for silence as well as the content of their speech play an important role in Plato's dramaturgy.

In crafting the conflict of philosophy and antiphilosophy Plato also employs history. The historical elements are mainly drawn from the last thirty years of the fifth century BCE. This period encompasses the first thirty years of Plato's life, a span of Athenian history marked by the Peloponnesian War and its immediate aftermath and concluding with Socrates' execution. More precisely, the early dialogues are set in a quasi-historical past; historical elements populate the dialogues, but the particular configuration of the historical elements is not historically accurate. The prevalence of anachronism confirms this—and the sort of anachronism to which I am referring is not unconscious.

Plato's interest was to create a pastiche of elements representative of the period. His concern with history is philosophical, as he conceived philosophy. In other words, it is ethical and political. Plato is not interested in the particularities of individuals or the contingent social and environmental conditions that shape their personalities. He is interested in character, its formation, and its influence on the city-state. His interest in history is not chronological; he is not concerned with how sociopolitical conditions came about. Indeed, he does present an analysis of sociopolitical conditions, but not in terms of antecedent events.

Much of the history to which Plato alludes surely is lost, and so the texts' historical dimensions are elusive. But surviving historical sources facilitate appreciation of certain examples and so suggest a more general significance for Plato's engagement with history. The setting and characters of *Protagoras* provide a concrete demonstration. Protagoras claims that he can teach excellence in both private and public spheres, specifically, how to manage one's household and be an effective citizen in speech and action. The ensuing inquiry concerning the relation of the parts of excellence exposes Protagoras' ignorance of excellence and undermines his claim. But before this inquiry begins, Plato intimates, through his choice of setting and characters, that Protagoras cannot teach excellence.

In the dialogue, Protagoras is staying at Callias' house. The historical Callias came from one of the wealthiest and most esteemed Athenian families. In the course of his life, he depleted his family's fortunes and disgraced their reputation. Callias was one of Protagoras' principal Athenian adherents. Therefore, the dialogue's setting at Callias' house undermines Protagoras' claim to teach excellence in a private capacity.

Many of the Athenians at Callias' house were notorious for political and social misdeeds. The collection of characters in *Protagoras*, the largest in a Platonic dialogue, contrasts with the collection in *Phaedo*, the second largest. None of the nineteen characters at Callias' house is present in Socrates' prison cell. The group in *Phaedo* consists of Socrates' disciples and adherents of philosophy who have come to share last moments with a dear friend and teacher. In contrast, the group in *Protagoras* are portrayed as adherents of sophists. Plato thereby loosely correlates their scandalous histories with the sophists' corrupt activity. Accordingly, their presence undermines Protagoras' claim to teach excellence in a public capacity. Early in the text Protagoras argues that the Athenians cultivate excellence; he concludes:

> The Athenians think that excellence is teachable in both private and public affairs . . . in matters where the death penalty or exile awaits their children if not instructed and cultivated in excellence—and not merely death, but the confiscation of property and practically the entire subversion of their households—do they not have them taught or take utmost care of them?[24]

The histories of the individuals represented in *Protagoras*, many of whom suffered death, exile, or confiscation of their property, undermine Protagoras' claim.

This example illustrates a basic criticism of Athens that pervades the early writings: The upper class lacks excellence, fails to recognize their ignorance of excellence, and fails to cultivate it. The criticism of the sophists who appear in many of these texts correlates the corruption in Athens with sophistry. The relation is not portrayed as one of cause and effect. Rather, the Athenian upper class's reception of sophistry is characterized as symptomatic of their antiphilosophical character and values. The members of the upper class employ sophists above all for rhetorical training in order to win the approval of the *dêmos*. Insofar as they seek political power through the approval of the *dêmos*, they ignore the proper role of leadership. In his most explicit attack on Athenian political leaders of the past, Plato has Socrates in *Gorgias* criticize Pericles for having made the *dêmos* idle, cowardly, gossiping, and avaricious.[25]

Generally speaking, by setting his dialogues in this quasi-historical past, Plato engages the histories of the individuals whom the characters represent and their reputations among posterity with the portrayal of the characters in the texts' settings. The early dialogues portray Athens and a segment of Athenian society

---

24. *Prt.* 325b–c.
25. *Grg.* 515e.

of a past generation with the hindsight of Athens' fate during this period. Plato's engagement of history dramatizes the opposition of philosophy and antiphilosophy because philosophy is a practical social and political enterprise. Therefore, not only the conduct of dramatic characters, but also the biographical activities of the individuals whom these characters represent serve as evidence that is evaluated in relation to the topics and problems that the texts explore.

Plato's realistic portrayal of character and engagement of history is remarkably compelling. But the treatment of character and history is not fundamentally psychological or historical; it is ethical and thus philosophical. Accordingly, the realism Plato employs to dramatize the opposition of philosophy and antiphilosophy and to demonstrate the value of the former over the latter is cunning. The dialogues incorporate representative elements of philosophy and antiphilosophy, including representative persons, but this incorporation involves manipulation. The realism of the dialogues conveys the impression that the portrayal of persons and their utterances is accurate. But the dramatic characters are constructions and entirely subject to their author's interests. This does not preclude aspects of the dialogues from being historically accurate. Still, the opposition of philosophy and antiphilosophy operates through a conquest of appropriation. Within the dialogues' dramatic worlds, the values embedded in the social and political life of Athens, its inhabitants and discursive forms, are reevaluated and recalibrated according to the authority of philosophy. In this respect, although philosophy emerges from within antiphilosophical contexts in the dramas, the antiphilosophical contexts are themselves framed and defined by the author's philosophical interests.

The role of characterology and history in the dialogues indicates that most every element and aspect of the dialogues is hermeneutically significant. And yet to avoid anachronism, the significance assigned to particular elements and dimensions of the texts must be historically warranted. Insofar as this is the case, it is also worth emphasizing the magnitude of the gap between the rich texts that we have and the vast and intricate background that we struggle to reconstruct.

6. The Mouthpiece Principle

The character Socrates is central to Plato's early dialogues, and he appears in all of them. The other characters appear in only one or two; and even when they appear in more than one, their role in the other is small; for example, Crito in *Crito* and *Euthydemus*, and Critias in *Charmides* and *Protagoras*. Hippias is a slight exception; he is Socrates' principal interlocutor in *Hippias Major* and *Hippias Minor*, and he has a small role in *Protagoras*. But Socrates not only appears in all the early dialogues, his role in all of them is central. All of the early dialogues, save *Laches*, begin with Socrates as a principal speaker. Furthermore, unlike some of Plato's middle and late dialogues, Socrates is the only figure in these texts who fits the description of a philosopher. Even Crito, a close friend of Socrates and among the Socratic and Pythagorean philosophers in Socrates' prison cell in *Phaedo*, advocates a conventional belief on conventional, antiphilosophical grounds when he appears in *Crito*. Socrates is, then, the main and, as far as Plato is concerned, most sympathetic character in these texts; he is Plato's favored character.

In view of the dichotomy of philosophy and antiphilosophy, in the early dialogues Socrates would seem to be philosophy incarnate. In that case, the conflict between philosophy and antiphilosophy in these texts might be divisible by character. Accordingly, the dialogues would constitute contests (*agônes*) between Socrates and Protagoras, Socrates and Gorgias, Socrates and Hippias, and so on. Some such conception has governed a good deal of interpretation of the early dialogues. Indeed, the idea goes back as far as Diogenes Laertius—and surely he inherited it from earlier commentators—that Socrates is Plato's mouthpiece and the site of the philosophy that Plato intended to endorse in the dialogues. More recently, the mouthpiece principle has been advocated by some of the most prominent Plato scholars. Consider the claim by Gregory Vlastos, the most influential scholar of Plato's early dialogues in the last half century, that "in any given dialogue Plato allows the persona Socrates only what he (Plato), at that time, considers true."[26]

Some scholars, more wary of leaping from the character to the author, restrict their interpretations to Socrates' utterances, but still find in Socrates the philosophical substance of the dialogues. In the introduction to their book *Plato's Socrates* Thomas Brickhouse and Nicholas Smith explain, "We do not, in this book, intend to answer the question of whose philosophy we are actually interpreting [Plato's or the historical Socrates']...We claim only that a distinct philosophy can be found consistently portrayed as Socrates' in Plato's early dialogues and that the philosophy so portrayed is itself consistent."[27] Although this view is in one important respect different from the view expressed in Vlastos's statement, both views imply that the interpretation of the dialogues involves the following hermeneutic procedure: assembly from all of the early dialogues all of Socrates' topically philosophical utterances and derivation from these, so far as possible, consistent and coherent propositions. This set then constitutes the philosophy of the early dialogues.

Such an approach to the dialogues distorts their content and, among other things, leads to the questions why Plato wrote dialogues and how the literary and dramatic dimensions relate to the philosophical, questions that, given the commitments of the interpreters, cannot be satisfactorily answered.

An interpreter may grant this, but object that his aim is merely to interpret one dimension of the dialogues. Moreover, this dimension, the philosophical—according to some conception of philosophy—is the one that, as a philosopher or historian of philosophy, matters to him. Such a reply might carry the day. Consequently, the interpreter will leave nonphilosophical dimensions of the texts to the ancient historian, the scholar of Greek literature, and the philologist.

But this maneuver fails. Several factors undermine the attempt to distill philosophical principles from the assembly of all of Socrates' topic-relevant utterances. The most significant of these are intratextual and intertextual inconsistencies among Socrates' philosophical utterances. By intratextual inconsistencies, I mean

---

26. (1991) 17; see also Vlastos (1994) 125.
27. (1994) viii.

inconsistencies among Socrates' utterances within a given dialogue; by intertextual inconsistencies, I mean inconsistencies among Socrates' utterances through two or more dialogues. Both types of inconsistency occur frequently. Among Anglophone scholars over the last half-century there have been three prevalent responses to these inconsistencies: argument for developmentalism within the set of the early dialogues; pursuit of subtle unifying principles; and interpretation some of Socrates' utterances as "ironic" (meaning "disingenuous").

Ultimately, problems of inconsistency have to be treated on a case-by-case basis because the informational content of each context is unique. Which set of inconsistent utterances? How inconsistent? What proposed solution? Some important cases will be discussed in the ensuing chapters. Still, the following two principles serve as rules of thumb. Intratextual inconsistencies tend to be the effects of α-structure, and intertextual inconsistencies tend to be the effects of the common doxastic base of the early dialogues.

As I noted above, in accordance with the operation of α-structure, the given dialogue or some portion of it begins with a conventional or traditional belief; in the course of discussion, this is criticized, rejected, and supplanted by some unconventional Platonic view. The concept of a *Platonic* view requires a precise formulation; by it I mean a view that Plato intended to advance as compelling within the discursive framework of the dialogue in contrast to a related conventional view. Hereafter, I will use the adjective "Platonic" in this specific sense. When I intend to attribute a belief or some other item to Plato otherwise and in a more conventional sense, I will use the possessive "Plato's."

The operation of α-structure conforms to the Platonic view that prereflective conventional beliefs ought to be scrutinized, that it is unwise to hold a belief merely because it is commonly held. Moreover, the process of rationally justifying belief is difficult. The character Socrates, who, as philosophical, is highly sensitive to these points, is sometimes shown in the course of an investigation to alter his own beliefs precisely because he finds substantive reasons to do so. For example, at the beginning of *Protagoras* Socrates suggests that excellence cannot be taught. He bases this belief on the argument that the Athenians are sensible people; in the Assembly they allow any citizen who wishes to contribute opinions to political debate; this is interpreted as evidence that effective contribution to political debate does not require special training, but that all citizens possess the ability; therefore, such excellence cannot be taught. By the end of the dialogue, Socrates' view has changed. It has been argued that excellence is a kind of knowledge; and since knowledge is teachable, excellence is teachable. Similarly, in *Lysis* Socrates generates the following conception of *philia* (friendship). *Philia* occurs between something that is neither-good-nor-bad and something that is good, on account of the presence of something bad in that which is neither-good-nor-bad. For example, a man (neither-good-nor-bad) pursues health (good) because he suffers from sickness (bad). Almost immediately after concluding this account, it occurs to Socrates that he is wrong and that a satisfactory account of *philia* must include desire and deficiency as its cause. Socrates then reforms his conception of *philia*. Similarly, in *Charmides*, in an attempt to define the kind of specialized knowledge that constitutes sound-mindedness, Socrates suggests, by analogy with other forms of productive expertise, that sound-mindedness must have a product. To this Critias objects that some forms of expertise do not have products. Socrates concedes the objection, and, instead of insisting that sound-mindedness differs from other forms of expertise in this sense, proposes that sound-mindedness may be akin to forms of nonproductive expertise that are distinguishable according to the objects with which they are preoccupied. In the case of *Charmides*, Socrates may or may not have changed his mind. Still, he has demonstrated open-mindedness, willingness to admit error, and appreciation that there may be more compelling conceptions than his immediate one. This is particularly noteworthy in contrast to the character of Critias, who enters the investigation with acute anxiety over admitting ignorance and error. In the case of *Lysis*, Socrates' revised conception of *philia* demonstrates the danger of complacency, the difficulty of the process of philosophical inquiry, the importance of reconsideration, and also the possibility of developing understanding. These are philosophical values themselves. Furthermore, they conform with the fact that throughout the early dialogues Socrates is, to a large extent, not portrayed as a doctrinaire or dogmatic thinker, in sharp contrast to the many alleged and selfprofessed experts and authorities whom he engages. Attempts to explain away intratextual inconsistencies undermine this aspect of the character Socrates as well as the broader operation of *a*-structure in conformity with which such inconsistencies occur.

Intertextual inconsistencies typically occur for quite a different, although related, reason. This has to do with what I call the common doxastic base of the texts. In discussing *a*-structure, it was emphasized that the early dialogues share a common cognitive point of departure, conventional or traditional belief. Accordingly, comprehension of any given early dialogue does not appear to require comprehension of any other. So, for instance, the concept of Form (*eidos*) is introduced in *Euthyphro*. It also occurs in *Meno* and *Hippias Major*, but in both cases, understanding of this unconventional, Platonic concept only requires the given text itself. Accordingly, the early dialogues are not arranged like a textbook in which the understanding of successive chapters depends upon the understanding of preceding ones. Rather, each dialogue serves as a fresh occasion to explore a given topic or problem.

From the common doxastic base of conventional or traditional belief in the dialogues, unconventional, Platonic views are developed. But at the same time, the development of these Platonic views depends upon conventional or traditional premises. Thus, the discussion proceeds throughout the dialogue. In any given instance, then, Socrates may introduce a conventional or traditional claim *whose content is not the focus of the present discussion*, but which is needed to advance the issue that is the focus of the discussion. Such premises might be conceived as lemmas that will require a more adequate justification at some later point or simply as convenient and provisional structures that must ultimately be replaced by more adequate ones. Likewise, the conclusions of Socrates' arguments that depend upon such premises might be conceived as tentative precisely according to the tentative status of these lemmas or provisional structures. The main point is that given the doxastic base of conventional or traditional belief of the dialogues,

Socrates himself inevitably introduces such premises. Plato simply cannot have Socrates asserting the unconventional, Platonic view of every concept that arises within the course of a discussion. This would result in a full-scale exposition of Platonic views and thus entirely transform the dialogues into treatises. Consequently, Socrates' assertions occasionally conform to conventional opinions, especially in cases where the subjects of those opinions are not the main subjects of the discussion. Such conventional opinions are, therefore, simply employed in passages whose objective is the investigation, problematization, or advancement of some *other* view. Indication that such a given Socratic assertion is not Platonic is the conjunction of that assertion with certain features: the opinion asserted is conventional or traditional; in another text Socrates does problematize or even refute it; Socrates does not repeat the assertion in several dialogues.

Consider two examples of intertextual inconsistencies explicable in this way. In *Gorgias* Socrates assumes that friendship is based on likeness. The assumption is employed, for convenience, to advance a different point, namely that in befriending a tyrant one corrupts one's soul. The argument begins with the assumption that in order to avoid suffering harm one must either be a ruler in one's own city or else a supporter of the government. Socrates then suggests that because friendship is based on likeness, to befriend a tyrant one must make oneself like a tyrant and thereby corrupt oneself. In *Gorgias* Socrates does not explicitly problematize the nature of friendship. In contrast, in *Lysis* Socrates does; this is a central topic of the text. Furthermore, Socrates' view of friendship in *Gorgias* is traditional, based on received wisdom, whereas early in the investigation in *Lysis*, Socrates argues against the view of friendship based on likeness and instead develops a view based on belonging (*oikeiotês*). Furthermore, the argument in *Gorgias* is dialectical; the view that in order to avoid suffering harm one must either be a ruler or supporter of the government is not Platonic. Rather, evidence from *Gorgias* and other dialogues such as *Apology* suggests that the Platonic view is that the conventional conception of harm is unsatisfactory and accordingly that a good person cannot suffer harm. These considerations support the view that neither in *Lysis* nor in *Gorgias* is the conception of friendship based on likeness Platonic— even though in *Gorgias* Socrates assumes that it is.

The second example is derived from *Euthyphro*. There, Socrates claims that holiness is a part of justice. In *Euthyphro* Socrates problematizes the nature of holiness. However, he does not problematize the relation of the parts of excellence. He does not argue that holiness is a part of justice; he merely asserts it. In *Protagoras* Socrates does problematize the relation of the putative parts of excellence; this topic is central to the discussion. Moreover, he argues for the unconventional view that holiness and justice are identical or at least as similar as can be. Furthermore, evidence from other early dialogues such as *Charmides* and *Laches* suggests that the view that the parts of excellence are identical or at least more closely related than according to the conventional conception Protagoras expresses is Platonic. In *Euthyphro*, Socrates' view of the relation between holiness and justice is conventional, at least within the legalistic context of the dialogue. Socrates and Euthyphro are engaged in cases concerning impiety. Insofar as matters of justice are conceived as coextensive with matters of positive law, matters of holiness do form a subset of judicial matters. In short, there is good reason to believe that the view that holiness is part of justice is not Platonic, even though in *Euthyphro* Socrates says it is.

In sum, Plato sometimes conveniently put conventional, traditional, or commonsensical views into Socrates' mouth, but without intending to advance those views. Of course, Socrates occasionally also asserts conventional or traditional views that are Platonic, for example, the view that the putative parts of excellence are good and fine. But in this case it is clear for a number of reasons that such views are Platonic. First, Socrates never objects to it. Second, Socrates repeats the view in several dialogues. Third, in *Republic* 1, when Thrasymachus suggests that justice is not an excellence and so neither good nor fine, Socrates is shocked and argues against him. In short, it is necessary to evaluate Socrates' conventional or traditional assertions in light of their functions within the dialogues. In particular, this involves the recognition that the early dialogues share a particular doxastic base.

It must be emphasized that these explanations of Socrates' intratextual and intertextual inconsistencies do not involve denying attribution to Socrates of sincere commitment to any particular claims. The explanations admit that at one point in a given dialogue Socrates is sincerely committed to a given position to which at another point in that dialogue he is not committed. Likewise, the explanations admit that in one dialogue Socrates is sincerely committed to a given position to which in another dialogue he is not committed. Consequently, Socrates' utterances are not entirely consistent among the early dialogues. Moreover, this inconsistency is not due to Plato's intellectual development or to Socrates' so-called irony, nor are such inconsistencies resolvable by subtle unifying principles. Rather, the interpretive approach to the dialogues that attempts to assemble all of Socrates' topic-relevant utterances and to distill from these unifying principles is naïve. It fails to recognize the complexity of Plato's dramaturgy, specifically the various ways in which Plato uses the character Socrates to achieve his philosophical-pedagogical objectives.

These criticisms of the mouthpiece principle have still further implications for the conception of the character Socrates in the early dialogues. It is necessary to relinquish the view that the Socrates of a given early dialogue is in a strong sense identical to the Socrates of another early dialogue. Instead, it is more reasonable to adopt a weaker view. Plato had his reasons for creating a main character named "Socrates" to serve as the philosophical protagonist in his early dialogues. These reasons clearly include debt and tribute to the historical Socrates. Still, Plato was not so bound to the historical Socrates that the character Socrates in any one of his dialogues had to be strictly identifiable with the historical Socrates, and that, as a result, the character Socrates in any one dialogue had to be strictly identifiable with the character Socrates in another early dialogue.

Clearly, a general body of commitments governs Plato's depiction of Socrates in every early dialogue. Socrates is not merely a vague stock character, the philosophical type. But Plato employs and manipulates Socrates in various ways to achieve various ends. Any interpretive project that aims to determine Platonic views in the early dialogues or in any given early dialogue must acknowledge and respect this fact.

In place of the mouthpiece theory it is more reasonable to regard Socrates as Plato's favored character. Socrates is the character to whom, of all dramatic characters, Plato is most sympathetic. Accordingly, Socrates often expresses or develops Platonic views. Socrates is the philosopher in texts that dramatize the opposition of philosophy and antiphilosophy and that argue for the superiority of the former over the latter. Yet not all the views that Socrates asserts are Platonic. And not all the views that are Platonic are captured in Socrates' utterances.

The mouthpiece principle is the central tenet of a theory of interpretation of Plato's early dialogues. In light of the preceding discussion, that theory must now appear to be a caricature of the truth. The theory depends upon the fundamental fallacious assumption that the dialogues belong to the genre of the philosophical treatise. Accordingly, dialogue is misguidedly reduced to monologue and the character Socrates to the authoritative voice. The concept of Plato's favored character reestablishes Socrates in his proper place; and the notion that the texts dramatize philosophy, more precisely, the conflict of philosophy and antiphilosophy and thus that they are as much metaphilosophical as philosophical restores their dialogicity.

7. Forms of Evidence

The words that constitute the early dialogues are embodied in the form of realistic and quasi-historical characters and sometimes also a quasi-historical narrator.[28] Thus, the words are composed as verbal activity. Characters speak to one another, or a narrator relates to an audience events of characters speaking to one another. The verbal activity may be distinguished according to three categories: Characters speak about the nonverbal activities of characters; characters speak about verbal activities of characters; and characters speak on topics.

Nonverbal activity is described in narrative passages. Such passages occur in all the early dialogues, even though only a few (for example, Republic 1 and Charmides) are framed as narratives.[29] The reason is that in many dialogues narration is embedded in dialogue; for example, in Protagoras Socrates describes to the anonymous associate the manner of Hippocrates' arrival at his house.

There are many kinds of nonverbal activity in the dialogues. For example, characters arrive at the scene of the dialogue (Critias and Alcibiades in Protagoras) and depart (Euthyphro in Euthyphro), temporarily fall silent (Lysis in Lysis) or shift roles from discussants to spectators (Melesias and Lysimachus in Laches), blush (Thrasymachus in Republic 1), applaud (the crowd at the Lyceum in Euthydemus), ogle (at Charmides in Charmides), fall down (off the bench in Charmides), and leap up (as Thrasymachus is described as doing in a predatory manner when he begins to rebuke Socrates).

Speech about the nonverbal activity of characters may itself be divided into two kinds insofar as the nonverbal activity may be one's own or another's. For example, at

---

28. This always happens to be the character Socrates.
29. Apology is peculiar in largely being a speech.

the beginning of *Republic* 1, Socrates says he went down to the Piraeus to watch the festival of Bendis, and in that case he speaks of a nonverbal action that he himself performed. In contrast, in *Protagoras* Socrates says that Hippocrates blushed.

The second category, speech about verbal activity, is similarly divisible according to whether a character speaks about what he himself has said or what another has said. In the former case, for example, Socrates sometimes reminds his interlocutor of something he, Socrates, has said. In the latter case, for example, an interlocutor says that he disagrees with something Socrates has said. Generally speaking, throughout passages of argumentation and inquiry, speakers refer to, reiterate, summarize, and comment upon points made previously.

Speech about topics includes verbal activity whose content is not about the verbal or nonverbal activities of characters. This category might be divisible into speech on philosophical topics and speech on nonphilosophical (including anti-philosophical) topics. However, this division cannot be sustained, above all since most of the speech on nonphilosophical topics is, dramaturgically, deliberately related to philosophical topics. Generally speaking, this conforms to the pervasive dramatization of the conflict of philosophy and its antithesis. Examples are ubiquitous and obvious. For example, I have mentioned that *Gorgias* begins with Gorgias' completion of a rhetorical performance. But the identity of rhetoric, its political function and value are immediately the focus of philosophical inquiry.

Verbal activity about topics may be divisible into claims about universals and claims about particulars. For example, in *Gorgias* Callicles asserts that goodness and pleasure are the same thing (a claim about universals), but elsewhere in the dialogue Socrates argues that Pericles was not a good statesman (a claim about a particular). As we will see in chapter 3, the distinction is methodologically and epistemologically significant, for the interpretation of claims about particulars depends upon the interpretation of claims about universals—for example, whether Pericles was a good statesman depends upon a theory or definition of statesmanship.[30]

I have said that within the early dialogues philosophy is conceived primarily as a kind of motivation, secondarily as an activity driven by that motivation, and finally

---

30. A general problem facing the interpretation of verbal activity is determining the speaker's attitude toward his utterance. Speakers are usually, but not always sincere. In the history of Platonic scholarship the most important species of such insincerity is Socratic irony. In this context, the word "irony" is used in various and sometimes unconventional ways. But, as I have noted, it is most commonly misused is to mean "disingenuousness." Observe that if Socrates were portrayed as characteristically disingenuous, this would seriously complicate the interpretation of the dialogues, for then the texts' central character's attitude toward his utterances would occasionally or persistently be unclear. My view of Socratic irony is unconventional. I refer the reader to appendix 2, where I discuss the subject. Presently, suffice it to say that Socratic irony is not an interpretive problem that troubles this study. In any event, the general point is that interpretation of verbal activity also requires interpretation of the attitude that the speaker adopts toward his utterance. In determining characters' attitudes toward their utterances, interpreters can appeal to two sources of information: the content of a character's utterance and other characters' responses to that utterance. In the first case, an utterance may be conventional for a person of that age, status, or situation. In that case, there is reason to treat the utterance as sincere. Similarly, an utterance may

as a condition resulting from that activity. The aim of this study is to clarify these claims. The discussion in the previous sections has articulated a framework according to which this can be done. The immediately preceding categorical distinctions in verbal activity suggest that the early dialogues inform our understanding of a given element or aspect of philosophy in various ways.

First, the verbal and nonverbal activity of the characters reveals their desires, values, and attitudes as well as their practices. As I have said, the conditions of the characters' souls are revealed through the conduct of their lives and thus their conduct in the dramas. Second, the characters explicitly state their desires and beliefs about what they think they know and do not know. In addition, they state what they value; and these values suggest motivations and practices. Third, within discussion participants make claims about elements and aspects of philosophy such as desire, knowledge, goodness, and the practice of philosophy itself. Fourth, participants engage in arguments about elements and aspects of philosophy, for example, about desire.

Among these sources of information about philosophy, the last is of paramount importance for understanding the Platonic conception of philosophy among the early dialogues. This is because the early dialogues convey that what we should believe on a given topic is what is most well reasoned, and the function of arguments is to provide reasons. This does not, however, imply that we should focus on passages of argumentation to the exclusion of nonargumentative passages or nonargumentative dimensions of passages of argumentation. That would be misguided for two reasons. First, most elements and aspects of philosophy are not treated as subjects of argumentation in the dialogues. Second, some arguments are not Platonic; and this is revealed by attention to pragmatic and dramatic aspects of an argument—as opposed to their relatively bare logical form. Accordingly, in attending to argument, we must ask ourselves how the argument functions within the dialogue and whether it is Platonic. The following considerations support the view that an argument is Platonic: The context of the argument indicates that the characters are making a sincere alethic effort; conclusions of such arguments are more worthy of belief than unreasoned views; the argument involves the rejection of conventional views; the conclusion of the argument itself is unconventional.

---

be consistent with the personality of the character, where personality is determined by consideration of a character's utterances and nonverbal activity in general. One character's response to the utterance of another character provides an implicit or explicit interpretation of the attitude toward the original utterance. For example, if an interlocutor agrees to a Socratic statement, then it may be assumed that the interlocutor interprets Socrates' attitude as sincere. Granted, the interpretation may be incorrect. But characters also explicitly remark on their attitudes toward their own utterances as well the attitudes toward utterances of other characters. For example, in *Euthydemus* Socrates suggests that Euthydemus and Dionysodorus are joking with Clinias; in *Charmides* Critias accuses Socrates of deliberately trying to refute him, and Socrates responds that this is false. Here, again, one character may misinterpret the attitude of another. Similarly, a character may deliberately misrepresent his own attitude. Thus, when problems of interpretation arise in considering this second source of information regarding characters' attitudes toward their utterances, the interpreter is bound to depend on the primary source.

Among the early dialogues Plato does not compose any arguments between Socrates and his interlocutors concerning the identity of knowledge or ethical knowledge specifically. Rather, the Platonic conception of ethical knowledge in these texts must be determined from the following aspects of the texts: concepts that Socrates and his interlocutors repeatedly employ in connection with epistemic concepts, for example, *technê*, as well as claims or arguments concerning or employing such concepts; unconventional claims that Socrates makes about knowledge or ethical knowledge, for example, that he has none or that definitional knowledge is epistemologically prior to relevant nondefinitional knowledge; the practice of philosophy itself since, as I have suggested, the form of the practice is related to its objective and the way its objective is conceived; the results of the practice, and comments that Socrates and his interlocutors make about the practice and its results.

Method or the practice of philosophy is, for the most part, not a subject of theorizing in the texts. In this case, my account is largely derived from the portrayal of the practice itself. However, in one importance case, which I will discuss at length in section 3 of chapter 4, Socrates explicitly introduces a method of reasoning that he derives from geometry.

Aporia is partially explicable in light of my conclusions concerning the treatment of knowledge; however, it is not wholly so explicable. Instead, aporia will be explained in view of the forms it assumes, that is, the forms of perplexity to which the dramatic characters fall victim in their investigations.

Finally, let me once again emphasize that my goal is not to determine the character Socrates' views about philosophy and its constituents. I seek Platonic views. I will have much to say about the claims and contributions of the character Socrates, for Socrates' utterances provide central evidence for Platonic views. But I will not be assembling all of Socrates' topic-relevant utterances and from these attempting to distill unifying principles. In emphasizing this fundamental point and in applying my critique of the mouthpiece principle, I will have occasion in the discussions of desire, knowledge, method, and aporia to introduce and discuss Socratic conduct, claims, and practices *inconsistent* with my conclusions and to provide explanations for why such conduct, claims, and practices do not jeopardize those conclusions. For example, I will consider passages in *Charmides* and *Gorgias* where Socrates makes claims about desire inconsistent with arguments and conclusions concerning desire in *Meno*, *Protagoras*, and *Lysis*. I will consider passages in *Laches* and *Apology* where Socrates makes ethical knowledge claims inconsistent with the epistemological views I characterize as Platonic. And I will argue that the aporiai in which many of the early dialogues end, aporiai to which Socrates himself in varying ways is subject, do not precisely correspond to Platonic perplexity. The cognitive disparity between Plato and his favored character is not radical, but satisfactory interpretation of the dialogues requires appreciation that to some degree disparity exists.

2

DESIRE

1. Socrates and Eros

It is often said that Socrates is an erotic figure. For example, in a fragment from the dialogue *Alcibiades* by Aeschines the Socratic, Socrates claims, "I knew no course of study (*mathêma*) by which I could teach and benefit him [Alcibiades], but I thought that by being with him I could make him a better person through love (*dia eran*)."[1] Among Plato's early dialogues, one interpretation of Socratic love occurs at the beginning of *Protagoras* in the brief exchange between Socrates and the anonymous aristocrat. The dialogue opens with the aristocrat: "Where are you coming from Socrates? But of course, from hunting the youthful beauty of Alcibiades."[2] He assumes that Socrates' interests are sexual.

Plato plays up this interpretation of Socratic eros in the introductory scene in *Charmides*. Socrates describes his first moments with Charmides:

> He arrived and caused much laughter, for each of us who were seated made room for him by pushing hard at the person seated beside us, until at one end one person had to stand up and at the other he tumbled off sideways. Charmides then came and sat down between Critias and me. But here . . . I began to fall into a state of perplexity, and my former confidence in expecting quite an easy time in talking with him was knocked out of me. And when Critias told him that it was I who knew the cure [for the headaches he had been suffering of late], he gave me such a look with his eyes as passes description. And he was just about to plunge into a question when all the people in the wrestling-school surged round us on every side. And

---

1. Ael. Aristid. *Orat.* 45, II 23–4D; cited from Giannantoni (1990) 610.
2. *Prt.* 309a1–2.

then—then, I saw inside his cloak, and I caught fire. I could no longer possess myself, and I thought that no one was so wise in matters of love (*ta erôtika*) as the poet Cydias, who in speaking of a beautiful boy, recommends to someone that he "beware of coming as a fawn before the lion and being seized as his portion of flesh . . ."[3]

Both passages serve to titillate the reader while introducing the suspicion that Socrates' real motive in engaging the youths of Athens was self-gratification. Yet in accordance with the function of *a*-structure Plato quickly disabuses his reader of this assumption. In *Protagoras* Socrates relates that he has just come from Callias' house, where, although he was in the company of Alcibiades, he hardly paid attention to the young man. Instead, Socrates was captivated by a much more compelling beauty. The anonymous aristocrat assumes, "Surely you did not find anyone else more beautiful there—not in this city-state."[4] Socrates explains that indeed the wisest is the most beautiful and that he has just come from conversation with the wisest man of his generation. Similarly, in *Charmides*, Socrates pulls himself together and proceeds to examine the condition of Charmides' soul, to determine whether Charmides possesses the sound-mindedness Critias has attributed to him.

The homoerotic moment in *Charmides* also indicates that Socrates himself has not achieved the ideal of sound-mindedness that he seeks. Nonetheless, he is *philosophos* (a lover of *sophia*), not *philhêdonos* (a lover of pleasure). Plato reserves the latter characterization for other characters, for example, Hippothales in *Lysis* and, above all, Callicles in *Gorgias*. Moreover, as I mentioned in chapter 1 and will discuss again in chapter 3, the Platonic view is that ethical hedonism, the identification of goodness with pleasure, is rife in Athens, among the *ochlos* (the masses) as well as the upper class and their educators. By "pleasure" is not meant the satisfactions of the contemplative life, but a kind of bodily sensation. Plato is alive to this distinction. In *Protagoras* the sophist Prodicus, whose special talent is fine semantic distinctions, says, "we listeners [to Socrates' and Protagoras' discussion] would, therefore, be most contented (*euphrainoimetha*), [I do not say] pleased (*hêdoimetha*); for to be contented is to learn something and to partake of understanding in the intellect alone, whereas to be pleased is to eat something or to experience some other pleasure (*hêdu*) in the body."[5]

Plato's Socrates does not educate his associates by endowing them with ethical knowledge, for he lacks such knowledge himself. At least in some cases, however, he shapes their desires by persuading them that excellence is knowledge and by revealing to them their lack of knowledge. Given the principle that all human beings desire the good, recognition of ignorance and of the goodness of knowledge engenders *philosophia*, the desire for knowledge. Thus in *Euthydemus*

---

3. *Chrm.* 155b9–e1.
4. *Prt.* 309c2–3.
5. *Prt.* 337c1–4.

Socrates concludes an argument with Clinias: "Since we are all desirous of well-being, and since we discovered that to achieve this we should not only use things, but use them correctly, and moreover that it is knowledge that provides this correctness [of usage]...then, it seems, every man ought by every means to provide himself so that he becomes as wise as possible."[6]

The principle that everyone desires the good is fundamental to early Platonic psychology. But its correct interpretation is controversial. Consider the following four interpretations. According to the so-called neoplatonic interpretation, the real or actual good is the object of desire of the true self or of the genuine or true motivational state of all people.[7]

According to Terry Penner, Socrates' conception of desire (that is, the Platonic conception) is radically at odds with most of the subsequent Western philosophical tradition and bound up with a distinct conception of the individuation of actions. For Socrates the ultimate end of all humans' desires is what is really good, namely true happiness, "even if [that] is different from what [they] think it is."[8] Yet Penner's view does not depend on reference to a true self or genuine motivational state:

> Consider what parents want for their children when, as usually, they "want what is best for them." Is this wanting what is best for one's children identifiable with wanting what one *thinks* is best for them? I think not. For it is an exceptionally obtuse parent that thinks it very likely that what the *parent* thinks best for the child will be what is in fact best for the child....
> [W]hat parents want for their children is what really *is* best for their children, even if what is really best differs from what the parents or children think best. So why shouldn't it be the case that what I want for *myself* is: what is really best for me *even if that differs from what I think it is?*[9]

Furthermore, Penner argues that Socrates "individuates actions by means of a totality of attributes *that includes consequences.*"[10] Accordingly, if a man pursues a course of action, falsely believing that action to be conducive to his true happiness, then that man does not desire that action.

Heda Segvic argues that Socrates is committed to a novel conception of wanting or desiring: "I (Socratically) want to ϕ only if my wanting to ϕ is linked to my recognition of the goodness of ϕ-ing; if it is a mere coincidence that I believe that ϕ-ing is the right thing to do and that ϕ-ing in fact is the right thing to do, my wanting to ϕ is not Socratic wanting."[11]

---

6. *Euthd.* 282a1–6.
7. See McTighe (1984) notes 8, 9, 11, 18, 19.
8. Penner (1991) 195.
9. Ibid., 193.
10. Penner and Rowe (1994) note 14, with my italics.
11. Segvic (2000) 11.

Furthermore, the principle that everyone desires the good is not trivially true just because Socrates stipulatively defines desire in an idiosyncratic way. Socrates' claim is "meant to express a truth about the underlying structure of human motivation."[12] "Socrates seems to propose his special notion of wanting...not as a notion we already have at work in our language, but rather as a notion that we occasionally grope for, and a notion that we need. We need it because it enables us to express something that is of relevance to all the willing, wishing, and desiring that we ordinarily do and ordinarily speak of."[13]

Finally, according to the subjectivist interpretation, desire depends upon a fallible evaluation of the desideratum as good.[14]

Four passages among the early dialogues have a special bearing on the question of the Platonic conception of desire: the argument in *Meno* (77–78) that everyone desires the good, the argument in *Gorgias* (466–68) that orators have least power in their city-states and that one may do what one thinks best without doing what one desires, the critique of *akrasia* (weakness of will) in *Protagoras* (352–57), and the argument in *Lysis* (220–22) that desire is the cause of friendship. I will begin the examination of desire in section 2 by focusing on the *Meno* argument. There I will defend a subjectivist interpretation of the principle that everyone desires the good. In section 3 I turn to the *Gorgias* argument, which many scholars have thought provides strong evidence against the subjectivist interpretation. I will defend the deflationary thesis that the passage actually sheds no light on the Platonic principle that everyone desires the good.

Some scholars have argued that in *Gorgias* and elsewhere Plato distinguishes two motivational states: *boulêsis* and *epithumia*, which they interpret as rational and irrational desire, respectively; for example, wanting to become a doctor and thirst. Indeed, Plato was alive to this distinction; it relates to the distinction between pleasure and contentment that Prodicus draws in *Protagoras*. In a passage in *Charmides* Socrates distinguishes pleasure and goodness as objects of *epithumia* and *boulêsis*, respectively. In section 4, I discuss the *Charmides* passage, but suggest that it provides no compelling evidence that the distinction between rational and irrational desire is Platonic.

The critique of *akrasia* in *Protagoras* provides the strongest evidence for the Platonic view that there are no irrational desires for particular objects or courses of action. This passage is the subject of section 5.

In section 6 I discuss *Lysis*, arguably Plato's most perplexing early dialogue. Here we find a remarkable development of the subjectivist conception of desire. The passages from *Meno* and *Protagoras* support the subjectivist interpretation, but neither wholly explains desires for particular objects or courses of action. In *Lysis*, Socrates argues that desire and so friendship (*philia*) arise from a condition of deficiency. But this deficiency is precognitive and so preevaluative. Explaining

---

12. Segvic (2000) 13.
13. Ibid., 19.
14. For example, Santas (1964) and (1979).

how the subjectivist conception can be integrated with the deficiency conception of desire will be a central task in my discussion of *Lysis*.

Section 7 concludes the chapter with a consideration of antiphilosophical desires. The Platonic view is that most Athenians are driven by two types of desire: *philotimia* (love of esteem) and *philhêdonia* (love of pleasure). I will identify various forms of textual evidence that reveal these antiphilosophical desires and discuss the Platonic conception of the psychology of these desires.

2. The Subjectivist Conception of Desire

The first movement of *Meno* is devoted to the question "What is excellence?" Meno offers three successive definitions, and Socrates responds with three successive criticisms. Meno's third definition is that excellence is the desire for fine things and the ability to acquire them. Socrates criticizes this definition in two stages. The first involves an argument for the view that everyone desires fine things. Given this, the desire for fine things cannot be a component of excellence, for it is assumed that excellence is not a universal human attribute. Socrates' first criticism of Meno's third definition of excellence, then, contains an account of desire for which Socrates provides an argument.

Socrates' argument against Meno's third definition begins with Socrates' redescription of fine things (*kala*) as good things (*agatha*).[15] Meno permits the redescription, and the discussion proceeds without further comment on the relationship between fineness and goodness. Still, it is a question why Socrates suggests and Meno accepts this redescription.

When he introduces his third definition, Meno says it is derived from some poet. It is unclear to whom Meno is referring—perhaps to Simonides since he had connections with Thessaly. But whoever the poet is, it has long been noted that the definition and particularly the concept of fineness (*kallos*) reflect an aristocratic ethos consonant with Meno's own social status.[16] For Meno, then, the definition suggests that the aristocrat, who is the best sort of person, values the right sort of things and has the means to obtain them.

I suggest that Meno accepts and understands Socrates' redescription of his definition to mean that good things are the sort of things traditionally valued by aristocrats. In other words, Meno understands goodness as he understands fineness. Accordingly, as the exchange continues, Meno initially understands badness as the contrary of fineness, that is, as baseness, with its corresponding class connotations.

In contrast, as the ensuing discussion will show, Socrates redescribes fine things as good things precisely to avoid the particular class connotations associated with the concept fineness and to focus on the non-class-specific positive

15. *Men.* 77b6–7.
16. The noun *kallos* and the corresponding adjective *kalon* and their contraries are difficult to translate. Throughout the study I use various words to suit the context. These include "beautiful," "fine," "admirable," "noble."

value that objects of desire may have. Quite the reverse of Meno, then, Socrates understands fineness in terms of his, that is, Socrates', conception of goodness.[17]

Following the redescription of fine things as good things, Socrates questions whether Meno believes that some people desire bad things and others desire good things.[18] He poses the question because he believes that all people desire good things; therefore, he does not believe that the desire for good things can be constitutive of excellence, an attribute few people possess. In defense of his definition, Meno responds that

(a) some people desire bad things.[19]

Socrates is surprised that Meno believes that some people desire bad things. This is because, as the ensuing exchange makes clear, Socrates regards bad things as harmful to oneself; therefore, he finds it remarkable that people would desire things harmful to themselves and that Meno would think that people desire things harmful to themselves.

This raises the question why Meno submits that some people desire bad things. As the argument continues, Socrates' comments elicit several reasons Meno has for maintaining (a). Initially, it seems that Meno, in accordance with his aristocratic values, regards most people, namely the lower classes, as having bad values. That is to say, he regards most people as believing that certain things are good that in fact are bad. Consequently, since Meno understands bad things as base things, following Socrates' redescription of his original definition, one of his reasons for committing to (a) is that he interprets desire in (a) de re.[20] In other

---

17. Note that agathos (good) and kakos (bad) are standardly conceived as contraries. Likewise, kalos and aischros (foul, base, ugly, disgraceful).

18. Men. 77b7–c3.

19. Note that here and throughout the study, when introducing a premise of an argument from the dialogues to which I subsequently refer, I symbolize the premise with a lowercase letter in alphabetic order. Premises mentioned once do not receive symbols. At the beginning of each section, I return to the letter "a." There are only a few cases where premises are referred to across sections. In those cases, I reiterate the meaning of the symbol.

20. The de re/de dicto distinction is used in reference to phrases, which are themselves used in intensional (contrast extensional) contexts. An intensional context is one in which substitution of coextensive expressions does not preserve truth-values. For example, Socrates believes he is standing on the earth; the earth is the third planet from the sun; therefore, Socrates believes he is standing on the third planet from the sun. But this is false. Contrast, Socrates is standing on the earth; therefore, Socrates is standing on the third planet from the sun. This is true. The proposi- tional attitude of belief introduces an intensional context, into which substitution of "the earth" with "the third planet from the sun" does not preserve truth-values. There are many types of propositional attitude that introduce intensional contexts. Desire is one such attitude. For exam- ple, Oedipus desires to sleep with Jocasta; Jocasta is Oedipus' mother; therefore, Oedipus desires to sleep with Oedipus' mother. This is false. In such cases, we speak of desire de dicto. Put simply and crudely, desire de dicto is desire for the desideratum under the desirer's description or conception. De dicto means "concerning the thing as spoken of." But there is an interpretation of the sentence "Oedipus desires to sleep with Oedipus' mother" according to which this sentence is true. It is the interpretation according to which the phrase "Oedipus' mother" is understood extensionally, that

words, one interpretation of (a) is that things that are actually bad are the objects of some people's desires. Socrates' response to Meno supports this interpretation: "Do you mean that [those who desire bad things] think that the bad things are good, or do you mean that [those who desire bad things] recognize that the bad things are bad, but still desire them?"[21]

Socrates makes explicit here a distinction between the objective value of an object of desire o and the subjective value of o, that is, the value that the desiring subject attributes to o. In short, Socrates' first interpretation of (a), which would allay his surprise at Meno's commitment to (a), is that Meno claims (a) only because he understands desire in (a) *de re*.

In response to Socrates' question, however, Meno replies that both types of psychological condition occur:

(b) some people desire things that are bad, but believe that these
    things are good;

(c) some people desire things that are bad and recognize that these
    things are bad.

Consonant with my suggested interpretation, Socrates is not unsettled by Meno's admission of (b). However, he is surprised that Meno also commits to (c). His surprise is reflected in the fact that he seeks Meno's reconfirmation of (c): "Does it really seem to you, Meno, that a person could desire bad things when he recognizes them to be bad?"[22] Meno confirms (c).[23]

It is questionable why Meno commits to (c). The reason has to do with Meno's conception of badness following his understanding of Socrates' redescription of his original definition. Again, Meno understands goodness in terms of his aristocratic conception of fineness. Accordingly, he understands badness as baseness. In committing to (c), then, Meno is claiming that some people, presumably some subset of the lower classes, are aware that the things they desire are regarded as base, yet they desire these things nonetheless. In other words, such people realize that the things they value are not valued by the best class of people, yet this does not stop them from desiring those things.

Socrates now proceeds to argue that no one who recognizes that an object o is bad can desire o. The argument ensues in three steps: clarification of the concept of desire, clarification of the concept of recognizing that o is bad, and consideration of whether some people knowingly desire to harm themselves.

---

is, as referring to the person who in fact and regardless of the beliefs of the agent satisfies that description. Thus, we might say that Oedipus desires to sleep with his mother, *although he falsely believes that Jocasta does not satisfy that description*. In such a case, we speak of desire *de re*, which means "concerning the thing." For a relatively concise, but deeper and more formal account of the *de re/de dicto* distinction, see McKay and Nelson (2005).

21. *Men.* 77c3–5.
22. *Men.* 77c5–7.
23. *Men.* 77c7.

Socrates first elicits Meno's agreement that by "desire" he means desire that one have o.[24] The significance of this clarification is partially explained by a nearly identical clarification in *Symposium*. There, Diotima explains that when one desires o, one desires that one have o and that one's possession of o affects one in a particular way.[25] Likewise, in *Meno* Socrates is clarifying and emphasizing that the people of (c) actually want to possess bad things *de dicto*. That is, people want to possess things that they regard as bad. Since Socrates understands badness to imply harmfulness, this implies that some people actually want to harm themselves, and Socrates finds this psychologically unintelligible.

Meno accepts Socrates' characterization of desire as desire that one obtain o. Consequently, Socrates proceeds to question Meno's understanding of the concept of recognizing that o is bad. He asks whether a person who desires what in fact is bad, recognizing that it is bad, thinks that the bad benefits him, or whether he recognizes that it harms him.[26] Socrates' question reflects his own belief that badness implies harmfulness. In posing the question, he is trying to ascertain whether Meno also appreciates this implication. Meno responds by claiming that some people who desire bad things, recognizing those things to be bad, think that those things are beneficial, whereas others recognize that those things are harmful.[27] In short, Meno distinguishes two types of people who conform to (c):

(d) some people desire things that are bad, recognize that these things are bad, but believe that these bad things benefit them;

(e) some people desire things that are bad, recognize that these things are bad, and recognize that these things harm them.

I will refer to the class of people who satisfy the description in (e) as masochists. Socrates does not immediately attend to the alleged masochists. Instead, he focuses on the people of (d), whom I will refer to as the base.

Consonant with my explanation of Meno's commitment to (c), I suggest that Meno commits to (d) for the following reason. Previously, he had accepted (b) as one legitimate interpretation of (a). According to that admission, some people desire bad things *de re*, that is, things that in fact are bad; but they think that the objects of their desire o are good. However, Meno also believes that people desire things that they recognize to be bad, in the sense that they recognize that o is regarded as base by the best sort of people. Still, the base believe—from Meno's perspective, misguidedly—that o is beneficial. In view of this interpretation, it is evident that the phrase "recognize that o is bad" in (c) and (d) is ambiguous. It may mean *recognize that o is held to be bad* or *recognize, in the sense of know, that o in fact is bad*. I suggest that Socrates poses the following question regarding the base in order to resolve precisely this ambiguity of the phrase: "And do you really

24. Men. 77c7–d1. I read *hautôi* for *autôi*, as in Smp. 204d, 205e.
25. Smp. 204d, 205e.
26. Men. 77d1–3.
27. Men. 77d3–4.

believe that they *recognize* that the bad things are bad when they believe that the bad things are beneficial?"[28] Given Socrates' own view that what is good is beneficial and what is bad is harmful, he is committed to the view that the base cannot recognize, in the sense of know, that *o* is bad, while at the same time believing that *o* is beneficial.

Meno evidently grasps the thrust of Socrates' question, for he concedes the point: "No, not at all, I grant you that [*ou panu moi dokei touto ge*]."[29] The particle *ge* here is concessive and limiting. Meno concedes Socrates' point about the base: According to Socrates' conception of recognizing that *o* is bad, the base do not in fact recognize that *o* is bad. Still, Meno maintains that the other class of people, the masochists of (e), do in fact desire bad things while recognizing that they are bad.

Given Meno's concession that the base do not recognize, in the sense of know, that *o* is bad, Socrates now draws the conclusion that the base do not desire bad things:

> Clearly, then, (1) these people who are ignorant that [the objects of their desire] in fact are bad do not desire bad things. (2) Rather, they desire those things that they have been considering good, (3) even though these things in fact are bad. (4) Consequently, those who are ignorant that the objects of their desire are bad and think them good clearly desire the good things. Right?[30]

I have inserted numerals to facilitate explication of the passage.[31] In view of the preceding discussion, it is clear that Socrates' aim here is to confirm that the base do not desire bad things. Once he has made this point, he turns to the only remaining set of people who allegedly desire bad things, the masochists of (e). In short, the function of the passage is conclusively to eliminate one of the last two sets of people from the class of those who, Meno alleges, desire bad things.

> (1) Clearly, then, these people (*houtoi men*) who are ignorant that
> [the objects of their desire] (*hoi agnoountes auta*) are in fact bad
> do not desire bad things.

The demonstrative pronoun *houtoi* refers to the base. The particle *men*, which follows the demonstrative pronoun, indicates that these people will be contrasted with another class of people, namely the masochists to whom Socrates addresses himself in the exchange following the passage.[32] Socrates' claim in (1) is that the base clearly do not desire bad things. The reason he gives is that the base are ignorant that *o* in fact is bad. The participial phrase *hoi agnoountes auta* is,

---

28. *Men.* 77d5–6, with my italics.
29. *Men.* 77d6–7.
30. *oukoun dêlon hoti houtoi men ou tôn kakôn epithumousin, hoi agnoountes auta, alla ekeinôn, ha ôionto agatha einai, esti de tauta ge kaka; hôste hoi agnoountes auta kai oiomenoi agatha einai dêlon hoti tôn agathôn epithumousin; ê ou?* (*Men.* 77d7–e4)
31. In this, I am following Penner and Rowe (1994).
32. Socrates' remarks following the passage begin *ti de?* I take the *de* here at *Men.* 77e5 to answer to the *men* of the passage.

accordingly, explanatory. In view of the preceding discussion—specifically Socrates' distinction between the objective and subjective values of *o* that emerges from his explanation of (a) as (b)—the participial phrase explains that the base do not desire bad things; they do not *because* they regard *o* as beneficial and so good. This indicates that desire for *o follows* an evaluation of *o* as good. This interpretation is further supported by (2) and (3):

(2) Rather (*alla*), they desire those things that they have been considering (*oionto*) good,

(3) even though these things in fact are bad (*esti de tauta ge kaka*).

Rather (*alla*), the base regard *o* as good and desire *o* because they believe that *o* is good. And yet *o* in fact is bad; (3) emphasizes the distinction between the objective value, bad, of the things that the base desire and the subjective value, good, that the base mistakenly attribute to those things. In short, the contrast precisely serves to distinguish the value that the desiring subject attributes to *o* and the objective value of *o*.

Note also the force of the imperfect *oionto* (have been considering) in (2). The desire of the base temporally follows upon the belief, previously formed and maintained from an indefinite point in the past to the present, about the value of *o*.

(4) Consequently (*hôste*), those who are ignorant that the objects of their desire are bad and think them good clearly (*dêlon*) desire the good things.

It follows from this (*hôste*) that clearly (*dêlon*) since the base are ignorant that the objective value of *o* is bad and that the value they attach to *o* is good, they desire good things. In other words, they desire *o* because they have the false belief that *o* is good.

In sum, the conception of desire implicit in Socrates' psychological explanation of the base is that desire for an object *o* results from an evaluation of *o* as good. I will speak of this as a subjectivist conception of desire insofar as the object desired is desired upon its evaluation by the subject as good.

Meno responds to the passage by conceding Socrates' point, that the base in fact desire good things: "In their case, at least, it seems so."[33] Having eliminated the base as candidates for the set of people who desire bad things, Socrates proceeds to the last remaining group, the masochists of (e). First, he confirms Meno's claim about such people: "I presume, then, as you say, that those who desire bad things and believe that the bad things are harmful to those who have them, recognize that they will be harmed by these bad things [that they desire]?"[34] Meno confirms that this follows from the previous admissions.[35] Consequently, Socrates elicits Meno's assent to the following implications. The alleged masochists believe that

---

33. *Men.* 77e4. I interpret the particle *ge* here in the same way as in 77d7, concessive and limiting.
34. *Men.* 77e5–7.
35. *Men.* 78a1.

those who are harmed are wretched (*athlioi*) insofar as they are
harmed;

and

the wretched are miserable (*kakodaimones*).[36]

From this it follows that some people desire to be wretched and miserable, and
Socrates now asks, "So is there anyone who desires to be wretched and miserable?"
Meno concedes that

(f) no one desires to be wretched and miserable.[37]

Consequently, masochists do not exist, and Socrates concludes and Meno admits
that therefore no one desires bad things.[38]

Terry Penner and Christopher Rowe raise a difficulty for this interpretation of
Socrates' argument against the masochists of (e) that pertains to (f) and to
Socrates' following comment related to (f):

(g) being wretched is desiring and getting bad things.[39]

If desire in (a) is interpreted subjectively, as for example in (b), then one must also
suppose that (e) is about desire for things *thought* bad. But then, Penner and Rowe
argue,

> The point [in (f)] that no one wants to be [miserable] must [consequently] be
> the point that no one wants what *appears* to them to be [misery]; and to be
> [miserable] must be [as in (g)] to desire *apparently* bad things and get them.
> But this is plainly unsatisfactory. What if the apparently bad things are really
> good? Will it really be [misery] to desire and get things which, though they
> appear bad, *are really good*? Surely that is not Socrates' intention. His intention
> must be that [misery in (f)] is desiring *really* bad things and getting them.[40]

Penner and Rowe's objection fails to appreciate two points. The first is that
the context in which (g) is introduced is the discussion of the masochists of (e).
These *hypothetical* psychological types—after all, Socrates argues that no such
people exist—are said to desire bad things *and to recognize that the things they desire
are bad*. Recall that in discussing the base of (d), who, Meno claimed, recognize
that the object of their desire *o* is bad, we observed that the phrase "recognize that
o is bad" is ambiguous between *recognize that* o *is held to be bad* and *recognize, in the
sense of know, that* o *is in fact bad*. Socrates, then, argues that the base do not
recognize, in the sense of know, that the object of their desire is bad. Accordingly,
the masochists of (e), in being said to recognize that *o* is bad, in contrast to the

---

36. Men. 78a1–4.
37. Men. 78a4–5.
38. Men. 78a5–b2.
39. Men. 78a7–8.
40. (1994) 16.

base of (d), do know that *o* is bad. Therefore, the masochists desire *o*, which they evaluate as bad, and their evaluation is correct.

Given this context, (f), no one desires to be wretched and miserable, and (g), being wretched is desiring and getting bad things, must be understood to mean

(f2) correctly judging that *o* brings or constitutes wretchedness and misery, no one desires *o*;

(g2) being wretched is desiring things that one correctly judges to be bad and getting those bad things.

The second point that Penner and Rowe miss is that since Socrates' argument against (e) is a *reductio*,[41] (f2) and (g2) need not reflect claims to which Socrates is committed or, more importantly, that are Platonic. Rather, Socrates derives them from Meno's commitment to the existence of masochists. Yet the conclusion of the argument is that masochists do not exist and therefore that no psychological types exist who desire bad things. But since no one desires bad things, the psychological conditions described in (f2) and (g2) do not exist.

In sum, the foregoing interpretation of the first part of Socrates' criticism of Meno's third definition of excellence involves a conception of desire according to which desire is for an object *o* evaluated as good. More precisely, desire for *o* follows upon the subject's evaluation of *o* as good. Since people may misjudge the objective value of *o*, they may pursue objects whose acquisition is not good for them. Consequently, well-being requires knowledge of what is good.

Finally, recall that Meno introduces his original definition through reference to a poet, perhaps Simonides. Since certain poets were traditionally regarded as reservoirs of wisdom, specifically wisdom reflective of aristocratic ideals, Socrates' criticism of Meno's definition can be viewed as targeting a traditional aristocratic ideal through a representative aristocrat's unreflective endorsement of that ideal and incapacity to provide an adequate defense of it. In short, by arguing that all people desire those things that they have evaluated as good, the force of Socrates' conclusion is that excellence requires the ability to accurately evaluate what is good.

3. Instrumental and Terminal Desires

At *Gorgias* 466e–468e Socrates and Polus engage in two arguments concerning the power of orators. In the course of the second argument Socrates employs the premise that everyone desires good things. This premise appears to be equivalent to Socrates' conclusion in *Meno*. However, in the context of the *Gorgias* argument, it does not mean that desiderata are evaluated as good, but that desiderata in fact

---

41. *Reductio* is, as here, typically short for *reductio ad absurdum*. *Reductio* is a type of argument where one assumes a thesis and argues on the basis of this assumption to some untenable (for example, self-contradictory, impossible, absurd, ridiculous) position. On the basis of the conclusion, one infers that the assumed thesis is false. As we will see, Plato deploys *reductiones* (plural of *reductio*) throughout the early dialogues. For a deeper and more formal account, see Rescher (2006).

are good. Socrates' premise in *Gorgias*, therefore, contradicts the Platonic conception of desire in *Meno*.

Socrates' arguments with Polus have been treated as important for the interpretation of Plato's conception of desire among the early dialogues, but substantial controversy surrounds their correct interpretation. I regard the importance that has been placed on the *Gorgias* passage for understanding desire in the early dialogues as misguided, for I believe that the premise that everyone desires what in fact is good is employed as a dialectical expedient. As such, it provides no evidence for a Platonic conception of desire. In this section, I will examine the argument and expose the interpretive error of identifying as Platonic the premise that everyone desires the good.

The stretch of argumentation at *Gorgias* 466a–468e develops in response to Polus' view that orators have great power in their cities. The passage is divisible into two arguments: 466a4–467a10 and 467c5–468e5. In the first, Socrates argues as follows that orators do not have power because they lack intelligence:

(a) Power is something good for its possessor.
(b) Orators do whatever they think best.
(c) When one lacks intelligence, doing what one thinks best is not good for oneself.
(d) Therefore, power is not the ability to do whatever one thinks best.
(e) Orators lack intelligence.
    Therefore, orators lack power.

The argument depends on the view that one may have the ability to do whatever one thinks best, but that this ability is not a power; it therefore requires the distinction between ability and power. The argument satisfies this requirement by identifying power in (a) as something good for its possessor and by indicating in (c) that some abilities are not good for their possessors.

Although (a) serves the argument, it may be objected that power is not necessarily good for its possessor. Indeed, Plato himself was well aware that the word *dunamis* (power) could be used to mean capacity for good or bad. In *Hippias Major*, Socrates suggests a definition of fineness as power, but then he rejects the definition on the grounds that since power may be instrumental to some bad end, power is not always fine.[42] However, in *Gorgias* Socrates does not simply introduce or stipulate an unconventional meaning of "power":

POLUS   Do [orators] not have the greatest power in their cities?

SOCRATES   No—not if by having power you mean having something good for one who is powerful.

POLUS   But of course that is what I mean.[43]

---

42. *Hp. Ma.* 295e5–296d7.
43. *Grg.* 466b4–5.

Socrates would not want to deny the obvious, that orators have power in the sense that they effect persuasion widely. They obviously have that ability. But Socrates recognizes that in claiming that orators have great power, Polus also intends to convey that this competence is valuable. Accordingly, Socrates correctly interprets Polus' claim to imply not merely that orators have the ability to effect persuasion among the citizenry, but that this particular competence is a good thing for them to have. As we see, Polus strongly assents to this interpretation of his claim.

Granted this, it may still be objected that the argument is ad hominem: Socrates employs (a), not because he believes it is true, but because he believes Polus will commit to it and that he can refute Polus by means of it. But this objection is misguided. Socrates' intention is not simply to refute Polus by whatever means he can. He honestly believes that the ability orators have—call it what one will—is not a good thing. It is more appropriate, then, to characterize Socrates as arguing that orators do not have power insofar as power is a good thing for its possessor.

This point is further elucidated by consideration of the relationship of Socrates' argument to the claims he makes about rhetoric as a type of flattery that immediately precede and prompt the argument. In his critique of rhetoric as a type of flattery, Socrates claims that rhetoric is not a craft (technê), but a competence (empeiria) that is a poor semblance of the genuine craft of justice or statesmanship. Crafts possess two components that rhetoric, therefore, lacks. First, crafts are epistemic. Specifically, Socrates distinguishes two aspects of the knowledge that constitutes a craft: physiological, that is, knowledge of phusis (nature) and aetiological, knowledge of aitia (cause).[44] For example, in the case of medicine, whose subject matter is bodily health, physiological knowledge is knowledge of the identity of bodily health (what bodily health is), and aetiological knowledge is knowledge of how to produce bodily health.[45] Second, crafts are ethical; that is, they serve some good or produce some benefit. For example, health is the good that medicine produces. Socrates maintains that pleasure is a semblance (eidôlon) of goodness and that rhetoric, and others forms of flattery such as cookery, fashion, and sophistry, are concerned with pleasure, not goodness.

The competence that the orator possesses is to be identified with his ability to effect persuasion among the citizenry. But this competence is not a craft, for it is neither epistemic nor ethical. For this reason, Socrates maintains that orators lack intelligence. And also for this reason his employment of (a) is not merely ad hominem.

In the course of the first argument, specifically in the context of (b), (c), and (d), Polus speaks indiscriminately of doing what one thinks best and doing what one desires. Socrates objects that the two are not the same. Polus strongly disagrees, and the disagreement prompts a second argument. Before I proceed to give an account of the second argument, it is worth considering why Plato has Socrates develop a second argument.

---

44. Grg. 465a. Note that Socrates repeats this point in his discussion with Callicles at 501a.
45. The example is based on Socrates' example at Grg. 501a.

In the first argument, Socrates maintains in (c) that when one lacks intelligence, doing what one thinks best is not good for oneself, and in (e) that orators lack intelligence. However, he does not specify how it is that when one lacks intelligence, doing what one thinks best is not good for oneself. Polus accepts (c); still (c) is susceptible to at least two interpretations. These two interpretations are explicable in view of Socrates' distinction between two epistemic components of a craft, *physiological* and *aetiological*. *Physiological* knowledge can be understood as knowledge of ends, whereas *aetiological* knowledge can be understood as knowledge of means. Accordingly, insofar as one's lack of intelligence entails lack of knowledge of ends, one might falsely think that pleasure is identical to goodness and therefore pursue pleasure as best for oneself. Alternatively, insofar as one's lack of intelligence entails lack of knowledge of means, one might know that health is good for oneself, but because one falsely believes that murdering one's fellow citizens is conducive to one's health, murder one's fellow citizens in pursuit of one's health.

Socrates' second argument with Polus focuses on the alternative interpretation of lack of intelligence, that is, on the significance of *aetiological* ignorance. There are two reasons for this. One relates to the immediate context of the dialogue; the other relates to the broader context of the dialogue. The first reason is that in the course of the first argument Polus identifies the capabilities of orators with certain types of action emblematic of tyranny or despotism:

SOCRATES   I think the orators have the least power of all in their city-states.

POLUS   What? Do they not, like tyrants, execute whomever they desire, confiscate property, and banish from their city-states whomever they think best?[46]

Polus need not be viewed as bloodthirsty, but evidently his attraction to having such capabilities is strong. Accordingly, in the second argument Socrates clarifies that political leaders do not (usually) pursue such courses of action as ends in themselves, but for the sake of goods such as health, wealth, and security. Accordingly, Socrates focuses on the relationship between actions as instrumental to desired ends.

The significance of Socrates' focus on *aetiological* knowledge in relation to the larger context of the dialogues is this. In the remainder of the Polus episode (468e–481b) and in most of the Callicles episode (481b to the end of the dialogue) Socrates' arguments focus on the nature of goodness, in other words *physiological* knowledge. From this perspective, the structure of the dialogue can be seen as moving from an examination of the problem of *aetiological* knowledge to an examination of the problem of *physiological* knowledge. There is a significant disparity in proportion between the space Plato allots to the two sections, and I take it that this correlates with the importance that Plato attributes to them. I regard this as related to Platonic endorsement of the epistemological priority of

46. Grg. 466b9–c2.

definitional knowledge: One must know what something is before one can know, for instance, how to achieve or bring that thing about.[47]

Seen in this light, Socrates' second argument with Polus is very much akin to his refutation of Thrasymachus' definition of justice as the good for the superior at *Republic* 1 339a5–340a2. Thrasymachus argues that rulers establish laws to serve their own interests and thus that justice entails their subjects' obedience to the laws. Socrates, however, argues that since rulers are fallible and may therefore establish some laws that are detrimental to themselves, their subjects' obedience to those laws is not good for the rulers. Accordingly, both this argument and Socrates' second argument with Polus draw attention to the potential for means to fail to achieve desired ends.

So much then for the reasons for Socrates' development of the second argument. Recall that the argument itself arises in response to the disagreement between Socrates and Polus that doing what one thinks best and doing what one desires are not the same. The basic construction of the argument is

(f) When one performs an action for the sake of some object, one desires the object,
and one desires the action insofar as it conduces to the object. Everything is either good, bad, or neither-good-nor-bad.

(g) Wisdom, health, wealth, and such things are good.

(h) Ignorance, illness, poverty, and such things are bad. Actions undertaken for the sake of some good are neither-good-nor-bad. People perform neither-good-nor-bad actions for the sake of good things.

(i) People desire good things, not neither-good-nor-bad things or bad things.

(j) If one performs an action, thinking that it is beneficial, yet it is harmful, then one does what one thinks best, but not what one desires.

(k) Therefore, one may do what one thinks best, but fail to do what one desires.

Premise (f) plays a crucial role in the argument. Both its content and function have been misunderstood. In the course of the argument, Socrates makes a number of claims, on the basis of which I have derived (f). He begins the argument by presenting Polus with a disjunctive question:

(1) do people desire that which they do on each occasion (*heka-sto te*), or

(2) do people desire that for the sake of which they do what they do . . . ?[48]

Socrates subsequently argues for and Polus agrees to (2).

---

47. This point will be discussed at length in chapters 3 and 4.
48. *Grg.* 467c5–7. I have inserted numerals to facilitate explication.

Kevin McTighe has interpreted (2) as claiming that "all action is such that if a person does something, he desires only that for the sake of which he acts, not the action itself."[49] I suggest that McTighe has misinterpreted (2). After introducing the disjunctive question, Socrates clarifies himself through two examples: taking bitter medicine for the sake of health and suffering danger on a merchant ship for the sake of profit. Polus agrees that in these cases the agent desires health, as opposed to medicine, and the agent desires profit, as opposed to the sea journey. Consequently, Socrates states and Polus agrees to

(f2) When a man performs an action for the sake of some object, he
　　　desires the object, not the action.[50]

I emphasize that in (f2) Socrates is speaking of occasions when a man performs an action for the sake of some object. Thus, although it is not explicit in his formulation of the original disjunctive question, Socrates is not making an argument about any action whatsoever. Rather, he is making an argument about instrumental action. The adverb *hekastote* in disjunct (1) must, then, be interpreted to mean that people desire that which they do *whenever they act for the sake of something*, rather than simply *whenever they act*.

Granted this, Socrates has been accused of inconsistency on the grounds that (f2) contradicts the following proposition to which Socrates subsequently commits:

(f3) When a man performs an action for the sake of some object, he
　　　desires the action insofar as the action conduces to the desired
　　　object.[51]

So, it is alleged, Socrates initially denies that action performed for the sake of some object is desired, but subsequently admits that it can be.

I suggest that in view of (f3), it is simply uncharitable to interpret Socrates as committed to (f2) such that Socrates contradicts himself in the space of what in fact is one Stephanus page.[52] I propose a more reasonable explanation of the relationship between (f2) and (f3). In the course of the second argument, Socrates is clarifying the motivational structure in action performed for the sake of some object. Hereafter I will refer to such action as instrumental action. Socrates first clarifies that when action is undertaken for the sake of some object, that action is not desired per se; in other words, that action is not desired for itself. Accordingly, Socrates initially introduces (f2) in order to highlight the distinction between means and ends in the interest of illuminating the deeper motivational structure operative in instrumental action. As such, the examples of taking medicine and

---

49. McTighe (1984) 203.
50. *Grg.* 467d6–e1.
51. *Grg.* 468c2–5.
52. The phrase "Stephanus page" refers to the pagination system used in the edition (1578) of the
　　Platonic corpus of Henri Estienne II (1531–1598), whose last named is Latinized as "Stephanus."

risking one's life at sea are employed, not in a cunning effort to compel upon Polus a fallacious belief. Rather, the stark contrast between taking bitter medicine or suffering danger at sea and recovering one's health or making a profit is intended to be particularly useful in conveying or at least developing these points. In short, (f2) is an imprecise formulation, but, like the examples on the basis of which it is inferred, it is dialectically expedient.

In clarifying the nature of desire in instrumental action, Socrates scrutinizes the accuracy of conventional desiderative reports. Polus believes that orators or tyrants may desire to execute, banish, or steal from citizens, and, as we have seen, he regards the ability to execute such desires as indicative of a valuable power. In developing (f), Socrates is claiming that orators and tyrants do not desire these actions per se: "Then we do not desire to execute or exile people from cities or confiscate their property simply so (haplôs houtôs), but if these things are beneficial [in other words, if these things conduce to something good], then we desire to do them."[53] Socrates' phrase haplôs houtôs corresponds to the phrase "per se." In contemporary philosophy of psychology it is common to make the terminological distinction between intrinsic and extrinsic desires. Plato, as usual, does not have Socrates coin terminology to facilitate exposition. Nonetheless, in view of the phrase haplôs houtôs and for the sake of clarity, it will be convenient to employ a terminological distinction between desires for things for their own sakes and desires for things as means to other things desired for their own sakes. I will, however, resist the familiar intrinsic/extrinsic desire distinction because, as Christine Korsgaard has argued,[54] the extrinsic/intrinsic distinction is not equivalent to the instrumental/end distinction. Instead, I will speak of instrumental and terminal desire.

In (f), then, Socrates is claiming that in the case of instrumental action, the action is instrumentally desired and that for the sake of which the action is performed is terminally desired. Granted this, it is a question what ends orators and tyrants do desire and, subsequently whether their actions are conducive to those ends.

Following Socrates' trichotomy of things as good, bad, and neither-good-nor-bad, Polus and he agree that neither-good-nor-bad things, which correspond to instrumental actions, are pursued for the sake of good things:

SOCRATES For we desire good things, as you yourself admit; we do not desire neither-good-nor-bad things, nor do we desire bad things. Right?...

POLUS True.[55]

In this passage, Socrates and Polus commit to (i), people desire good things, not neither-good-nor-bad things or bad things. Before we proceed to consider the proposition that people desire good things, it is worth commenting on the rest of

53. Grg. 468c2–4.
54. Korsgaard (1983).
55. Grg. 468c5–8.

the content of (i). In view of (f), Socrates cannot mean that people do not desire neither-good-nor-bad things at all. Rather, he must mean that people do not terminally desire neither-good-nor-bad things.

The claim that people do not desire bad things is somewhat odd, for the idea that people desire bad things has not been entertained in their exchange; thus, denial of it would seem to be unnecessary. I suggest that Socrates' introduction of the point relates to the fact that the passage in which Socrates and Polus commit to (i) begins with Socrates remarking, "Then we do not desire to kill people, exile them from our cities, or steal their property simply so, but if these things are beneficial, we desire to do them, and if they are harmful, we do not desire to do them." Accordingly, in eliciting Polus' assent to the claim that people do not desire bad things, Socrates is stressing that these sorts of actions that orators or tyrants may perform, which are conventionally conceived as horrible, are not undertaken for the sake of badness. Thus, while the actions themselves are atypical—in that few citizens ever perform them—insofar as the discussion concerns desire in instrumental action, the psychology of the despots or tyrants does not differ from the psychology of others.

We come to the claim that people desire good things. I will refer to this as (i2). First, (i2) must be understood to mean that people terminally desire good things. Second, note that (i2) is not submitted as claim about all human desire. In other words, in committing to (i2), Socrates and Polus are not committing to the proposition that all human desires are for the good. Rather, (i2) pertains to those occasions when people undertake action for the sake of some good—even granted that such occasions constitute a large subset of the events that constitute human lives.

Granted then that the context in which it is affirmed implies that (i2) has a more specific meaning than that all desire is for the good, still, particularly in view of (g)—wisdom, health, wealth, and such things are good—the context indicates that Socrates and Polus understand (i2) to mean that the objects for the sake of which instrumental action is undertaken are objectively good.

This contradicts my interpretation of the Platonic conception of desire in *Meno*. I suggest that in *Gorgias*, while Socrates is being sincere, the view that desiderata are objectively good is not Platonic. There are two reasons for thinking so. The main reason is that in *Meno* and *Euthydemus* Socrates develops arguments that health and wealth are not objectively good.[56] Socrates conceptualizes such things as facilitators, for they may facilitate good as well as bad action.[57] Indeed, I think it is for this reason that in the first argument with Polus Socrates claims not merely that orators and tyrants have no power, but that they have the least power of anyone in their city-states. Insofar as power is good for its possessor, orators and tyrants, who have the greatest ability to do bad, have the least of what is good for them.

---

56. *Men.* 78c; *Euthd.* 281d–e. See also *Ap.* 28b5–9, 29d7–e2, 30a7–b4; *Cri.* 48c6–d5.
57. I discuss these arguments in section 3 of chapter 3. See Dimas (2003).

There is, then, good reason on the basis of arguments elsewhere among the early dialogues to think that (i2) is not Platonic. But there is also good reason to think that (i2) is not Platonic on the basis of the immediate context of *Gorgias*. As I emphasized above, Socrates' second argument with Polus concerns instrumental reasoning. Accordingly, Plato does not here have Socrates investigate and challenge conventional conceptions of what is good. Rather, he simplifies the discussion by granting the conventional list of good and bad things, and he focuses on instrumental reasoning in terms of these. At the same time, this circumscription of the discussion is itself innocuous since most of Socrates' and Polus' contemporaries would regard the items Socrates lists as goods, and they would describe their actions as motivated toward them. Accordingly, (g), (h), and (i) should be understood as commonsensical propositions. They are not introduced as axioms of human psychology, but as claims that, on empirical grounds, are generally true. In short, they should be interpreted to imply that

> When people undertake actions for the sake of certain ends, generally, people undertake those actions for the sake of things such as wisdom, health, and wealth.

Granted this, Socrates and Polus now continue their exchange:

SOCRATES   ... if one man, be he a tyrant or an orator, kills or banishes from a city another man or confiscates his property, and [he performs the action] believing that it is better for himself [that is, that the action is conducive to some good that he desires], yet it is worse [that is, it conduces to something bad], then that man, I take it, does what he thinks best—correct?

POLUS   Yes.

SOCRATES   Then is it also the case that he does what he desires if these things in fact are bad [that is, if what he does conduces to something bad]? ...

POLUS   Okay, I think he does not do what he desires.[58]

In short, Socrates infers (j):

> If someone performs an action, thinking that it is beneficial, yet it is harmful, he does what he thinks best, but he does not do what he desires.

And he concludes (k):

> One may do what one thinks best, but fail to do what one desires.

Finally, then, let us specify how Socrates' argument clarifies the distinction between doing what one thinks best and doing what one desires.

---

58. *Grg.* 468d1–7.

"Doing what one thinks best" is vague; it might be interpreted in at least one of two ways: undertaking the means that one believes are conducive to a given end, or achieving the end that one believes is good. Likewise, at least before the second argument, "doing what one desires" might be interpreted in at least one of two ways: undertaking the means that one desires in order to achieve a given end, or achieving the desired end. The second argument reveals that in (j), by "doing what one thinks best" Socrates understands undertaking the means that one believes are conducive to a given end, and by "doing what one desires" he understands achieving the desired end. Accordingly, (j) should be interpreted as

If someone performs an action, thinking that it is beneficial, yet it is harmful, he does what he thinks best, that is, he acts according to his—in this case false—belief about how his action will achieve his terminal desire, but he does not do what he terminally desires, that is, he does not satisfy his terminal desire.

Accordingly, (k) should be interpreted as

One may do what one thinks best, that is, perform the act that one believes is conducive to the satisfaction of one's terminal desire, but fail to do what one terminally desires, that is, fail to satisfy one's terminal desire.

In sum, Socrates has argued that doing what one thinks best is not the same as doing what one desires. The argument depends upon the premise that everyone desires the good. And this premise is to be interpreted *de re*, not, as in *Meno*, *de dicto*. The contradiction between the two interpretations is, however, hermeneutically innocuous; it does not compromise the Platonic subjectivist view of desire, for in *Gorgias* the premise is used as a dialectical expedient.

4. Rational and Irrational Desires

There is another passage among the early dialogues that might be used to argue that the subjectivist interpretation of the principle that everyone desires the good is not Platonic. At *Charmides* 167e1–5 Socrates speaks of pleasure as the object of *epithumia* and goodness as the object of *boulêsis*. Both Greek words may be translated as "desire." But here Socrates clearly distinguishes these motivational states. I suggest, however, that his employment of the distinction in *Charmides* is, Platonically speaking, a dialectical expedient. In other words, Socrates evidently commits to the distinction in *Charmides*. But I do not regard the distinction as Platonic. In fact, I will argue that Plato probably adopted the distinction from the sophist Prodicus.

In *Protagoras* Socrates also refers to a distinction between *epithumia* and *boulêsis*. The context in which the reference occurs is the interpretation of Simonides' ode. Protagoras has presented his interpretation, and Socrates claims to be overwhelmed. To bide time so that he can generate an adequate response, Socrates calls on Prodicus' assistance; he says that in order to defend Simonides against

Protagoras' critique, he needs that education by which "[Prodicus] distinguishes *boulesthai* and *epithumein* as not being the same,[59] as well as the many fine distinctions [Prodicus] recently made."[60] Socrates' last phrase refers to Prodicus' speech at 337a1–c4, in which Plato, parodying Prodicus' interest in subtle linguistic distinctions, makes Prodicus distinguish between common and equal, listening and heeding, disputing and contending, being well reputed and being praised, and, as I noted in the first section of this chapter, being contented and being pleased. Consider also that at the conclusion of his critique of *akrasia*, which occurs later in *Protagoras*, Socrates requests that Prodicus overlook the distinctions between pleasurable (*hêdu*), delightful (*terpnon*), and joyful (*charton*).[61] The distinction between *boulêsis* and *epithumia* in *Protagoras* is, then, specifically identified as Prodicean, and it is introduced within a comic context.

The distinction of *epithumia* and *boulêsis* in *Charmides* does not occur in a comic context. On the other hand, the distinction is not vital to and hardly important for the broader argument. The concepts of *epithumia* and *boulêsis* play no significant role in the investigation of sound-mindedness. Furthermore, Socrates does not argue for this distinction. Rather, he employs it in passing, along with a number of other distinctions between kinds of powers (*dunameis*) and their objects.

In examining whether knowledge of knowledge and all other knowledges and lack of knowledge exists, Socrates considers hypothetical instances of the principle that a power may have itself as the object upon which it acts. For example, he questions whether a vision of vision could exist, for vision itself would have to have properties that belong to objects of vision such as color and shape. In arguing that powers most likely cannot act upon themselves, he does not require the particular distinction between *epithumia* and *boulêsis*; he merely needs a broad set of kinds of powers, including psychological states. Accordingly, I regard the distinction between *epithumia* and *boulêsis* as a convenience and, therefore, particularly with regard to the argument in the *Meno* passage, hermeneutically innocuous.

Note further that within *Charmides*, Critias, in explaining his definition of sound-mindedness as doing one's own thing, introduces a distinction between working (*ergazesthai*), doing (*prattein*), and making (*poiein*). It becomes clear that Critias is unable to maintain this distinction,[62] and in response Socrates says, "In fact, I have heard Prodicus drawing innumerable distinctions between words. Indeed, I will allow you any application of words that you want—just make clear what it is to which you attach a given word!"[63]

There is still a further reason why Socrates' use of the words *epithumia* and *boulêsis* to refer to two distinct motivational states is not Platonic. Given the subjectivist conception of desire in *Meno*, particular objects, courses of action, or

---

59. *boulesthai* and *epithumein* here are verbs used in infinitival constructions equivalent to the nouns *boulêsis* and *epithumia*, respectively.
60. *Prt.* 340a7–b2.
61. *Prt.* 358b.
62. I discuss this passage in greater detail in section 3.4 of chapter 5.
63. *Chrm.* 163d3–7.

conditions are desiderata as a result of their fallible evaluation as good. Accordingly, the desire for pleasure would be understood as a desire for that sensation or sensation-producing thing as a consequence of its evaluation as good. Therefore, the view that there is a particular motivational state whose object is pleasure is not Platonic. In short, while I grant that Socrates sincerely distinguishes *epithumia* and *boulêsis* at *Charmides* 167e1–5, I deny that this is good evidence that the distinction is Platonic.

5. Desire in the Critique of *Akrasia*

The claim in *Meno* that all people desire the good means that all people desire objects as a result of fallibly evaluating them as good. This suggests that every desire for a particular course of action or object *o* is rational just insofar as it follows an evaluation of *o* as good. I suggest that this subjectivist conception of desire in *Meno* is Platonic since it is argued for and since the argument is not contradicted by any other conception of desire among the early dialogues that we should consider Platonic. Furthermore, Socrates argues for the conclusion against a conception of desire that is conventional, at least from within the sphere of aristocratic values. Accordingly, the conclusion is unconventional.

The subjectivist conception of desire is inconsistent with what are commonsensically conceived as brute impulses or irrational desires, which may not depend on evaluations of their objects as good or which may override subjectivist desires. In fact, one scholar has argued that in the *Meno* passage itself Socrates distinguishes irrational desires or impulses, which he refers to as *epithumiai*, from rational evaluative desires, which he refers to as *boulêseis*.[64] I do not see any evidence in the *Meno* passage that Socrates employs this distinction. For example, consider that when he clarifies the meaning of "desire" as desiring to obtain *o*,[65] he uses the verb *epithumein*. Furthermore, as we saw in the preceding section, there is no compelling evidence elsewhere among the early dialogues that such a distinction between rational and irrational desires is Platonic. In particular, the view that the view that the subjectivist conception of desire explains all desires for particular objects or courses of action is Platonic is strongly supported by Socrates' critique and intellectualist analysis of *akrasia* (weakness of will) in *Protagoras*, for cases of *akrasia* are supposed to be paradigms of irrational desire or brute impulse.

Socrates' critique and intellectualist analysis of *akrasia* occurs in the final movement of *Protagoras* (from 349a on). This movement is devoted to an examination of the relationship between courage and knowledge. At 349e1–351b2 Socrates presents an argument for the identity of courage and knowledge, and Protagoras rejects this argument. At 352b3–360e5 Socrates presents a second argument for the identity of courage and knowledge, which Protagoras grudgingly concedes. In section 2 of chapter 3, I will have more to say about why Socrates

---

64. Weiss (2001) 35. *epithumiai* and *boulêseis* are plurals of *epithumia* and *boulêsis*, respectively.
65. *Men.* 77c.

develops two arguments and how Protagoras criticizes the first. My present focus will be on the second argument, specifically on Socrates' critique and intellectualist analysis of *akrasia* within it.

To be precise, Socrates criticizes the condition that the many (*hoi polloi*) characterize as knowingly being overcome by pleasure.[66] In other words, he criticizes the popular conception of knowledge-*akrasia* of a particular kind. Contrast this, for example, with criticizing belief-*akrasia* of a particular kind, such as the condition of a man who believes that a course of action is good, but who, because he is overcome by fear, fails to execute the action. For convenience, I will speak of Socrates' criticism simply of *akrasia*, but it should be kept in mind that the criticism is of *akrasia* of a particular kind, once again, knowledge-relative-to-pleasure.

Socrates' criticism employs the argument form *reductio*,[67] which he uses twice. The structure of his critique of *akrasia* and its immediate context is

352b1–353b6	Socrates and Protagoras maintain that knowledge is invincible
353c1–354e2	Ethical hedonism is determined to be a popular view
354e3–355c1	Socrates prepares the *reductio* arguments
355c1–e3	Socrates' first use of *reductio* with commentary
355e4–356c3	Socrates' second use of *reductio* with commentary
356c4–357e8	Socrates' intellectualist analysis of being overcome by pleasure
358b3–d4	Socrates' introduction of the principle that no one willingly does what is bad

In the first *reductio*, given ethical hedonism and the following description of the weakness of being overcome by pleasure

(a) A man willingly[68] performs an act, knowing it to be bad,[69] because he is overcome by pleasure,[70]

Socrates redescribes "pleasure" in (a) as "goodness":

(b) A man willingly performs an act, knowing it to be bad, because he is overcome by goodness.[71]

Socrates then suggests that (b) is ridiculous (*geloion*) and comments on (b). In the second *reductio* Socrates redescribes "bad" in (a) as "painful":

(c) A man willingly performs an act, knowing it to be painful, because he is overcome by pleasure.[72]

---

66. Why Socrates examines a popular conception, rather than Protagoras' view, will be discussed in section 2 of chapter 3.
67. See note 41 in section 2 of this chapter.
68. That is, the agent can freely choose to pursue or avoid the act.
69. That is, while that act contains aspects of both goodness and badness, on balance the act contains more bad than good.
70. *Prt.* 355a7–b1.
71. *Prt.* 355d1–3.
72. *Prt.* 355e5–356a1.

And Socrates comments on (c).

The central problem for the interpretation of Socrates' critique is why Socrates thinks the popular conception of *akrasia* is ridiculous, in other words, why he rejects the popular conception of *akrasia*. I will argue that Socrates' conception of the ridiculousness of the popular conception is made explicit through his comments on (b). There Socrates explains that

> being overcome by goodness implies that the quantity of goodness on balance of the akratic action is greater than the quantity of badness on balance. However, by definition the quantity of the badness on balance of the akratic action is greater than the quantity of goodness on balance. Thus, the popular conception is ridiculous because it is self-contradictory.

Reductio is typically used to refer to *reductio ad absurdum*. But there are other kinds of *reductiones*: *reductio ad impossibile*, *ad falsum*, *ad ridiculum*, and *ad incommodum*. In fact, the phrase *reductio ad absurdum* is sometimes liberally used to refer to these other forms. Strictly speaking, however, *reductio ad absurdum* entails self-contradiction, whereas *reductio ad impossibile* entails impossibility, *ad falsum* falsehood, *ad ridiculum* implausibility, and *ad incommodum* anomaly. I maintain that Socrates indeed employs *reductio ad absurdum*.

Furthermore, the popular view holds that *akrasia* occurs often; indeed, the frequency of putative *akrasia* is repeatedly emphasized. Socrates too thinks that there is some kind of common weakness. Following his *reductiones*, he therefore proceeds to give his own explanation of *akrasia*. This explanation is based on the view that agents often misjudge, or more precisely mismeasure, the relative quantities of goodness and badness of their actions as a result of their propinquity to and distance from these aspects of the action. Finally, following this explanation, Socrates introduces the principle that no one willingly does what is bad. Given ethical hedonism, which remains operative throughout the discussion, this principle implies that it is psychologically impossible knowingly to do what is bad. Ultimately, then, Socrates' critique presents two different reasons for rejecting the popular conception of *akrasia*. The first argues that the concept of being overcome by pleasure is ridiculous because self-contradictory. The second suggests that knowingly doing what is bad is psychologically impossible.

Let us turn now to Socrates' treatment of (b). Following the redescription of (a) as (b), Socrates says that an arrogant interlocutor will laugh at (b) and say, "What a ridiculous thing you are saying, that someone does bad things, knowing that they are bad, and not having to do them, because he is overcome by good things."[73] In other words, this passage expresses that (b) is ridiculous. I suggest that the arrogant interlocutor and Socrates find (b) ridiculous in virtue of the concept of being overcome by good things and that the immediately subsequent passage 355d3–e3, in which Socrates comments on the *reductio*, explains why (b) is ridiculous as such.

---

73. *Prt.* 355d1–3.

The passage 355d3–e3 begins with a question: " 'Is this,' [the arrogant inter-locutor] will ask, 'in your judgment (*en humin*), with the good things not being worthy (*axiôn*) of conquering the bad things, or worthy?' "[74] One interpretive difficulty with the arrogant interlocutor's question is the adjective *axiôn*, since it is a question what it means to ask whether the good things are *worthy* of conquering the bad things or vice versa. The adjective implies that the good things have a certain value. Accordingly, I take the question to ask whether the value of the good things is superior to the value of the bad things. The answer given to this question is that the good things, namely the pleasures by which the akratic is allegedly overcome, are *not* worthy of conquering the bad things: "Clearly we will reply that they [namely, the good things] are not worthy [of conquering the bad things], for then (*gar*) he whom we say is overcome by pleasures would not have erred (*exêmartanen*)."[75] This passage explains that the value of the good things is inferior to the value of the bad things because if the value of the good things were superior to the value of the bad things, then the action would not be an error. In other words, the action qua error is understood to contain more badness than goodness on balance.

It is made explicit in the subsequent passage that the relative worth or value of good and bad things is indeed understood in terms of their relative quantities: "And in what sense . . . are the good things unworthy of the bad things or the bad things unworthy of the good things? Can it be otherwise than that the ones are greater and the others smaller, or that the ones more and the others less? We will not be able to say anything other than this."[76] In short, this passage confirms that the akratic action on balance contains a larger quantity of badness than goodness. Consequently, a conclusion is drawn: " 'Then it is clear,' he will say, 'that this being overcome of which you speak is the taking of greater bad things in exchange (*anti*) for lesser good things.' "[77]

At this point, commentary on (b) ceases, and Socrates turns to (c). I suggest that the reason commentary on (b) ceases here is that the self-contradiction has now been fully revealed. The original claim was that the agent was overcome by good things. It has been explained that being overcome by good things implies that the quantity of good things is superior to the quantity of bad things. But by definition the akratic agent erred, and this implies that his action contains a greater quantity of bad things than good things. Thus, the popular conception is self-contradictory, and so ridiculous.

We turn now to (c). In the introduction to the *reductiones* Socrates says, "It will be clear that these things are ridiculous if we do not use many words at once, pleasant and painful, good and bad.[78] But since these things appeared to be two,

---

74. *Prt.* 355d3–4.
75. *Prt.* 355d4–6.
76. *Prt.* 355d6–e2.
77. *Prt.* 355e2–3.
78. Here and for the most part elsewhere, since the use/mention distinction is not employed, I will not import it.

let us speak of them using two words, first good and bad, *and then in turn pleasant and painful*."[79] Thus, after Socrates has commented on (b), he redescribes "bad" in (a) as "painful." In other words, Socrates expresses (c), and then at 356a1–356c3 he comments on (c). Clearly, then, Socrates regards his treatment of (c), as well as (b), as part of the critique of the popular conception. Accordingly, an explanation of the critique should incorporate Socrates' comments on (c).

Given the redescription of (a) as (c), it should follow that the agent knowingly takes greater pains in exchange for lesser pleasures. This does follow; Socrates speaks of the pleasure as unworthy of defeating the pain,[80] and he explains the unworthiness in terms of relative quantities.[81]

But at this point, Socrates considers a potential objection: In estimating the value of a course of action, it is not merely the respective sum quantities of pleasure and pain that count, but also the relative temporal propinquity to and distance from the agent in the present of the pleasure and pain.[82] The objection suggests that although a course of action may be more painful than pleasant on balance, the immediacy of the pleasure versus the remoteness of the pain may count in favor of pursuing the action. Socrates anticipates the potential objection:

[Does the immediately pleasant differ from the remotely pleasant or painful] in anything other than pleasure and pain? There is no other distinction. But like a man good at weighing, once you have assembled the pleasures and the pains and set on a scale the near and the distant, tell me which ones are greater. For if you weigh pleasures against pleasures, the greater and the more are always to be chosen; whereas if you weigh pains against pains, the smaller and fewer should be chosen (*lêptea*). And if you weigh pleasures against pains and the pleasures exceed the pains, be it the remote exceeding the near or the near exceeding the remote, that course of action should be taken (*prakteon*). But if the pains exceed the pleasures, then they should not be done (*praktea*).[83]

Socrates asserts that the agent's temporal relationship to pleasures and pains does not affect the value of the pleasures and pains. Rather, the value of pleasures and pains depends only on their relative magnitudes. Thus, the relative quantities of pleasures, aggregated from those both near and remote, and pains, aggregated from those both near and remote, should guide one's course of action. I emphasize that Socrates' statement here is not simply a dogmatic assertion that the agent's temporal relationship to the pleasures and pains does not affect the values of those pleasures and pains. His point implies the distinction between the objective and the subjective values of things. In other words, he will grant an objector that a

---

79. *Prt.* 355b3–c1, with my italics.
80. *Prt.* 356a1.
81. *Prt.* 356a1–5.
82. *Prt.* 356a5–7.
83. *Prt.* 356a7–c1.

proximate pleasure may seem more attractive to an agent than a remote pleasure. But, again, the actual values of the proximate and remote pleasures are independent of their temporal relationships to the agent.

The verbal adjectives *lêptea*, *prakteon*, and *praktea* in this passage have been a source of controversy, namely whether they should be taken as implying prudential obligations and so meaning *should be taken* and *should be done* or whether they should be taken as implying psychological necessity and so meaning *must be taken* and *must be done*. The significance of the dispute is that if they are taken in the latter sense, then they may be employed as evidence that psychological hedonism implicitly operates throughout the *reductio*.[84]

There is evidence elsewhere among the early dialogues of these verbal adjectives being used in both ways, so it is a question how the interpretation of these verbal adjectives is to be decided. Clearly we must look to the broader context of the argument. Some scholars point to the principle that no one willingly does what is bad, which features in the discussion immediately following Socrates' intellectualist analysis of *akrasia*, and which in the context of the discussion implies psychological hedonism. However, up to the point in the argument where the verbal adjectives occur, psychological hedonism has not been introduced. Indeed, in view of the argument up to this point, Socrates could not reasonably expect the verbal adjectives to be understood otherwise than as implying prudential obligations. Accordingly, I have translated the passage "if you weigh pains against pains, the smaller and fewer *should be chosen*. And if you weigh pleasures against pains and the pleasures exceed the pains, be it the remote exceeding the near or the near exceeding the remote, that course of action *should be taken*. But if the pains exceed the pleasures, then they *should not be done*."

In view of this conclusion and the preceding remarks on the content of Socrates' comments on (c), the function of (c) within the critique emerges. In the commentary on (b), Socrates explains that (b) is ridiculous because being overcome by pleasure implies both that the quantity of goodness of the akratic action on balance is greater than the quantity of badness, but also the contrary. In the commentary on (c), Socrates adds that the agent's temporal relationship to goodness or pleasure and badness or pain does not affect the value and so magnitude of the goodness or badness. As such, this point addresses a potential objection to Socrates' explanation of the ridiculousness of (b). It also serves as preparatory to Socrates' subsequent intellectualist explanation of *akrasia*, for it introduces the concept of the agent's temporal relationship to the good and bad aspects of the action. Although Socrates maintains that the value of the good and bad aspects of the action does not depend upon the agent's temporal relationship to them, he does argue that an agent's estimation of the value of the good and bad aspects of the action may be affected by his temporal relationships to them.

So much for Socrates' *reductiones* of the popular conception of *akrasia*. We come now to Socrates' intellectualist explanation of putative *akrasia*. In the

---

84. Psychological hedonism is the view that everyone naturally desires pleasure.

course of his critique, Socrates describes the popular conception of *akrasia* in four passages:

> The masses think that often (*pollakis*) when a person has knowledge, the knowledge does not rule him, but something else does, sometimes passion, sometimes pleasure, sometimes pain, occasionally love, and often fear...[85]

> ...Most people...say that many men (*pollous*), who know what the best thing to do is and are able to do it, are unwilling to do it and do something else...They say [the reason for this is] that they are overcome by pleasure or pain or by one of those things by which I was just saying that agents are overpowered when they act.[86]

> ...Do you people not say that this occurs in the following circumstances. For instance, often (*pollakis*) being overpowered by the pleasures of food or drink or sex, although people know that these are wrong, still they do them? They would agree.[87]

> ...you say that often (*pollakis*) a person knowing that bad things are bad, still does them, when he is able not to do them, because he is driven and compelled by pleasures.[88]

The adverb *pollakis* (often) occurs in three of these four passages. In the one where it does not occur, the quantifier *pollous* (many) serves a similar function. The many do not claim that whenever a person with knowledge is tempted to act on account of pleasure, pain, or the like, knowledge is *always* overpowered. Such a view is highly counterintuitive and so could hardly represent popular opinion. Rather, the many suggest that *akrasia* occurs *often* and that *many* people experience it.

In contrast, Socrates commits to the proposition in the question, "Do you agree with this view of knowledge, or do you consider that knowledge is something fine and able to govern a person and that if ever (*eanper*) someone knows what is good and bad, he will not be overpowered by anything so as to do anything other than those things that his knowledge commands?"[89] According to Socrates, and to Protagoras who agrees with him, the many are wrong in thinking that knowledge-*akrasia*-through-pleasure occurs often. But since Socrates and Protagoras claim that knowledge is never overcome by pleasure, they owe the many an explanation of what in fact does occur often, which the many misconceive.[90] Following his remarks on (c), Socrates proceeds to supply this explanation.

---

85. *Prt.* 352b5–8.
86. *Prt.* 352d5–e2.
87. *Prt.* 353c5–8.
88. *Prt.* 355a6–b1.
89. *Prt.* 352c2–6.
90. The request for this explanation is first expressed at 353a4–6.

Socrates' account is that, contrary to popular opinion, the man who acts akratically does not have knowledge. It is not the actual quantity of the goodness or badness of the action on balance that motivates the man, but the perceived, or more precisely misperceived, quantity. By analogy with visual perception, Socrates suggests that the propinquity to the agent of the good aspect of the action makes the good aspect appear greater than it is. Likewise, the remoteness from the agent of the bad aspect makes the bad aspect appear smaller than it is. Consequently, in akratic action, there is no conflict between knowledge's authority and pleasure's attraction. Instead, being overcome by pleasure is explained as a form of ignorance:

> You [the many] said that pleasure often (*pollakis*) overpowers a person who has knowledge. But when we disagreed with you, you proceeded to ask us, "Protagoras and Socrates, if this condition is not being overcome by plea-sure, what on earth can it be, and what do you claim that it is? Tell us." If at that point we had right away said, "Ignorance," you would have laughed at us. But now if you laugh at us, you will be laughing at your very selves.[91]

More precisely, then, the ignorance of the akratic agent consists of having beliefs about the quantities of the good and bad aspects of the action, which are false on account of the agent's failure to distinguish apparent from real value. Socrates explicitly states this point following his intellectualist explanation of *akrasia*: "Do you agree, then, that ignorance is this: having a false opinion (*pseudê doxan*) and being deceived in matters of great value?"[92] He then introduces his principle that no one willingly does what is bad:

> (d) Then it must be the case . . . that (1) no one willingly pursues bad things (*epi ta kaka*) or things that he thinks are bad (*epi ha oietai kaka*), (2) nor, it seems, is it in human nature to want to pursue things that one thinks are bad (*epi ha oietai*) in preference to good things. And whenever one is forced to choose one of two bad things, no one will choose the greater when he is able to choose the lesser.[93]

The principle (d1) contains the disjunction of not pursuing bad things or things one thinks are bad. This disjunction echoes a remark of Socrates' shortly preceding:

> (e) If pleasure is good . . . then no one who knows (*eidôs*) or believes (*oiomenos*) there are other things he can do that are better than those he is doing persists his action when he is able to do the better things.[94]

---

91. *Prt.* 357c4–d3.
92. *Prt.* 358c4–5.
93. *Prt.* 358c6–d1. I have added the numerals to facilitate exegesis, and I will accordingly refer to the embedded premises as (d1) and (d2).
94. *Prt.* 358b7–c1.

It is implied by (e) that people always pursue the course of action that they know or believe to be best, which is equivalent to the principle in (d) that no one willingly does what is bad. The disjunction in (e) of knowing or believing there to be a better course of action is to be explained in view of Socrates' preceding intellectualist explanation of *akrasia*. Socrates has argued that weakness is false belief. Thus, there will be people who pursue courses of action that they know, and therefore truly believe, to be good and people who pursue courses of action that they falsely believe to be good.

The disjunction in (d1) is to be explained similarly. Not pursuing "bad things or things one thinks are bad" should be understood as not pursuing things one *knows* are bad or things one *falsely* thinks are bad. In other words, the first disjunct, not pursuing "bad things," is expressed as such precisely because Socrates has in mind the agent who knows: Since the knowledgeable agent's belief is true, the things that he does not pursue, in the belief that they are bad, in fact are bad. Furthermore, since each disjunct in (d1) implies pursuing things one thinks (or believes) are bad, in (d2) Socrates simply employs the one form, not pursuing "things one thinks are bad." Here, then, not pursuing "things one thinks are bad" should be understood as not pursuing things one *truly or falsely* thinks are bad. In short, in this passage immediately following his intellectualist explanation of *akrasia*, Socrates introduces the psychological principle that everyone desires and pursues what he believes is good. This principle is, then, equivalent to the subjectivist conception of desire in *Meno*. Accordingly, Socrates' critique and intellectualist analysis of *akrasia* in *Protagoras* underscores that there are no irrational desires, for akratic actions would be paradigms of irrationally motivated actions. As he argues, the knowledgeable are distinct from the ignorant (or false believers) in that the knowledgeable will actually do what is good.

Finally, there is good reason to think that Socrates' denial of *akrasia* in *Protagoras* and the denial of the sort of irrational desire that it entails are Platonic. The position is argued for; it is an unconventional view; it explicitly involves the rejection of a conventional view; and it is consistent with the subjectivist conception of desire that I have also argued to be Platonic. The *Protagoras* and *Meno* passages, then, mutually support the view that the subjectivist conception of desire is Platonic.

6.1. Interpreting *Lysis*

Lysis contains one further important treatment of desire among the early dialogues, and it occurs within the context of an investigation of *philia*. *Philia* is typically translated as "friendship." For reasons that will become clear momentarily, this translation is misleading. A more accurate translation in the context of *Lysis* would be a more general and abstract one that encompassed relations between nonhuman entities, for example, "the relationship of bonding." Unfortunately, this is clumsy. Moreover, it is unclear how to translate the cognate noun *philos*, usually translated as "friend," and the verb *philein*, usually translated as "to befriend" or "to love." To avoid English sentences overpopulated by awkward constructions and transliterated Greek, I will retain the standard translations. The point of mentioning this is just to warn the reader to resist importing unwarranted content.

Interpretation of *Lysis* as a whole has been seriously hampered by a number of understandable, but mistaken, assumptions. Readers have consistently approached the text with presumptions about the nature of friendship, as this reciprocal, often exclusively human psychological, and particularly emotional relationship is commonly experienced and conceived. This is anachronistic and otherwise misguided. Consider, for instance, that the psychological conditions of empathy and compassion so common and fundamental to our experiences of love and friendship find no place in the discussion. Granted, the dramatic dimensions of the text seem to encourage the view that the dialogue in essence concerns friendship insofar as the dramatic characters, Socrates, Ctesippus, Hippothales, Menexenus, and Lysis, are all involved in various forms of what the Athenians would describe as *philia*. However, there are two reasons for caution. One is that in *Lysis* Plato develops the view that human friendship is one instance, albeit for us humans an especially important one, of a much more general condition. Remarkably, the conception of *philia* advanced in the dialogue is not necessarily psychological or even human. It is also, in most instances, not reciprocal, and so it is not necessarily reciprocal. Once this is appreciated, it becomes clear that one must be careful in applying familiar ethical concepts and concerns. The other reason is that although *philia* is not explicitly discussed as a part of excellence—as justice, courage, sound-mindedness, and holiness are among other early definitional dialogues—it is conceived as good. Throughout *Lysis*, it is maintained that *philia* is beneficial, at least to one participant in the relationship. Thus, especially in the case of humans, *philia* is an ideal. Consequently, like the dearth of excellence among the Athenians, which, for example, Socrates rues at the beginning of *Meno*,[95] there is a dearth of *philia*.

In sum, throughout *Lysis philia* is examined as a two-place relationship whose participants (*philoi*) may or may not be humans or even have what we would call mental states. Even though most examples considered in fact do involve humans and the investigation of *philia* in part attempts to explain the relationships between the dramatic characters, *philia* is more broadly understood as a condition that pervades nature or the cosmos. Moreover, in the same way that what we call "friendship" is conceived as one manifestation of the broader condition of *philia*, so what we call "desire" is conceived as one manifestation of the broader condition of *epithumia*. Entities that do not have souls, or at least that we would not assume to have souls, are described as subject to desire. For instance, Socrates claims that the body desires medicine, that the wet desires the dry, and the cold the hot. Indeed, it might be possible to translate *epithumia* as "attraction," but for convenience I retain "desire."

6.2. The Deficiency Conception of Desire

So much for a general orientation to the problem of *philia* in *Lysis*. Hereafter I will translate *philia* as "friendship," and the cognate nouns and verbs accordingly. I now turn to the conception of friendship that Socrates himself develops in the

---

95. *Men.* 71b.

dialogue. Note that although Socrates develops this conception in discussion with Lysis and Menexenus, relative to other passages in the dialogue, the passages upon which I will be focusing are relatively monologic. My treatment of the text will reflect this.

Following the rejection of the popular conception of friendship based on likeness (*homoiotês*), Socrates develops his own account. This I will call Socrates' first account of friendship. According to the first account, friendship entails that that which is neither-good-nor-bad loves that which is good on account of the presence of that which is bad in that which is neither-good-nor-bad. For example, Socrates himself, who is neither-good-nor-bad, loves wisdom, which is good, on account of the presence within him of ignorance, which is bad. Hereafter, that which is neither-good-nor-bad will be referred to as the neither-good-nor-bad, that which is good as the good, and that which is bad as the bad.

Socrates' account of desire (220b6–222b2) occurs in that section of the dialogue following the conclusion of his first account of friendship. As soon as he has concluded his first account, he is struck by its deficiency, and he proceeds to criticize it. In fact, his criticism does not involve a complete refutation of his first account. Rather, he focuses on two problems with the first account: the object of friendship and the cause. In the process of examining these two aspects, Socrates develops a second account of friendship. This account retains elements of the first, but now identifies the cause of friendship as desire (*epithumia*) and the object as the first friend (*to prôton philon*).

Socrates introduces the concept of the first friend in order to halt a potential regress. It is assumed that one entity *a* may befriend another entity *b* for the sake of yet another entity *c*. For example, a sick man befriends a doctor for the sake of health. In such cases, *a* is understood also to befriend *c*. But if *a* befriends *c* and one entity may befriend another for the sake of a third, then *a* may befriend *c* for the sake of yet another entity *d*. Accordingly, Socrates asks, "Are we not bound to go on in this way wearing ourselves out unless we can arrive at some governing entity (*archên*) that will not keep leading us to some other friend, but which will reach the first friend, for the sake of which all other things can be said to be friends?"[96] The first friend is, then, that entity for the sake of which all others are befriended and which is befriended only for its own sake. I will speak of it as an intrinsic friend. Precisely what entity satisfies these conditions in *Lysis* will be discussed below. Socrates speaks of the first friend as *really* and *truly* a friend[97]—specifically in contrast to friends that are not befriended for their own sake. Those friends he characterizes as "like phantoms (*eidôla*)" of the intrinsic friend.[98]

Insofar as Socrates speaks of the first friend as a true friend, it might seem that phantom friends are false friends. However, he does not speak of phantom friends as false friends. Moreover, as we will see below, he subsequently introduces a class

---

96. *Ly.* 219c5–d2.
97. *Ly.* 220b4, 219d5.
98. *Ly.* 219d3.

of inauthentic friends that do not meet the same conditions as phantom friends. Therefore, it is necessary to distinguish the first friend from phantom friends as intrinsic and extrinsic friends, respectively. Hereafter, I will speak of phantom friends as extrinsic friends.

I now turn from the objects of friendship to the cause. In Socrates' first account of friendship, the bad implicitly plays the role of the cause insofar as it is said to be on account of (*heneka*) the bad, that is, the presence of the bad, that the neither-good-nor-bad befriends the good. In the criticism of the first account, another cause of friendship emerges, for Socrates describes extrinsic friends as befriended on account of (*heneka*) other friends. He then distinguishes extrinsic friends from the first friend, which is not befriended *on account of* another friend, but *on account of* the bad: "Then that friend of ours in which all the other friends terminated . . . does not resemble these friends. These are called friends on account of a friend. But it appears that the real friend in its nature is entirely opposite, for it has been revealed to be a friend on account of an enemy."[99]

I suggest that Socrates' main problem here is that extrinsic friendship and intrinsic friendship have different causes. This might seem unproblematic, for extrinsic friendship differs from intrinsic friendship; therefore, one should not expect the two to have the same cause. Still, the causes here specified are of remarkably different kinds. On the one hand, the bad, which is said to be the cause of intrinsic friendship, loosely corresponds to an Aristotelian efficient cause, whereas the intrinsic or extrinsic friend for whose sake an extrinsic friend is befriended, and which thereby is the cause of extrinsic friendship, loosely corresponds to an Aristotelian final cause. Plato does not explicitly draw such Aristotelian distinctions, and it would be wrong to attribute to him the distinction between these two causes in these very terms. Nonetheless, it is reasonable to attribute to him some sort of distinction between these two causes. Consider that the bad is said to be the cause of intrinsic friendship; this implies that an opposite causes an opposite. But evidence from other dialogues indicates that the Platonic view of causation is that like causes like.[100] The consequent difficulty in the case of the bad causing desire for the first friend is particularly striking when one compares the presently conceived causes of extrinsic and intrinsic friendship, for in the case of extrinsic friendship an intrinsic or extrinsic good is the cause, whereas in intrinsic friendship something bad is the cause. I suggest that Plato would find this unacceptable.

The peculiarity of the idea that the bad causes intrinsic friendship, that an opposite causes an opposite, and that the causes of extrinsic friendship and intrinsic friendship are so distinct all, I suggest, implicitly motivate reconsideration of the cause of friendship and specifically prompt the question, which Socrates now asks, whether friendship would survive the extinction of the bad. As Socrates puts the question, "For if there were nothing left to harm us, would we

---

99. *Ly.* 220d8–e5.
100. See Wolfsdorf (2005a) as well as Sedley (1998) and Hankinson (1998).

feel any want of assistance?"[101] In other words, Socrates begins with the following argument: *a* befriends *b* under the assumption that *b* can benefit *a*, but if the bad and so the harmful is extinct, *a* should have no reason to befriend anything. His answer to the argument engages the concept of desire (*epithumia*). He begins by posing three questions:

> (1) If the bad ceases to exist, will it be impossible still to be hungry or thirsty or any other such thing? (2) Or will hunger exist so long as humans and other animals exist, but just without being harmful (*blabera*)? (3) And thirst and the other desires (*epithumiai*), will these not be bad (*kakai*) if the bad has ceased to exist?[102]

At least two interpretations of Socrates' description of thirst and hunger as harmful and bad are possible. On an ethical hedonist reading, Socrates could mean that the pains of hunger and thirst, which are bad, will cease to exist. On what I will call an object-oriented reading, Socrates could mean that objects of hunger and thirst that are bad will cease to exist. I endorse the object-oriented interpretation. The ethical hedonist interpretation requires that Socrates believes that the pains of hunger and thirst are themselves bad. But I see no reason to maintain that Socrates believes this. Moreover, there is no evidence in *Lysis* that Plato intended to portray Socrates as committed to ethical hedonism; and, as I will discuss below, there is evidence that he intended to portray him as not committed to it.

The object-oriented interpretation has the following evidence in its favor. Note that Socrates uses the words *blabera* in (2) and *kakai* in (3). *Blabera* (harmful) implies instrumentality, specifically, a relationship between the desire and its consequence. *Kakai* (bad) is ambiguous; something that is *kakon* can be intrinsically or extrinsically bad. I suggest that since in (2) hunger and thirst are described as harmful, that is, extrinsically bad, *kakai* in (3) must be understood to mean extrinsically bad as well. Accordingly, Socrates is asking whether, with the bad extinct, it will be possible to have desires that are bad in the sense that the objects of desire, which would be acquired upon the satisfaction of the desire, are bad.

Socrates observes that it might be ridiculous to attempt to answer these questions on the grounds that it is hard to know what would result in the case of the extinction of the bad.[103] Nonetheless, he proceeds to answer the questions:

> But this at any rate we do know, that even now it is possible for one who is hungry to be harmed (*blaptesthai*) and also to be benefited (*ophelesthai*)... So also when one is thirsty or has desires of all other sorts, sometimes one will desire beneficially (*ophelimôs*), sometimes harmfully (*blaberôs*), and

---

101. *Ly.* 220c7–d1.
102. *Ly.* 220e7–221a4. I have inserted numerals to facilitate exegesis.
103. "Or is this a ridiculous question, what will be possible or impossible then, for who knows?" (*Ly.* 221a4–5).

sometimes neither... Now if bad things cease to exist, should it be the case that those things that are not bad cease to exist along with the bad? [Lysis and Menexenus agree that they shouldn't.] Then there will be neither-good-nor-bad desires even if bad things cease to exist.[104]

Socrates' use of *blaptesthai*, *ophelesthai*, *ophelimôs*, and *blaberôs* further supports the object-oriented interpretation.[105] Accordingly, he introduces the concepts of desiring beneficially, harmfully, and neither-beneficially-nor-harmfully. And given the inference in the passage cited immediately before this one from harmful desire to bad desire, we can infer the concepts of good, bad, and neither-good-nor-bad desires, that is, desires for objects that are good, bad, and neither-good-nor-bad. With the extinction of the bad, both good and neither-good-nor-bad desires should survive. And this is Socrates' point. In short, the extinction of the bad does not imply the extinction of all desire.

Subsequently, Socrates claims that when a subject desires an object, the subject loves and befriends that object. Therefore he identifies desire as the cause of friendship. I note two general points about this reconceived cause of friendship, and one apparent problem. First, throughout his discussion of the cause of friendship, Socrates intends to include both extrinsic friendship and intrinsic friendship. This is clear from the examples of hunger and thirst that he uses, for the objects of these obviously are not the first friend. The second point is that the identification of desire as the cause of friendship more closely unifies extrinsic and intrinsic friendship. Recall that Socrates previously spoke of the bad as the cause of intrinsic friendship and the friend for the sake of whom the extrinsic friend was befriended as the cause of extrinsic friendship. But now both extrinsic friendship and intrinsic friendship can be conceived as caused by desire. Moreover, the identification of desire as the cause of friendship also enables an explanation of how this common cause can generate two related but not identical kinds of friendship. Intrinsically good desire is the cause of intrinsic friendship, whereas extrinsically good desire is the cause of extrinsic friendship.

There is a problem with this account, however; for Socrates infers that *a* befriends *b* from the fact that *a* desires *b*. But if friendship must be beneficial and *a* may desire *b* falsely believing *b* to be (intrinsically or extrinsically) good, then friendship between *a* and *b* will not benefit *a*. To preserve his conception of friendship, then, Socrates must distinguish genuine from inauthentic friendship, whereby inauthentic friendship occurs precisely when the desideratum is *misconceived* as good. I will develop this point below.

First, given that desire is the cause of friendship, Socrates submits a set of claims about desire:

---

104. *Ly.* 221a5–b6.

105. Note that according to the object-oriented interpretation, Socrates must be assuming that so long as bad things exist, there are bad desires. This assumption is confirmed by Socrates' claim here that as things are now people sometimes desire harmfully as well as the concept of bad desires in the passage cited immediately preceding this one.

The subject desires that in which it is deficient.
That which is deficient is deficient in that of which it is deprived.
That of which that which is deficient is deprived is its belonging (*oikeion*).
The subject desires its belonging.[106]

I will describe these claims as constituting a deficiency conception of desire. This conception of desire is indebted to Empedocles—a point that sheds light on the composition of *Lysis* more broadly. Assuming that *Lysis* was in fact composed early in Plato's career, the principal philosophical treatment of friendship prior to the dialogue occurs in Empedocles. At the beginning of the investigation of friendship based on likeness in *Lysis*, Socrates remarks to Lysis, "And you have come across the writings of the most wise which say these very things, that like is necessarily friend to like. I am speaking of those who talk and write about nature (*peri phuseôs*) and the whole (*tou holou*)."[107] That Plato is here alluding to Empedocles has often been noted. Moreover, Plato's treatment of friendship also resembles Empedocles' insofar as human friendship in *Lysis* is treated as merely one, albeit for humans centrally important, type of a much broader condition.

Specifically regarding Empedocles' conception of desire, Aëtius (1st or 2nd c. CE) reports that

> Empedocles says that desire (*orexin*) occurs because of a deficiency of nourishment (*elleipsei trophês*) . . . Empedocles says that things have pleasures because of things like themselves and that on account of deficiency [they aim at] replenishment (*anaplerosin*). Consequently, desire for what is like is caused by deficiency.[108]

> Empedocles says that animals have desires according to their deficiencies in those elements that complete (*apotelountôn*) each. And pleasures come from what belongs (*ex oikeiou*) according to the blending of kindred (*sungenôn*) and like [elements], while disturbances and <pains from what does not belong (*ex anoikeiou*)>.[109]

In *Lysis*, as I have noted, Socrates argues against the conception of friendship based on likeness. Furthermore, the notion that pleasure accompanies the satisfaction of desire plays no part in Socrates' conception. Still, Plato has Socrates retain the Empedoclean notion that deficiency causes desire. Moreover, Plato appears to adapt the concept of belonging (*oikeion*) to the object of desire. In Empedocles what belong are kindred and like elements. Since Plato rejects the conception of friendship based on likeness, belongings must be conceptualized otherwise.

---

106. *Ly.* 221d6–e5.
107. *Ly.* 214b2–5.
108. Aët. 4.9.14–15; *Dox. Graec.* 398.
109. Aët. 5.28; *Dox. Graec.* 440. The last phrase is corrupt. The reading here is based on Diels' reconstruction. The translations of both passages are influenced by Inwood (2001) 206.

It is difficult to clarify the conception of belongings as desiderata in Socrates' second account of friendship. Socrates elicits the boys' assent to the four claims that constitute the deficiency conception of desire in rapid succession, and he offers no commentary on or explanation of them. A basic interpretive problem is whether belongings are types or tokens. Desiderata may, of course, be either. For instance, Menexenus may desire this particular fishcake in the fishmonger's stall in the agora or, more generally, fishcake, fish, or food. Empedocles' deficiency conception of desire indicates that desiderata principally are kinds—more precisely, we can assume, the four kinds that constitute the basic elements in his ontology. For instance, an animal's lack of water or earth causes desire for water or earth. Socrates, for his part, is not explicit about whether belongings are types or tokens, but a charitable interpretation suggests that his belongings also principally are types. The reason for this is simply that the alternative is absurd. Menexenus' desire for the particular fishcake he sees is caused by a deficiency of some sort. But this cannot be a deficiency of the particular fishcake that Menexenus sees. So it cannot be that belongings principally are the particular objects of every desire.

Assuming that Socrates' belongings principally are types, desire for tokens can be explained. Desire for a token is governed by desire for a type of which that token is a member. For example, Menexenus' desire for this particular fishcake is governed by Menexenus' deprivation of fishcake, fish, or food and so desire for fishcake, fish, or food. Accordingly, then, particular objects of desire may be belongings, but only in that they instantiate types.

A further problem of belongings qua types is that Plato does not have Socrates present any explicit taxonomy of them. More precisely, it is unclear with what degree of generality and specificity belongings are distinguished. As in the preceding example, it is unclear whether the belonging is fishcake, fish, or food. Moreover, it is unclear how coordinate belongings, that is, belongings on the same level of descriptive generality, are categorized; for instance, food and drink versus food, relish (*opson*), and drink. In answering this question, passages from elsewhere among the early dialogues, such as the following from *Gorgias*, are helpful only to a limited degree:

SOCRATES   Tell me now, are you speaking of such things as being hungry and eating when one is hungry?

CALLICLES   Yes.

SOCRATES   And being thirsty and drinking when one is thirsty?

CALLICLES   Certainly, and having all the other desires and being able to satisfy them with enjoyment.[110]

SOCRATES   You spoke of hunger ... and thirst also? [It is implied that eating is satisfying hunger.] And drinking is the satisfaction of the desire (of being thirsty)?[111]

---

110. *Grg.* 494b7–c3.
111. *Grg.* 496c6–e2.

SOCRATES   ... that is how the body is provided with food when it is hungry, drink when it is thirsty, clothes, blankets, and shoes when it is cold, and all other desires the body has.[112]

Such passages suggest certain coordinate categorical divisions, but they do not enable us to determine that, say, food, drink, and warmth are, so to speak, the properly general categories of belongings.

We cannot, then, be sure of the details of the divisions in a Socratic taxonomy of belongings in Lysis, but we can sure of certain broad divisions in any Platonic taxonomy. For instance, the distinction of body and soul is common among the early dialogues. There must, then, be somatic desires as well as psychological desires.[113] Objects of somatic desire such as food, drink, and warmth are subsumed under the more general category of somatic health.[114] Moreover, knowledge concerning the satisfaction of such more specific and more general desires is appropriate to the domains of medicine and gymnastics.[115] Consider the statement by Socrates that occurs immediately after the last passage cited above in Gorgias: "[Medicine and gymnastics] have the proper claim to rule over all those [subordinate] crafts because they know what is healthful and harmful in food and drink for somatic excellence."[116]

In contrast, it is much less clear how desires of the soul are distinguished and organized. Still, it is clear that they must be hierarchically organized in some manner and that all desires are ultimately subsumed under the psychological desire for psychological fulfillment. The argument in Lysis in which the first friend is introduced and extrinsic and intrinsic friends are distinguished makes evident some hierarchical organization of desiderata.[117] In Euthydemus, Socrates suggests that well-being (eudaimonia) is the ultimate object of desire.[118] Accordingly, a number of scholars have employed this Euthydemus passage to suggest that in Lysis the first friend is well-being. I think the evidence is more ambiguous. I will discuss the identity of the first friend below.

For the moment, in sum, Socrates' second, or rather revised, account of friendship, is based on belonging (oikeiotês). According to this conception, deprivation and deficiency cause desire. Moreover, objects of desire, belongings (oikeia),[119] principally are types, rather than tokens. A Socratic, or rather Platonic, taxonomy of belongings is not entirely clear. However, belongings are hierarchically ordered in some manner, and psychological fulfillment is the first friend or ultimate belonging. Since friendship is necessarily beneficial and friendship based on likeness

---

112. Grg. 517d2–5.
113. See Grg. 505a–b.
114. Grg. 504c. Here the phrase hê aretê tou sômatos (the excellence of the body) is used.
115. Grg. 517e.
116. Grg. 517e4–518a1.
117. It is noteworthy that the opening sections of book 1 of Aristotle's Nicomachean Ethics discuss the goods of the various crafts in a hierarchical order, reminiscent of Gorgias, and that this is accompanied by the claim, strongly reminiscent of Lysis, that desire must have an ultimate object.
118. Euthd. 278e.
119. oikeia is the plural of oikeion.

has been rejected, friendship based on belonging occurs between the neither-good-nor-bad and the good.

6.3. Inauthentic Friendship

Since desire causes friendship and desires may be bad in the sense that the objective value of desiderata may be bad, such conditions cannot constitute friendship, but merely some semblance of it. It is necessary, then, to distinguish friendship from its semblances.

Immediately following the articulation of his deficiency conception of desire, Socrates applies his conception of friendship based on belonging to the relationship between Lysis and Menexenus, then more generally to the conventional Greek homosexual relationship between a lover (*erastês*) and his darling (*paidika*). This might seem puzzling, for Lysis and Menexenus or lovers and their darlings qua people are neither-good-nor-bad; therefore, on Socrates' conception, they cannot be friends. In fact, Socrates does not claim that they are friends; he speaks hypothetically: "Then *if* you both are friends with one another, in some way by nature (*phusei*) you belong to one another..."[120] Even so, Socrates' account does permit friendships among people, albeit extrinsic ones. Granted that a person on the whole is neither-good-nor-bad, certain aspects of his soul may be extrinsically good; therefore, he may be befriended in this respect. This, I think, is what Socrates means when he says, "if one person desires or loves another...he would not desire, love, or befriend the other unless he belonged to him in soul *or in some character or aspect or form of soul.*" Given this, he suggests that "what belongs to us by nature (*phusei*)...is something we must befriend"[121] and that "the darling (*tôn paidikôn*) of a genuine (*gnêsiôi*), as opposed to a inauthentic (*prospoiêtôi*), lover (*erastêi*) must befriend the genuine lover."[122] This brings us to the distinction between a genuine and an inauthentic lover and thus between genuine and inauthentic friendship. In clarifying these concepts, it will also become clear how the genuine/inauthentic friendship distinction relates to the extrinsic/intrinsic friendship distinction.

According to Socrates' conception of friendship based on belonging, conventional Greek homosexual friendship is explicable as a condition where two males, one relatively immature, one relatively mature, desire one another and in some way belong to one another. The question is how each is a belonging to the other. The text offers no explicit help here. Moreover, comparison of humans' interrelations with humans' relationships to, say, food and drink underscores the difficulty of identifying the type of belonging that a male person qua object of male desire instantiates. It is clear to what deprivation a given edible or potable answers. We might even explain the reciprocal desire of male and female of a species as a

---

120. *Ly.* 221e5–6.
121. *Ly.* 222a5–6.
122. *Ly.* 222a6–7.

desire to procreate and thereby as answering to the species' defect of mortality.[123] Still further, male-male relationships in accordance with occupational or vocational roles such as patient and doctor, student and teacher, buyer and merchant are easily intelligible; and elsewhere in the dialogue Socrates makes use of such examples. The explanation of male-male homosexual relationships, however, remains opaque.

In *Symposium* it is claimed that the beauty of the beloved evokes the lover's desire for the Form of beauty. Assuming that the Form of beauty is identical to the Form of goodness, the lover's desire for the beloved may, in its own way, be conceived as continuous with the lover's attraction to the good. The attraction of the *erômenos* (the subordinate partner in a relationship) to the *erastês* (the dominant partner in a relationship), in turn, is explicable insofar as the lover is perceived to be capable of serving as an educator or model of excellence to the beloved. Thus, the beloved may desire the lover insofar as the beloved pursues his own excellence. Compare Socrates' question in *Cratylus*: "Is there any desire greater than the desire to associate with someone whose company one believes will make one a better man?"[124]

If this suggestion is correct, then the type of belonging that the male person as object of desire may instantiate is human excellence. In considering this point, I note, in passing, the variety of modes by which desiderata of different kinds are pursued. Whereas, say, food and drink are *consumed* to satisfy desire for food and desire for drink and, say, clothes are *worn* to satisfy the desire for warmth, the male person is *engaged in activity and discourse* to satisfy the desire for excellence. Accordingly, I suggest that the inauthentic lover is the lover whose pursuit of a beloved is not for genuine excellence. For example, a lover might pursue a beloved for pleasure. This suggestion is supported by a close reading of the following passage:

> "So then, boys, (1) *if one person desires or loves another*," I said, "*he would not desire, love, or befriend the other unless he belonged to him in soul or in some character or aspect or form of soul*." "Entirely," said Menexenus, but Lysis was silent. "Well," I said, (2) "*it has become clear that we must befriend that which belongs to us by nature*." "It seems so," he [that is, Menexenus] said. (3) "*Then the darling must befriend the genuine, not the inauthentic, lover*." Then Lysis and Menexenus gave a faint nod, and Hippothales, out of pleasure, turned all manner of colors.[125]

I have inserted numerals to facilitate reference to Socrates' claims, which I have also italicized; and I want to address three questions in this passage. Why does Menexenus agree to but Lysis fall silent at (1)? Why do Lysis and Menexenus subsequently agree to (3), but with a "faint nod"? And why is Hippothales

---

123. This, at least, is how Aristotle explains sex drive in *De Anima*. Empedocles explains sex drive as a desire for unity.
124. *Cra.* 403d4–5.
125. *Ly.* 221e7–222b2.

described as turning all manner of colors out of pleasure at (3)? The answer to these questions depends upon the broader context of the discussion. The examination of friendship in *Lysis* began when Socrates encountered Hippothales and Ctesippus by Miccus' palaestra. Socrates learned that Hippothales was in love with Lysis, but that Lysis had rejected his various advances. Socrates subsequently rebuked Hippothales for his manner of treating Lysis and offered to demonstrate how a lover ought to treat his beloved.

I suggest that Menexenus accepts (1) and (2) because they follow from Socrates' account of friendship based on belonging. To be more precise, (2) does not exactly follow from Socrates' preceding account. The concept of a natural belonging was not explained in Socrates' articulation of the deficiency conception of desire. Socrates does introduce the concept (at 221e5–6) when he suggests that Lysis and Menexenus may be friends. But he does not at that point explain it; nor does the context itself make its meaning clear. I believe that the meaning of the phrase only becomes clear once Socrates has introduced the distinction between the genuine and the inauthentic lover and so friend. Accordingly, Menexenus' assent to (2) must be based on his intuition of this distinction or, more plausibly, on the ground that he initially (inaccurately) interprets a natural belonging as equivalent to a belonging.

In contrast to Menexenus, Lysis is said to fall silent at (1) and to remain silent at (2). I suggest that Lysis' silence is due to the fear that (1) and (2) imply unattractive consequences for his relationship to Hippothales: Lysis interprets (1) and (2) to mean that Hippothales would not desire Lysis unless Lysis in fact belonged to him.[126] Therefore, Lysis fears that he must yield to Hippothales' desire. This is especially puzzling and disconcerting to Lysis because he feels no attraction to Hippothales. Claim (3) distinguishes the genuine from the inauthentic lover and explicitly, for the first time in the passage and, more generally, since the inception of Socrates' investigation of friendship, applies the concept of friendship to conventional homosexual relationships. Neither boy entirely grasps the significance of this, hence their faint nods (*mogis pôs epeneusatên*). But the very introduction of the inauthentic lover and the notion that a darling or beloved is not bound to an inauthentic lover gives Lysis vague encouragement that he may not be bound to Hippothales if Hippothales is an inauthentic lover. Thus, Lysis, by giving a faint nod of assent, positively reengages the exchange.

Hippothales' response to (1) through (3) markedly differs from Lysis'. I suggest that mention of homosexual relations arouses him. He assumes that he is a genuine lover; therefore, he is delighted that, according to Socrates' view, Lysis is bound to accept his advances. But Hippothales is quite mistaken here. Earlier in the dialogue Socrates had criticized Hippothales for his treatment of Lysis. Ctesippus had also ridiculed Hippothales for his incessant talk of Lysis and his bathetic poems about him. When Hippothales denies these compositions, Ctesippus

---

126. Accordingly, Lysis' silence at (2) suggests that he also fails to appreciate the meaning of the phrase "natural belonging."

speaks of Hippothales as raving (*lêrei*) and crazed (*mainetai*).[127] Conventionally speaking, Hippothales is madly in love with Lysis. I submit, however, the passage under discussion subtly indicates that Hippothales is not a genuine lover of Lysis. The crucial evidence is the phrase "out of pleasure" (*hupo tês hêdonês*). That is, I suggest that Hippothales is driven to Lysis by a desire for sexual gratification. Evidence among the early dialogues of the association of sex with base pleasure in particular occurs in *Hippias Major* and *Gorgias*. In *Hippias Major*, pleasures through taste and touch, and specifically sex, are excluded from fineness on the grounds that they are base.[128] In *Gorgias* Socrates uses the example of the catamite to elicit from Callicles the view that some pleasures are base.[129]

Accordingly, if this suggestion about Hippothales' motivation is correct, the genuine lover is distinguishable from the inauthentic lover on the grounds that the genuine lover, that is, the active and dominant partner in a homosexual relationship, pursues true excellence, while the inauthentic lover pursues an object that is not beneficial.

Having distinguished genuine from inauthentic friendship, it is clear how this distinction also differs from the distinction between intrinsic and extrinsic friendship. Intrinsic and extrinsic friendships may be genuine or inauthentic. In sum, Socrates' second account of friendship distinguishes four conceptions of friendship:

Intrinsic friendship: The neither-good-nor-bad befriends the first friend, which is befriended for its own sake and which is that entity for the sake of which all others are befriended.

Extrinsic friendship: The neither-good-nor-bad befriends an extrinsic friend, in other words, an entity that is not befriended for its own sake, but for the sake of some other friend, be it an intrinsic friend or an extrinsic friend.

Inauthentic friendship: The neither-good-nor-bad "befriends" an entity that is not objectively either extrinsically or intrinsically good.[130]

Genuine friendship: The neither-good-nor-bad befriends an entity that is objectively either extrinsically or intrinsically good.

Finally, I suggest that the distinction between a genuine and an inauthentic friend also serves to explain the introduction of the concept of a natural belonging (*phusei oikeion*). According to the deficiency conception of desire, the objects of desire are belongings. But since there may be bad desires, that is, desires whose

---

127. *Ly.* 205a7–8.
128. *Hp. Ma.* 299a.
129. *Grg.* 494e. Admittedly, Callicles does not at this point concede. However, he is at first appalled by the baseness of Socrates' example. Subsequently, he chooses to allow that the life of a catamite is good explicitly in order to remain consistent in his identification of pleasure and goodness.
130. The verb "befriends" is in quotes since inauthentic friendship is not in fact friendship.

objects are objectively bad, and genuine friendship is beneficial, the relationship between the desiring subject and the desideratum cannot be one of genuine friendship. In order to distinguish belongings that are bad from belongings that are good, Socrates introduces the concept of natural belonging. In short, a natural belonging is beneficial and so a genuine friend.[131]

6.4. Platonic Desire

Socrates argues for his second account of friendship based on belonging and the deficiency conception of desire fundamental to it. The conception of friendship based on belonging is specifically contrasted with the traditional conception of friendship based on likeness against which Socrates argues. This suggests that friendship based on belonging and the deficiency conception of desire are Platonic.

In view of the foregoing interpretation of desire in *Lysis* as well as the subjectivist interpretation from *Meno* and *Protagoras*, we find three Platonic conceptions of desire among the early dialogues:

Object-oriented conception of desire: A desire is good, bad, or neither-good-nor-bad in virtue of the value of the desideratum.

Subjectivist conception of desire: The desideratum is desired as a result of its fallible evaluation as good.

Deficiency conception of desire: The desideratum is a kind in which the subject is deficient.

These correspond to three elements of desire: the subject's evaluation of the desideratum, the objective value of the desideratum, and the desideratum qua belonging. These three elements are compatible. Their compatibility in part depends on a conception of ethical properties as objective. The value of an object of desire is independent of its being desired. The desiring subject may evaluate that object correctly or incorrectly. Given the subjectivist conception, there is a need for knowledge that enables its possessor to evaluate correctly. Plato's interest in

---

131. The introduction of the concept of the natural belonging raises the question why Plato has Socrates use the word "natural" to play this role; in other words, how Plato here conceives the natural. In one sense, Plato's treatment of desire and friendship in *Lysis* is naturalistic. As we have seen, examples such as hunger and thirst figure prominently in the dialogue, and, as I have emphasized, friendship is conceived as a condition widespread throughout nature or the cosmos. We might speak of this notion of the natural as the "actual natural." Desire and friendship are described according to the way things actually are in the natural world and the cosmos more broadly. But the notion of the natural in the concept of natural belonging is not equivalent to this notion of the actual natural. A natural belonging is a beneficial and so good belonging; and since a natural belonging is also a genuine friend, the concepts of the good, the genuine, and the natural in some sense run together. This conception of the natural is of the ideal. It is noteworthy that the ideal natural order is never wholly realized within the actual natural order. But it must be emphasized that Plato never has Socrates speak of I am calling the "actual natural" order as "natural." Interestingly, the ideal natural is the natural.

distinguishing subjectivist and object-oriented elements of desire depends, then, precisely on the notions of objective value and subjective evaluative fallibility.

Plato's interest in the deficiency conception of desire may be twofold. First, the subjectivist conception of desire does not explain the cause of desire. Precisely, it does not explain why a subject, upon the evaluation of an object as good, desires that object. The evaluation of an object as good is insufficient for desire. For instance, when one is sated in the relevant respect, one may evaluate an object as good, but not desire it. Fundamentally, desire is conceived as a response to deficiency and deprivation. Observe that, in this respect, desire, that is, desire for a belonging, is preevaluative and to that extent prerational. It is subsequent to the presence of desire for a belonging that reason evaluates whether a particular object of the type desired is good and so choiceworthy. Accordingly, I am suggesting the following sequence of psychological events:

Deficiency of, for example, food (qua belonging)

(Preevaluative) desire for food (qua belonging)

Fallible evaluation of some object as good food

Desire for that evaluated object

The other relevant aspect of the deficiency conception is the broad Platonic theme of human imperfection and the imperfection of the sensible world. Granted, the metaphysical dichotomy of Forms and participants[132] and its attendant values falls wholly outside of the discursive context of *Lysis*. But this metaphysical apparatus is unnecessary for the point. The theme is conventionally Greek as well, and the conventional Greek dichotomy of divine and mortal and of the self-sufficient and the dependent suffice. It is this gap that human desire ultimately, though vainly, seeks to transcend. As Socrates says early in the investigation in *Lysis*, "there is a certain possession that I have been desiring since my youth."[133] We may add that only the divine, perfect and rational, possess true fulfillment.

With this, we come to the identity of the first friend. Scholarly interpretations principally divide over whether the first friend is well-being (*eudaimonia*) or the Form of goodness. As just noted, within the discursive context of *Lysis* there is no mention of Forms whatsoever. For this reason I regard the former option as misguided. I mentioned earlier that a number of scholars have identified the first friend with well-being, but that the evidence is rather ambiguous. Granted, in *Euthydemus* Socrates suggests that everyone desires well-being. But among the early dialogues *eudaimonia* is conceptualized as activity, not psychological fulfillment.[134] *Aretê* is the optimal condition of the soul (*psychê*).

---

132. Here and elsewhere I use the word "participant" rather than "particular" to refer to entities that participate in Forms. "Participant" is more accurate since kinds as well as particulars participate in Forms.

133. *Ly.* 211d7–8.

134. The point will be discussed further in sections 3 and 4 of chapter 3.

The problem is complicated by the fact that there is controversy over the Platonic conception of the relationship between *aretê* and *eudaimonia*. For example, some scholars claim that these two are identical. In that case, there is no need to adjudicate between the claim that excellence is the first friend and the claim that well-being is the first friend. But, as I will argue in section 4 of chapter 3, the relationship between excellence and well-being is not one of identity. Rather, excellence is a psychological capacity responsible for the activity of living well. As such, I prefer the view that the first friend is excellence, rather than well-being. Once excellence is attained, one will inevitably live well.

The first friend is the end of psychological desire. Insofar as the desire for such a belonging arises naturally as a consequence of our deficient psychological condition, something like the neoplatonic conception is correct: By nature we desire genuine psychological fulfillment. However, since desire for belongings is preevaluative, we do not naturally desire psychological fulfillment under the description of the good. Instead, we fallibly evaluate this or that as psychologically fulfilling and desire it as the good. In other words, the natural desire for psychological fulfillment is like the natural desire for, say, food, a relatively general sort of wanting. I emphasize, moreover, that the subjectivist conception is compatible with this version of the neoplatonic conception. The subjectivist conception has to do with fallible evaluation of objects that fall under types of belonging, whereas the neoplatonic conception has to do with belongings to which one is preevaluatively drawn.

7. Antiphilosophical Desires

In this chapter we have examined arguments and Socratic claims concerning the nature of desire in an effort to determine the Platonic conception of desire among the early dialogues. I have shown that three passages, from *Meno*, *Protagoras*, and *Lysis*, provide compelling evidence for a Platonic conception of desire, according to which nature orients deficient humans toward the correct type of belonging, but leaves them to use their cognitive powers to determine which objects will genuinely satisfy their natural desires. Insofar as *aretê* is wisdom, *philosophia* is the form of desire that will enable us to achieve psychological fulfillment. In chapter 3, I will examine the Platonic conception of this desideratum. In this section, I conclude my discussion of desire by considering antiphilosophical desires and their psychology.

Several views of excellence are expressed among the early dialogues. In addition to the Platonic conception of excellence as wholly epistemic, we encounter popular and traditional views. According to what I will call the standard view—which serves as Socrates' point of departure in his inquiry into the relationship between the parts of excellence in *Protagoras*—excellence consists of justice, holiness, sound-mindedness, courage, and intelligence. More precisely, justice is understood as conducting oneself well with respect to other humans; specifically, as Polemarchus defines it in *Republic* 1, justice is aiding friends and harming enemies. Holiness is conducting oneself well with respect to the gods, specifically, knowing when, to whom, and how to worship and pray.

So, in *Euthyphro*, Euthyphro claims that holiness, understood as service to the gods, involves praying and sacrificing and thus doing what pleases the gods. Sound-mindedness is resisting indulgence in pleasures. For example, in *Charmides*, Charmides defines sound-mindedness as restraint. Courage is resisting fearful circumstances, especially on the battlefield. Accordingly, in *Laches*, Laches defines courage as paradigmatic hoplite conduct. And intelligence is managing one's household well and conducting oneself well in political office. So, in *Protagoras*, Protagoras claims to be able to teach Hippocrates how to manage his private and public affairs, a thing that Socrates recognizes as civic expertise (*politikê technê*).

Note that all of these descriptions concern types of action, rather than the psychological capacities for such action. I do not mean to suggest that the average Athenian aristocrat would deny that these components of excellence also entail states of the soul. However, it is remarkable that, when initially asked to define excellence, most of Socrates' interlocutors respond by describing types of action, rather than psychological capacities.

A number of interlocutors also express conceptions of excellence that differ from this standard conception in various ways. For example, Nicias endorses an epistemic conception of courage, which he seems to inherit from Socrates. In virtue of his prosecution of his father for the unintentional death of a hired laborer, Euthyphro's conception of holiness differs from the standard conception in some respect, which unfortunately he cannot adequately clarify. More radical are Callicles' and Thrasymachus' views. Callicles endorses ethical hedonism and wholly rejects sound-mindedness: "In truth, Socrates... indulgence, licentiousness and freedom are excellence and well-being!"[135] Thrasymachus endorses cunning and boldness as a means to get more (*pleonexia*) than others. This itself may be consistent with nonegalitarian aristocratic values, but Thrasymachus' crudeness and utter lack of concern for the well-being of others is radical.

Given the Platonic conception of desire, we would expect Socrates' interlocutors to be motivated in accordance with their views of excellence. And indeed, in most cases they are. For example, Euthyphro is prosecuting his father on the basis of his conception of holiness. On the other hand, the grasp of the conceptions of excellence that the interlocutors express is invariably tenuous and limited. In other words, the interlocutors tend not to understand what they really are about. This is amply born out by their repeated failures to provide adequate explanations or defenses of their views when Socrates asks them to do so. From this it follows that the interlocutors' opinions about excellence reveal their motivations in a merely superficial way.

In order to understand the motivations of Socrates' interlocutors, one additionally needs to consider their conduct, and by this I mean to include two things. On the one hand, there is activity during conversations with Socrates, specifically, the interlocutors' attitudes toward inquiry and the ways they respond to its challenges.

---

135. *Grg.* 492c4–6.

This, of course, constitutes the bulk of the action in the dialogues. But there is also activity that is referred to, but not actually performed, within the dialogues. For example, *Hippias Minor* begins with Hippias having just completed an epideictic speech; Ion is an itinerant rhapsode who spends his time performing and commenting on Homer's epics; Laches and Nicias are prominent military generals; Hippothales is madly in love with Lysis and preoccupied with that erotic pursuit.

In light of the various forms of evidence, the early dialogues convey that Socrates' interlocutors, and the Athenians in general, are motivated by two principal desiderata: *timê* (honor, esteem, recognition) and *hêdonê* (pleasure). Accordingly, *philotimia* (love of *timê*) and *philhêdonia* (love of pleasure) are the two principal forms of antiphilosophical desire among the early dialogues.[136]

The psychology of *philotimia* relates to the desire to be considered valuable, that is, to be recognized and esteemed. Honor, esteem, and reputation are relational properties. One gains a reputation, honor, or esteem insofar as others generally have a certain attitude toward one. As the adverb "generally" suggests, esteem, honor, or reputation depend on popular attitudes, that is, the attitudes of the many (*hoi polloi*) or the majority of the social group of which one identifies oneself as a member. In this respect, *philotimia* may also be understood as a basic desire to belong. Noteworthy here is Plato's identification of the desideratum in *Lysis* as an *oikeion* (belonging), a word whose root, *oikos* (home, family), clearly reveals the social dimension of desire. From this vantage point *philotimia* may be seen as a prosocial desire. Indeed, David Whitehead has suggested that in Athens of the fifth and fourth centuries *philotimia* served democratic interests by motivating wealthy citizens to compete in funding various public projects.[137]

But *philotimia* also has an antisocial dimension. It is closely related to *philonikia* (love of winning or ambition) since characters driven by *philonikia* often seek *timê*. But if *nikê* (victory) is achieved, there will typically also be losers. Insofar as the pursuit of status is a zero-sum game, *philotimia* engenders social distress and antagonism.[138] For example, in *Gorgias* Socrates explains that he is afraid to challenge Gorgias' position because in discussions people tend to be motivated by victory (*philonikountas*). Consequently, Gorgias might assume that Socrates is striving for victory (*philonikounta*) against him.[139]

Given the relationship between status and power, *philotimia* may assume the form of a desire for power. For example, in *Protagoras* Socrates introduces Hippocrates to Protagoras as a youth who desires to gain renown (*epithumein ellogismos genesthai*) in the city.[140] Hippocrates' ambition might be to serve the best interests

---

136. Note that none of Socrates' interlocutors denies that knowledge is valuable. However, it is evident that many regard knowledge as merely instrumentally valuable to the attainment of *timê* or *hêdonê*.
137. (1983); see also Roberts (1986).
138. This idea has been developed in Gouldner (1965).
139. *Grg.* 457d4, e4.
140. *Prt.* 316c.

of the people. But political prominence can also be achieved and maintained in pernicious and oppressive ways. In *Gorgias*, Polus' description of Archelaus' murderous rise to the throne in Macedonia is a signal example.[141] Indeed, as we have seen, Polus admires the despotic power to do as one will, emblematic of which, as he claims, is executing and exiling citizens and confiscating their property.

The early dialogues diagnose different kinds of philosophical maladies with the different forms that *philotimia* assumes. The nefarious form of despotic *philotimia* is inconsistent with justice. Indeed, Polus uses the example of the Macedonian ruler Archelaus to argue that well-being does not depend on justice. More deeply, if *timê* is a genuine good and the pursuit of *timê* is a zero-sum contest, then goodness is a scarce commodity. Consequently, in principle—not merely as a matter of contingent fact—the cosmos, of which society is a part, must perpetually suffer from a state of imbalance and disharmony.

The philosophical problem to which the more benign form of *philotimia* is victim is precisely that one's self-esteem, values, and corresponding activity depend upon the values and attitudes of others. Accordingly, if those who constitute one's social group have false conceptions of the good, then one's sense of one's self and accordingly one's conduct in life will be misguided. As such, to seek *timê* is to seek a possession of dubious worth.

My discussion of Critias in *Charmides* in section 3 of chapter 5 will include one of Plato's principal reflections on *philotimia* among the early dialogues. Here I offer a few other salient examples. Hippias of Elis, particularly as portrayed in *Hippias Major* but also in *Hippias Minor*, is the most conceited character among the early dialogues. His polymathy in particular enables him to represent himself as a sort of paradigm of *autarkeia* (self-sufficiency and self-mastery). But Hippias' self-esteem heavily depends upon the recognition he receives from others. He competes in verbal contests at the Olympic games, and he travels throughout the Mediterranean performing and teaching for cash.

The governing question of *Hippias Major* is "What is *to kalon*?" One common sense of *to kalon* is "beauty." Accordingly, Hippias' initial definitions, a beautiful maiden and gold, relate to visual appearance. But *kalon* also commonly bears the ethical sense of "admirable" and "estimable." Thus, Hippias' third definition is to be rich, healthy, honored (*timômenôi*) by the Greeks, to reach old age, and after providing an admirable burial for one's parents to be admirably and splendidly buried by one's own children. The aesthetic and ethical senses of *kalon* are related insofar as in both cases value is identified with conditions external to the soul. In the aesthetic sense, *to kalon* is the external appearance of the object. In the ethical sense, value is conferred upon activity by observers—a point strongly confirmed by the following example from *Gorgias*. Polus and Socrates debate the relative values of doing and suffering injustice. Polus maintains that doing injustice is more shameful (*aischron*), while suffering injustice is worse (*kakon*). Here and in general the antonym of *aischron* is *kalon*, whereas the antonym of *kakon* is *agathon* (good).

---

141. *Grg.* 471a–d.

Polus' position is that suffering injustice is worse because it is more painful, while doing injustice is more shameful because others condemn it. In other words, *agathon* and *kakon*, here identified with pleasure and pain, are conceived as qualities internal to the agent, whereas *kalon* and *aischron*, here identified with esteem and disgrace, are conceived as qualities externally conferred upon the agent.

All this suggests that Hippias' conception of value is associated with and thus dependent upon conditions over which he has limited control. As such, his life actually is a perversion of *autarkeia*. Moreover, Hippias' self-conceit is especially noxious because it renders him impregnable to criticism and self-examination.

Applause is a form of distributing *timê*. Thus, *Hippias Minor* opens with Hippias having just completed an epideictic performance at the home of Eudicus son of Apemantus.[142] Socrates stands in silent thought, and Eudicus asks: "But why are you silent, Socrates, when Hippias has just finished such a display? Either join us in praising what he has said or challenge him if you think there is something he has not said admirably."[143] In *Euthydemus*, the crowd of spectators at the Lyceum periodically burst into applause to show their approval for the discursive maneuvers of Euthydemus and Dionysodorus. Similarly, in *Protagoras* the company at Callias' house cheers (*ethorubêsan*) at Protagoras' speech on the relativity of goodness.[144]

Since esteem depends upon the views of others, the psychodynamics of *philotimia* are particularly prominent in dialogues in which, as in the preceding examples, there are multiple interlocutors or at least witnesses to the discussion. Indeed, when Socrates accompanies Hippocrates to inquire about Protagoras' instruction, Socrates asks Protagoras whether he wishes to discuss the subject alone or among the company. Protagoras requests that the discussion occur among the other sophists, students, and Athenians at Callias' house. Socrates now remarks to the anonymous associate to whom he is recounting the event: "And then I said—for I suspected that Protagoras wanted to make a display and appear marvelous (*kallôpisasthai*) before Prodicus and Hippias insofar as we had come as admirers of his—'Why then, let's invite Prodicus and Hippias and their followers so that they can listen to us.'"[145]

In considering the operation of *philotimia* among the dialogues, we should also bear in mind the antithesis of *timê*, namely *aischunê* (shame or disgrace). While *timê* may be a condition of recognition and acceptance, *aischunê* is a condition of rejection and devaluation by those who constitute the social group with which one identifies oneself.

---

142. Note that there is no need to assume that Hippias has a transtextual identity between *Hippias Major* and *Hippias Minor*. But as a matter of fact, Plato's portrayal of him in these two dialogues is quite consistent.
143. *Hp. Mi.* 363a1–3.
144. *Prt.* 334c.
145. *Prt.* 317c6–d3.

Again in *Protagoras*, after Socrates has completed his interpretation of Simonides' ode and condemned the practice of interpreting poetry as befitting boorish
wine-parties, Protagoras is silent "and gives no indication of what he will do."
Alcibiades now asks Callias reproachfully, "Do you think Protagoras is behaving
well now...?" Socrates describes Protagoras' reaction: "Then Protagoras was
ashamed (*aischuntheis*) at Alcibiades' words and when Callias and almost all the
others present asked him..."[146] Here Protagoras' desire for the esteem of the
company and expectation that the outcome of a philosophical examination with
Socrates will undermine his competence in teaching excellence evokes shame.

Earlier in *Protagoras*, when Hippocrates and Socrates walk in the courtyard
of Socrates' house discussing Hippocrates' intentions in studying with Protagoras,
Socrates reasons that if one were to study with a sculptor, one's intention would be
to become a sculptor. Accordingly, Socrates proposes that Hippocrates intends to
become like Protagoras. But when Socrates asks Hippocrates to identify Protagoras' profession, Hippocrates blushes (*eruthriasas*) at the implication that he
would intend to become a sophist.[147] The implicit principle in Socrates' example
of sculpting concerns apprenticeship among laborers. But as a member of the
leisure class, it would be shameful for Hippocrates to make a living as a sophist.
Accordingly, Socrates explains, "Yet, Hippocrates, this is not the sort of learning
you expect to receive from Protagoras, but the sort that you received from your
grammar teacher, music instructor, and athletics coach. For you did not learn
these things as a craft in order to become a laborer (*dēmiourgos*), but for the sake of
education (*paideia*), as befits (*prepei*) a private and free man."[148]

In *Crito*, one of Crito's reasons in favor of Socrates escaping from prison is that
if he does not and is executed, Crito will be thought to have preferred money to his
friendship: "And yet what reputation could be more shameful (*aischiôn*) than that
of considering one's money of more importance than one's friends?"[149] Socrates
responds that Crito should not care what people think. Crito objects that the
concerns of the public do matter, for that is precisely why Socrates is now
imprisoned. Once Crito has completed his argument, Socrates begins his response
by claiming that we ought to esteem (*timan*) the opinions of some, but not others;
the opinions to be esteemed are the useful opinions of those who have knowledge.[150] In other words, Socrates is stating that what matters is what is truly
valuable, not what people think is.

From the perspective of the reader, especially the modern reader, who stands
outside of both the fiction of the drama and the social-psychological pressures of
the cultural-historical milieu in which the dialogues are embedded, it may be easy
to look down upon such characters for their psychological failings. But while

---

146. *Prt.* 348b1–c3.
147. *Prt.* 312a2.
148. *Prt.* 312a7–b4.
149. *Cri.* 44c2–3.
150. *Cri.* 47a.

condemnation of the *philotimic* spirit that contradicts *philosophia* is Platonic, the early dialogues also demonstrate an appreciation of the difficulties of extricating oneself from social pressures. Protagoras' livelihood depends upon the esteem of those like the company at Callias' house, and, as Crito suggests, rejecting the opinions of the many can be deadly.

In this light, *Apology* offers some important observations on the social psychology of belief and action. Socrates begins his defense, not with his immediate accusers, but, as he describes them, his old accusers. The latter were men of the preceding generation whose influence predisposed the jury to assume that Socrates was guilty. They purveyed false beliefs about Socrates for many years (*polla etê*) and at a time when the jurors were children (*ek paidôn*).[151] Implicit here is the idea that repeated exposure to ideas enforces acceptance and conviction and that children are especially susceptible to persuasion. Later in the dialogue, Socrates explicitly states that it is difficult, in the short span of a daylong trial, to disabuse people of prejudice under which they have been influenced for a long time.[152] Furthermore, youth tend to believe and follow their elders. This is why Socrates finds it remarkable that foreigners such as Gorgias, Hippias, and Prodicus are able to persuade Athenian youth to associate with them.[153] Indeed, the Athenians are angry with Socrates because they believe Socrates has influenced the youth of his own generation to challenge the views of their elders.[154] Generally speaking, unconventional conduct is apt to be regarded with suspicion. And yet Socrates explains that he was compelled to conduct his philosophical activity outside of the customary political fora: "If I had attempted to go into politics, I would have been executed a long time ago ... the fact is that no man will spare his life if he ... opposes you or any other populace."[155]

In a portion of his Great Speech in *Protagoras* (325c–326e), Protagoras relates in considerable detail the various contexts in which from infancy through adulthood Athenians are informed with the values of their society. In view of this, it may be questioned just what sort of person would be immune to the social pressures of *timê* and *aischunê*. In *Gorgias* and *Republic* 1 Plato explores the idea through his portrayals of selfish, insensitive, and antisocial characters.

Among the early dialogues, shame plays the most prominent role in *Gorgias*. Polus attributes Gorgias' self-contradiction to his sense of shame.[156] Likewise, Callicles attributes the refutation of Polus to his sense of shame.[157] In contrast, Callicles presents himself as a person who will not be cowed by conscience. In articulating his radical thesis of natural justice, he abjures any sense of

---

151. *Ap.* 18b.
152. *Ap.* 24a.
153. *Ap.* 19e.
154. *Ap.* 23c.
155. *Ap.* 31d7–e4.
156. *Grg.* 461b–c; compare 482c–e.
157. *Grg.* 482e.

shame.[158] Indeed, Socrates presses Callicles, on the basis of his ethical hedonism, to consider whether the life of a catamite is a good one:

SOCRATES   Consider what you will answer, Callicles, if someone should ask you all that follows from this [commitment to ethical hedonism]—even the extremity of such things, the life of catamites. Is this not awful, shameful (*aischros*), and wretched? Or will you dare (*tolmêseis*) to say that they live well if they can satisfy their wants without inhibition (*aphthonôs*)?

CALLICLES   Are you not ashamed (*aischunêi*) to lead the discussion to such things, Socrates?[159]

But in the face of the "many shameful (*aischra*) consequences"[160] of ethical hedonism, Callicles stands his ground.

More extreme still is the characterization of Thrasymachus, who repeatedly insults Socrates and disregards the well-being of others. In Socrates' narration of the event, Thrasymachus' demeanor is characterized by reference to animals. As he enters the conversation, he is described as "preparing to pounce (*sustrepsas*) like a beast (*thêrion*)."[161] Socrates then relates that if he had not beheld Thrasymachus before Thrasymachus had seen him, he would have lost his voice.[162] The statement is explicable as an allusion to the superstition that being seen first by a wolf would render one mute.[163] Later, when Thrasymachus challenges Socrates to outwit him, Socrates says he is not so crazy as to try to beard a lion (*xurein leonta*).[164] The point of this language is to suggest that in his violent and insensitive conduct Thrasymachus stands at the edge of the human community.[165]

Thrasymachus' demeanor is consistent with the radical conception of justice that he endorses. He claims that justice is a sort of naiveté, whereas injustice is excellence. Even so, Socrates' arguments ultimately prove effective; Thrasymachus is compelled to concede that justice is a good thing. Moreover, however unethically Thrasymachus blusters and conducts himself during the inquiry, the fact that his concession to Socrates is accompanied by sweating (*hidrôtos*) and blushing (*eruthriônta*)[166] reveals his concern for *timê* and thus with others—even if that concern is not for the well-being of others.

---

158. He extols the man whose *andreia* (vigor) and *phronêsis* (intelligence) enable him to gain mastery over others (*Grg.* 491b).
159. *Grg.* 494e2–8.
160. *Grg.* 495b4–5.
161. *R.* 1, 336b5.
162. *R.* 1, 336d.
163. See Shorey (1930) 41, n. c.
164. *R.* 1, 341c.
165. Compare Callicles' reference to young lions in his defense of natural justice at *Grg.* 483e and to animals more generally at 483d.
166. *R.* 1, 350d.

Among the characters in the early dialogues, only one might be said to be relatively immune to the social pressures of esteem and shame. That character is Socrates. Yet morally speaking Socrates is antithetical to Thrasymachus. Indeed, in *Euthyphro* Socrates speaks of his *philanthrôpia* (love of humanity),[167] and throughout *Apology* he explains how he has devoted his life to encouraging his fellow citizens to care for their souls. We may wonder, then, about the source of Socrates' love of humanity. I presume it must be his love of excellence, in other words, his *philosophia*. But this must mean that Socrates loves people not as they are, but for what they may become. In that case, Socrates may perceive himself as part of a larger deficient whole.

We turn now to the psychology of *philhêdonia*. The Platonic conception of the psychology of *philhêdonia* is revealed above all in *Gorgias*. As we have seen, Socrates distinguishes crafts (*technai*) from competences (*empeiriai*) and claims that the former are concerned with the good, while the later are concerned with pleasure. Moreover, pleasure is a semblance (*eidôlon*) of the good. In *Protagoras* Socrates argues that the many are committed to ethical hedonism. In short, the Platonic conception is that pleasure motivates many people. Less clear is why people generally are so motivated.

The Platonic view is that ethical hedonism is a misidentification of goodness and thus a cognitive failing. Evidence for this thesis comes from several passages and sources. Consider first Socrates' intellectualist account of *akrasia* in *Protagoras*. Here, as we have seen, putative *akrasia* actually is a condition of mismeasurement. In other words, apparent irrational drives actually are cognitive defects. Furthermore, cognitive deficiency is conceived as a failure to realize oneself as a man. This clearly follows from the Platonic conception of *aretê* as a form of knowledge because the pursuit of excellence in the early dialogues principally targets the *aretê* of an *anêr* (man).[168] But it is further confirmed by a number of passages where cognitive failure and susceptibility to pleasure and fear—that is, fear of pain—are associated above all with childishness, but also with the conditions of slavery and unmanliness. Within the critique of *akrasia* itself, Socrates scoffs at the popular view of *akrasia*-through-pleasure according to which knowledge is "overpowered" and "dragged about like a slave."[169] In *Crito* Socrates insists that the question of his escape must be subjected to examination and that the power of the multitude, threatening imprisonment, death, and confiscation of property, should not allow him and Crito to be frightened "like children (*hôsper paidas*)."[170] The word he uses for being frightened is *mormoluttêtai*, which is derived from the proper noun Mormô, the name of a bogey-monster with which adults scared children. The verb also occurs in *Gorgias* in Socrates' discussion with Polus. Socrates claims that it is better for one who commits injustice to be punished

---

167. *Euthphr.* 3d7.
168. Meno's first definition and Socrates' reaction to it is exceptional.
169. *Prt.* 352c.
170. *Cri.* 46c4.

than to escape punishment. Polus is incredulous, and he graphically describes the kinds of gruesome physical tortures to which criminals could be subjected. In response Socrates says, "You are trying to spook me (*mormolutthê*), Polus, rather than test (*elencheis*) me."[171] Later in *Gorgias* Socrates claims, "No one fears death, unless he is completely irrational (*alogistos*) and unmanly (*anandros*)."[172]

In *Gorgias* Socrates describes Callicles' hedonism in a number of revealing ways. As I have mentioned, he cites the condition of a catamite, a passive sexual position associated with that of a women, slave, or youth. Socrates likens the hedonistic life to that of a plover, one of constant consumption and excretion; in other words, a life more befitting an animal than a human being. Generally, Socrates speaks of the hedonist as lacking self-control. This conception resonates with portrayals of the dissoluteness and excitation of two other youthful characters among the dialogues. In *Protagoras* Plato spends considerable time conveying an impression of Hippocrates as an impetuous and intemperate soul. Hippocrates arrives at Socrates' house before sunrise; he knocks forcefully (*panu sphodra*) at the door with a stick; he rushes inside (*euthus epeigomenos*); he shouts (*têi phonêi mega*). He would have come to Socrates before he went to bed, but having gone to the district of Oenoë in search of his runaway slave Satyrus, he returned home too late. Plato's inclusion of Hippocrates' failure to control his slave may also suggest a failure of self-control. Alternatively, the names Oenoë and Satyrus may conceal the real reason Hippocrates returned home so late: He was out drinking.[173] When Hippocrates finishes his story, Socrates says, "Then I, recognizing his spirit and excitement (*ptoiêsin*)...."[174]

Hippothales, in *Lysis*, is another dissolute youth. In the previous section I noted his hedonism. When Hippothales is first introduced in the dialogue, Ctesippus characterizes his conduct: "If Socrates spends even a little time with you, he will be tormented by your incessant repetition. He has deafened our ears at least, Socrates, cramming them with Lysis. And if he should be a little drunk, we will surely be roused from sleep thinking we hear the name of Lysis."[175]

More generally, in *Gorgias* Socrates describes political and forensic rhetoric, as it is typically practiced in Athens, as akin to gratifying children. Socrates asks Callicles: "Do the orators seem to you always to speak with a view to what is best...or are they rather set on gratifying the citizens...like children (*hôsper paisi*)?"[176] Later in the dialogue Socrates says that if he is ever brought to trial it will be like a doctor tried by a jury of children (*paidiois*).[177] In that case, his prosecutor, a cook whose competence—not craft—aims to gratify the body, would

---

171. *Grg.* 473d3.
172. *Grg.* 522e1–2.
173. The place name Oenoë is cognate with the word for wine, *oinos*, and the slave's name evokes the figure of the satyr.
174. *Prt.* 310d2–3.
175. *Ly.* 204c5–7.
176. *Grg.* 502e2–7.
177. *Grg.* 521e.

claim, "Children, this man has done you many wrongs. He corrupts even the youngest among you by cutting and burning [medical techniques] ... not like me who has gorged (êuôchoun) you with a bounty of sweets (hêdea) of all kinds."[178]

In *Charmides*, Charmides introduces a definition of sound-mindedness, doing one's own thing (*to ta heautou prattein*), which he heard from Critias. Socrates is puzzled by the meaning of the phrase, and Charmides is unable to clarify it in a plausible way. Socrates turns to Critias: "Why, Critias, my good man ... it is no wonder that [Charmides] at his age (*têlikouton onta*) is ignorant, but I would think that you would know on account of your age (*hêlikias heneka*) and experience."[179] Socrates and his mature interlocutors assume the weaknesses of children and youth, including cognitive weaknesses. This is why in *Laches* Lysimachus and Melesias are unwilling to allow their sons to "run loose as their fancy leads them."[180] But the philosophical problem is not merely that the youth are not being well educated; their elders themselves lack the knowledge and pedagogical skills. Critias is no more able than Charmides to effectively clarify sound-mindedness. And Laches and Nicias, to whom Lysimachus and Melesias turn for advice in cultivating excellence in their sons, are unable to provide a consistent or compelling account of manliness.[181] Thus, the dialogue concludes with Socrates' statement:

> I tell you, men, and I say this in confidence, it is necessary that we all seek out the best teacher available, first for ourselves, for we need it, and then for our boys ... And if anyone should ridicule us for deeming it worthy to go to school at our age (*têlikoide ontes*), I think we should refer to Homer who said that shame is no good mate for a man in need. So let us pay no attention to what one may say, but let us take care of ourselves as well as our boys.[182]

Finally, given that among the early dialogues pleasure is understood as a kind of bodily sensation, there appears to be a disparity between the Platonic explanation of pleasure as a misconception of excellence and what I described in *Lysis* as the natural desire for psychological fulfillment. The problem is that, as I said, nature orients individuals toward proper types of belonging. Thus, we would expect nature to orient hedonists toward a psychological kind. Yet pleasure is conceived as somatic, not psychological. *Philhêdonia*, thus, appears to be a perverse desire.

The implicit treatment of *philhêdonia* as a kind of puerility among the early dialogues offers a possible Platonic explanation of *philhêdonia* as a perversion. Let us grant that children need psychological and specifically cognitive development. In view of their cognitive deficit, children may, then, more plausibly be identified

---

178. *Grg.* 521e6–522a3.
179. *Chrm.* 162d7–e2.
180. *La.* 179a. The translation of *aneinai autous ho ti boulontai poiein* is Lamb's (1924) 9.
181. The word *andreia*, which elsewhere I have translated as "courage," is cognate with the Greek word for man, *anêr*.
182. *La.* 201a2–b5.

with their somatic than with their psychological natures. In other words, ontologically speaking, children, in contrast to mature adults, are to a greater extent somatic than psychological beings.[183] In that case, the fulfillment that the children tend to seek is somatic. Moreover, given their psychological deficiency, the somatic fulfillment that they seek is not genuine health, but pleasure. Accordingly, some adults—indeed, for Plato, many adults—are like children; their identities are to a greater extent somatic than psychological. Thus, their *philhêdonia* manifests their failure to have developed their true natures.

---

183. Of course, I do not mean to suggest that this is sound, just sound exegesis.

3

KNOWLEDGE

1. Excellence as Wisdom

The questions "How ought one to live one's life?" and "What ought one to do with oneself?" are often treated as points of departure for philosophical reflection on ethics. But in the early dialogues, the implicit question is "What sort of character should one cultivate?" The Platonic, as well as traditional Greek and conventional Athenian, answer to this question is "An excellent character." Accordingly, the dialogues attempt to determine what excellence of character is.

The answer that the dialogues suggest, even while their discussions end aporetically, is that a sound-minded, courageous, just, and holy person is excellent. This view is not especially controversial. Indeed, at the end of chapter 2, I spoke of it as standard and voiced piecemeal by several of Socrates' interlocutors. On the other hand, the way these putative components of excellence are elucidated among the early dialogues is controversial. The Platonic view is that an excellent person is one who has the capacity or power to resist the inclination to pursue bad pleasures, to resist the inclination to capitulate to bad fears, to conduct oneself well with respect to other human beings, and to conduct oneself well with respect to the divine. Moreover, this capacity is wholly epistemic, that is, a kind of knowledge. In short, excellence is wisdom, the knowledge of the good.

There is considerable evidence among the early dialogues that an epistemic conception of excellence is Platonic. Arguments from *Euthydemus* and *Meno* suggest that among putative somatic, psychological, and social goods, only knowledge (= wisdom = intelligence) is invariably beneficial. In *Protagoras*, Socrates develops four arguments to support the view that holiness, justice, sound-mindedness and courage are knowledge.[1] In the course of the investigation of sound-mindedness

---

1. Admittedly, the arguments for the identity of justice and holiness and for the identity of justice and sound-mindedness are rejected by Protagoras and incomplete, respectively.

in *Charmides*, Socrates, in criticizing the definitions of his interlocutors, introduces conditions that the *definiens* must satisfy. One of these conditions is that sound-mindedness entails knowledge; the remaining definitions discussed are epistemic. Similarly, in the course of the investigation of courage in *Laches*, Nicias introduces an epistemic definition of courage, knowledge of what is to be feared and pursued, and supports it by citing a claim by Socrates that a man is good insofar as he is wise (*sophos*). In *Protagoras*, Socrates himself develops the view that courage is the knowledge of what is to be feared and pursued. In *Republic* 1, Socrates develops an argument for the view that justice is an excellence. In the course of his argument he articulates the view that justice is like knowledge and then that justice is knowledge. In short, there is more compelling argumentative evidence for view that the epistemic conception of excellence is Platonic than for another other weighty philosophical position among the early dialogues.

Furthermore, the Platonic conception is that the knowledge that constitutes excellence is a unity. Observe that the conception of excellence as a unity is important because it is consistent with the unity of character. For example, if sound-mindedness and justice were components of excellence, but components that compelled persons to act in contradictory ways in a given situation, then the ideal of human excellence would be unrealizable—indeed, as the Attic dramatists sometimes suggest, tragically so.

At the end of the last chapter we examined the principal forms of anti-philosophical desire among the early dialogues. Granted that *philotimia* and *philhêdonia* are not Platonic motivations, if we ask why *philosophia* is Platonic, we can now formulate an answer. Everyone regards the objects of their desires as good. But pleasure and goodness are not the same; more generally, the values of the many tend to be misguided. As examples in other domains of knowledge indicate, the many have mere opinions; it is the few who know. The human good is wisdom.

Precisely why Plato and the historical Socrates came to doubt conventional forms of ethical knowledge is, surely, a long and complex story, one that involves sociopolitical change in Athenian society of the fifth century and the activities of the sophists and other intellectuals, among other things. We will not pursue this story here. Suffice it to say that the early dialogues emphasize that there is a fundamental problem of ethical knowledge in the polis. On the one hand, they expose this problem; on the other hand, they attempt, although ultimately without success, to overcome it.

Section 2 of this chapter examines the Platonic conception of excellence as an epistemic unity. The section begins with the epistemic nature of excellence; it then turns to the unity of the knowledge that constitutes excellence. Given the Platonic conception of *aretê* as an epistemic unity, sections 3 and 4 examine the two basic aspects of this epistemic condition, knowledge itself and goodness, respectively.

In conceptualizing *aretê* as a kind of knowledge, Plato appeals to the concept of *technê* (craft, expertise) and specifically to the nonethical *technai* (plural of *technê*), for example, medicine and architecture, whose epistemic authority was established within the city-state. *Technê*, in turn, is conceptualized as a kind of *dunamis* (power, capability), and *dunameis* (plural of *dunamis*) are identified by their activities or functions (*erga*) and products (also called *erga*) as well as by their objects or contents (*relata*). Accordingly, section 3 focuses on the Platonic conceptualization of *aretê* qua knowledge as a *technê* (craft) and *technê* itself as a *dunamis* (power).

The examination of goodness in section 4 is motivated by the goal of providing a noncircular and nonvacuous account of *aretê* itself as well as its relation to well-being or living well (*eudaimonia*). Observe that *aretê*, which is understood as human goodness, is identified as knowledge of goodness. Moreover, insofar as *aretê* is responsible for *eudaimonia*, knowledge of goodness is responsible for living a good life. One solution considered, but rejected involves the identification of goodness with pleasure, where *aretê* is understood as the knowledge that enables its possessor to live pleasantly. Instead, it is argued that the Platonic view of goodness is order. Consequently, ethical knowledge, a kind of psychological order, is responsible for living an orderly life. It remains questionable, however, to what extent this solution is noncircular and nonvacuous.

Having thus clarified the concept of the knowledge of the good, section 5 focuses on a special epistemological condition associated with ethical knowledge in particular, but arguably with *technê* more generally, namely the epistemological priority of definitional knowledge. According to this principle, definitional knowledge is necessary for pertinent nondefinitional knowledge. For example, in order to know that Euthyphro's prosecution of his father is holy, Euthyphro must know what holiness is. (Note that the explanation for why the epistemological priority of definitional knowledge is Platonic is postponed until section 5 of chapter 4.)

Section 6 concludes the chapter by considering an objection to the view that the epistemological priority of definitional knowledge is Platonic. Occasionally Socrates avows some nondefinitional ethical knowledge; yet Socrates disavows pertinent definitional knowledge. I argue that such Socratic avowals of nondefinitional ethical knowledge are hermeneutically innocuous. The discussion in this section, thus, provides another significant example of Socratic inconsistencies and a demonstration of the distinction between Socratic and Platonic views.

2. The Epistemic Unity of Excellence

The early dialogues reveal two principal sorts of reason for the Platonic view that excellence is epistemic. The first relates to the idea that wisdom is the only invariably good human possession; upon it the goodness of all other human possessions depends. Arguments in *Euthydemus* and *Meno*, which I will discuss in section 3 of this chapter, provide the principal evidence for this view. The goodness of wisdom also figures in Socrates' arguments with Polus and Callicles in *Gorgias* that it is worse to do than to suffer injustice. Socrates' position in *Gorgias* is essentially to be explained on the grounds that suffering injustice entails somatic harm, whereas doing injustice implies corruption of the agent's soul. Similarly, as Socrates in *Apology* claims, no harm can come to a good man.[2] In short, these lines of argumentation suggest that the human good is psychological, specifically

---

2. *Ap.* 30c8–d1, 41d1–2.

epistemic, not somatic, material, or social. I will not discuss this line of argumentation further here.

The second principal reason for the Platonic conception of excellence as epistemic relates the view that knowledge is psychological strength. Courage and sound-mindedness—as standardly conceived and, arguably, in contrast to justice and holiness—appear to entail a certain fortitude, in addition to any cognitive component they might entail.[3] Plato designed Socrates' critique of *akrasia* in *Protagoras* precisely to challenge this idea.

As I mentioned in section 5 of chapter 2, the argument that Socrates develops for the identity of courage and knowledge in *Protagoras* is divisible into two arguments (349e1–350c5 and 351b3–360e5). Protagoras criticizes the first argument (350c6–351b2), and Socrates develops an argument in response to Protagoras' criticism. Socrates' first argument basically runs as follows:

> Courageous men are confident.
> Courage, qua part of excellence, is fine (*kalon*).
> Knowledgeable men are confident.
> Some without knowledge are confident.
> Ignorant confidence is base (*aischron*).[4]
> Therefore, courage is knowledge.

According to this description, Socrates attempts to identify courage and knowledge on the ground that both are fine confidence. In turn, Protagoras' criticism of Socrates' argument is based on the view that there may be two distinct sources of fine confidence: knowledge and courage. Protagoras initially makes this point in this way: "You show that those who have knowledge are more confident than those who lack knowledge and thereby you take courage and knowledge to be the same. But if you go about it that way, you might maintain that strength is the same as knowledge."[5]

This statement is rather elliptical. Observe that the argument form is *reductio*. Protagoras is claiming that if one argues as Socrates does, then one can conclude that strength is knowledge; but this, so Protagoras thinks, is absurd; therefore, Socrates' argument is fallacious.

We can clarify the ellipses in Protagoras' statement: "Socrates has tried to show that since knowledge [versus ignorance] is a form of [fine] confidence [and courage is a form of fine confidence], it follows that knowledge and courage are

---

3. On certain conceptions, holiness or piety might also require fortitude, for instance, the strength of faith or conviction. But such conceptions seem alien to classical Greek piety. Note also that justice might require a noncognitive component, namely compassion. But this virtue is strikingly absent from the early dialogues. There are, of course, contexts where justice and holiness overlap with courage and sound-mindedness; and in such cases, we might want to say that the psychological fortitude required for courage or sound-mindedness is also required for justice and holiness; for example, the ability to resist the temptation to steal or cheat.

4. As noted in chapter 2, *kalon* and *aischron* are understood as contraries.

5. *Prt.* 350d3–6.

identical." Protagoras now proceeds to clarify why this is false. He proposes that strength is a type of power and that the source of strength is the conjunction of nature (*phusis*) and good nurture of the body. For other kinds of power, there are three sources: knowledge, craziness, and rage. Analogously, Protagoras grants that courage is a type of confidence; however, he claims that the source of courage is the conjunction of nature and good nurture of the soul; whereas for other kinds of confidence, there are three sources: craft or skill (*technê*), craziness, and rage.

Let us be clear what Protagoras is suggesting in this analogy. By strength he means the sort of brute physical power that some people can develop through training their bodies because their bodies are naturally suited to such cultivation, for example, the strength of a professional boxer or weightlifter. Contrast this with the use of ingenuity to move a large object: A strong man lifts the object, while Archimedes devises a fulcrum. Furthermore, in episodes of craziness and rage the body is temporarily able to achieve more than usual, but such cases do not exemplify strength. Analogously, Protagoras understands courage to be a kind of psychological toughness cultivated through training of the soul of an individual whose soul is naturally suited to such training. A professional soldier may exemplify this. Moreover, the confidence of the courageous person differs from confidence derived from the acquisition of knowledge or through some delusion or passion. For example, a doctor may have confidence in performing a surgery, and a parent may confidently lash out in response to some attack on his child.

Accordingly, Protagoras can consistently maintain that knowledge is a form of fine confidence, but not identical to courage, since although courage is also a form of fine confidence, courage is engendered by natural constitution and good nurture of the soul, and not by knowledge.

Furthermore, we can see how Protagoras thinks Socrates' form of argument, when applied to the relation between knowledge and strength, will yield the conclusion, absurd according to Protagoras, that strength is knowledge. On the grounds that strength is a form of power and fine and knowledge is a form of power and fine, Socrates would have us believe that strength and knowledge are identical. But just as courage is engendered by natural constitution and good nurture of the soul, not by knowledge, so strength is engendered by natural constitution and good nurture of the body, not by knowledge.

In view of this account of Protagoras' rejection of Socrates' first argument, Socrates' second argument, and specifically his critique of *akrasia* within that argument, can be seen as a response to Protagoras' criticism of the first argument: Socrates argues that knowledge itself is the source of fine psychological strength.

We have seen that Socrates' critique of *akrasia* specifically targets the popular conception of *akrasia*-through-pleasure and in the process identifies ethical hedonism as a popular view. This is a peculiar move in several respects, and the peculiarity has generated puzzlement among scholars. First, it has been thought that Socrates himself commits to ethical hedonism in the process of this argument, yet elsewhere among the early dialogues Socrates strongly rejects ethical hedonism. I will resolve this problem in section 4 of this chapter. Second, it is unclear why Socrates criticizes *akrasia*-through-pleasure rather than *akrasia*-through-fear (and thus pain), which would seem to be directly relevant to the question of the epistemic nature of courage and Protagoras' criticism of his first argument. And third, it is unclear why Socrates criticizes the popular view of *akrasia*, rather than Protagoras' view directly.

If Socrates attempted to criticize *akrasia*-through-fear by arguing that a person with knowledge would not be overcome by fear, Protagoras would immediately block his line of argument, for it would directly contradict his previous objection that there are two sources of fine confidence. Consequently, Socrates turns to pleasure and to the popular conception of *akrasia*. Protagoras does not perceive the connection between *akrasia*-through-pleasure and *akrasia*-through-pain. Indeed, he complains that consideration of *akrasia*-through-pleasure is unrelated to the subject of investigation:

> SOCRATES Come, then, try with me to persuade and teach people what this affection of theirs is, which they call becoming overcome by pleasures . . .
>
> PROTAGORAS But, Socrates, why should we investigate what the many think . . . ?
>
> SOCRATES I think . . . it will aid our inquiry into courage and how the parts of excellence are related.[6]

In turning to pleasure Socrates is not attempting to deceive Protagoras into conceding that courage is wholly epistemic. Rather, he is approaching problem from a relevant angle, but one to which Protagoras is amenable. The shift is ad hominem, but the light that it throws on the subject is Platonic. Conventionally conceived, courage is the capacity to master fear; and fear entails the expectation of pain. Sound-mindedness is the capacity to master temptation, and temptation entails the expectation of pleasure. Therefore, clarification of *akrasia*-through-pleasure promises to illuminate *akrasia*-through-pain and thus fear and courage. Consequently, when, following the critique of *akrasia* (359a–360e), Socrates directly reengages the relationship between courage and knowledge, his first step is to clarify that fear is the expectation of badness. Given ethical hedonism, this implies that fear is the expectation of pain. Socrates then proceeds to argue *not* that courageous men master their fears in the sense that they pursue courses of action that are bad, despite their recognition of the badness. Rather, courageous men master fear in the sense that they know which situations on balance will yield more goodness than badness; and they, unlike cowardly men, pursue those.

The function of the critique of *akrasia* in *Protagoras* is, then, to show that courage does not require a noncognitive component of psychological fortitude; knowledge itself provides the psychological strength that the excellent person needs. It also explains what may be considered a gap between Laches' and Nicias' contributions in the investigation in *Laches*. Laches' second definition of courage is toughness of the soul (*karteria tês psychês*). Socrates ultimately refutes this view on the ground that some forms of toughness are foolish. Observe that this point

---

6. *Prt.* 352e5–353b3.

resembles Socrates' claim in the first argument regarding the relationship between courage and knowledge in *Protagoras*, that courage is a form of fine confidence. In *Laches*, following the refutation of Laches' definition, Nicias assumes the role of Socrates' principal interlocutor. Nicias' first definition of courage is the knowledge of what is to be feared and pursued, a definition that, as I mentioned above, Nicias admits he owes to Socrates' view that a man is good insofar as he is wise. The gap, then, is between Laches' noncognitive and Nicias' epistemic conceptions of courage. Socrates' intellectualist explanation of *akrasia* in *Protagoras* fills that gap.

The investigation in *Laches* in turn complements the investigation in *Protagoras* by developing the epistemic definition of courage as knowledge of what is to be feared and pursued. In examining Nicias' definition, Socrates argues, as in *Protagoras*, that fear is the expectation of badness. Thus, knowledge of what is to be feared entails knowledge of what is bad. It follows that courage is the knowledge of what is bad and its contrary good. At this point, Socrates suggests to Nicias, "Do you think, my good man, that such a man [namely, one who possessed the knowledge of good and bad] would in any way be lacking in excellence...? Do you think he would need sound-mindedness or justice or holiness...?"[7]

Since it was assumed at the beginning of the investigation in *Laches* that courage was a part of excellence, the investigation, which leads to a conception of courage as identical to excellence as a whole, ends in perplexity. Granted, then, that the view of excellence as wholly epistemic is Platonic, it remains a question whether and how the putative parts of excellence are unified. Many scholars who have examined the question of the unity of excellence begin with the assumption that the partition of excellence is Socratic (and therefore Platonic) because there are a few passages among the early dialogues where Socrates speaks of parts of excellence. For example, in chapter 1, I discussed the passage in *Euthyphro* where Socrates claims that holiness is a part of justice. In *Meno* Socrates speaks of justice, sound-mindedness, and courage as parts of excellence. But the inference from such Socratic claims to a Platonic position is naïve and results from a failure to appreciate the contexts and functions of Socrates' utterances. Accordingly, I dismiss as misguided claims such as that of Gregory Vlastos that the partition of excellence is "standard Socratic [= Platonic] doctrine" on the grounds that in *Meno* and *Euthyphro* Socrates explicitly speaks of the parts of excellence.[8]

Occasional Socratic statements about parts of excellence do not imply that the partition of excellence is Platonic. To pursue the question of the partition of excellence, it is necessary to look elsewhere. A common point of departure is the passage in *Protagoras* with which Socrates and Protagoras begin their investigation of the relationship between the parts of excellence (329c–330b). Here Socrates presents Protagoras with three options: The excellence-terms are co-referring; the excellences are related as the parts of an ingot of gold; the excellences are related as the parts of a face.[9]

---

7. *La.* 199d4–8.
8. Vlastos (1981) 225 and n. 8.
9. *Prt.* 329c–e.

With respect to the first option, observe that co-referring terms may have different meanings. However, there is no good reason to think that Plato conceived of Socrates' WF questions or the question about the relation of the excellences as concerning the meaning of "F" or the relation between the meanings of the excellence-terms. The parts of excellence are conceived as psychological conditions or states of the soul.[10]

With regard to the second option, observe that Socrates has in mind here a mereology[11] according to which parts are spatial and distinguishable in size, but not in quality. Note that Socrates does not speak of distinction in location, although this is another obvious way in which spatial parts are distinguishable. The problem with this mereology for the question of the unity of excellence is that since the putative parts of excellence are psychological, they are not spatial. It is unclear, then, how the relative sizes of psychological parts are to be conceived. This is a problem to which I will return below.[12]

The third option involves a distinction based on power (dunamis) as well as being: "Are the parts of excellence unlike one another both in themselves (auto) and in their powers (dunamis)?"[13] This is why, for example, eyes and ears are different parts of the face and have different powers. Unfortunately, the distinction in being is unclear in the text; among other things, it could be material or even structural.[14] But the distinction in power is clear. The power of the eyes is to see; the power of the ears is to hear. In other words, these facial parts are able to do different things. And the fact that these facial parts do different things is taken to be attributable to their having different powers. Excellence is a power; and, as we have seen, the putative parts of excellence were conventionally conceived as related to various types of action. Accordingly, Protagoras chooses this third option. In short, the parts of excellence are to be distinguished in terms of their dunameis (plural of dunamis).

In considering how the parts of excellence qua dunameis may be distinguished, it is useful to consider the first movement in Gorgias, especially 449c9–455a4. This movement is governed by the question of the identity of Gorgias' craft, rhetoric. As such, this first movement strongly resembles the pursuit of a WF question. Socrates himself first frames the answer to the question "What is Gorgias' craft

---

10. So Penner (1973). For a recent discussion of this point, see Wolfsdorf (2005a) and (2005c).

11. "Mereology" means "a conception or theory of the relation between parts and wholes."

12. Note that it is also a question what it would mean to speak of their qualities. Indeed, the early dialogues do not contain a concept of quality per se. But clearly whatever might be said of the excellences, it cannot be said that they are perceptible and therefore have sensory qualities. (It is true, however, that sensory language is occasionally used for them. For example, in Charmides Socrates tells Charmides to look into himself and see what perception his sound-mindedness yields. Surely, though, we are to understand Socrates' language as metaphorical.) Of course, we may speak of nonsensory qualities, and Socrates certainly speaks of things that we would speak of as nonsensory qualities, for example, being good and being fine.

13. Prt. 330a7–b1.

14. See Wolfsdorf (2005c).

and what is its *dunamis?*" by using references to the products of weaving and music. Accordingly, Gorgias' first attempt to define rhetoric is as a producer of speeches. In short, the underlying principle appears to be that a *dunamis* is distinguishable by its particular product.

Socrates, however, criticizes the definition of rhetoric as a producer of speeches on the ground that other crafts produce speeches. Consequently, he requests that Gorgias specify what sort of speeches (*poious toutous*) rhetoric produces. Socrates' response, which is typical of the ensuing examination, is noteworthy. Compare Socrates' response to Charmides' first definition of sound-mindedness, restraint (*hêsuchiotês*). There he argues that sound-mindedness is fine in all instances, whereas restraint is not fine in all instances. Therefore, sound-mindedness is not restraint—and Socrates encourages Charmides to try again to define sound-mindedness. Observe that Socrates does not suggest that the definition is not, so to speak, specific enough. In other words, he does not suspect that sound-mindedness is a kind of restraint, restraint in certain circumstances. In contrast, he does respond in this way to Gorgias here and throughout his examination with Gorgias. Gorgias claims that rhetoric differs from other speech-producing crafts in that its activity is entirely oral, whereas, for example, the activity of medicine is, to a large extent, manual. But Socrates argues that the activity of counting and other mathematical crafts is entirely oral as well. Thus, rhetoric must be distinguished as a kind of craft whose production is entirely oral.

Socrates assists Gorgias by distinguishing the objects—we might call them contents—of speeches. For example, counting produces speeches concerning the odd and the even; astronomy produces speeches concerning the rotations of the celestial spheres and their relative speeds. Note, furthermore, that Socrates recognizes that calculation (*logistikê*), like counting or numeration (*arithmêtikê*), produces speeches both of whose objects are the odd and even. However, the latter is concerned with the magnitude of a single quantity—for example, how many fingers Socrates has on his right hand[15]—while the former is concerned with the relationship between numbers. Gorgias then specifies that rhetoric produces speeches whose objects are justice and injustice.

Although it might be anachronistic to argue that the pursuit of the definition of rhetoric here proceeds by the diairectic method of *Sophist* and *Statesman*,[16] implicitly there is a strong resemblance. At least, it may be heuristic to bear this correlation in mind. One is also reminded of the work of sculpting, in which successive cuts are made whose effect is to produce a particular form. There are crafts that produce speeches and crafts that do not. There are crafts whose entire production is oral and those whose production is not. Among crafts that produce entirely orally, some are concerned with numbers and some are not. Among crafts that produce entirely orally and are concerned with numbers, one is concerned

---

15. The example is drawn from *Ion* 537e.
16. The diairetic method in these late dialogues is a method of definition by division.

with numbers in themselves and one is concerned with numbers in relation to one another. With this final cut, we have distinguished counting and calculation.

Furthermore, there is evidence that this procedure in *Gorgias* is conceptualized mereologically. The evidence comes from the movement of the dialogue immediately following the one we have been considering (461–66). Polus replaces Gorgias as Socrates' principal interlocutor, and he requests that Socrates himself define rhetoric. Socrates describes rhetoric as a competence (*empeiria*) that produces pleasure, rather than as a craft.[17] But Socrates also describes cookery as a competence that produces pleasure. Here Polus attempts to deploy the sort of criticism of Socrates that Socrates had repeatedly used in examining Gorgias' definitions; Socrates is then compelled to admit that rhetoric is the same thing as cookery. Polus' argument is a *reductio*. Socrates had used such *reductiones* with Gorgias, but to assist in refining his definition, not to refute it. Likewise, here Socrates responds by saying that cookery and rhetoric are not the same thing, but that each is a part (*morion*) of the same practice, namely flattery. This is significant for the question of the epistemic unity of excellence, for it suggests that Plato might conceptualize the relation between, let us momentarily call them, species and genera of crafts as one of parts and wholes. Thus, for example, counting and calculation would be conceived as parts of a more generic craft, say, the craft that produces speeches whose objects are the odd and even. In other words, given that excellence is wholly epistemic, the question of the partition of excellence qua *dunamis* should be examined in light of Platonic conceptions of the partition of *technai*.

Plutarch relates an explanation of the unity and partition of excellence given by the Stoic Ariston of Chios (3rd c.):

> [He] made excellence essentially one thing, which he called health. It was by relativity that he made the excellences in a way different and plural, just as if someone wanted to call our vision white-seeing when it apprehended white things, black-seeing when it apprehended black things, and so on . . . [Likewise,] as the knife, while being one thing, cuts different things on different occasions, and fire acts on different materials although its nature is one and the same.[18]

A number of modern scholars have followed Ariston's lead. For example, Thomas Brickhouse and Nicholas Smith argue that the parts of excellence are one in *dunamis*, but various in action (*ergon*).[19] But this line of interpretation for the early dialogues is problematic in two ways. First, there is no indication among the texts that the identity of F *includes* its action. Although a product or activity can clarify a correlative *dunamis*, F is *identified* as a *dunamis*. Second, the early dialogues suggest that different kinds of product or action have different *dunameis*. And this suggests that even when a given *dunamis* is applied in different kinds of

---

17. *Grg.* 462c7.
18. *De virt.* 440e–441a; cited from the translation in Long and Sedley (1987) 61.
19. (1997).

situation, the Platonic conception of the consequent products or activities would be to subsume those products or activities under a single species. Indeed, this appears to be Socrates' strategy in his argument in *Protagoras* for the identity of sound-mindedness and wisdom (332a4–333b5). The basic argument runs:[20]

> Foolishness and wisdom are opposites.
> Things done F-ly are so done because of F.[21]
> Things done rightly are so done because of sound-mindedness.
> Things done rightly are the opposite of things done foolishly.
> Each opposite has only one opposite.
> Therefore, sound-mindedness is wisdom.

The argument depends on the idea that sound-minded, right, and wise actions are equivalent. But it might be objected that although sound-minded actions are right and wise, not all right and wise actions are sound-minded. In other words, sound-minded actions are a subset of wise actions. Recall the conventional conception of sound-mindedness as the capacity to resist temptation. A wise action, for example, a judge's correct distribution of goods to contending parties, might require no capacity to resist temptation.

The force of this line of objection will be significantly weakened, however, if we follow the Platonic intellectualist critique of *akrasia*. In that case, it will be seen that the objection depends upon an appeal to a substantive distinction between the psychologies of sound-minded and wise people. But the critique of *akrasia* precisely denies this. In short, the unity of the *dunamis* collapses the distinction between types of action that depend upon it.

Socrates and Protagoras' argument over the relation between justice and holiness (330b7–332a3), which immediately precedes the argument for the identity of sound-mindedness and wisdom, provides further support for this line of explanation. Their discussion of justice and holiness is divisible into two parts: 330b7–d1 and 330d1–332a3. In the first part, Socrates tries to persuade Protagoras that justice and holiness are the same or very much alike. But Protagoras is unwilling to accept two crucial premises. And in the second part, Protagoras offers a counterargument in support of the distinctness of justice and holiness. The first part begins with two premises:[22]

> (a) Justice is just.
> (b) Holiness is holy.

Socrates now attempts to elicit Protagoras' assent to two further premises:

> (c) Holiness is just.
> (d) Justice is holy.

---

20. Note that I have simplified and reorganized the premises for the sake of exposition.
21. For example, sound-minded actions are due to sound-mindedness.
22. I have simplified the argument to facilitate exposition.

Socrates then attempts to infer from (a)–(d) that justice and holiness are the same (*tauton*) or most similar (*homoiotaton*).[23] But Protagoras refuses to accept (c) and (d). Instead, he presents a counterargument:

> Justice resembles (*proseoike*) holiness.
> (e) But whatever (*hotioun*) resembles whatever (*hotôioun*).

In view of (e) Protagoras cites examples: white and black, hard and soft, and "other things that are most contrary (*enantiôtata*) to one another."[24] He also refers to the parts of the face, each of which, as was earlier agreed, has a distinct power (*dunamis*).[25] Protagoras continues:

> These various things (white, black, and so on) are alike (*homoion*) in a small (*smikron*) way.
> But it is unjust on that ground to claim therefore that they are alike.

Socrates expresses surprise that Protagoras would claim that justice and holiness are alike in a small way. Accordingly, Protagoras qualifies himself by admitting that they are not alike in a small way, but neither are they alike in the manner that Socrates claims. At this point, Socrates suggests that since the problem is difficult to manage, they leave it, and the argument ends inconclusively.

The central difficulty of Socrates' argument is the self- and inter-predications of justice and holiness in (a)–(d). Elsewhere I have argued that while the subjects *dikaiosunê* (justice) and *hosiotês* (holiness) refer to the psychological powers of justice and holiness that people possess, the predicates *dikaion* (just) and *hosion* (holy) mean "conducive to right conditions between people" and "conducive to right conditions between people and gods," respectively. Thus, "justice is just" means that a certain psychological power is responsible for certain conditions between humans; likewise, "holiness is holy" means that a certain psychological power is responsible for certain conditions between humans and gods. As such, the self-predications are syntactically, but not semantically, self-predicative. In other words, although the subjects and predicates are cognates, they do not have the same meanings.[26]

Given this, it easy to see why Socrates endorses the self-predications and why Protagoras accepts them without question. The psychological powers of justice and holiness clearly are responsible for just and holy conditions, respectively. On the other hand, it remains unclear why Socrates endorses (c) and (d). I suggest that Socrates believes that one and the same psychological power is responsible for both right conditions between people and right conditions between people and

---

23. *Prt.* 331b4–5.
24. *Prt.* 331d5.
25. *Prt.* 331d5–8. This was agreed to at 330a4–b3.
26. Wolfsdorf (2002). Observe also that on this interpretation the self- and inter-predications are consonant with the premise, things done F-ly are so done because of F, that occurs in the argument for the identity of sound-mindedness and wisdom.

gods. As such, Socrates' argument should be seen as countering Protagoras' assumption that because activities relate to different sorts of party, humans, on the one hand, and humans and gods, on the other, there are distinct *dunameis* responsible for those activities.

Granted this, it must be emphasized that Socrates does not clarify why he believes that a single *dunamis* is responsible for right conditions among humans and between humans and gods. And indeed this is where Protagoras resists. Consequently, understanding why Socrates maintains the inference, while Protagoras resists it, is crucial to interpreting the argument and Protagoras' counterargument.

Justice and holiness were conventionally conceived as contraries insofar as the former concerned human interrelations, while the latter concerned relations between humans and gods. I suggest that Protagoras assumes that the ability to conduct right relations between humans differs from the ability to conduct right relations between humans and gods. Indeed, in the account of the creation of humans and society in his Great Speech, Protagoras states that holiness came into existence before justice.[27] Accordingly, the psychological capacity for right relations between humans is not a part of the broader sphere of right relations between humans and gods. Moreover, it is in view of the conventional opposition of justice and holiness that in his objection to (c) and (d) Protagoras cites the sets of contraries as well as the parts of the face. Black and white are colors; hard and soft are degrees of tactile resistance. But although each of the two contraries in a given pair belongs to the same sort or kind, and are alike as such, within that kind they are polar opposites. Likewise, eyes, ears, and so on belong to the kind facial part; and as such they are alike. However, within that kind their powers markedly differ. Accordingly, Protagoras maintains that while justice and holiness belong to the same kind, excellence, within that kind they markedly differ.

In contrast, I suggest, Socrates is tacitly committed to the view that justice, that is, right relations between humans, is favorable to the divine, while injustice is unfavorable to the divine. Likewise, the condition of holiness conforms to just relations between people. This suggestion is supported by the conception of piety that Socrates describes in *Apology*, but, above all, by passages in *Gorgias* where he argues for a conception of the cosmos as an order.[28] Accordingly, Socrates believes that there are not two fundamentally different psychological capacities, one for conducting right relations between humans and another for right relations between humans and gods. Indeed, in the climactic movement of *Gorgias*, when he has finally refuted Callicles' conception of excellence and well-being as luxury, licentiousness, and freedom by arguing against ethical hedonism, for the identification of goodness with order, and therefore the value of sound-mindedness, Socrates claims:

---

27. See *Prt.* 322a.
28. I will discuss the *Gorgias* passages in section 4 of this chapter.

And so, the sound-minded man would do what is fitting with respect to gods and with respect to humans... And so, doing what is fitting with respect to men he would do just things; and with respect to gods, holy things... And necessarily he would also be courageous. For it is characteristic of a sound-minded man neither to pursue nor to avoid what is not fitting, but what he ought to pursue and avoid, be they deeds, people, pleasures or pains... Therefore... Callicles, the sound-minded man, being just and courageous and holy, is the perfectly good man.[29]

In sum, the evidence suggests that there is a single epistemic *dunamis* responsible for all right action. This *dunamis* has as its object the good; in other words, it is knowledge of the good. To this extent, the attempt to explain the partition of excellence on the basis of a distinction between products or activities is not going to work.

Returning to the analogy with the ingot of gold, I noted above that it is unclear how the analogy of spatial extent is supposed to map onto psychological entities. We might entertain the possibility that distinction in spatial extension is supposed to be analogous to the scope of activity. For example, the scope of courageous actions might be smaller than that of just actions. However, there is simply no evidence in favor of this view.

There remains the distinction between the *technai* of numeration and calculation in *Gorgias*, which presents an intriguing case of distinct epistemic *dunameis* with the same object. Admittedly, it is hardly clear how Plato conceptualized the distinction between the operation of counting, for instance, how many fingers Socrates has on his left hand, and the operation of calculating, for instance, that ten minus five is five. Still, I did suggest that numeration and calculation might be conceived as species of a more general *technê* whose object is the odd and even. Accordingly, sound-mindedness, courage, justice, and holiness might all be conceived as species of the knowledge of the good, each distinguished by relating to the good in a distinct way.

On this interpretation, the most obvious way of partitioning the excellences would be to say that justice is knowledge of the good with respect to interhuman relations; holiness is knowledge of the good with respect to human-divine relations; courage is knowledge of the good with respect to fear; and sound-mindedness is knowledge of the good with respect to temptation. But such distinctions strike me as inconsistent with the evidence of the texts. Consider courage and sound-mindedness. The intellectualist analysis of *akrasia* and consequent epistemic conceptions of courage and sound-mindedness annihilate non-cognitive dimensions that would otherwise be present to these putative excellences and thereby distinguish them from one another and from justice and holiness. Indeed, it is not even clear that, for example, the fear of the wise man will have a phenomenological dimension. For example, when in *Apology* Socrates

---

29. *Grg.* 507a7–c3.

says he does not fear death, he should be interpreted to mean that he has no reason to expect that death is a bad thing.[30] But if fear and temptation reduce to anticipations of bad and good things, then courage and sound-mindedness reduce to knowledge of future goods and bad things and thus collapse into one another. Furthermore—soothsaying aside—there is no compelling reason to think that there is a techné of future goods as distinct from a techné of the good without temporal qualifications. Indeed, Socrates argues as much at the end of Laches. Finally, there is no reason to think that knowledge of the good with respect to the gods is any different from knowledge of the good with respect to humans. On the contrary, as Socrates makes clear in Apology, his political-philosophical activity is service to Apollo. In short, the most reasonable account of the Platonic epistemic conception of excellence as a unity is that "justice," "holiness," "courage," and "sound-mindedness" are co-referring; moreover, justice, holiness, courage, and sound-mindedness are one and the same thing. In sum, the Platonic view is that excellence is an epistemic unity. Excellence is wisdom, knowledge of the good.

3. Dunamis and Techné

In Gorgias, Callicles disdainfully remarks, "By the gods, [Socrates,] you simply cannot stop talking about cobblers and fullers, cooks and doctors, as though our discussion concerned them!"[31] Throughout the early dialogues Plato uses the various forms of techné of the laborers in his society as models for conceptualizing wisdom. David Roochnik cites a number of salient features as constitutive of the "primitive," pre-Platonic conception of techné: Techné is knowledge of a specific field; that is, its subject is determinate; it produces something useful; it is reliable; the knowledge is commonly recognized as such; it is certifiable, for instance, by its products; it is teachable.[32] As we will see, these criteria are explicitly or implicitly operative throughout the treatment of techné in the early dialogues. But Plato's conceptualization of techné also has a more theoretical basis. Admittedly, as difficulties of inconsistency and incompleteness will show, there is no systematic theory of techné latent in the texts. Nevertheless, we do find rudiments of a conceptual scheme informing Plato's treatment of the subject.

Within the early dialogues techné is conceptualized as a kind of dunamis. There is one passage in the Platonic corpus where Socrates explicitly defines dunamis:

> Shall we agree that dunameis are a type of thing by which we, as well as everything else, are capable of whatever we are capable of and whatever anything else is capable of? For example, sight and hearing are dunameis—if

---

30. Note that I do not mean to imply that Socrates is wise, but that he is relatively wise.
31. Grg. 491a1–3.
32. Roochnik (1996) 20.

you understand the type of thing I want to describe... Listen, then, to what I think of them. I do not see the color of a *dunamis*, nor its shape, nor any such thing, as I do in the case of many other things I look at to define. But in the case of a *dunamis* I look only at *that to which it is related* and at *what work it effects*. In this way I come to call each of them a *dunamis*. And that which is connected to the same thing and effects the same thing I call the same *dunamis*; and that which is connected to a different thing and effects a different thing I call a different *dunamis*.[33]

This passage occurs in book 5 of *Republic*. Nonetheless, as we will see, the implicit conception of *dunamis* among the early dialogues largely conforms to this explicit definition.

Socrates states that in the case of a *dunamis* he looks only at "that to which it is related" and at "what work it effects." Accordingly, *dunameis* are conceived as having *relata* and works.[34] What is meant by the *relatum* and work of a *dunamis* can be clarified from the immediate context as well as from elsewhere among the dialogues. The definition of *dunamis* occurs in the course of Socrates' effort to distinguish opinion from knowledge. He argues that insofar as knowledge and opinion are distinct *dunameis*, they have distinct *relata*. The *relatum* of knowledge is being, the *relatum* of opinion is that which is intermediate between being and nonbeing. In these cases, we would say that the *relata* are objects of knowledge and opinion, respectively.

Here the work (*ergon*) of a *dunamis* is the mode by which the *dunamis* relates to or, as Socrates also says, connects to its *relatum*. Thus, knowledge *knows* being, while opinion *opines* an ontological kind that is intermediate between being and nonbeing. Loosely speaking, we may say that the *ergon* of a *dunamis* it its characteristic action or function. In *Republic* 1, Socrates defines an *ergon* in this way: "Would you be willing to establish that the work (*ergon*) of a horse or anything else is that which one can do only with it or best with it?" "I do not understand," he said. "Consider this. Do you see by anything else than the eyes?... Do you hear by anything else than the ears?... Would we not justly say that these are the works of these entities?"[35] Elsewhere in *Republic* 1, Socrates says that it is the *ergon* of heat to make things hot and the *ergon* of dryness to make things dry. He also says that it is the *ergon* of the good (*to agathon*) to benefit.[36]

Sight and hearing are particularly salient examples of *dunameis* for Plato. By sight (*opsis*) is meant the power that enables the eye to see. The act of seeing, then, is the *ergon* of sight. The *relatum* of sight is color; sometimes, shape is included.

---

33. *R.* 477c1–d5, with my italics.
34. The word *relatum* is my own.
35. *R.* 1, 352e2–9. Socrates continues: " 'You could cut vine branches with a dagger or carving-knife or many other things?' 'Of course.' 'But, I think, with nothing so well as a pruning-knife, one made for this [task].' 'True.' 'Must we not establish that this is the work (*ergon*) of the pruning-knife?' 'We must' " (*R.*'1, 353a1–8).
36. *R.* 1, 335d3–6, 335d7–8.

Similarly, the *ergon* of the *dunamis* hearing, the capacity of the ear to hear, is the action of hearing; and the *relatum* of this *dunamis* is sound.

In *Republic* 6, Socrates suggests that the *dunameis* of sight and hearing differ in the way that they relate to their *relata*. Hearing occurs through a simple relation of the *dunamis* hearing and its *relatum* sound; but, for its operation, sight requires, in addition to a visible object, the presence of light:

> "Do hearing and sound need some other kind of thing for the one to hear and the other to be heard; or if some third entity is not present, does the one not hear and is the other not heard?" "There is need of nothing else," he said. "I think so too," I said, "and this is the case with many other [*dunameis*]—although not with all of them... Although sight is present in the eyes and its possessor tries to use it and color is present, without the presence of a third thing specifically and naturally for this, sight will not see and colors will remain invisible... The sense of seeing and the *dunamis* of being seen are yoked together not by a trivial kind of thing, but by a yoke more honorable than that by which other entities are yoked—if light is not a dishonorable kind of thing."[37]

This passage suggests that multiple elements may be necessary for the operation of a subset of *dunameis*. It also suggests that *relata* themselves are conceived as having particular *dunameis* such that they can relate to the *dunameis* of which they are the *relata*. For instance, the *relata* of sight have *dunameis* such that they can be seen. This distinction between the two types of *dunamis* may conveniently be described as active versus passive. F. M. Cornford has remarked that

> [*dunamis*] is the substantive answering to the common verb "to be able" [*dunasthai*] and it covers the ability to be acted upon as well as the ability to act on something else, whereas most of the corresponding English words— power, force, potency, etc.—suggest active, as opposed to passive, ability. [*Dunamis*] includes passive capacity, receptivity, susceptibility, as well.[38]

So, again, in *Republic* Socrates asks, "Have you considered how exquisitely the creator has created the *dunamis* of seeing and of being seen?"[39]

In Greek literature, *dunamis* is principally used to mean "power to act" and thus to describe what we are calling active *dunameis*.[40] It is also so used among the early dialogues. In *Charmides* Critias defines sound-mindedness as the knowledge of knowledge. Socrates is dubious that this definition can be correct because he assumes the existence of sound-mindedness, but doubts that such a thing as the knowledge of knowledge could exist. His argument against the existence of knowledge of knowledge hinges on the principle that "whatever has its own

---

37. *R.* 507c10–e2, 507e6–508a2.
38. (1935) 234, commenting on the meaning of *dunamis* at *Sophist* 247e.
39. *R.* 507c6–8.
40. On the common use of *dunamis*, see Souilhé (1919)1–23, reprinted in (1987).

dunamis related to itself will not have the being (*ousia*) to which its own *dunamis* is related."[41]

Socrates applies this principle to a variety of cases, including sensation (sight, hearing), motivation (desire, want), emotion (love, fear), and cognition (opinion, knowledge). Regarding sight and hearing, Socrates says that since hearing is of sound, for a hearing of hearing to exist, hearing would have to have sound of its own. Similarly, since sight is of color, for a sight of sight to exist, sight itself would have to have color. In light of the concepts we derived from *Republic*, Socrates is arguing that the bearers of (active) *dunameis* do not have the *relata* of those *dunameis*; therefore, the *dunameis* cannot perform their characteristic functions in relation to themselves. Note that Socrates does not argue that the bearers of active *dunameis* do not have the passive *dunameis* that would enable the realization upon themselves of their active *dunameis*. Presumably this is to avoid abstruseness in an already complex argument. Still, again, throughout the early dialogues *dunamis* is treated as active.

The argument in *Charmides* culminates a series of arguments in which Socrates attempts to clarify the knowledge with which Critias identifies sound-mindedness. Critias had previously suggested that sound-mindedness is a kind of *epistêmê* (specialized knowledge). Here, as often in the early dialogues, *epistêmê* is treated as equivalent to *technê*. Socrates tries to identify the kind of knowledge Critias claims sound-mindedness to be by comparing it with other kinds of knowledge. He first suggests that certain kinds of knowledge effect works (*erga*, plural of *ergon*), and he questions the kind of work sound-mindedness effects: " 'If, then, you should ask me,' I said, 'wherein medicine, being the knowledge of health, is useful and what it effects, I would say that it is a great benefit. For it effects health, a fine work for us... And if you should ask me with respect to architecture, it being the knowledge of building, what work it effects, I would say houses.' "[42] Here, unlike the definition of *ergon* in *Republic* 1, Socrates understands a work (*ergon*) to be a physical object or condition that results from activity for which the knowledge is responsible. This indicates that the Greek word *ergon*, like the English word "work," is ambiguous between activity or process and product.

In response to the examples of medicine and architecture, Critias criticizes Socrates for assuming that sound-mindedness can be analogized with types of knowledge that effect works qua products; and he cites geometry and calculation as counterexamples. Socrates concedes that not all types of knowledge have such a work (*toiouton ergon*). On the other hand, the expression "such a work" allows that although Socrates concedes the point, Plato might have him argue that geometry and calculation have other kinds of works. It is difficult to speculate here whether such works would be construed along the lines of activity as in the definition of *ergon* in *Republic* 1 or rather in some accordance with the notion of work qua product. For example, we would say that arithmetical or geometrical knowledge

41. *Chrm.* 168d1–3.
42. *Chrm.* 165c10–d6.

facilitates the mental activity of problem solving. As we saw in the previous section, in *Gorgias* Socrates allows that the mathematical crafts do have an *ergon* qua product, which is entirely oral. Like rhetoric, the mathematical crafts produce speeches.

The discussion in *Charmides* does not pursue the question of how the *erga* of forms of knowledge such as geometry and calculation are to be construed. I suggest that this is because Plato intends to introduce another means by which kinds of knowledge, and *dunameis* in general, can be distinguished. Specifically, Socrates grants that although types of knowledge such as geometry and calculation may not produce such works qua products, these types of knowledge are *of* entities that are distinct from themselves. That is to say, they have distinct objects and thus can be distinguished according to these objects:

> But I can point out that of which each of these types of knowledge is, which is different from the knowledge itself. For instance, calculation is of the odd and the even, their magnitudes with respect to themselves and one another …And you grant that the odd and even are different from calculation itself…Moreover, weighing is of the lighter and the heavier weight. But the heavy and the light are different from weighing itself.[43]

In view of the treatment of *dunamis* in *Republic*, it should be clear that these objects of knowledge are what we have called the *relata* of the respective *dunameis*.

In sum, the various evidence from *Charmides*, *Republic* 1, and the later books of *Republic* is compatible, with the qualification that in the early dialogues Socrates' use of *dunamis* is limited to active *dunameis*, and *ergon* is used ambiguously between activity or process and product. *Dunameis* are powers whose possession enables their bearers to act or to be acted upon in a distinctive way. The characteristic actions or operations of *dunameis* are *erga*. Additionally, certain *dunameis* enable their bearers to produce objects or conditions, also described as *erga*. Clearly some *dunameis* effect *erga* of both kinds, activity and product. For example, medicine both knows health and is productive of health. Finally, note that there seems to be a disanalogy between the *relata* of sight and knowledge. Sight is the capacity to connect to color, but knowledge is not the capacity to connect to beings. Knowledge entails a connection to its *relatum*, even if that connection enables the generation of other cognitions.

Technai qua *dunameis* should be distinguishable from one another by their *relata*. For example, as we saw in *Charmides*, calculation is of the odd and even, while weighing is of the heavy and light. But, as we also saw in the preceding section, Socrates suggests a complication when in *Gorgias* he claims that both numeration and calculation are concerned with the odd and even. Since the former is concerned with the odd and the even in themselves and the latter is concerned with their interrelations,[44] we may suppose that some *technai* may

---

43. *Chrm.* 166a3–b3.
44. *Grg.* 451c.

share *relata*, but nonetheless be distinguishable by the nature of their relation to the *relata*.

We have also seen that in *Charmides* a distinction is drawn between productive *technai* such as medicine and architecture and *technai* such as geometry and calculation that are not productive in the same way. In *Gorgias*, Socrates, with productive *technai* in mind, claims that a *technê* includes both knowledge of the *phusis* and *aitia* of its *relatum*. Recall that by *physiological* knowledge we understand knowledge of what the *relatum* is; for example, in the case of medicine, knowledge of the nature of health. By *aetiological* knowledge we understand knowledge of how the *relatum* can be produced as an *ergon*, for example, how health can be achieved.

Plato nowhere makes explicit how *technai* differ from other *dunameis*. The obvious distinguishing feature is that *technai* are epistemic. Consequently, for instance, they can be taught and learned. The question of whether excellence is teachable, which is central to a number of dialogues, in particular *Protagoras* and *Meno*, can accordingly be understood as inquiring whether there is a *technê* of excellence. But additionally, among the early dialogues Plato seems particularly concerned with two features of *technai* that may distinguish them from other *dunameis*: *Technai* provide benefits and may have contrary ends.

Technai have functions or ends, namely their characteristic *erga*. The *erga* of *technai* appear to be beneficial or good. At least, in *Republic* 1 Socrates claims that each *technê* is distinguished by its power and that each provides a particular benefit (*ôpheleia*). Similarly, in *Gorgias* Socrates argues that *technai*, in contrast to the *empeiriai* that resemble them, aim at the good. As we will see, there is reason to doubt that this view is Platonic. Nonetheless, it is worth examining Socrates' grounds for making the claim.

Socrates' conception of *technê* as beneficial is explicable in view of certain Greek anthropological and sociological views. *Technê* is central to the Greeks' conception of civilization. It was widely believed that *technai* were a divine gift to humanity for the purpose of survival and flourishing. In this context, the mythological figure of Prometheus plays a central role. For example, in *Prometheus Bound* Aeschylus presents Prometheus as glorifying the *technai* that support civilization:

> I am the huntsman of the mystery, the great resource that taught technology, the secret fount of fire put in the reed and given to humanity to serve its need ... I made humanity conscious and intelligent ... All they did was mindless until I revealed the dubious rise and setting of the stars ... I was the first to yoke animals in service to the strap ... Of those great utilities below the earth, copper and iron, silver and yellow gold, who before me dared to claim discovery of these, unless a madman?[45]

In *Protagoras* Plato incorporates the myth of Prometheus in Protagoras' Great Speech: "[Prometheus] stole Hephaestus' skill of fire and every other *technê* from

---

45. 436–40, cited and translated from Burford (1972) 189, on which see also n. 534.

Athena; he gave them to humanity, and from this, humanity has its means of life."[46] Consider also the more general statement from the treatise of the anonymous sophist preserved by Iamblichus: "Men are by nature unsuited to living in isolation and have formed associations with one another through necessity, and . . . the whole of life and its specialized skills (technêmata) have been developed by them for this end . . ."[47]

As I noted above, in his review of the pre-Platonic treatment of technê Roochnik consistently cites utility as a criterion.[48] Thus, the view of the benefit of technê that Socrates expresses in Republic 1 was conventional.

The second feature that distinguishes technai from other dunameis is that technai enable their possessors to effect contrary erga. Aristotle makes this point in Metaphysics: "Every one of the nonrational dunameis can have but a single ergon, whereas the rational [dunameis] can have contrary erga."[49] By nonrational dunameis Aristotle means to include such things as heat and cold, whose powers are to make hot and to cool. By rational dunameis he means technai. So, for instance, a doctor can, with greater skill than anyone lacking medical knowledge, render a human body sick as well as healthy. Although Plato himself never has Socrates explicitly make the point, it clearly preoccupied him. For example, in Hippias Minor Socrates first argues that the liar and honest person are the same; then he and Hippias struggle with the paradoxical conclusion that the excellent person is most capable of wrongdoing. Likewise, in a semicomic passage in Republic 1, Socrates argues that the just man is a thief precisely because his great capacity for honesty and safekeeping possessions implies an equally great capacity for the contrary.[50]

Later in Republic 1, Socrates effectively corrects this view of the just person when he argues, against Polemarchus' definition of justice as aiding a friend who is good and harming an enemy who is bad, that as the function of the musician is not to make men unmusical, the function of the just person is not to harm, since harming implies making unjust. In short, Socrates is arguing that the just person insofar as he is just does not produce injustice. Likewise, still later in the dialogue he argues that a shepherd qua shepherd fulfills the function of his technê when he cultivates his flock. Thrasymachus finds Socrates' position repugnant, but this is because he fails to appreciate the distinction between the function of a technê and the technê-independent interests of its possessor. For example, the shepherd may use his technê to serve technê-independent interests, as when he sells the sheep off for profit; however, in doing that, the shepherd is not acting qua shepherd, but qua profiteer.

---

46. Prt. 321e1–322a1.
47. 100.5–101.6 (Pistelli).
48. Roochnik (1996) 20, 26, 41, 44–45, 50, 52, 70. The Solonic treatment (31) is exceptional in this regard.
49. 1048a.
50. R. 1, 334a.

The paradox in *Hippias Minor* that the good man is most capable of wrongdoing is not resolved. I suggest that its resolution depends upon recognizing a
disanalogy between ethical and nonethical *technai*. As Aristotle claims, (most)
rational *dunameis* can have contrary *erga*. This is precisely because the function of
nonethical *technai* need not coincide with the *technê*-independent interests of
their possessors. But ethical *technê* is exceptional. While possession of a nonethical
technê does not ensure its proper use, ethical conduct follows from possession of
ethical *technê*. The reason relates to principles of the psychology of action, which
were discussed in chapter 2. All choose the particular course of action that they
evaluate as good; *akrasia* is a failure of knowledge, not of will; therefore, one who
possesses knowledge of the good will do it.

This disanalogy between ethical and nonethical *technê* suggests one reason for
the superior value of ethical *technê* to nonethical *technai*. The possessor of ethical
technê has a key capacity to ensure fulfillment of the functions of nonethical *technai*.

A passage in *Laches* suggests another reason for the superior value of ethical
technê to nonethical *technai*. There Socrates claims that while experts such as
doctors know the good and bad within the sphere of their *technê*, namely health
and sickness, they do not know in any particular case whether health is preferable
to death.[51] The text does not offer an example to clarify the point, but the
following may do: It may be better not to heal an ailing tyrant.

The *Laches* passage suggests that although nonethical *technai* have particular
ends, in any given situation it is questionable whether that end should be realized,
in other words, whether the given nonethical *technê* should be applied. Accordingly, the *Laches* passage suggests that nonethical *technai* require guidance from
some other form of knowledge. In the ensuing discussion, this is identified as
the knowledge of good and bad, in other words, ethical *technê*. Thus, the value
of ethical *technê* is indicated to be superior to that of nonethical *technai* because
ethical *technê* can guide the application of nonethical *technai*.

In one respect, this second reason for the relative value of ethical *technê*
complements the first reason. Ethical *technê* can play a crucial role in ensuring
fulfillment of the functions of nonethical *technai*, and ethical *technê* can also
determine whether the function of a nonethical *technê* should be fulfilled. But
the *Laches* passage also undermines the view that the ends of nonethical *technai*
per se are goods. Again, it may be better that a doctor not heal an ailing tyrant.
While conflicting with the view of Socrates in *Republic* 1 that all *technai* provide
some benefit, the idea that the ends of nonethical *technai*, in contrast to ethical
technê, are not necessarily good provides another explanation for the superior
value of ethical *technê* to nonethical *technai*.

Two passages in *Meno* and *Euthydemus* explicitly argue for the superior value
of wisdom, that is, ethical *technê*, to the putative goods provided by what we are
here characterizing as nonethical *technai*. At *Meno* 87b–89c Socrates develops an
argument with Meno concerning whether excellence is teachable, whose structure

---

51. *La.* 195c–d.

may be summarized as: Excellence is good; if knowledge is the only good, then excellence is knowledge; if excellence is knowledge, then it is teachable. The success of the argument, thus, turns on whether knowledge is the only good. In examining whether knowledge is the only good, Socrates considers two sets of conventionally conceived goods: health, strength, beauty, and wealth (bodily and social goods); sound-mindedness, justice, courage, intelligence, memory, and magnificence (psychological goods). It is agreed that what is good is beneficial (ôphelimon).[52] Therefore, if these conventionally conceived goods in fact are good, they are beneficial.

Socrates argues that while health, strength, beauty, and wealth sometimes are beneficial, sometimes they are harmful. Likewise, regarding the putative psychological goods, he argues that those that are distinct from knowledge (epistêmê) are sometimes beneficial and sometimes harmful. Socrates identifies the knowledge under discussion as wisdom (phronêsis),[53] and he specifies that the various putative goods are beneficial when wisdom guides and correctly employs them: "So it is in every case, in a human being all things depend upon the soul, and the things of the soul depend on wisdom if they are going to be good."[54]

The interpretation of the Meno argument is complicated by the fact that it assumes a distinction between psychological goods such as sound-mindedness, justice, courage, and intelligence, on the one hand, and wisdom, on the other. As I argued in the previous section, a number of other early dialogues suggest that these putative parts of excellence are identical to wisdom. Accordingly, both the assumptions that sound-mindedness, courage, and so on are distinct from one another and that they are distinct from wisdom should be understood as dialectical expedients, employed in conformity with the doxastic base of the text.

At Euthydemus 278e–282a Socrates develops an argument similar to that in Meno. The point of departure is psychological eudaimonism, the view that everyone desires well-being (eudaimonia). Note that here and throughout the early dialogues well-being is understood as well faring, living or doing well (eu prattein). In other words, well-being is an activity, not a psychological state. Given this, Socrates and Cleinias consider the requirements for well-being. It is agreed that the possession of goods is necessary. These are clarified according to three sets: health, beauty, and "other things pertaining to the body (bodily goods)";[55] good birth, talents, and honors in one's country (social goods); sound-mindedness, justice, courage, and wisdom (sophia) (psychological goods). There follows a subargument concerning the good of success (eutuchia) whose conclusion is that the possessor of wisdom does not require success as an independent good since wisdom makes men successful.[56]

---

52. Men. 87e.
53. Men. 88b.
54. Men. 88e4–89a1.
55. Euthd. 279b1.
56. Euthd. 280a. I follow Dimas (2003) in translating eutuchia as "success" rather than "good luck."

Given this, the claim that the possession of goods is necessary for well-being is twice revised. First, it is agreed that mere possession of goods does not yield well-being; rather, goods possessed must be beneficial, and in order to be beneficial they must be used. Second, Socrates suggests that in order to be beneficial, goods must not merely be used, but used rightly. Finally, it is agreed that knowledge (*epistêmê*) guides and orders correct use of all things. This knowledge is identified as wisdom (*sophia*, *phronêsis*, and *nous*). Moreover, the remaining items from the original list of goods are now said to have "no worth by themselves" (*kath' hauta . . . oudenos axia*),[57] but only to be beneficial if wisdom governs them.[58] Conversely, Socrates argues that when one lacks wisdom, use of putative goods is more harmful than when one lacks them. Socrates concludes, "Since we are all intent upon well-being and we have seen that we achieve this from using things correctly and that knowledge provides correctness and success, it seems that every man must prepare himself in every way in order to become as wise as possible."[59]

As in the *Meno* argument, the interpretation of the *Euthydemus* argument is complicated by its assumptions that sound-mindedness, courage, and so on are distinct from one another and that they are distinct from wisdom. Again, I suggest that these assumptions should be understood as dialectical expedients, employed in conformity with the doxastic base of the text.

Both the *Meno* and *Euthydemus* arguments claim that wisdom is the only human possession that is invariably beneficial.[60] Commentators have argued that Plato, therefore, distinguishes two kinds of goods, and they variously describe these as unconditional and conditional, independent and dependent, or moral and nonmoral. Against such views, and particularly on the basis of the *Euthydemus* argument, Panos Dimas emphasizes that Socrates' point is that putative goods such as health are just as capable of being harmful as beneficial. Thus, there is no more reason to think of them as qualified goods than as qualified bad things.[61] The concept from among the early dialogues that best seems to capture this idea—granted, Plato does not apply it here—is the neither-good-nor-bad; for example, in *Gorgias* Socrates characterizes the neither-good-nor-bad as "such things as sometimes partake of the good, sometimes of the bad, and sometimes of neither."[62] Dimas himself uses the concept of a facilitator. He convincingly argues that health, wealth, honor, and so on are conceived as facilitating activity, whereas their contraries are conceived as inhibiting it. For this reason, facilitators are more harmful when the agent lacks wisdom than when the agent who lacks wisdom lacks them as well. Accordingly, Socrates asks: "Would not a man do less wrong if

---

57. *Euthd.* 281e1.
58. *Euthd.* 281b.
59. *Euthd.* 282a.
60. The notion of invariable beneficence is derived from Ferejohn (1984); see also Santas (1993).
61. Dimas (2003) 3.
62. Of course, in that context health, wealth, and so on are considered to be goods, but as I have argued, they are treated so for dialectical reasons.

he did less?"[63] I suggest that this is also why in *Gorgias* Socrates thinks that orators have *least* power in their cities, where power is something good for its possessor: Orators have the most competence—not power—to do wrong. In short, facilitators, the putative bodily, social, and psychological goods (excluding wisdom and so the putative parts of excellence that are wisdom), are neither-good-nor-bad; they merely facilitate activity, be it good or bad; and wisdom itself is good because it invariably makes activity good.

Observe, then, that the basic difference between the neither-good-nor-bad things in *Gorgias* and the facilitators qua neither-good-nor-bad things in *Euthydemus* and *Meno* is that the neither-good-nor-bad things in *Gorgias* may be instrumental to the attainment of (putative) goods, whereas those in *Euthydemus* and *Meno* may facilitate well-being.

In light of the *Meno* and *Euthydemus* arguments it must be concluded that the ends of nonethical *technai* per se are not necessarily good. Accordingly, in *Republic* 1, Socrates' claim that all *technai* provide some benefit must be regarded as non-Platonic and as a dialectical expedient conforming to the doxastic base of the text. From this it also follows that *technai* cannot be distinguished from other *dunameis* because their *erga* are beneficial. In distinguishing *technai* from other *dunameis* we are left with the obvious point that *technai* are epistemic, thus teachable and learnable, and the principle that epistemic *dunameis* enable contrary *erga*—although, ironically, ethical *technê* will be the exception.

Finally, it may be argued that the idea that epistemic *dunameis* enable contrary *erga* preoccupied Plato on account of his commitment to the principle that like causes like.[64] The idea that, for example, medicine produces sickness contradicts this. But in light of our distinction between ethical and nonethical *technai*, we can identify the following Platonic solution to the problem. Nonethical *technai* enable contrary *erga*, but they are not chiefly responsible for realizing contrary *erga*. Since everyone desires the good, ethical *technê* or lack thereof, ethical ignorance, is responsible for, is the *aitia* of, good or bad *erga*.

4. Goodness and Form

The argument at *Euthydemus* 278e–282a introduces the principle of psychological eudaimonism, that everyone desires well-being. Throughout the early dialogues *eudaimonia* is conceived as a synonym of *eu prattein* (doing or faring well). The common translation of *eudaimonia* as "happiness" can, thus, easily obscure the fact that *eudaimonia* is not a psychological affect, but an activity. Accordingly, it can also obscure the fact that *eudaimonia* is the characteristic *ergon* qua activity of ethical *technê*. In other words, the relationship between ethical *technê* or excellence and well-being is that of *dunamis* and *ergon*, where *ergon* is understood in the sense of activity.

---

63. *Euthd.* 281b8–c1.
64. Recall the discussion of this principle of causation in the context of *Lysis* in section 6.2 of chapter 2.

Precisely how the relation between excellence and well-being should be conceived, then, depends upon how Plato conceives the *dunamis-ergon* relation. A natural suggestion is that the *dunamis-ergon* relation is one of causation. However, it is questionable whether Plato had a conception of causation per se. For several decades now, it has been debated whether Plato anticipated Aristotle in distinguishing different kinds of *causae* (that is, *aitiai*),[65] specifically whether Plato distinguished causal and logical relations.[66] Elsewhere, I have argued that Plato nowhere clearly distinguishes these types of relation.[67] Rather, Socrates or the principal interlocutor of the dialogue refers to both kinds as *aetiological*— notably, sometimes conflating the two. Consequently, since logical relations are not identical to causal relations, we cannot, without anachronism, claim that, for Socrates or Plato, excellence qua *dunamis* causes well-being. Instead, we are compelled to accept the more vague claim that excellence is the *aitia* of well-being.

This might seem like a pedantic point. But consider its significance in view of the argument in *Charmides* where the knowledge of knowledge is defined as sound-mindedness. Recall Socrates' principle, introduced in the previous section: Whatever has its own *dunamis* related to itself will not have the being (*ousia*) to which its own *dunamis* is related. As explained above, Socrates uses the examples of sight of sight and hearing of hearing, among other psychological states, to confirm the principle. In addition, Socrates uses examples of relational quantities: the double, more, heavier, and older. For example, Socrates argues that the double of itself could not exist, for then the same entity would be both double and half of itself. These examples are puzzling. As Hugh H. Benson writes, "a Socratic *dunamis* is typically associated with particular types of activities. (I say 'typically' because it is unclear what activities are associated with the *dunameis* of the greater, the double, the heavier, the lighter, the older, and the younger in *Charmides* [168b–d]) . . . A thing that possesses a *dunamis does* various things."[68]

A problematic passage such as this—and there are others in the corpus— encourages caution in interpreting Plato's concept of *dunamis* as causal. Again, strictly speaking, Plato would conceptualize the relation as *aetiological*. That is, excellence qua *dunamis* is the *aitia* of the *ergon eudaimonia*. Responsibility is a more general concept than cause; *aitiai* needn't be events; and we would not identify as causes all the entities that Plato, among the early dialogues and in the corpus in general, conceptualizes as *aitiai*.

In contrast to the account I have just given, scholars have variously argued that excellence and well-being are identical, that excellence is sufficient for well-being, that excellence is necessary for well-being, that excellence is neither necessary nor

---

65. *aitiai* is the plural of *aitia*.
66. On the history of the discussion, particularly in the wake of Vlastos (1969), see Wolfsdorf (2005a).
67. Wolfsdorf (2005c).
68. Benson (1997) 80–81 and n.5. The sentence in parentheses is from n.5.

sufficient for well-being, and that excellence is instrumental to well-being. I will briefly comment on these claims.

It is clear that excellence and well-being are not identical. It is also clear that excellence is necessary for well-being. Furthermore, strictly speaking, excellence is not instrumental to well-being. Ends and means are logically interdependent concepts, but ends may be ontologically distinct from means. In contrast, actions are not ontologically distinct from a relevant psychological state of the agent. Rather, a relevant psychological state is a constituent of the action. Therefore, excellence is a constituent of well-being. Finally, it is questionable whether excellence is sufficient for well-being. We can derive the answer to this question from the conclusion of the arguments in *Euthydemus* and *Meno* that excellence invariably makes one be well. Excellence is insufficient for well-being insofar as well-being requires facilitators. On the other hand, at a minimum living entails activity. Since activity of some extent is a given, excellence may be logically insufficient for well-being, but actually or practically sufficient.[69]

Having clarified the relation between excellence and well-being in terms of the relation between *dunamis* and *ergon*, it remains to consider whether excellence and well-being can be explained noncircularly or nonvacuously, for it has been argued that Plato's treatment here runs aground.[70] *Eudaimonia* and *eu prattein* (doing well) both contain the adverb *eu*, which means "well" and corresponds to the adjective *agathos* (good). As the *ergon* of the *dunamis* excellence or ethical *technê*, *eudaimonia* can be described as living in accordance with excellence. As such, an explanation of *eudaimonia* rests on an explanation of *aretê*. *Aretê* is a nominalization of the superlative of the adjective *agathos*. Therefore, excellence, at least lexically, is superlative goodness. In this context, however, Plato did not intend to distinguish between excellence and goodness or being good and being excellent. For example, in *Meno* Socrates claims that we are good (*agathoi*) because of excellence (*aretê*).[71] In short, human excellence is human goodness. Excellence is, of course, identified with wisdom or ethical *technê*. Thus, human excellence is an epistemic state. On the other hand, wisdom is identified as the knowledge of the good, most explicitly in *Laches*. Thus, excellence is the knowledge of goodness, and well-being is living in accordance with it. In other words, living well is living in accordance with the knowledge of goodness.

One solution to this problem is ethical hedonism. In that case, *aretê* can be understood as the knowledge that enables one to achieve pleasure, and *eudaimonia* as living pleasantly. The problem with this view is that there is no good evidence in the early dialogues that it is Platonic. The principal evidence derives from *Protagoras*, where Plato makes Socrates develop an argument for ethical hedonism

---

69. Consistent with this conclusion is the view that there is no difference in value between an excellent life amply facilitated and one diminutively facilitated. Nevertheless, this seems paradoxical.

70. Santas (1993) and (2001).

71. *Meno* 87d.

that he employs in the rejection of the popular conception of *akrasia*. On the other hand, in *Gorgias* the argument for the value of philosophy and against conventional politics and rhetoric depends upon Socrates' vigorous rejection of Callicles' identification of goodness with pleasure.

Consequently, scholars who attribute ethical hedonism to Plato in *Protagoras* are at least compelled to the view that Plato's conception of goodness shifted over the course of his early career. But most recent discussions reject the view that Plato endorses ethical hedonism in *Protagoras*. I believe this is correct, and when one considers the Platonic conception of philosophy as politics throughout the early dialogues, it becomes clear that ethical hedonism is anathema to Plato's project. As Socrates suggests in *Gorgias*, the political leaders of Athens, that is, the demagogic orators who largely came from the upper classes, catered to the people and therefore—for Plato, appallingly—were actually led by the people. Their political influence fundamentally depended upon their rhetorical abilities, and it was the need for rhetorical training to which the sophists principally responded. Sophists, masses, and political leaders were thus complicit in corrupting the city-state and, as Callicles characterizes Socrates' diagnosis, turning life utterly upside-down.[72]

We have seen that the argument against *akrasia* specifically targets the weakness of being overcome by pleasure, but that argument can easily be generalized to other forms of *akrasia*. For example, being overcome by fear is explicable as mistaking the quantity of future pain on balance of a course of action. But the choice of *akrasia*-through-pleasure is explicable on the grounds that Plato believed that—practically, whether or not theoretically—the many (*hoi polloi*) were committed to the identity of goodness and pleasure. In other words, the many were motivated to maximize pleasure. The argument for ethical hedonism in *Protagoras* is explicitly addressed to the many. Indeed, the whole argument against *akrasia* is addressed to the many. It is they who commit to ethical hedonism, and it is on the basis of this commitment that Socrates subjects their conception of *akrasia*-through-pleasure to ridicule.

Following the *reductio* and Socrates' intellectualist explanation of weakness, which vindicates the strength of knowledge and shows that knowledge is not "like a slave" able to be dragged about by any force whatsoever, Socrates turns to all the sophists present for their confirmation of his conclusion: "And I ask you now, Hippias, Prodicus, and Protagoras—for I would have you make a joint reply." They agree: "They all thought that what I had said what absolutely true."[73] Immediately Socrates asks whether the sophists agree that pleasure and goodness are identical and pain and badness are identical. Whereas previously Protagoras had resisted the identification by claiming that only fine (*kalai*) pleasures are good, now he and the others agree.

Evidently, all are swept up in the success of Socrates' vindication of the authority of knowledge against the masses. At the same time, it is deeply ironic

---

72. *Grg.* 481c.
73. *Prt.* 358a1–5.

that the *politikê technê* (political craft) that Protagoras claims to teach, which among other things will enable Hippocrates to be most politically powerful in speech and action, is precisely the pseudo-knowledge, characterized as flattery in *Gorgias*, that is enslaved and dragged about by the pleasure of the people.

Assuming, then, that ethical hedonism is not Platonic in any of the early dialogues, the problem of circularity or vacuity pertaining to *aretê* and *eudaimonia* remains. In book 6 of *Republic*, Plato makes Socrates criticize the account of excellence as knowledge of goodness precisely for its circularity:

> SOCRATES   Furthermore, you certainly know that the majority believe that pleasure is the good, while the more sophisticated believe that it is knowledge . . . But you also know that those who believe this can't tell us what sort of knowledge it is; ultimately they are compelled to say that it is knowledge of the good.
>
> ADIMANTUS   And that's ridiculous.
>
> SOCRATES   Of course it is. They blame us for not knowing the good and then turn around and talk to us as if we did know it. They say that it is knowledge of the good—as if we understood what they're speaking about when they utter the word "good."[74]

Granted that among the early dialogues ethical hedonism is not Platonic, arguably Plato fell victim to the problem of circularity, and Socrates' criticism in *Republic* 6 reflects genuine self-criticism. I suggest that this is not so, that the early dialogues suggest an alternative conception of goodness, and that this alternative conception is continuous with Plato's middle period metaphysics.

There is no passage among the early dialogues where Plato has Socrates explicitly criticize the identification of excellence with the knowledge of goodness as he does in *Republic* 6. But there are a couple of suggestive passages. In *Gorgias* Callicles claims that according to nature, justice entails that the better rule over and have more than the worse.[75] Socrates seeks clarification of the better. Callicles' first clarification is the superior, but Socrates shows that this implies a contradiction of Callicles' view that it is worse to suffer than to do injustice.[76] Callicles then claims that by the better (*beltious*) he means the more excellent (*ameinous*). To this Socrates replies, "Don't you see that you are giving these men mere names and making nothing clear? Won't you say whether by the more excellent and superior you mean the wiser or something else?"[77] Socrates' suggestion that the better be identified with the wiser does not address our

---

74. *R.* 505b5–c4.
75. *Grg.* 488b; see also 483d.
76. More precisely, in a democracy the majority of weaker citizens achieve political power and endorse principles such as that it is worse to do injustice than to suffer injustice.
77. *Grg.* 489e6–8.

more fundamental problem that wisdom itself is identified as the knowledge of goodness. However, it does indicate an awareness of the problem of circularity in defining ethical kinds by ethical terms.

In *Republic* 1, Socrates rejects Polemarchus' definition of justice as aiding a friend who is good and harming an enemy who is bad. Thrasymachus now bursts into the discussion and criticizes Socrates for rejecting the views of others without offering his own position. He commands Socrates to say what justice is, and he insists that Socrates comply with his condition: "And don't tell me that it is the obligatory (*to deon*) or the beneficial (*ôphelimon*) or the profitable (*lusiteloun*) or the gainful (*kerdaleon*) or the advantageous (*xumpheron*), but tell me clearly and precisely what you maintain it is, for I won't accept it if you speak that sort of nonsense."[78] Thrasymachus' criticism certainly is more powerful than Socrates' criticism of Callicles, for here Socrates' manner of pursuing definitions is under attack.

I am not suggesting that the *Gorgias* and *Republic* 1 passages alone provide strong evidence of Plato's awareness of problems of circularity in the definitions of excellence and its parts and in the ethical investigations of the early dialogues more generally.[79] However, these passages are suggestive, especially upon reflection on the broader contents of these two dialogues.

Callicles and Thrasymachus are often compared. They are aggressive and coarse; they contemn Socrates and his philosophical activity. Above all, they have been characterized as notorious immoralists, advocates of ruthless power-seeking, tyranny, and opposition to the well-being of others. Such descriptions may not be entirely accurate. Moreover, there are important differences between the two characters. Nevertheless, the similarities are strong. Both interlocutors enter their respective dialogues in the contexts of discussions of justice. *Republic* 1 is devoted to investigating the identity of justice and its value. In *Gorgias* Callicles enters the conversation after Socrates has rejected Polus' claim that it is worse to suffer than to do injustice and that it is better to do injustice and escape punishment than not to do injustice at all.

Justice, as it is conventionally conceived, entails consideration of others. This is precisely why Thrasymachus characterizes justice as the good of another and has little sympathy for it. In his view, to act justly is to do what is good for another at the expense of oneself. Accordingly, both Callicles and Thrasymachus claim that injustice is more profitable for the agent. In contrast, in *Charmides*, Socrates rejects both of Charmides' definitions, restraint and modesty, on the grounds that they are not fine or good for the agent. Similarly, he stumps Laches with the argument that since courage is a part of excellence and therefore good and

---

78. *R.* 1, 336c6–d4.
79. Indeed, in response to Thrasymachus Socrates says, "You know very well that if you asked a man how many are twelve and in putting the question warned him—don't tell me, man, that twelve is twice six or thrice four or six times two or four times three, for I won't accept any such drivel from you as an'answer—it was obvious that no one could give you an answer to a question framed in that fashion" (*R.* 1, 337b1–5).

fine, it cannot be courageous for a soldier in a weak position to dig in and defend himself against the enemy. Such toughness is foolish because it is harmful to the agent. Furthermore, consider that although *akrasia* may entail a conflict between morality and self-interest, it is not treated in this way in *Protagoras*. The correlate to Socrates' principle of psychological hedonism, that everybody pursues what is pleasant—in other words, given ethical hedonism, what is good for himself—is the principle that no one willingly does what is bad. The latter principle is often characterized as the dictum that no one willingly errs (*hamartanei*). But erring is ambiguous between doing wrong, that is, doing what is immoral, and doing what is bad, that is, harmful to oneself. As we saw in our earlier examination of the rejection of the popular conception of *akrasia*, in *Protagoras* Socrates speaks of doing what is bad, where this is understood as what is bad for the agent; and so, again, he is not concerned with morality.

As we also saw in the previous section, in *Meno* and *Euthydemus* arguments are made specifically for the view that wisdom is invariably beneficial. But in *Republic* 1 and *Gorgias* consideration of justice raises the question, good for whom? For insofar as justice is not good for the agent, as Thrasymachus argues, it cannot be a part of excellence. The treatments of justice in *Gorgias* and *Republic* 1, particularly in view of Callicles' and Thrasymachus' radical positions, can thus be seen as pressing for clarification of goodness. It is inadequate for Socrates to identify the good with the obligatory, useful, beneficial, or profitable, for these locutions obscure the beneficiary. Compare the relativism in Protagoras' speech in *Protagoras*:

> I know a number of things that are not beneficial to humans, namely, foods, drinks, drugs, and countless others, and some that are beneficial; some that are neither one nor the other to men, but are one or the other to horses; and some that are beneficial only to cattle, or again to dogs; some also that are not beneficial to any of those, but are to trees; and some that are good for the roots of a tree, but bad for its shoots, such as dung... Goodness is such diverse (*poikilon*) and multifarious (*pantodapon*) thing... [80]

More fundamentally, the nature of the advantage, whomever the beneficiary, remains unclear.

Among the early dialogues Plato's most explicit expression of the solution to this problem occurs in *Gorgias*. There, as I have said, Callicles commits to ethical hedonism, and he identifies the satisfaction of desire with pleasure. Callicles, therefore, believes that insofar as an individual must restrain his desires, his well-being will be impaired: "He who would live rightly (*orthôs*) should allow his desires to be as strong as possible, should not chasten them, and should be able to minister to them when they are at their height..." [81]

Socrates defeats Callicles' position by arguing against the identity of pleasure and goodness (495c–499b). Then, in an elaboration of his critique of rhetoric as a

---

80. *Prt.* 334a3–b7.
81. *Grg.* 491e8–492a1.

form of flattery from earlier in the dialogue, he condemns as forms of flattery those pursuits, especially rhetoric as it is conventionally practiced, whose objective is pleasure (500a–503d). He subsequently contrasts conventional rhetoric with an idealized form of rhetoric that, like the *technai*, has goodness as its objective:

SOCRATES   The good man, whose aim is the best when he speaks, does not speak at random (*eikêi*), but with a view to some object. He is just like all the other craftsmen, each of whom looks toward (*apoblepôn*) his particular work (*ergon*) and does not select the things he applies to his particular *ergon* at random (*eikêi*), but with the purpose that the object upon which he works have a certain form (*eidos*). For example, consider the painters, architects, shipwrights, and all the other craftsmen, whomever you like—see how each arranges his object into a certain order (*taxin*)... So also those who are concerned with the body, the athletic trainers and doctors; they order and structure the body... And what is the name of order and design (*kosmou*) in the body?

CALLICLES   Health and strength.[82]

In view of the central role that the metaphysical concept of Form plays in Plato's thought, including some of the early dialogues, the use of the concept *eidos* here and the related concepts *kosmos* (design) and *taxis* (order) are remarkable. The metaphysical concept of Form is commonly understood as akin to the concept of universal. But in this passage of *Gorgias* there is no theorization of universals. Rather, *eidos* is understood as the idealized *ergon* of a craftsman.[83]

Socrates subsequently identifies order and design as goodness:

We and all things are good (*agatha*) insofar as we are good through the presence of some excellence (*aretê*)... The excellence of each thing, be it equipment, the body, the soul, or any living thing, is not best produced just at random (*eikêi*), but through an order (*taxei*), correctness (*orthotêti*), and craft (*technêi*) that is assigned to each thing... The excellence of each thing is its being arranged (*tetagmenon*) and designed (*kekosmenon*) according to an order (*taxei*)... And so a certain design (*kosmos*) appropriate (*oikeios*) to each thing being present in each thing renders each thing good (*agathon*).[84]

Socrates' identification of goodness with order and design at this climactic moment in the refutation of Callicles reveals a Platonic conception of goodness within the early dialogues that reflects a broad metaphysical vision. This metaphysics

---

82. Grg. 503d6–504b9.
83. Both Dodds (1959) 328 and Irwin (1979) 214 agree that Plato is here alluding to the metaphysical concept of Form. For the use of the verb *apoblepein* for the apprehension of Form, see *Euthphr.* 6e; *Cra.* 389a–c; *R.* 596b.
84. Grg. 506d2–e4. My translation is influenced by Dodds's notes (1959) 334.

involves, first, an ordering of individuals, natural and artificial, into kinds; second, the idea that each kind has its own excellence or optimal condition; and third, the idea that this excellence is an order or design appropriate (*oikeion*) to that kind. As we have seen in *Republic* 1, Socrates defines an *ergon* as an entity's characteristic function or activity. Accordingly, the excellence of each entity or rather each kind of entity endows it with a *dunamis* that enables it to perform its *ergon* properly. For instance, consider Socrates' question to Thrasymachus in *Republic* 1: "Could the eyes perform their own *ergon* well if they lacked their appropriate excellence (*oikeian aretên*)?"[85] Such passages indicate that the broad metaphysical vision of the early dialogues is informed by reflection on *technê*. One might call it a metaphysics of craftsmanship.

The metaphysical scheme, whose details are never elaborated among the early dialogues,[86] but whose fundamental concepts are expressed in *Gorgias* and elsewhere, resolves the problem of justice: Justice is conceived in terms of what may be called cosmic norms.[87] The idea is that the cosmos is designed with a particular structure and that entities within the cosmos are allotted specific places and functions within this grand design. Political structure, that is, the order of the polis, is continuous with cosmic structure, and the structure of the human being is continuous with that of the polis. Optimal functioning of larger wholes depends upon optimal functioning of their respective integrally designed parts. As such, the good of the agent is consistent with the good of others. Thus, there is no conflict between self-interest and morality.

This conception of the cosmos as a whole consisting of integral parts also well conforms to Socrates' conception of friendship based on belonging (*oikeiotês*) in *Lysis*. At the end of the discussion in *Lysis*, Socrates suggests that the good belongs, that is, is *oikeion* to all humans who are neither-good-nor-bad. As we have just seen, in *Gorgias* Socrates assumes that all that is good—"we and everything else that is good"—is good through the presence of a certain excellence.[88] Thus, in *Lysis* it is excellence that humans lack and that would enable them to function optimally, which is to say, to be well. Note further that since the *ergon* of excellence or wisdom is well-being, there is a correlation among the early dialogues between the treatments of desire and friendship in *Lysis* and the relation between nonethical *technai* and their ends, on the one hand, and ethical *technê* and its end, on the other. The ends of nonethical *technai* are extrinsic friends, and the end of ethical *technê* is the first friend. Moreover, the distinction between genuine and inauthentic friendship accommodates the fact, discussed in the previous section on the basis of the *Meno* and *Euthydemus* arguments, that the ends of nonethical *technai* are themselves not necessarily beneficial.

---

85. *R.* 1, 353b14–c2.
86. The individual human and political details are elaborated in *Republic* and the natural and cosmic details in *Timaeus*, where the creator of the cosmos is described as a *dêmiourgos* (workman).
87. Compare White (2002) 148–54.
88. *Grg.* 506d2–4.

In *Gorgias* Socrates also makes a general statement about the nature of the cosmos: "Wise men tell us, Callicles, that heaven and earth and gods and men are held together by communion and friendship (*philia*) and orderliness and sound-mindedness and justice, and this is the reason why they call this universe a cosmos."[89] The concept of belonging or appropriateness (*oikeiotês*) is, thus, central to the metaphysical scheme I am sketching. It suggests a propriety of relations between entities. In other words, it suggests the concept of harmony that is also implicit in the concepts of order and design. In short, then, among the early dialogues, specifically in *Gorgias*, goodness is explained as form, order, organized structure. Moreover, I am suggesting that form is Form.[90] In other words, the concepts of organized structure and order that emerge through reference to *technê* are concepts that are elsewhere elaborated as Form. As such, wisdom or ethical knowledge can be explained as knowledge of Form.

The explanation of goodness in terms of order and Form helps clarify and unify a number of elements in the early dialogues. At the same time, it raises a number of problems of its own. I will consider two problems in particular: the value of the *erga* of nonethical *technai* and the ethical circularity of goodness qua Form.

In the previous section I observed that Socrates' claim in *Republic* 1 that the products of nonethical *technai* are beneficial conflicts with Socrates' conclusions in *Meno* and *Euthydemus* that wisdom alone is invariably beneficial. Since the claim in *Republic* 1 is conventional and the claims in *Meno* and *Euthydemus* are unconventional and conclusions from arguments, I maintain that the view that the products of nonethical *technai* are beneficial is not Platonic. But this view also conflicts with the view that goodness is Form and order. For example, health is the Form and order of the human body. But if the character of the soul of the possessor of health is unjust, then health will simply facilitate injustice.[91] Consequently, there is a conflict between the view that all Forms are good and the view that, at least in the case of humans, only one Form is good, namely wisdom.

We encounter a similar difficulty in regard to another problem: Is the explanation of goodness in terms of order successful as a reductive account? In other words, is the concept of order intelligible independently of ethical concepts? If not, then Plato never overcomes the problem of circularity that it was hoped the explanation of goodness in terms of order would achieve.

In considering this problem, I begin with a related one concerning the range of Forms. For instance, in *Euthyphro* Socrates uses the word *idea*, a synonym for *eidos*, to refer to the contrary of the Form of holiness, the Form of unholiness. At least, for every positive property or condition there is a contrary negative property or condition. Such negative conditions or properties are not *eidê* (plural of *eidos*) in the sense in which the word *eidos* is used in *Gorgias*, but they are universals.

---

89. *Grg.* 507e6–a3.
90. To avoid confusion, hereafter I will tend to use the word "order" in place of "form."
91. *R.* 505a2–4.

Furthermore, the kinds (or bearers), which are recipients of Forms, are themselves universals. For instance, the body can be healthy or sick. The soul can be wise or ignorant. These considerations suggest that the early dialogues include two different senses of *eidos*, *eidos* as excellence and *eidos* as universal, and that there is a tension between these two senses. A passage from the middle period dialogue *Parmenides* may be evidence for such a tension:

> "Are there also," said Parmenides, "Forms of the following, justice itself, fineness, goodness and all such things?" "Yes," I said. "And is there a Form of man separate from us and those who are such as we are, and of fire and water?" "Parmenides," I replied, "I have often been perplexed about whether there are Forms of these things." "And what about these things, Socrates, which you may think are ridiculous, such as hair, dirt, and mud, or anything else particularly disdainful and worthless? Are you perplexed over whether it is necessary to say that there is a separate Form of these things, which is distinct from the things that we deal with?" "Not at all," Socrates replied, "these things are just as they appear to us; and it would be too strange to think that there is a Form of them. And yet, the thought has sometimes troubled me that the same applies to all things. But then when I assume this position, I run away from it, fearing that I should fall into some abyss of nonsense. So when I have come to those things which we were saying do have Forms, I stay and busy myself with them." "Yes, for you are still young," said Parmenides...[92]

It is one thing to explain negative conditions in terms of *eidos*. Negative conditions may simply be deviations from corresponding Forms. For example, sickness is a deviation from the Form of health. But the admission of Forms of badness undermines the conception in *Gorgias*. Like the argument against ethical hedonism that elicits the existence of bad pleasures, Forms of badness imply that excellence or goodness cannot to be identified with order.

Plato's self-criticism in *Parmenides*, if in fact that is what it is, suggests that the conceptualization of the sense of *eidos* as excellence preceded the conceptualization of the sense of *eidos* as universal. Assuming this, we may question the motivation behind this original conception of *eidos*. We also come to the objection that Plato tacitly smuggles the concept of goodness or optimality into his concept of *eidos*. For instance, health may be the *eidos* of the body, but a diseased body is also one whose elements have some sort of structure or organization. Likewise, the particular tuning of the lyre in which it is in a state of harmony is an organized structure, but when a lyre is out of tune, the condition and relation of its strings is also some sort of structure. Accordingly, the objection runs, Plato cannot mean by *eidos* any structure or organization whatsoever. But the problem is whether he can have a conception of *eidos* of the sort that he needs that does not assume goodness.

---

92. *Prm.* 130b7–e1.

The motivation for Plato's conceptualization of *eidos* as excellence depends, as we have seen, on reflection upon *technê*. The works that craftsmen effect are conceived as having orders or organized structures. These concepts are and should be understood very generally, for it is one thing for a musician to arrange strings or notes in a particular way, another for an architect to structure building materials, and another for a doctor to bring the quantities of bodily humors or elements into balance. Plato evidently conceived the relations in such structures as quantifiable in mathematical or specifically geometric terms, for immediately following his comment that wise men call the universe a *kosmos* (design), Socrates criticizes Callicles: "But it has escaped you that geometrical equality has great power among humans and gods; and you think it is necessary to exercise greed because you neglect geometry."[93]

This comment appears to be of neo-Pythagorean influence, and it has been suggested that *Gorgias* was composed shortly after Plato's return from his first trip to Southern Italy and Sicily. Other Pythagorean ideas are introduced in the dialogue, for example, the claim, involving a play on words, that the body (*sôma*) is a tomb (*sêma*) and the parable of the jars, which Socrates explicitly attributes to a Sicilian or Italian.[94] Generally speaking, the reference to geometry is significant, for it suggests that the *eidê* of the craftsmen may be understood in terms of mathematical properties, above all, I suppose, symmetry and proportion. And insofar as this is the case, form will indeed be explicable in nonethical terms. It must be admitted, however, that this is not a wholly adequate solution, for it may still be questioned which proportions, symmetries, equalities, and so on are appropriate for particular kinds.

5. The Epistemological Priority of Definitional Knowledge

The WF question is central to the investigations in *Charmides*, *Laches*, *Lysis*, *Euthyphro*, and *Hippias Major*. It is the point of departure in *Meno* and *Republic* 1. And while in these two dialogues Socrates and his interlocutors subsequently pursue other related questions, Socrates remains insistent on the importance and, in a sense to be clarified shortly, the epistemological priority of the WF question. The heart of the investigation in *Protagoras* focuses on the identity of excellence, although here through the relation of its parts. In *Gorgias*, the Gorgias episode focuses on a question akin to the WF question: "What is rhetoric?" And in the Callicles episode of *Gorgias*, Socrates initially responds to Callicles' position as though he were engaged in the pursuit of a WF question: "What is natural justice?"[95] In short, more than half of the early dialogues

93. Grg. 508b5–7.
94. Grg. 493a. Consider also the reference to Epicharmus at 505e, one of only two among the corpus.
95. For instance, consider Socrates' use of the words *horos* (definition) and *diorison* (to define) at Grg. 488d–e.

are preoccupied with the WF question or its like; and, given that *Hippias Minor, Crito*, and *Ion* are the shortest of the early dialogues, *Euthydemus* and *Apology* are the only texts of length in which the WF question or its like plays no role.

The WF question is, then, central to the early dialogues. Moreover, the question is related to the metaphysics of Forms since the pursuit of the WF question is, at least in three early dialogues (*Euthyphro, Meno*, and *Hippias Major*), explicitly conceived as the pursuit of a Form. Accordingly, epistemologically speaking, there is a clear link between the Platonic conception of goodness as *eidos* and the pursuit of the WF question. Yet we must also acknowledge that, dramaturgically, there is a disparity between the pursuit of the WF question and the Platonic identification of goodness as *eidos*. The WF questions in the early dialogues pursue *human* goodness (= excellence), not the Form of the good. The former is merely a type of the latter, as horse is a type of animal. As we have seen, the pursuit of human goodness ultimately leads to the question of the Form of the good, since the Platonic view is that excellence is the knowledge of the good. But this is a result of inquiry into WF questions, not their point of departure.

Granted this, it is controversial whether the principle of the epistemological priority of definitional knowledge itself is Platonic. So in this section my objective is limited to clarifying the principle and to confirming that it is Platonic. In chapter 4 I will say more about the epistemological and methodological grounds of the pursuit of definitional knowledge.

The epistemological priority of definitional knowledge has been analyzed as consisting of two principles:

> (a) If one does not know what F is, then one cannot know for any x
> whether x is an instance of F.

In other words, (a) states that without definitional knowledge of F, that is, without knowing what F is, one cannot know any instances or examples of F. For instance, if Cephalus does not know what justice is, he cannot know whether Polemarchus' act of returning to him a borrowed shield is just. The second principle is:

> (b) If one does not know what F is, then one cannot know for any
> property P whether F has P (where the attribution of P to F is
> substantive).

In other words, if one lacks definitional knowledge of F, one cannot know any of F's properties. For example, if Meno lacks definitional knowledge of excellence, he cannot know whether excellence is teachable. The reason for the parenthetical qualification in (b) is that, otherwise, in a discussion of, say, justice, Socrates could not claim to know that his interlocutor and he were speaking of justice or whether the name of justice was "justice." The fact is that Plato does not entertain such matters. Presumably, he would find them trivial.

The conjunction of (a) and (b) yield the following principle:

(π) If one does not know what F is, then one cannot know anything
of substance about F (such as that x is an instance of F or that
P is a property of F).[96]

If (π) were Platonic, it might well explain the prominence of theWF question
among the early dialogues. However, it remains controversial whether (π) is
Platonic. In this section, I examine the evidence for (π). I begin with (a), then
turn to (b).

In *Hippias Major* Socrates describes his alleged friend, who is actually himself,
as rebuking him:

> How do you know what sort of things are fine (*kalon*) and base (*aischron*)?
> Come now, can you say what the fine is?[97]

> He asks me if I am not ashamed to talk about fine practices when I have
> clearly been refuted concerning the fine, to the effect that I don't know what
> the thing itself is. "And yet," he will say, "how will you know whether or not
> someone has spoken finely, or done any other thing whatsoever, when you
> do not know the fine?"[98]

These two passages frame the investigation of the fine. The first initiates the
investigation. On the grounds given in the first passage, Socrates says that he was
determined to inquire of one of the wise men what the fine is. The second
passage follows the failed investigation. Socrates hereby reemphasizes the importance of reaching the correct account of the fine. In short, both of Socrates'
rebukes suggest that without knowing the fine he cannot know instances of the
fine. The principle (a), therefore, explains the motivation for the investigation of
the fine.

At the conclusion of the investigation in *Lysis*, Socrates says, "We have
become ridiculous... For those who leave us will say that we think we are friends
with each other—yet we have not been able to discover what a friend is."[99]
Socrates is here contrasting a commonsensical conception of friendship on
whose basis Lysis, Menexenus, and he may be considered friends, with the fact
that the three have failed to identify what friendship is. The ridiculousness of this
contrast admits of several interpretations. For example, Socrates may be referring
to the funny and odd condition that we can in some way correctly grasp certain
things without being able to articulate them. However, it is more plausible that
Socrates is suggesting that there is a problem with the common conception,
namely that insofar as a defense of the common conception cannot be given,
there is no good reason to maintain that it is correct.

---

96. I symbolize the principle of the epistemological priority of definitional knowledge as (π) because
   I will refer to it in later sections as well.
97. *Hp. Ma.* 286c8–d2.
98. *Hp. Ma.* 304d5–e2.
99. *Ly.* 223b4–8.

A related passage occurs in *Charmides*. The investigation begins with the assumption that Charmides possesses sound-mindedness. By the end of the investigation, it is unclear what sound-mindedness is. Socrates remarks that although the investigation has ended inconclusively, sound-mindedness surely is something good; therefore, if Charmides possesses sound-mindedness, he possesses something of value. In response Charmides replies, "I don't know if I have sound-mindedness or if I don't have it. How would I know when neither of you is able to determine what it is, or so you say?"[100] The passage is noteworthy in that one of Socrates' interlocutors rather than Socrates himself makes a claim akin to (a). But the very fact that Charmides is the speaker serves to clarify why Plato would tend to portray Socrates as making claims akin to (a). In view of the failed investigation, Charmides realizes that in a case where one recognizes that one does not know what *F* is, one will not know whether one possesses *F*. Socrates, unlike his interlocutors at the beginning of the investigation, is typically portrayed as beginning with a keen awareness of the difficulties of defining excellence. Consequently, he is already a veteran of the state in which Charmides finds himself.

A set of passages in *Euthyphro* is indicative of (a). The first occurs at the beginning of the dialogue. Euthyphro has recounted the nature of his suit. By Athenian standards, Euthyphro's prosecution of his father is extraordinary. Socrates and Euthyphro continue their exchange:

EUTHYPHRO   [My relatives say] that it is unholy for a son to prosecute his father for murder—knowing poorly, Socrates, how the divine is disposed to the holy and the unholy.

SOCRATES   Euthyphro, do you think that you have such accurate knowledge concerning divine affairs and concerning holy and unholy things that, the situation being as you say, you do not fear that by prosecuting your father you may be doing something unholy?

EUTHYPHRO   I would be useless, Socrates, and no different from the average man if I did not accurately know all such things . . .

SOCRATES   Then tell me what you just now asserted you clearly knew, what sort of things you say the sacred and the sacrilegious are, in the case of murder and all other actions.[101]

At the end of the investigation, Socrates makes similar remarks:

For if you did not clearly know the holy and the unholy, it is not possible that you would attempt to prosecute your aged father for murder on behalf of a hired laborer, but you would have feared the gods, risking that you did not

---

100. *Chrm.* 176a6–b1.
101. *Euthphr.* 4d9–5d1.

do this correctly, and would have been ashamed before men. Now, I know well that you think you know clearly the holy and the unholy.[102]

It has been suggested that these passages do not provide good evidence of (a). Euthyphro's case is extraordinary. In general, definitional knowledge may be required to adjudicate controversial or borderline cases, but most cases do not require definitional knowledge.

But this view is contradicted by further evidence in the dialogue. Socrates has posed the WF question, and Euthyphro has given his first unsatisfactory definition; Socrates again poses the WF question: "Then teach me what this Form itself is, so that looking to it and using it as a paradigm, I can say that that which is such as it is, whether done by you or someone else, is holy and that which is not is unholy."[103] Socrates makes clear here that definitional knowledge of holiness is useful for evaluating not merely Euthyphro's case, but any action. Granted this, it can still be objected that although definitional knowledge is sufficient for knowledge of relevant examples, it is not necessary. Again, some sort of nondefinitional grasp of holiness will suffice to identify most instances. We ought to consider whether the early dialogues license and encourage such a view.

First, the investigations of F in the early dialogues typically involve the rejection or problematization of conventional views about F, and they advance or advance in the direction of unconventional views about F. As such, the investigations suggest that conventional, especially prereflective, assumptions about F, and specifically assumptions of knowledge about F, tend to be undermined. Note that often alleged experts have their pretensions to knowledge of F repeatedly undermined. Accordingly, the early dialogues suggest that it is not merely borderline cases that warrant scrutiny, but mundane cases as well. A striking example is Socrates' novel conception of justice in Republic 1. Most Greeks would assume that instances of harming one's enemy exemplified justice. But Socrates argues that it is never just to do harm. In short, the early dialogues suggest that while everyone may have beliefs and strong convictions about what counts as an instance of F, few if any have ethical knowledge.

Second, consider the common Greek practice of seeking or acquiring information from the divine. If a person believed that he received a message from a divine source, perhaps he would believe that he knew the content of that message. But the early dialogues undermine the view that such a person would have knowledge. In Apology Socrates claims that the divine does not lie: "[The god] cannot be lying, for that it not lawful for it."[104] Elsewhere in Apology Socrates criticizes the jurors for fearing death, since they do not know what death is.[105] This rebuke suggests a principle related to (b): If one does not know what death is, one cannot know whether death is good or bad. Toward the end of his speech, Socrates

102. *Euthphr.* 15d4–e1.
103. *Euthphr.* 6e3–6.
104. *Ap.* 21b5–7.
105. *Ap.* 29a3–b2.

claims that death is a good thing and that he has strong evidence of this. His divine monitor did not prevent him from coming to court and delivering his speech; yet it would have prevented him if the outcome of the action were to have been bad.[106] Since Socrates is being condemned to death, death cannot be a bad thing. However, even though Socrates expresses his strong belief in this, in the final line of the text he claims that whether death is a good thing is unclear to all but the divine.[107] Accordingly, he concludes his speech by stating that he does not know whether death is good. Yet the divine cannot be deceiving him.

Consequently, although, strictly speaking, the *Euthyphro* passages only suggest the sufficiency of definitional knowledge for knowledge of instances of F, the foregoing considerations suggest that in fact there are no other means of acquiring knowledge of instances of F.

In sum, the evidence from *Hippias Major*, *Charmides*, *Lysis*, and *Euthyphro*, as well as *Republic* 1 and *Apology*, suggests that (a) is Platonic.

I now turn to the evidence for (b). The investigation in *Meno* begins with Meno's question to Socrates whether excellence is teachable. Socrates replies:

> I am so far from knowing whether or not excellence is teachable that I do not know at all what excellence itself is... Not knowing at all what a thing is, how would I know what sort of thing it is? Or do you think that it is possible for someone who is completely unacquainted with Meno to know whether he is beautiful or wealthy or well-born or the opposite of these?[108]

Consequently, Socrates poses the WF question. After three failed attempts to define excellence, Meno presents his infamous epistemological paradox: The pursuit of definitional knowledge is motivated by ignorance of F; but if one is ignorant of F, how can one achieve knowledge of it? Socrates' account of recollection (*anamnêsis*) satisfies Meno that it is reasonable to pursue knowledge. However, when Socrates suggests that they return to the WF question, Meno proposes that they instead pursue the question whether excellence is teachable. Socrates grants the request and pursues the question using a method inspired by geometrical analysis. The results ultimately are inconclusive, and at the end of the dialogue Socrates says, "We shall know clearly concerning this [that excellence comes to us by divine inspiration] when, prior to the attempt to seek how excellence comes about in men, we attempt to seek what excellence itself is by itself."[109]

The geometrically inspired method does not, then, enable Socrates and Meno to dispense with the WF question altogether. Definitional knowledge of F is conceived as having a certain epistemological priority over other questions pertaining to F. Precisely what this priority amounts to is controversial. Scholars have

---

106. *Ap.* 40c1–2.
107. *Ap.* 42a2–5.
108. *Men.* 71a5–b7.
109. *Men.* 100b4–6.

drawn attention to Socrates' question, "Not knowing at all (*parapan*) what a thing is, how would I know what sort of thing it is?" It has been suggested that the pursuit of knowledge about F is indeed impossible if we know nothing whatsoever about F. Yet it is possible to know something substantive about F without having definitional knowledge of F; and indeed that substantive nondefinitional knowledge is precisely what enables us to pursue definitional knowledge.

The wording of the *Meno* passage is echoed in *Laches*. The topic of the pertinent *Laches* passage is, again, excellence and its acquisition. Lysimachus and Melesias have invited Laches and Nicias to counsel them on whether training in fighting-in-arms, specifically with Stesilaus, is valuable for cultivating excellence in their sons. Socrates, who happens to be present, contributes the following advice:

> For if we happen to know concerning anything whatever that its being added to something makes that thing to which it is added better, and further, we are able to cause that thing to be added to it, then it is clear that we know that thing itself concerning which we advise how someone might best and most easily attain it . . . Then isn't it necessary for us to begin by knowing what excellence is? For if we do not know at all (*parapan*) what excellence happens to be, how would we consult with anyone as to how he might best acquire it?[110]

This passage suggests that a relatively broad principle motivates Socrates' claim about the acquisition of excellence.[111] That is to say, Socrates is not merely talking about excellence, but about the acquisition of anything. Moreover, as in the case of *Meno*, the language is qualified: "If we do not know at all what excellence happens to be . . . "

The similarity of the *Meno* and *Laches* passages lends some support to the view that some knowledge about F is possible in the absence of definitional knowledge of F. It will be convenient to refer to this position as

(c) It is possible to have knowledge of some of F's properties in the absence of definitional knowledge of F.

On the other hand, a passage in *Republic* 1 undermines or at least complicates endorsement of (c) as Platonic. The investigation in *Republic* 1 is governed by the question "What is justice?" After Thrasymachus' first failed definition, the good for the stronger, the investigation shifts to the questions whether justice is an excellence and whether justice is strong and conducive to well-being. As in *Meno*, the WF question is suspended for consideration of related questions. While the argument ultimately suggests that justice is an excellence and that the just person is strong and well, at the end of the dialogue Socrates rebukes himself:

---

110. *La.* 189e3–190c2.
111. I owe this point to Benson (1990).

"When I do not know what justice is, I will not possibly know whether or not it happens to be an excellence or whether or not one who has it is well."[112]

Lack of definitional knowledge of justice disables Socrates from knowing whether justice is an excellence and whether justice is conducive to well-being. Moreover, the qualification "[not knowing] at all" does not appear in the *Republic* passage. This suggests the following alternatives. The qualification "at all" in *Meno* and *Laches* does not carry the sort of epistemological weight that has been attributed to it; in other words, (c) is a misinterpretation of the *Meno* and *Laches* passages, and (b) carries the day. Or, on the basis of *Meno* and *Laches*, a similar qualification should be read into the *Republic* 1 passage, and (c) should be maintained against (b). How then should we adjudicate between these options?

One problem for supporters of (c) is that the actual course of the investigation in *Meno* does not follow from (c). That is to say, the investigation in *Meno* does not proceed to identify something known about F on the basis of which more knowledge of F is pursued. Yet perhaps this can be explained on the grounds that Meno insists upon pursuing the question whether excellence can be taught, contrary to Socrates' will that the WF question should be pursued.

Further support for (c) comes from the fact that the investigation in *Laches* proceeds precisely as would be expected given (c). Socrates and Laches confirm their assumption that they know what excellence is and that courage is a part of it. On the basis of these epistemic assumptions, they proceed to the WF question regarding courage.

Although this supports (c), it is by no means conclusive. The investigation in *Laches* ends in aporia precisely because the final definition of courage proposed is revealed to be identical to excellence. Of course, this could indicate that the reasoning that led to that conception of courage was faulty. But, as we have argued, a number of other early dialogues suggest that excellence is a unity and that the conventional conception of its partition is mistaken. In that case, Socrates' and Laches' epistemic assumptions about excellence and courage are mistaken. Indeed, this is the most plausible interpretation of Socrates' presumption to know what excellence is and that it has parts. Consequently, the investigation in *Laches* reveals that neither Socrates nor Laches has definitional or nondefinitional knowledge about courage or excellence. And thus, despite the ostensible form of the investigation in *Laches* in its initial movement, the dialogue as a whole winds up undermining (c) rather than supporting it. The preceding considerations suggest that the *Meno*, *Laches*, and *Republic* 1 passages should be read as supporting (b). Indeed, I will maintain that it is most reasonable to infer that (b) is Platonic. Granted this, let us examine the passages more closely to clarify the motivation for (b).

Consider again the properties of F to which reference is made in the *Meno*, *Laches*, and *Republic* 1 passages. In *Meno* Socrates distinguishes the WF question from the question "Is excellence teachable?" Similarly, in *Laches* Socrates

---

112. R. 1, 354c1–3.

distinguishes the WF question from the question of how F is attainable. In *Meno*, the distinction is understood as being between questions that ask "What (*ti*) is F?" and "What sort of thing (*poion*) is F?" Socrates does not attempt to explicate the *ti/poion* distinction; it remains intuitive and pretheoretical. However, some explication can be derived from *Euthyphro*. There, in refuting Euthyphro's third definition of that which is holy qua holy as that which is loved by all the gods qua loved by all the gods, Socrates claims that Euthyphro has given an account of an affection (*pathos*) of that which is holy, namely being loved by all the gods, rather than an account of its being (*ousia*). Some scholars have thought that the *ousia/pathos* distinction is equivalent to the essence/accident distinction. But this is not quite right. Evidence from the rest of the Platonic corpus suggests that Plato conceives of *ousia* and *pathos* as two elements of a trichotomy, the third member of which is *poiêma* (action).[113] Affection and action are contraries, and beings (*ousiai*) may be subject to one or the other or both. In *Euthyphro* Socrates conceives of being loved by all the gods, like being seen, led, and carried, as something that holiness has done to it.[114] Moreover, he is clear that this *pathos* of holiness is in part due to what holiness itself is. However, being loved by all the gods does not identify the *ousia* of holiness. Likewise, I suggest that Plato would explain the teachability or lack thereof or any other mode of acquisition of F as something that F has the potential to have done to it. That is, being taught may be a *pathos* of excellence, and the question whether F can be taught is a question about whether F has the capacity to suffer that *pathos*. But in order to answer that question, it is necessary determine the *ousia* of F.

The point of these considerations is to show that, strictly speaking, the passages we have considered suggest a principle weaker than (b); they suggest

> (b2) If one does not know what F is, then one cannot know for
> any affection (*pathos*) or action (*poiêma*) P, whether F
> experiences or effects P.

Let us now return to the evidence from *Republic* 1. There it is claimed that definitional knowledge of justice is epistemologically prior to knowledge of whether justice is an excellence and whether its possessor is well. In other words, definitional knowledge of justice is epistemologically prior to knowledge of the relation between justice and excellence and justice and well-being (*eudaimonia*). Socrates' point here must be understood in relation to the preceding investigation: Thrasymachus, in claiming that justice is the good of another, challenged Socrates' assumption that justice is a good thing for its possessor. That is, Thrasymachus argues that justice, one form of which he understands to be a subject's following the laws of his polis, may be detrimental to its possessor, for the laws of one's polis may be designed to benefit the government rather than the

---

113. This point is discussed in Wolfsdorf (2005a).
114. Note that Plato does not seem to be concerned with or aware of the distinction between mental acts such as seeing and loving and physical acts such as leading and carrying.

subjects. Both Socrates and Thrasymachus assume that excellence is beneficial to its possessor. Thus, if justice did not benefit its possessor, it would not be a part of excellence. Similarly, if justice did not benefit its possessor, it would not be conducive to its possessor's well-being. Accordingly, given Thrasymachus' challenge to Socrates, the WF question indeed requires a satisfactory answer before the discussants can know whether justice is an excellence or whether it conduces to well-being. As I argued in section 3 of this chapter, the relation between excellence and well-being is that of *dunamis* and *ergon*. Given that *eudaimonia* is activity, at least part of Socrates' expression of the epistemological priority of definitional knowledge in *Republic* 1 might be understood as concerning the relation of *ousia* and *poiêma*. But in fact, I do not think this well captures Socrates' point. To see why, let us turn to the relation of justice and excellence. This relation clearly cannot be understood as being between *ousia* and *poiêma*, for excellence is not an action. Moreover, being an excellence is not a *pathos* of justice. Here it is helpful to consider two passages from *Protagoras* and *Gorgias*, respectively, akin to (b):

> I would be surprised if you knew what a sophist is. But if you don't know this, then you don't know whether the person to whom you are giving your soul is good (*agathon*).[115]

> I will not answer him whether I think rhetoric is fine (*kalon*) or base until I answer first what it is, for it would not be right.[116]

In these cases, knowledge of the subjects, a sophist and rhetoric, is claimed to be in some sense prior to knowledge of ethical properties of the subjects. I suggest that the sense in which knowledge of the subjects is claimed to be prior is epistemological priority. In *Protagoras* and *Gorgias*, the nature of sophistry and rhetoric, respectively, is fundamentally questioned such that it is unclear what the value of these things is.

Likewise, in *Republic* 1 Thrasymachus' position fundamentally questions the nature of justice such that it becomes unclear what justice is. In other words, these dialogues attempt to examine sophistry, rhetoric, and justice in a way that does not beg the question of their value. Accordingly, when in *Republic* 1 Socrates says, "When I do not know what justice is, I will not possibly know whether or not it happens to be an excellence," he should be understood as saying that he recognizes the need to define justice in a way that does not beg the question of its value for its possessor. Indeed, I think that Socrates' doubts about the conduciveness of justice to well-being amount to the same thing. If justice is not good for its possessor, it will not conduce to its possessor's well-being.

How then does the *Republic* 1 passage relate to (b)? Taking the *Protagoras* and *Gorgias* passages into consideration, the *Republic* 1 passage suggests that

---

115. *Prt.* 312c1–4.
116. *Grg.* 463c3–6 (compare 462c10–d2).

(b3) If one does not know what F is, one cannot know the value of F.

Strictly speaking, the conjunction of (b2) and (b3) does not imply (b). But the point of the foregoing consideration of the evidence for (b) has not been to suggest that the Platonic view is that it is possible to know some properties of F in the absence of definitional knowledge of F, in other words, that a principle weaker than (b) is Platonic. Rather, it has been to illuminate the motivation for Socratic claims in *Laches*, *Meno*, and *Republic* 1 akin to (b). The weight of the evidence in these dialogues encourages the inference that (b) is Platonic. In that case, (π) is Platonic.

6. Ordinary Ethical Knowledge

In the early dialogues Socrates occasionally avows nondefinitional ethical knowledge. Insofar as he disavows ethical expertise and definitional knowledge of F, Socrates' occasional avowals of nondefinitional ethical knowledge are inconsistent with the epistemological priority of definitional knowledge (π). Indeed, this is one reason some scholars have rejected (π), and have argued for a distinction between ordinary ethical knowledge and ethical expertise in the early dialogues. Definitional knowledge is necessary for expertise, but not for ordinary ethical knowledge. Socrates' occasional avowals of nondefinitional ethical knowledge, therefore, present a problem for defenders of (π). In this section we consider Socrates' occasional avowals of ethical knowledge and thus the status of ordinary ethical knowledge in the early dialogues.

I will begin by briefly canvassing Socrates' disavowals of ethical knowledge. Socrates tends explicitly and implicitly to disavow knowledge of the ethical subjects central to the discussions. In *Apology* and *Laches* He disavows knowledge of a *technê* of excellence.[117] In *Charmides*, *Hippias Major*, *Laches*, *Lysis*, *Meno*, and *Republic* 1, he disavows knowledge of the identity of excellence or a part of it.[118] In addition to these explicit denials of ethical knowledge, there are numerous implicit denials. For example, in *Euthyphro* Socrates never explicitly says that he does not know what holiness is, but it is clear from his request to Euthyphro to learn what holiness is as well as the aporetic conclusion of the investigation that he does not know or think that he knows.[119] Likewise, the aporetic conclusions in *Protagoras* and *Hippias Minor* indicate that Socrates does not know or think that he knows the answer to the questions governing the investigations. Furthermore, in dialogues such as *Gorgias* and *Crito*, which are not aporetic, at least not in the same way as those just mentioned, Socrates maintains, but never claims to know, the conclusions he reaches and maintains, namely that it is better to suffer than to do injustice and that he should not escape from prison.

---

117. *Ap.* 21d2–6, 20c1–3; *La.* 186b8–c5, 186d8–e3.
118. *Chrm.* 165b5–c1,166c7–d3; *Hp. Ma.* 304d5–8 (compare 286d1–3); *La.* 200e2–5; *Ly.* 223b7–8 (compare *Ly.* 212a4–6); *Men.* 71a5–7, *Men.* 80d1; *R.* 1, 337e4–5.
119. See in particular *Euthphr.* 5a7–c5, 15c12, 15e5–16a4.

Arguably, these disavowals of ethical knowledge are compatible with avowals of some ethical knowledge. Specifically, it might be argued that while Socrates disavows ethical expertise and pertinent ethical knowledge (for instance, definitional ethical knowledge), as well as knowledge of particularly controversial ethical positions, he nonetheless avows some ordinary ethical knowledge. Collectively, scholars have claimed that Socrates avows ordinary ethical knowledge at least thirty-three times in the early dialogues. Granted, our concern is with the question whether the view that there is ordinary ethical knowledge is Platonic, not whether Socrates avows ordinary ethical knowledge. But the two questions are related. For if Socrates does avow ordinary ethical knowledge at least thirty-three times among the early dialogues, it is difficult to deny that the view that there is ordinary ethical knowledge is Platonic.

In fact, most of the attributions to Socrates of avowals of ordinary ethical knowledge are misguided. To demonstrate this in every case would be tedious.[120] It should suffice here to offer a set of representative examples. First, a number of alleged avowals of ordinary ethical knowledge are not ethical in content. The first is from *Euthydemus*: " 'Come then, answer me this,' he [Dionysodorus] said, 'Do you know (*epistasai*) anything?' 'Yes, of course,' I [Socrates] replied, 'many things, in fact, though insignificant ones.' "[121] Here Socrates makes a general claim about what he knows, namely that he knows some things. At the same time, he qualifies the scope of his knowledge by its value. Although he does know some things, they are insignificant. Since the content of what Socrates is claiming to know is not expressed, it should not be assumed that ethical propositions are among the things he claims to know. Therefore, this passage should not be used as evidence of Socrates avowing ordinary ethical knowledge.

A second passage occurs in *Protagoras*: "For I know (*oida*) that if this were clear [that is, what excellence is and whether it has parts], then that other question concerning which you and I have drawn out such a long discussion—I denying and you claiming that excellence can be taught—would be cleared up satisfactorily."[122] Here Socrates is claiming to know something about the epistemological relation between two ethical propositions, that knowing the one, that is, whether excellence is knowledge, would enable a person to know the other, that is, that excellence is teachable. This passage may provide support for the claim that Socrates is committed to the sufficiency, if not necessity, of definitional knowledge of excellence for pertinent nondefinitional ethical knowledge. But Socrates is not claiming to know either one of the ethical propositions.

A third passage is from *Apology*:

Besides, these accusers are many and have already been making their accusations for a long time, and moreover, they spoke to you when you were at an age when you would most easily believe them—some of you as

---

120. Those interested in such a demonstration should consult Wolfsdorf (2004b).
121. *Euthd.* 293b7–8.
122. *Prt.* 360e8–361a3.

children and youths—and the case they prosecuted went completely by default since there was no defense. But the most unreasonable thing of all is this, that it is not possible to know (*eidenai*) and speak their names, except when one of them happens to be a comic poet.[123]

Here Socrates is implying that members of the jury and he know that Aristophanes was partly responsible for the impression of him that the jurors received when they were young. The content of the knowledge claim simply is not ethical.

In addition, Socrates makes a number of claims that have ethical content and that seem to be knowledge claims, but in fact are not. Consider two passages from *Apology*:

For know well (*eu gar iste*) that if you kill me, I being such a man as I say I am, you will not injure me so much as yourselves, for neither Meletus nor Anytus could injure me. That would not be possible; for I believe it is not permitted by the divine that a better man be injured by a worse man.[124]

For know (*eu gar iste*), men of Athens, if I had tried to go into politics, I would have been put to death long ago and should have done no good to you or myself.[125]

And compare these with three from the same dialogue, whose form is similar, but whose content is not ethical:

Know well (*eu iste*) that what I said before is true, that great hatred has arisen against me and in the minds of many persons. And it is this that will cause my condemnation—if it is to cause it—not Meletus or Anytus, but the prejudice and dislike of the multitude.[126]

For know well (*eu iste*) that the divine commands these things [that is, Socrates' philosophical activity].[127]

but if anyone says that he has ever learned from me or heard anything privately from me that all the others did not, know well (*eu iste*) that he is lying.[128]

Rather than claiming to know something, in all five passages Socrates is commanding his audience to know it. The expression "know well" (*eu iste*) is idiomatic and akin to our expression "rest assured [that]." The speaker uses the expression to instill confidence in his audience of the proposition that follows. For

---

123. *Ap.* 18c4–d2.
124. *Ap.* 30c6–8.
125. *Ap.* 31d6–e1.
126. *Ap.* 28a4–8.
127. *Ap.* 30a5.
128. *Ap.* 33b6–8.

instance, in responding to the WF question, Laches says, "Know well (*eu isthi*) that if a man were willing to remain in rank, defend against the enemy, and not flee, he would be courageous."[129] And Hippias says, "Know well (*eu isthi*), Socrates, if I must speak the truth, a beautiful young woman is beautiful."[130] W. R. Lamb and Harold Fowler translate the expressions as "you may be sure" and "rest assured," respectively.[131] Of course, in both instances, the speakers, Laches and Hippias, do believe that they know the propositions they are persuading Socrates to accept. But it cannot be inferred in general that one who uses this form of expression believes that he knows the proposition he is persuading his audience to accept.

The first passage cited from *Apology* supports this point. There Socrates encourages his audience to accept that if they kill him, they will injure themselves more than him. But then he expresses his explanation of this as a belief claim rather than a knowledge claim: "For I believe (*oiomai*) it is not permitted by the divine that a better man be injured by a worse man." Moreover, in his ensuing statements Socrates continues to explain himself with belief claims rather than knowledge claims: "Perhaps he thinks he would thus inflict great injuries on me...but I do not believe so (*oiomai*)";[132] "For I think (*moi dokei*) the divine fastened me upon the city."[133] In short, one who employs the expression *eu isthi* or *eu iste* may believe he knows what he is persuading his audience to accept, but he need not. And given the particular difficulties of Platonic epistemology, it is most reasonable not to assume that when Socrates uses these expressions, he is implying that he knows the given propositions.

Consider two more passages in which Socrates seems to be avowing ethical knowledge. The first is from *Apology*:

> But, judges, you must also be disposed toward death with good hope and must bear in mind this truth: Nothing bad can come to a good man, neither in life nor after death, and the divine does not neglect his affairs. So, too, that which has now befallen me has not occurred by chance, but it is clear to me that it was better for me to die now and to be freed from troubles. That is the reason why the sign never interfered with me.[134]

C. D. C. Reeve cites this as an "explicit" knowledge claim. If it were, it would be of an ethical proposition. But it is not. Nowhere does Socrates claim to know that nothing bad can befall a good man in life or death. He clearly does claim this to be true. But that he is convinced of its truth on account of the silence of his

---

129. *La.* 190e5–6.
130. *Hp. Ma.* 287e3–4.
131. (1924) 47; (1926) 361.
132. *Ap.* 30d2–4.
133. *Ap.* 30e5–6.
134. *Ap.* 41c8–d6.

divine sign does not imply that he believes that he knows it. Compare Socrates' attitude in *Gorgias* toward the proposition that it is better to suffer than to do injustice:

> These matters, as has become evident to us in our preceding exchange, are fixed and, to put it rather crudely, bound with claims of steel and adamant— or so it would at least seem—claims that unless you or someone more vigorous than yourself can unfasten, no one can assert otherwise than I do and still assert well. For my position is the same as always: I do not know (*oida*) how these matters stand, but of all whom I have encountered, as now, no one is able to state it otherwise and not look ridiculous. And so, once again, I assert that these things are so.[135]

Socrates' claims appear contradictory. Yet however firmly Socrates is convinced of the truth of the proposition that it is better to suffer than to do injustice, his conviction and strong affirmation are not in his eyes equivalent to a knowledge claim. This, I suggest, is precisely the point that the passage conveys: Although Socrates may strongly believe an ethical proposition to be true and with great confidence assert it as true, still, this does not imply and it should not be inferred that he believes that he knows that proposition. Compare Hugh H. Benson: "The fact that Socrates frequently expresses extreme confidence in various truths . . . is simply a red herring in this context. It has been no part of my account to suggest that Socratic knowledge is to be identified with confidence, extreme or otherwise."[136]

Finally, in considering Socrates' alleged claims of knowledge, it is important to respond to a contention that John Beversluis raises regarding the scope of Socrates' knowledge claims:

> The case for ascribing some moral knowledge to Socrates does not depend on a handful of texts containing a tiny range of strong epistemic verbs such as *oida, epaiô, epistêmai,* or *gignôskô.* In addition to these passages in which Socrates advances explicit knowledge-claims, there are numerous others which contain implicit knowledge-claim indicators, i.e., semantically different but epistemically equivalent modes of expression.[137]

Consequently, Beversluis cites a number of passages where Socrates does not explicitly claim to know a given proposition, but which, as he believes, contain implicit knowledge claim indicators. It is worth pausing over this point and these passages to clarify why in evaluating Socrates' alleged knowledge claims, I reject those that do not contain "strong epistemic verbs." The passages Beversluis cites in suppot of his argument are:

---

135. *Grg.* 508e6–509b1.
136. (2000) 227.
137. (1987) 219.

(1) "it has been proved (*apodedeiktai*) true."[138]

(2) "the just man has revealed (*anapephantai*) himself to us as good and wise and the unjust man as ignorant and bad."[139]

(3) "[the previous argument] has rightly compelled (*orthôs anangkasthênai*) them to agree that no one does what is bad willingly."[140]

(4) "the self-controlled man, being, as we have now demonstrated (*diêlthomen*), just and courageous and holy, must be completely good."[141]

(5) "we can now tell who our friends are, for the argument shows (*sêmainei*) us that it must be those who are good."[142]

(6) [In response to Polus' admission that it will be difficult to refute the Socratic thesis that, of all wrongdoers, those who escape punishment are the unhappiest, Socrates replies] "Not difficult... but impossible (*adunaton*), for the truth is never refuted."[143]

Here it is useful to refer back to the *Gorgias* passage we just considered in conjunction with the *Apology* passage that Reeve cites as an explicit avowal of ethical knowledge. In the *Gorgias* passage, Socrates explicitly contrasts the fact that "these matters, as has become evident to us in our preceding exchange, have been fixed and bound with claims of adamant and steel," and the fact that "as always, I do not know how these matters stand." That is to say, despite the force of the argument, which compels Socrates to accept the conclusion, and the fact that he has reached the same conclusion numerous times and therefore believes that "no one can assert otherwise than I do and still assert well," he still disavows knowledge of the matter. I interpret the passage as among the most compelling evidence in the early dialogues, outside of *Meno*, that the distinction between knowledge and true belief or knowledge and strong conviction in the truth of a proposition on the basis of a putatively strong argument for it is Platonic. Accordingly, although Socrates may strongly believe that a given argument compels him to accept a given conclusion and in fact he does strongly accept that conclusion, this does not imply that he, therefore, believes that he knows the conclusion.

It should be added that interpretations of *apodedeiktai* (it has been proved) and *anangkê* (necessarily) that imply proof and necessity in the strict deductive sense in which philosophers use these concepts now is anachronistic. Consider passage (4), which Beversluis cites from *Gorgias*. Actually, Socrates' expression in the passage is even stronger than Beversluis indicates. Socrates begins by saying that "therefore, it follows of much necessity (*pollê anangkê*) that..." The phrase *pollê*

---

138. *Grg.* 479e8.
139. *R.* 1, 350c10–11.
140. *Grg.* 509e4.
141. *Grg.* 507c1–5.
142. *Ly.* 214d8–e1.
143. *Grg.* 473b10–11.

anangkê is revealing, for what sense is there in conceiving of necessity as coming in degrees?[144] Such a phrase should be interpreted as implying that the argument strongly convinces the discussants. Similarly, verbs such as *apodedeiktai* should be interpreted as implying that on the basis of the argument a certain proposition appears to the discussants to be the case.

This point is well brought out by consideration of the larger passage in which Beversluis' passage (3) is embedded, for it undermines the force Beversluis would ascribe to it. The broader passage is: "I really must have your answer on this particular point, Callicles—whether you think that Polus and I were correct in finding ourselves forced to admit, as we did in the preceding argument, that no one does injustice of his own will, but that all who do injustice do it against their will."[145] The fact that Socrates allows the possibility that Callicles could disagree indicates that the "force" of the argument that compelled Socrates and Polus to the particular conclusion might not be persuasive to another person—not necessarily because that person is irrational, but because the argument itself may have weaknesses that those who have accepted the argument cannot see.

In sum, then, the passages Beversluis cites are not evidence of Socrates avowing ethical knowledge. And, more generally, few of the many passages that commentators have cited as evidence of Socrates avowing ethical knowledge are genuine. In fact, there are only five passages among the early dialogues where Socrates avows some ordinary ethical knowledge: *Euthydemus* 296e3–297a1, *Gorgias* 521c7–d3, *Protagoras* 310d3–4, *Apology* 29a4–b9 (with 37b2–8), and *Apology* 22c9–d3. In addition there is one passage where Socrates presumes to possess some ordinary ethical knowledge: *Laches* 190b7–c5. I will not discuss all of these passages here. Instead, I will consider a couple of salient cases.[146]

One instance of Socrates avowing ordinary ethical knowledge occurs in *Apology*:

> For fearing death, men, is nothing other than thinking one is wise when one is not, for it is thinking that one knows what one does not know. For no one knows whether death is not, in fact, the greatest good for a person; and yet people fear it as though they knew well that it was the worst thing. Yet is this not the most reprehensible ignorance, not to know what one thinks one knows? But I, men, differ from most people perhaps in just this way, and if I am to some degree wiser than others, it would be in this: While I do not adequately know about things in Hades, I do not think I know. *But I do know that to do injustice and to disobey someone better than myself, whether god or man, is bad and foul.*[147]

Later in the text Socrates reaffirms this knowledge claim in a similar way by contrasting it with his ignorance of the value of death and the afterlife:

144. Obviously, distinctions such as logical and nomological necessity have no place here.
145. *Grg.* 509e2–7.
146. The other cases are discussed in Wolfsdorf (2004b).
147. *Ap.* 29a4–b9, with my italics.

Since, then, I am convinced that I have not done anyone an injustice, I am hardly going to do myself injustice and to say of myself that I deserve something bad and to propose some such penalty for myself. What should I fear? That I should suffer the penalty Meletus proposes, of which I say I do not know if it is good or bad? Instead of this, *should I choose to suffer something that I know is bad*...?[148]

In short, in *Apology* Socrates explicitly once and somewhat more obliquely again affirms knowledge that it is bad and foul to commit injustice and to disobey anyone better than oneself. Moreover, in both cases Socrates makes the affirmation in clear contrast to some other proposition of which he disclaims knowledge.

The occasion on which Socrates presumes to possess some ethical knowledge occurs in *Laches*:

SOCRATES   Then we must begin by knowing what excellence is, for if we had no idea what excellence is, then how could we serve as counselors regarding how best to acquire it?

LACHES   We couldn't by any means, Socrates.

SOCRATES   Then we agree that we know what it is.

LACHES   Yes, we agree.[149]

Here Socrates assumes that Laches and he know what excellence is.

Although such passages are quite rare, in view of Socrates' disavowals of ethical knowledge elsewhere among the early dialogues, they raise an interpretive question. The complete set of Socrates' disavowals and avowals of ethical knowledge contains inconsistencies.

Numerous strategies for resolving these inconsistencies have been proposed. For example, some scholars claim that when Socrates avows ethical knowledge, he is using words for "knowledge" in one sense, and when he disavows ethical knowledge, he uses words for "knowledge" in another sense. Other scholars argue that Socrates denies definitional knowledge of ethical kinds, but maintains nondefinitional ethical knowledge.

On the basis of the textual evidence, such proposals cannot be sustained; Socrates' avowals and disavowals of ethical knowledge are inconsistent. Yet this is a problem only if it is assumed that the correct way to interpret the early dialogues is to assemble all of Socrates' topic-relevant utterances and to distill from these unified principles. Given that almost all of the discussions in the early dialogues focus on ethical topics and that Plato uses Socrates in various ways, some inconsistency among Socrates' avowals and disavowals of ethical knowledge is to be expected. Furthermore, while commentators have sought to determine Socrates' ethical and epistemological commitments, it is more sensible to attend to Plato's

---

148. *Ap.* 37b2–8, with my italics.
149. *La.* 190b7–c5.

reasons for composing Socrates' various ethical or epistemological assertions and ultimately to Platonic ethical or epistemological views.

Again, I emphasize that Socrates' ethical knowledge claims are rare. On only a few occasions in the early dialogues does Socrates claim or presume to have some ethical knowledge. His explicit and implicit disavowals of ethical knowledge are much more common. Consequently, although from the perspective of the ancient Athenians Socrates' disavowals of ethical knowledge are unconventional, from the perspective of the early dialogues his avowals of ethical knowledge are anomalous. In other words, Plato intended to portray Socrates fairly consistently as disavowing ethical knowledge.

The few occasions on which Socrates avows ethical knowledge must be explained in view of their local contexts. Here I will provide explanations of such avowals in *Apology* and *Laches* to serve as representative treatments.

As discussed previously, occasionally, for the sake of convenience, Plato makes Socrates express conventional or traditional positions that are not Platonic. Such assertions fit into the stream of dialogue without disrupting it. As such, they do not provoke a need for further justification, which would detract from the aims of the text. Moreover, Socrates' ethical knowledge claims are conventional, in terms of both their content and their epistemic attitude. Again, it is Socrates' disavowals of ethical knowledge that are unconventional.

Socrates' claims in *Apology* are typically taken as the strongest evidence among the early dialogues of Socrates avowing ethical knowledge. In these passages he explicitly and directly contrasts his knowledge that it is wrong to do injustice by disobeying a superior with his ignorance of the afterlife. In these passages the emphasis is on both the aspect of the propositional attitude as epistemic and the propositional content itself. Accordingly, in explaining the passages, it is necessary to address a number of questions. How can Socrates' ethical knowledge claims in *Apology* be consistent with his distinction of human and divine wisdom and his disavowals of knowledge in *Apology*? What is the function of this distinction in *Apology*, and is it significant for Platonic epistemology? Finally, why did Plato make Socrates assert such a strong ethical knowledge claim in *Apology*?

In *Apology*, Socrates makes several disavowals of ethical knowledge. He disavows a *technê* of human and political excellence. He disavows knowledge of death and the afterlife; he disavows rhetorical skill; and he disavows nonethical *technê*. In all but one of these cases, he disavows expertise of some kind. On two other occasions, his disavowals appear to be more sweeping. "Finally, I went to the craftsmen, for I was aware that I knew nothing, so to speak (*hôs epos eipein*), but that I would discover that they knew many fine things";[150] "I am aware of being wise (*sophos*) in nothing great or small."[151] In these two cases Socrates is disavowing expertise, not all knowledge.

---

150. *Ap.* 22d1–2.
151. *Ap.* 21b4–5.

In the former case, Socrates says that he knows nothing, but he qualifies this statement with the phrase "so to speak." I suggest that by this qualification he means that relative to the kind of knowledge the craftsmen have, namely nonethical expertise, he knows nothing. In short, Socrates has no expertise. This interpretation is supported by the fact that Socrates here is explicitly contrasting his epistemic state with that of craftsmen and by the more general fact that he clearly commits himself to a number of common knowledge claims throughout his defense speech.

The latter case occurs in response to the Delphic oracle's pronouncement that Socrates is the wisest of men. After Chaerephon informed him that Delphi had stated that he was the wisest of men, Socrates says that he was baffled because he was aware of "being wise (*sophos*) in nothing great or small." Socrates' disavowal of all *sophia* cannot be interpreted here as a disavowal of all knowledge. If that were the case, then this would blatantly contradict his commonsensical knowledge claims elsewhere in *Apology*. Instead, I suggest that the word *sophia* and its cognates are being used here to refer to expertise, not merely to the knowledge of any given proposition. This usage of *sophia* is perfectly acceptable Greek. And while Plato does not always have Socrates use *sophia* in this particular way, the reason just given as well as the broader content of Socrates' speech support this interpretation.

When Socrates takes up the accusations against him, beginning with his first accusers, he defends himself against a view of himself as a sophist.[152] That is to say, he defends himself against a view of himself as having a certain kind of expertise and as occupying himself with certain fields of understanding and as teaching in those fields. So when he disavows this knowledge, Socrates identifies Gorgias, Prodicus, Hippias, and Evenus as the kind of people who possess it.[153] Once he has distinguished himself from this group of well-known sophists, Socrates explains how he acquired the kind of reputation that would lead to his being associated with such figures. Here he defines the knowledge he does have as "a kind of wisdom,"[154] more specifically as "human wisdom."[155] However, he qualifies this identification by saying that "perhaps (*isôs*)" he has human wisdom, and immediately afterward he says: "my *sophia*—if it is *sophia*."[156] Socrates' point in these qualifications is that the oracle identified him as the wisest Greek; thus, he is bound to consider himself wise. However, at the time that he received the message he was "aware of himself as being *sophos* in nothing great or small." Socrates' claim here suggests, then, that he is not disavowing all knowledge, including common knowledge—say, that his name is Socrates and that he is an Athenian. Rather, he

---

152. Socrates' prosecutors' statement is characteristic of sophistic intellectual activity: "Socrates is a criminal and a busybody, investigating the things beneath the heavens and making the weaker argument stronger and teaching others these same things" (*Ap.* 19b4–c1).

153. *Ap.* 19e1–4, 20a2–c3.

154. *Ap.* 20d7.

155. *Ap.* 20d8.

156. *Ap.* 20e7.

is disavowing that he has a specialized body of knowledge that would distinguish him from his peers in the way that the sophists or other experts are distinguished. Furthermore, the expression "nothing great or small" characterizes the relative importance of various kinds of expertise. For instance, Socrates regards ethical expertise as great, indeed, divine, whereas he regards the common crafts, say, cobbling and pottery, as relatively unimportant.[157] Thus, in denying *sophia* great or small, he means to deny having any specialized knowledge whatsoever. Finally, when Socrates does explain what his human *sophia* amounts to, he describes it as involving not thinking one knows what one does not know.[158] He interprets the oracle's pronouncement as indicating that "human wisdom is of little or no value" and that human wisdom lies in recognizing that one is "like Socrates... truly of little worth with respect to *sophia*."[159] Thus, the kind of wisdom Socrates admits he has is really no wisdom at all. Rather, it is an appreciation of the limitations of human understanding and, above all, an appreciation of his ignorance of true *sophia*, the *sophia* that the gods possess, the *sophia* of the most important thing, excellence.

Socrates' ethical knowledge claims in *Apology* are consistent with his distinction of human and divine wisdom insofar as in claiming to know that it is wrong to do injustice and so forth he is not claiming to have ethical expertise. Still, it may be wondered why Plato makes Socrates assert such strong ethical knowledge claims in *Apology*. Here it is useful to consider the content of the claims and the contexts in which they occur. Socrates' first claim of ethical knowledge occurs in response to the question whether Socrates is not troubled by the fact that he has engaged in a pursuit that may lead to his death. His response is that, just as it would have been wrong for him through fear of death to have abandoned his military posts at Potidaea, Amphipolis, and Delium, it would have been wrong through fear of death to abandon the post to which the divine appointed him.[160] He supports this claim by two further points: He does not know whether death is to be feared, and he does know that it is wrong to commit injustice by disobeying

---

157. Of course, Socrates does characterize craftspeople as knowing many fine things, but, again, he relativizes the value of their knowledge: "But, men of Athens, the good craftsmen also seemed to me to have the same failing as the poets. Because of practicing his art well, each one thought he was very wise in other *most important* matters, and this folly of theirs obscured that wisdom" (*Ap.* 22d4–e1, with my italics).

158. With regard to the politicians: "I am wiser than this man, for neither of us really knows anything fine and good, but this man thinks he knows something, when he does not; whereas, as I do not know anything, I do not think I do. I seem then, in just this little thing to be wiser than this man at any rate, that what I do not know I do not think I know either" (*Ap.* 21d2–7). With regard to the poets: "So I went away from them also thinking that I was superior to them in the same thing in which I excelled the politicians" (*Ap.* 22c6–8). Finally, in the case of the craftsmen, Socrates determines he is wiser than they, for, although he does not possess their craft-knowledge, they additionally believe they have wisdom that they do not. Thus, Socrates' awareness of his epistemic limitations makes him wiser than they (*Ap.* 22d4–e5).

159. *Ap.* 23a6–7, b2–4.

160. *Ap.* 28d6–29a1.

one's superior whether god or man. In asserting these two points Socrates is also assuming that the divine would not have compelled him to follow a course of action that was harmful; and since the divine is superior to him, it would be wrong for him to disobey the divine injunction upon him to philosophize. Thus, these points also reflect Socrates' assumption, already introduced in his speech, that the divine has ethical expertise.

For the jurors and the intended audience of Apology, Socrates' avowal is itself a commonsensical ethical knowledge claim. As one must obey one's superior in, say, military rank, so humans must obey the divine. From a conventional perspective, then, Socrates' claim to know this is unremarkable. It would not, in the eyes of the jurors, signify that he had ethical expertise; nor, of course, does he conceive of it as such. In contrast, his claim that he does not know about death and the afterlife is unconventional. The strong contrast Socrates makes in claiming to know the one and not know the other is, among other things, supposed to highlight the relative piety and justice of his conduct in contrast to that of the jurors. Since Socrates has suggested that he is superior to his peers insofar as he does not think that he knows what he does not know, their prosecution of him for impiety is an act of injustice, for they are disobeying their human superior. In contrast, Socrates' philosophical activity is an act of piety to the extent that it is divine service. Thus his peers, by condemning him, are acting both unjustly and impiously. Furthermore, Plato, by calling into question the justification for fearing death, is conveying Socrates' relative courage and the extent to which reason governs Socrates' conduct. In contrast, Socrates' peers, in wondering how he could risk his life for philosophy, reveal both their cowardice in respect of their apprehension of death and their twofold ignorance in thinking they know that death is bad when they do not. Thus, Socrates analogizes his suggestion that death may not be something bad with his earlier point about human wisdom, that is, not thinking one knows what one does not know.

In sum, then, Socrates' ethical knowledge claims in Apology are consistent with his distinction of human and divine wisdom because they are conventional claims that neither constitute nor reflect ethical expertise. Moreover, they do not conflict with his claim of human wisdom simply because they are unrelated to this claim. Furthermore, the consistency of Socrates' avowals and disavowals of ethical knowledge and his distinction of divine and human wisdom in Apology need not be interpreted as supporting a different interpretation than the one I am suggesting of Socrates' avowals and disavowals of ethical knowledge more generally. Specifically, one can interpret Socrates' ethical knowledge claims in Apology in particular as serving specific objectives that Plato has in this dialogue, while also acknowledging that the strict intertextual inconsistency between these claims and Socrates' disavowals of ethical knowledge in other texts would not have bothered Plato and so, relative to Platonic epistemology, is insignificant.

The content of Apology is often treated as a kind of hermeneutic guide for the interpretation of the other early dialogues, especially for the early definitional dialogues. This tendency is rooted in the assumption that in its portrayal of Socrates' own defense of his discursive activity, the text is especially serviceable for clarifying the nature of the discursive activity in which Plato portrays Socrates as engaged in the other early dialogues. The fact that Socrates says nothing about definitional knowledge, the epistemological priority of definitional knowledge, or the WF question should encourage the view that Apology does not present a hermeneutic guide, or an especially precise one, for the interpretation of the other early dialogues as such. Moreover, although in my view the distinction between human and divine wisdom in Apology unproblematically maps onto Platonic epistemology in other dialogues, the phrase "human wisdom" simply does not occur outside of Apology. This suggests that although Apology is consistent with other early dialogues in this respect, Plato did not think it important to advance this manner of characterizing epistemology elsewhere. And yet if Apology were a guide for interpreting the other early dialogues, one would expect some reference to the distinction elsewhere. In fact, it seems that Plato simply found the distinction useful for conveying a particular point in Apology.[161]

I turn now to Socrates' assumption of knowledge of excellence in Laches. This assumption is remarkable in that it is the only passage in the early dialogues where Socrates claims or presumes to know the identity of excellence or a component of excellence. Furthermore, the claim is not tangential to the broader discussion in the text; it is important for the ensuing investigation insofar as Socrates later employs his view of excellence in the refutation of the final definition of courage. On the other hand, the context in which this assumption is expressed is distinctive in the way that Socrates defines the character of the investigation according to popular views of courage and excellence. I suggest that Socrates' assumption can be explained accordingly.

The investigation in Laches conforms to a-structure: It begins with popular conceptions of excellence and courage, but by the end of the investigation the conception of courage is unconventional. Yet this unconventional conception is refuted precisely because it conflicts with the conventional view that excellence has parts and that courage is a part of excellence. In this respect, the aporetic conclusion in Laches is similar to that in Lysis, where the investigation moves from the popular conception of friendship as based on likeness to an unconventional conception of friendship based on belonging. However, the investigation ends in aporia, without confirming this novel conception of friendship, because in the final stage of the discussion Lysis and Menexenus express a position that commits them to the view of friendship based on likeness that has already been rejected. The conflict from which the aporia results is thus between a conventional and an unconventional conception of friendship; however, Socrates endorses the latter and rejects the former, while his interlocutors—however consciously—commit themselves to the former. But in Laches, unlike Lysis, although Socrates plays an important role in developing the novel conception of courage described at the end of the investigation,[162] he himself is portrayed as committed to the conventional

---

161. But consider Socrates' claim in Euthydemus that he possesses the technê of a private person (295e).

162. In particular, Nicias' conception of courage is based on Socrates' view that a person is good only insofar as he is knowledgeable (La. 194d1–2).

view of F, that courage is a part of excellence, with which the unconventional view ultimately conflicts. More generally, the portrayal of Socrates at the beginning of the investigation is distinctive among the early definitional dialogues precisely in the way I have described. So while Socrates rejects the final conception of courage because it conflicts with the view he expressed at the beginning of the investigation that courage is a part of excellence, this view of courage is not Platonic. Rather, as I argued in section 2 of this chapter, Plato intended to advance (as a compelling alternative to the related conventional view) that the conception that excellence has parts and that courage is one of these parts is a conventional, prereflective view that, upon consideration of the identity of courage, emerges as untenable. Insofar as people are good because they are knowledgeable and insofar as the knowledge of what is to be feared and dared essentially is the knowledge of good and bad, courage is identical to excellence.

Socrates' claim in *Laches* contradicts a claim he makes in *Meno* not to know and not to have ever met anyone who knows what excellence is.[163] But I suggest that this very inconsistency is evidence that Plato was not troubled by some degree of inconsistency in Socrates' avowals and disavowals of ethical knowledge among the early dialogues. More specifically, due to the pedagogical-dramaturgical objectives to which a-structure is put, in *Laches* Plato felt free to portray Socrates as committed to the very conventional positions that Plato intended to problematize in that dialogue as well as to a view—that he knows what excellence is—that is remarkably atypical in light of his views elsewhere. Finally, such inconsistencies should not be resolved by some appeal to developmentalism or by ascribing to Socrates some subtle epistemological position that unifies disavowals of some ethical knowledge with avowals of other ethical knowledge. Rather, it should simply be recognized that Plato took the liberty of portraying Socrates in various ways in various texts for various ends. In short, although on a few occasions among the early dialogues Socrates avows or presumes to know some ethical knowledge, the view that there is no ordinary ethical knowledge is Platonic. Therefore, there is no reason to qualify (π). Definitional knowledge of F is necessary for all pertinent nondefinitional knowledge.

Recall that we began this chapter with the question "How should one develop an excellent character?" The Platonic view is that excellence is a single unified epistemic state, knowledge of the good. Thus, one should philosophize. Ethical knowledge is conceptualized in terms of nonethical *technê*, and *technê* is conceived as a kind of *dunamis*. Ethical knowledge qua *technê* qua *dunamis* has a distinct *ergon* (activity), namely *eudaimonia* (well-being or living well). Ethical knowledge qua *dunamis* has a distinct *relatum*, the good. The good is conceived as order. This means that ethical knowledge, which itself is a sort of psychological order, is responsible for living in an orderly way. Whether this view is noncircular depends on whether the notion of order can be explained in nonethical terms. Whether

---

163. *Men.* 77a–c.

this view is nonvacuous depends on whether the notion of order can be given a substantive explanation.

The Platonic view is that no one has knowledge of the good. Moreover, Socrates' rare avowals of ethical knowledge do not undermine this point, for they are hermeneutically innocuous. The reason that no one has ethical knowledge is that the principle of the epistemological priority of definitional knowledge (π) is Platonic, and no one has definitional ethical knowledge. Accordingly, many early dialogues portray pursuits of definitional ethical knowledge. They do not, however, portray pursuits of the definition of knowledge itself, let alone the definition of the knowledge of the good itself, since the view that *aretê* is an ethical epistemic unity is one of their central developments, not one of their points of departure.

4

METHOD

1. The Socratic Fallacy

There is a methodological problem for the very pursuit of the definitional knowledge that (π) prioritizes and requires. There seem to be only two means by which to attain definitional knowledge of F. One involves the assembly of a set of instances of F and the determination of F on the basis of common features of those instances. The other is the assembly of a set of properties possessed by F and the determination of F on the basis of those properties. But (π) insists that lacking definitional knowledge, one cannot know F's properties or entities that instantiate F. Consequently, (π) has been labeled the Socratic fallacy. Peter Geach, who is responsible for this label, puts the point this way:

> [If] the parties to a discussion are agreed, broadly speaking about the application of a term, then they can set out to find a criterion for applying it that shall yield the agreed application. On the other hand, if they are agreed on the criterion for applying the term, then they can see whether this criterion justifies the predicating ["F"] of a given example. But if there is no initial agreement either on examples of things that [possess F] or on criteria for predicating ["F"], then the discussion is bound to be abortive; the parties to it cannot know what they are about—they do not even know whether each of them means the same by saying ["F"]. Any profit they gain from the discussion will be *per accidens*; *per se* the discussion is futile.[1]

In fact, Geach's criticism is akin to a criticism Meno makes of Socrates in *Meno*: "How, Socrates, will you search for something about which you know nothing at

---

1. Geach (1966) 372.

all? For what sort of thing, among those of which you are ignorant, will you establish as the object of your search? Or if, in the best case, you happen to hit upon it, how will you know that it is the very thing of which you are ignorant?"[2] Meno is suggesting here that the pursuit of definitional knowledge of F requires *some* knowledge of F—and we might interpret this to mean knowledge of instances of F or of some of F's properties.

In view of Meno's criticism, it has been thought that in *Meno* Plato himself is acknowledging a methodological problem, namely that he is acknowledging that the pursuit of ethical knowledge in the other early dialogues is futile. Accordingly, it has been argued that *Meno* is a transitional dialogue written late in Plato's early period and that a method, standardly called the hypothetical method, which is introduced in this dialogue, is supposed to supersede the so-called elenctic method of the earlier early dialogues. Indeed, this widespread conception of Plato's epistemological development is attested as early as Richard Robinson's *Plato's Earlier Dialectic* of 1941: "With the introduction of this method [of hypothesis] he is passing from destructive to constructive thinking, from elenchus and the refutation of other men's views to an elaboration of positive views of his own."[3]

This chapter examines the elenctic and hypothetical methods. Throughout the discussion we will have the epistemological priority of definitional knowledge in mind. Since (π) is Platonic, we want to understand how Socrates and his interlocutors pursue definitional knowledge and whether Plato has an answer to Geach. I begin in section 2 with the elenchus and argue that the elenchus is not an adversarial or refutative method. In section 3, I turn to the so-called hypothetical method in *Meno*. I reject the standard account of the hypothetical method. Indeed, I argue that *hupothesis* means "postulate," that is, a cognitively secure proposition. In section 4, I argue that the method of reasoning from a postulate does not supersede any method of argumentation deployed elsewhere among the early dialogues. Rather, the so-called elenctic and hypothetical methods are, for the most part, consistent.

Section 5 explains why Plato was compelled by (π). I suggest that, for Plato, one who knows a proposition p must be able to explain why p is the case. In other words, one who knows that p must be able to give the *aitia* (cause, explanation) of p. In the sphere of ethical knowledge, definitions serve as the *aitiai* (plural of *aitia*) of pertinent nondefinitional ethical propositions. This view, in turn, provokes the question: What kind of *aitia* grounds definitional knowledge? In pursuing an answer to this question, in section 6, I examine the manner in which Socrates and his interlocutors pursue definitions of F in the early definitional dialogues. I argue that fundamental to these pursuits are identity conditions for F, which I call F-conditions, that Socrates introduces through the course of the investigations. In section 7 I examine whether these F-conditions are postulates or cognitively

2. Men. 80d5–8.
3. Robinson (1941).

secure propositions and whether, as such, they may serve to ground the pursuit of definitional knowledge.

2. Socrates' Pursuit of Definitions

Here is a common conception of the way that Socrates pursues definitional knowledge in the early definitional dialogues. Socrates asks an alleged expert to answer the WF question. The alleged expert proposes a definition of F; Socrates criticizes and rejects the proposed definition; the alleged expert proposes a second definition; Socrates criticizes and rejects this, and so on, until both discussants are fatigued or frustrated, and the investigation suspends in aporia.

This conception of the pursuit of definitions well accords with a widespread conception of the way Socrates generally pursues ethical knowledge among the early dialogues. This manner of inquiry or method of philosophizing has been called the elenchus. "Elenchus" is a Latinized form of the Greek word *elenchos*, which was used in Athenian legal contexts to mean "cross-examination" and "refutation." Conceived as such, Socrates' elenctic method is adversarial and agonistic. Socrates attempts to undermine his interlocutor's specific claim and general assumption that he possesses ethical knowledge. Gregory Vlastos is responsible for a seminal analysis, which characterizes the Socratic elenctic method according to the following conditions:

(1) Socrates' interlocutor asserts a thesis p.

(2) Socrates considers p false and targets p for refutation.

(3) Socrates secures his interlocutor's agreement to a premise set Q that includes one or more premises q, r, etc. relevant to p.

(4) Argument is from Q not to it.

(5) It is agreed that Q entails not-p.

(6) Socrates concludes not-p.

Consider an example of the elenchus in a passage from *Charmides*. Charmides' first definition (p) is that sound-mindedness is restraint. Socrates refutes this definition: He elicits Charmides' agreement to the claim (q) that sound-mindedness is always fine, and he then elicits Charmides' agreement to the claim (r) that restraint is not always fine. The set Q that includes q and r entails the negation of p. Socrates then concludes that restraint is not sound-mindedness.

In fact, Socrates' mode of inquiry, the mode in which he engages his interlocutors in the early dialogues and specifically in the definitional dialogues, is not elenctic, as Vlastos claims. It is not "a search for moral truth by question-and-answer adversary argument in which a thesis is debated only if asserted as the answerer's own belief and is regarded as refuted only if its negation is deduced from his own beliefs."[4]

---

4. (1994) 4.

Condition (1) states that Socrates' interlocutor asserts a thesis p. In the present context, this will be the proposed definition of F—in the case of *Charmides*, sound-mindedness. One common conception of the early definitional dialogues, which accords with Vlastos's conception of the Socratic elenctic method, is that Socrates tests and refutes definitions proposed by alleged experts. This view is inspired by Socrates' description of his activity in *Apology*. There he says that in order to interpret the oracle's claim that he is the wisest Greek, he went around the city examining alleged experts and, in most cases, found that they did not possess the knowledge they claimed. Accordingly, in the definitional dialogues, Socrates uses the WF question to test his interlocutor's expertise. Expertise regarding F entails having a consistent set of beliefs about F. Therefore, if the interlocutor cannot maintain a consistent set of beliefs about F, in other words if Socrates can reveal that the interlocutor is committed to p and Q and that Q entails not-p, then Socrates has shown that the interlocutor lacks expertise.

In the early definitional dialogues, Euthyphro, Laches, Nicias, Hippias, Thrasymachus, and arguably Critias are alleged experts who propose definitions of F. But if Socrates' purpose were to test these interlocutors for knowledge, it is questionable why after one or two exposures of inconsistency, the discussion of F would continue. One or two exposures of inconsistency would suffice to show that Socrates' interlocutor lacked the relevant knowledge. In this respect, only *Laches* conforms to this conception of Socrates' role in the dialogue, for after two definitions Socrates switches from Laches to Nicias as his principal interlocutor. In contrast, in *Hippias Major* Socrates allows Hippias to formulate three definitions, and in *Euthyphro* he allows Euthyphro to formulate four definitions. Note, furthermore, that Socrates never speaks of testing these interlocutors' knowledge.

Another problem with this conception is that alleged experts propose less than half of the definitions evaluated in the early definitional dialogues. Approximately twenty-nine definitions are proposed [5] Four are in *Charmides*: restraint, modesty, doing one's own thing (which is reinterpreted as doing good things), and self-knowledge (which is reinterpreted as knowledge of knowledge); three in *Laches*: paradigmatic hoplite conduct (remaining in rank, defending against the enemy, and not fleeing), toughness of the soul, and knowledge of what is to be feared and pursued; four in *Lysis*: between likes, between opposites, the neither-good-nor-bad loves the good on account of the presence of the bad, and the neither-good-nor-bad loves the first friend on account of desire; four in *Euthyphro*: prosecuting one who commits sacrilege regardless of the prosecutor's relation to

---

5. I say "approximately" because it is arguable whether given contributions constitute definitions or distinct definitions. For example, in *Euthyphro* Euthyphro's initial response to Socrates' WF question is that what he is doing now, prosecuting his father for the death of the hired laborer, is holy. Socrates replies by explaining that Euthyphro has not understood the WF question. Arguably, then, Euthyphro's response is not even intended as a definition of F. Should it be considered a definition? In *Charmides* it is considered whether sound-mindedness is doing one's own thing. In the process, doing one's own thing is reinterpreted as doing good things. Do doing one's own thing and doing good things constitute two definitions or one? Little hangs on the resolution of such questions for the present discussion.

the offender, that which is god-beloved, that which is loved by all the gods, and attention to the gods (which is reinterpreted as service to the gods); seven in *Hippias Major*: a beautiful woman, gold, paradigmatic male life (to be rich, healthy, honored by the Greeks, to live to old age, and to bury one's parents), decorousness or propriety, utility, benefit, aesthetic pleasure (reinterpreted as beneficial pleasure); three in *Meno*: managing political affairs (for a man) and managing domestic affairs (for a woman), being able to govern people, and desiring what is fine and being able to procure it; and four in *Republic* 1: telling the truth and returning what one takes, doing what is fitting (reinterpreted as aiding friends and harming enemies), aiding a friend who is good and harming an enemy who is bad, and what is good for the stronger.

Socrates himself introduces eight of these twenty-nine definitions. He introduces all four in *Lysis* and the last four in *Hippias Major*. Among these, the first two in *Lysis* are not intended to represent Socrates' own conceptions; rather, they represent conventional or traditional views or the views of some putatively wise person who is not a party to the discussion. The remaining six definitions reflect Socrates' own beliefs at the given stage of the investigation. To this it may be added that the third definition in *Laches*, which is offered by Nicias, depends upon a principle that Nicias attributes to Socrates, that a person is good insofar as he is wise. And in *Euthyphro* Socrates aids Euthyphro in the formulation of the fourth definition since, following the refutation of the third definition, Euthyphro finds himself at a loss over how to proceed. Consequently, the pursuit of definitions in the early dialogues does not always involve Socrates testing definitions proposed by his interlocutor.

Furthermore, some of Socrates' interlocutors who propose definitions are not alleged experts: Charmides in *Charmides*, Meno in *Meno*,[6] and Cephalus and Polemarchus in *Republic* 1. In fact, of the twenty-nine definitions considered in the early definitional dialogues, alleged experts propose only thirteen. In other words, more than half of the definitions proposed in the early dialogues are not proposed by alleged experts; and among those that aren't, about half are proposed by Socrates himself. *Euthyphro* and *Laches* are the only two definitional dialogues that conform fairly well to the common conception. And even in these cases, as noted, Socrates assists in the formulations of some definitions.

Regarding (2), it may be that Socrates considers *p* false and targets *p* for refutation. But put this way, Socrates' attitude in the investigation emerges somewhat misleadingly. For the most part, his attitude in the investigations is constructive and cooperative, not adversarial and refutative. He tests and evaluates definitions because he wants to determine whether they are sound. He is critical of himself and others because he is particularly sensitive to the difficulty of achieving stable well-reasoned beliefs.

---

6. Meno may derive his first definition from Gorgias, who is an alleged expert. However, there is no reason to think that he derives his other two definitions from Gorgias.

First, consider Socratic statements that indicate that Socrates' principal motive is to achieve truth, not to undermine his interlocutor. In response to Euthyphro's second definition, Socrates says, "Excellent, Euthyphro, you have now answered as I asked you to answer. However, whether it is true, I am not yet sure; but of course, you will show me that it is true."[7] In Lysis Socrates responds in dismay to his first account of friendship: "A most unaccountable suspicion came over me that the conclusion to which we had agreed was not true."[8] In Republic 1, Socrates tells Thrasymachus, "But it is clear that we must investigate to see whether or not it [Thrasymachus' definition] is true."[9] In Charmides, Charmides introduces a definition that Socrates suspects he has heard from Critias. Charmides asks whether it should matter from whom he heard it; and Socrates replies, "It makes no difference at all...One ought not to consider who said it, but whether or not it is true."[10]

Further support for the claim that Socrates seeks true definitions of F can be gained from consideration of the explicit reasons he gives in each dialogue for pursuing the definition of F. Indeed, to cite all the available evidence would be tedious. I offer a representative sample from Hippias Major and Meno.

In Hippias Major, Socrates recounts an experience he recently had listening to speeches. He judged parts of these foul and parts fine. But when he recognized that he was making these judgments, he chastised himself for assuming to know what was fine or foul without knowing what the fine itself was. To avoid this error in the future, he promised himself that if he happened to meet a wise man, he would learn from him what the fine is. Believing that Hippias is such a person, Socrates wishes to learn from him.[11] Clearly, then, in pursuing a definition of the fine with Hippias Socrates wants to gain a true definition of the fine.

In Meno, Meno, assuming Socrates to be knowledgeable, asks him how excellence can be acquired. Socrates professes not even to know what excellence is and not to have ever met a person who does. Meno, who had been a pupil of Gorgias and who is surprised by Socrates' claim, suggests that Gorgias knows. Socrates, confirming that Meno shares Gorgias' views, invites him in Gorgias' absence to tell what excellence is and so to prove him wrong in claiming never to have met anyone who knows what excellence is. In short, then, Socrates' motivation in pursuing a satisfactory definition of excellence is that he lacks knowledge of it, has never been able to find someone who possesses that knowledge, and then encounters someone who claims to have it. Clearly, then, Socrates wants to know whether the definitions Meno proposes are true.

Now consider a set of Socratic statements as evidence that Socrates' intention is not to refute his interlocutors. In Republic 1, when Thrasymachus claims that

---

7. Euthphr. 7a3–4.
8. Ly. 218c5–7.
9. R. 1, 339b2–3.
10. Chrm. 161c5–6.
11. Hp. Ma. 286c3–e4.

justice is not an excellence, Socrates says he is convinced that Thrasymachus has finally expressed his true opinion. Thrasymachus responds, "What difference does it make to you whether I believe it or not, aren't you testing the account?" And Socrates replies, "It makes no difference to me."[12]

In *Charmides*, when Critias accuses Socrates of deliberately trying to refute him without attending to the content of the investigation, Socrates answers:

> If I am thoroughly refuting you, how can you think I am doing so for any other reason than that on account of which I would scrutinize what I myself say—from a fear of carelessly supposing at any moment that I knew something without knowing it. And so I assert that here and now this is what I am doing, I am examining the argument, mostly for my own sake, but also perhaps for that of my fellows. Or do you not think it is basically a common good for all people that the nature of every entity be made clear?[13]

I take Socrates to be saying here that the fact that Critias is being refuted is incidental, that Socrates is concentrating on the argument—rather than on refuting Critias—and that he is concerned to determine what sound-mindedness is and whether sound-mindedness is what Critias says it is. Socrates' attention is so focused just because it is beneficial to have a true belief about this rather than a false one.

Compare Socrates' remark in *Gorgias*: "I think we should be contentiously eager to come to know what is true and what is false about the things we discuss, for it is a common good for all that the truth should be made evident."[14] Elsewhere in *Gorgias* Socrates says, "And why, when I have my suspicions, do I ask you and refrain from expressing them myself? It's not you I'm after; it's our discussion, to have it proceed in such a way as to make the thing we're talking about most clear to us."[15] Again, later in the dialogue Socrates explains himself:

> What's my point in saying this? It's that I think you're now saying things that aren't very consistent or compatible with what you were first saying about rhetoric. So I'm afraid to pursue my examination of you, for fear that you should take me to be speaking with eagerness to win against you, rather than to have our subject become clear. For my part, I'd be pleased to continue questioning you if you're the kind of man I am; otherwise, I would drop it. And what kind of man am I? One of those who would be pleased to refute anyone who says anything untrue, and who, however, wouldn't be any less pleased to be refuted than to refute.[16]

---

12. *R.* 1, 349a9–b2.
13. *Chrm.* 166c7–d4.
14. *Grg.* 505e4–6.
15. *Grg.* 453c1–4; compare also 454c1–5.
16. *Grg.* 457e1–458a5.

Similarly, in *Protagoras* Socrates claims, "Provided you give the answers, it makes no difference to me whether it is your own opinion or not. I am primarily interested in testing the argument, although it may happen both that the questioner, myself, and my respondent wind up being tested."[17] "I don't want you to think that my motive in talking with you is anything other than to take a good hard look at things that continually perplex me. I think that Homer said it all in the line, 'Going in tandem, one perceives before the other.'"[18] Consider also an exchange between Socrates and Protagoras:

> PROTAGORAS   I think that you just want to win the argument, Socrates...
>
> SOCRATES   I have no other reason for asking these things than my desire to answer these questions about excellence, especially what excellence itself is.[19]

In sum, the evidence suggests that Socrates is typically portrayed as cooperatively engaged in the pursuit of ethical knowledge with his interlocutors. Note, however, that in citing this evidence I do not want to claim that in discussion Socrates always pursues the truth and never attempts to refute his interlocutor. There are a few occasions where Socrates does attempt to refute his interlocutor. For example, in his exchange with Hippocrates early in *Protagoras* Socrates explicitly says to the anonymous aristocrat that he was attempting to test Hippocrates. However, Socrates' objective clearly is not to make himself look good at Hippocrates' expense. Indeed, there are no other people present at their discussion. Rather, Socrates uses argumentation to caution Hippocrates insofar as Hippocrates intends to submit his soul to Protagoras' instruction. Likewise, early in *Lysis* Socrates engages in a deliberately fallacious exchange with Lysis, the conclusion of which is the stunning claim that Lysis' parents will only love him insofar as he is knowledgeable. But here, again, Socrates' objective is philosophical, not self-aggrandizing. Also, in *Apology* Socrates deliberately refutes Meletus, and in this case he does not seem to be concerned with Meletus' education, but principally with his own self-defense. Granted such cases, in his discussions Socrates predominantly exhibits a cooperative spirit, not a critical one.

The tendency, represented by Vlastos, to view Socrates' method in the early dialogues as critical or adversarial rather than cooperative probably owes to the *results* of Socrates' examinations of his interlocutors' opinions. To a significant extent, these are negative. However, it is important to distinguish Socrates' intentions in inquiry from the results of inquiry. Furthermore, while Plato, in composing the early dialogues, sought to dramatize the conflict between Platonic philosophical views and attitudes and antiphilosophical views and attitudes (often represented by Socrates' interlocutors), the dramatization of such a conflict is consistent with Socrates having a cooperative attitude toward his interlocutors in the inquiry.

---

17. *Prt.* 333c5–9.
18. *Prt.* 348c5–d1.
19. *Prt.* 360e3–8.

Finally, it must also be emphasized, as I have to some extent shown in preceding chapters, that many of Socrates' arguments reach positive conclusions. For example, in *Ion* Socrates argues that Ion lacks a *technê*. In *Hippias Minor* he argues that the liar and honest man are the same. In *Crito* he argues that it is unjust for him to escape from prison. In *Gorgias* he argues that orators have least power in their cities and that doing what one thinks best is not the same as doing what one desires, and also that it is worse to do than to suffer injustice. In *Apology* he argues that he is innocent of impiety and corruption of the youth, and that death is not a bad thing. In *Euthydemus* he argues that knowledge is the only human good. In *Meno* he argues that knowledge is the only human good, and that everyone desires the good. In *Protagoras* he argues that sound-mindedness and intelligence are the same thing, that putative *akrasia* is a failure of knowledge, and that courage and knowledge are the same thing. In *Republic* 1, he argues that it is not the function of justice to harm people, and that justice is better, stronger, and more conducive to well-being than injustice. Indeed, in view of such examples, the idea that the Socratic method in the early dialogues merely entails the demonstration of an interlocutor's ignorance by exposing inconsistency in his belief-sets is wide of the mark.

Regarding (3), Socrates does secure his interlocutor's agreement to a premise set Q that includes one or more premises *q*, *r*, and so forth, relevant to *p*. But again, in the context of Vlastos's analysis, this may be misleading. According to Vlastos, Socrates chooses premises to which he believes his interlocutor is committed and which are inconsistent with the proposed definition. But in cases where Socrates himself has proposed the definition this makes little sense. Moreover, given the evidence for Socrates' constructive and cooperative involvement with his interlocutor in the investigation, this does not make sense in general. Rather, Socrates elicits his interlocutor's assent to a set of premises Q relevant to *p*, albeit one that entails the negation of *p*, because, more often than not, he himself is committed to Q and seeks his interlocutor's judgment of Q. Since Socrates is investigating with his interlocutor, he wants to know if his interlocutor agrees with him that Q.

In (4), Vlastos claims that argument is from Q not to it. In fact, conditions vary. Sometimes Socrates does argue for some of the premises constituting the set Q. To take the *Charmides* case again, one of the premises is that restraint is not always fine. Socrates draws this as a conclusion on the basis of a set of examples where restraint is not fine, to which he elicits Charmides' assent.

Finally, it is the case, as (5) and (6) claim, that Socrates and his interlocutor agree that Q entails not-*p* and that Socrates then concludes not-*p*. But an important qualification must be made regarding the way Socrates draws the conclusion. Consider the following question. On what grounds can Socrates conclude not-*p* on the basis of Q? The set of Q plus *p* is inconsistent. However, it is possible to reject Q rather than *p*; and Plato is well aware of this. For example, in *Protagoras* Socrates and Protagoras examine the relation between knowledge and sound-mindedness. Protagoras proposes that the two are not identical. In the course of the examination, it is agreed that each contrary has only one contrary and that both knowledge and sound-mindedness are contraries of ignorance. Consequently, Socrates says, "Then which statement are we to give up? The claim 'one thing one contrary' or the statement that knowledge and sound-mind-edness are distinct...The two statements are not very harmonious; they don't chime well together or fit in with one another."[20] In conformity with Vlastos's model, Socrates and Protagoras relinquish p, not Q or some subset of Q. But why? Vlastos considers this to be the basic puzzle of Socrates' method of inquiry; he calls it "the problem of the elenchus."

The simple solution to the problem of the elenchus is that Protagoras' commitment to the view that each contrary has only one contrary is stronger than his commitment to the view that knowledge and sound-mindedness are not the same. More generally, the fact that people are more strongly committed to some beliefs than others explains why Socrates' interlocutors and Socrates himself, when confronted with the fact that Q entails not-p, relinquish p rather than Q or some subset of Q. Moreover, commitment to a proposition entails belief that the proposition is true; therefore, one concludes that p is false, not-p true.

This resolves the problem of the elenchus in one respect, but it also exposes a deeper problem. Although Socrates or his interlocutor is relatively deeply committed to Q, the truth of not-p depends upon the truth of Q. Vlastos claims that in evaluating p, Socrates argues from, not to, Q. In that case, Q seems to include lemmas. The *Charmides* passage again provides an example. As noted above, one of the premises of Q, q, that restraint is not always fine, is a conclusion based on an argument. The other premise, r, that sound-mindedness is always fine, is an assumption that Socrates and Charmides make. Consider the way Socrates draws the conclusion of the argument: "Then sound-mindedness would not be a sort of restraint...at least (*ge*) according to this argument...for we submitted that sound-mindedness was a fine thing."[21] He is saying that sound-mindedness is not restraint, on the assumption that sound-mindedness is always fine. In short, Socrates does not categorically conclude not-p; he concludes not-p conditionally.

In fact, many of the conclusions in the definitional dialogues are qualified in this way, or, more generally, they are qualified as relative to the particular argument developed. For instance, in concluding his response to Euthyphro's second definition, Socrates says, "Then the same things would be both holy and unholy according to this argument."[22] The conclusions to the second definition in *Laches*, the first, second, and fourth definitions in *Charmides*, the second definition in *Lysis*, the fourth and, as mentioned, the second definition in *Euthyphro*, the second and seventh definitions in *Hippias Major*, and the second definition in *Republic* I are also expressed conditionally.[23]

On the other hand, Socrates does not always conclude his arguments with conditional qualifications or by relativizing the conclusions to the particular

---

20. *Prt.* 333a1–8.
21. *Chrm.* 160b7–d2.
22. *Euthphr.* 8a7–8.
23. *La.* 193d4–10; *Chrm.* 160d1–2, 174d3–7; *Ly.* 222d1–e3; *Euthphr.* 15c8–9; *Hp. Ma.* 291c6–8; *R.* 1, 331e1–2 and 334d5–8.

argument developed. Many of Socrates' conclusions are expressed categorically. In response to Laches' and Meno's first definitions, as well as Meno's second definition, Socrates more or less simply tells his interlocutor that the response is inadequate.[24] Moreover, Socrates' conclusions to the arguments in response to the third definition in *Laches*, the first definition in *Lysis*, the first and third definitions in *Euthyphro*, the first, third, fourth, fifth, and sixth definitions in *Hippias Major*, the third definition in *Meno*, and the first, third, and fourth definitions in *Republic* 1 are all unqualified.[25] For instance, in concluding his response to the first definition in *Republic* 1, Socrates says, "Then this is not the definition of justice, telling the truth and returning what one takes."[26] And in concluding his response to the third definition in *Laches*, he says, "So, what you are now describing, Nicias, will not be a part, but the whole of excellence... But, you know, we agreed that courage was a part of excellence... Then, Nicias, we have failed to discover what courage is."[27]

An obvious explanation for this mix of conditional and categorical conclusions is that Socrates has different attitudes toward the different arguments. Some he finds more compelling, others less so. Reasonable as this would seem, in fact, there isn't a compelling correlation between the character of Socrates' conclusions and the character of his commitments to Q that he employs in the arguments. For instance, in developing his arguments in response to Hippias' first and second definitions in *Hippias Major*, Socrates uses the same argument. However, his conclusion to the former is categorical, whereas his conclusion to the latter is conditional. Similarly, both the sixth and seventh definitions are rejected on the same grounds. But the conclusion to the latter argument is expressed conditionally, whereas that to the former is expressed categorically.

It is also significant that however conditionally Socrates concludes an argument, he never proceeds to reconsider the definition or to investigate the soundness of his commitment to Q. Once it has been concluded that a definition is unsatisfactory—whether or not the conclusion is expressed conditionally— Socrates suggests that his interlocutor try again to answer the WF question by posing a new definition, or he himself offers a new definition.

In view of this, it is unreasonable to infer as a general principle that the way Socrates concludes an argument in response to a proposed definition, that is, either conditionally or categorically, relates to the degree of his conviction in the soundness of the argument.[28] The deeper problem of the elenchus, therefore,

---

24. *La.* 190e7–9; *Euthphr.* 6d6–11; *Men.* 72a6–73c8, 74a7–10.
25. *La.* 199e3–11; *Ly.* 218c4–7; *Euthphr.* 6d9–e6, 10e9–11a4; *Hp. Ma.* 289d2–5, 293b10–c7 (see also 293d6–8), 294e7–9, 296d2–3, 297d3–6; *Men.* 79d6–e2; *R.* 1, 331d2–3, 335e1–5, 347d8–e1 (see also 342e6–11).
26. *R.* 1, 331d2–3.
27. *La.* 199e.
28. However, this is not to say that in *some* cases Socrates' tentativeness in drawing a given conclusion does not correlate with the strength of his conviction in the soundness of the argument. For instance, in response to the fourth definition in *Charmides*, although his argument concludes that

remains. What is the epistemic or cognitive status of assumed and undefended premises in Socratic arguments? This is a problem to which we will return in section 6 of this chapter.

In sum, however, it is misguided to view Socrates' mode of inquiry or manner of philosophizing in the early dialogues as elenctic in the sense in which Vlastos characterizes the Socratic elenchus. Rather, at least in the early definitional dialogues, when it comes to evaluating proposed definitions of F, Socrates' mode of evaluation tends to have the following form:

(1) Socrates or his interlocutor proposes a definition p.

(2) Socrates questions whether p is true.

(3) Socrates elicits his interlocutor's agreement to a premise set Q consisting of one or more premises q, r, etc. relevant to p.

(4) There may or may not be argument to Q.

(5) Q entails not-p.

(6) Socrates and his interlocutor conclude not-p conditionally or categorically.

In one respect, it is to be expected that Socrates' mode of evaluating definitions would tend to have this form. The evaluations depend on a logical principle akin to Leibniz's Law,[29] or more precisely on a pretheoretical, higher-order form of the distinctness of discernibles. According to this principle, for any two first-order properties A and B, A and B are not identical if one has a second-order property C that the other lacks. But it is not surprising that the evaluations tend to depend upon this principle, since the evaluations are of identity claims about universals, and they invariably conclude that the alleged identicals are discernible.

3.1. Hupothesis

So much for a first pass at the elenchus. We turn now to the so-called hypothetical method. At Meno 86e1–87b2, Socrates introduces Meno to a method of reasoning, which he derives from geometry and calls ex hupotheseôs. Socrates' illustration of the method ex hupotheseôs in Meno employs a geometrical construction problem: to inscribe a given area as a triangle in a given circle. Having introduced the method, Socrates applies it to the ethical problem governing his and Meno's discussion, the teachability of excellence. The application of the method to the ethical problem proceeds in two steps of uneven length. The gist of the first, brief step is the claim that if excellence is a kind of knowledge, then it is teachable. The

---

the knowledge of knowledge and all other knowledges and lack of knowledge does not exist, Socrates admits that he is not entirely competent to judge the matter (Chrm. 169a7–b1).

29. According to Leibniz's Law in its positive form, the indiscernibility of identicals, for any two putative individuals a and b, if a and b share all the same properties, then they in fact are identical. In its negative form, the distinctness of discernibles, if a and b do not share some property, then they are not identical.

second, lengthier step examines whether excellence in fact is a kind of knowledge. This step itself has two parts. The gist of the first, brief part is that if knowledge is the only psychological good, then excellence is a kind of knowledge. The second, lengthier part argues that knowledge in fact is the only psychological good. Thus, Socrates concludes that excellence is a kind of knowledge and therefore teachable. In short, the structure of this stretch of the dialogue is

86e1–87b2	Geometrical problem
87b2–c10	First step of ethical problem
87c11–87d8	First part of second step of ethical problem
87d8–89c4	Second part of second step of ethical problem

My discussion of this passage will begin with the meaning of the word *hupothesis*. In section 3.2 I will identify the *hupotheseis* (plural of *hupothesis*) in the first part of the second step of the ethical problem and in the first step of the ethical problem. In section 3.3, I will turn to the *hupothesis* in the geometrical problem. Finally, in sections 3.4 and 3.5, I will clarify how the method of reasoning introduced in the geometrical problem, which is indebted to geometrical analysis, is applied to the ethical problem.

We begin with the word *hupothesis*, whose semantic root is "something laid down." But instances of *hupothesis* typically have the more specific sense of "something underlying." The distinction of the latter sense is that the thing laid down stands in a relation of priority or fundamentality to something else. So, physically, a *hupothesis* may be an object, but, qua underlying thing, more precisely a base or foundation. Conceptually, it may be a proposition, proposal, or subject matter, but, again, more precisely a postulate, plan of action and thus source or point of departure, or the topic about which discussion is oriented.

The word *hupothesis* does not occur in Andocides, Antiphon, Lysias, Dinarchus, Demades, Lycurgus, Isaeus, Hyperides, Aeschylus, Sophocles, Euripides, Aristophanes, or Thucydides. It does occur three times in Xenophon and Aeschines, seven times in Demosthenes, and thirty-one times in Isocrates. Among these, the most common sense (occurring twenty-nine times) is "subject matter" and hence "theme" or "topic."[30] For example, authors speak of returning to and trying not to stray from their given *hupotheseis*. Nine occurrences mean "foundation."[31] For example, in the *Second Olynthiac* Demosthenes insists that "in affairs of the state, the principles (*archas*) and foundations (*hupotheseis*) must be true and just." Likewise, in the oration *To Archidamos* Isocrates writes, "but each must follow the principles which from the beginning (*ex archês*) they have made the foundation (*hupothesin*) of their lives." Another notable instance occurs in Xenophon's *Memorabilia*, book IV: "Whenever anyone argued with him on any point

---

30. Dem. 3.1, 19.242; [Dem.] 60.9; Isoc. 5.10, 83, 138, 7.63, 77, 8.18, 145, 11.9, 49, 12.4, 35, 74, 88, 96, 108, 161, 175, 15.57, 60, 68, 138, 177, 277; Aesch. 3.76, 176, 190.
31. Dem. 2.10; 10.46; [Dem.] 44.7, 60.27; Isoc. 1.48, 4.23, 6.90, 7.28; Xen. *Mem.* 4.6.13. The instance at Isoc. 15.276 seems akin to these, although more in the sense of "support" than "foundation."

without being able to make himself clear, asserting but not proving, that so and so was wiser or an abler politician or braver or what not, he would lead the whole discussion back to the *hupothesin.*"[32] Xenophon provides an illustration. An anonymous interlocutor claims that one man is a better citizen than another. To resolve the question, Socrates proposes first to consider the function of a good citizen.[33] In light of the example, the word *hupothesis* seems to mean the basic principle or concept upon which the debate turns.

Finally, four instances of *hupothesis* have the sense of "proposal."[34] Indeed, one might propose something as a foundational principle, but this is not required by the use of *hupothesis.* Rather, like "subject matter" or "topic," the thing proposed may simply be a point of orientation in a discussion or inquiry.

Hupothesis occurs thirty-four times in Plato, excluding several instances in *Meno.*[35] The three instances among the early dialogues, again excluding *Meno*, all mean "proposal" or "thesis." In *Euthyphro* Socrates refers to Euthyphro's proposed definitions of holiness as *hupotheseis.* Similarly, in *Gorgias* Socrates refers to Gorgias' definition of rhetoric as a *hupothesis.* And in *Hippias Major* Socrates refers to the definition of beauty as pleasure through sight and hearing as a *hupothesis.*

These Platonic instances in particular, but the range of uses in canonical Attic authors of the fourth century indicate that *hupothesis* does not entail hypotheticality. Consider Webster's primary definition of "hypothesis": "a tentative assumption made in order to draw out and test its logical or empirical consequences." Thus, a hypothesis is a proposition about the truth of which the hypothesizer is unsure. But, for instance, Socrates' interlocutors assert their definitions confident of knowing their subject matters.

Carl Huffman has recently discussed the verb *hupotithesthai* (to make a *hupothesis*) and the noun *hupothesis* in pre-Platonic intellectual contexts, specifically in Philolaus and in the Hippocratic corpus.[36] Huffman claims that here the concept of *hupothesis* is linked to the concept of *archê* (beginning) such that to make, literally lay down, a *hupothesis* (*hupotithesthai*) is equivalent to positing *archai* (plural of *archê*). For example, the author of *On Ancient Medicine* criticizes medical theorists for the use of *hupotheseis* in their theories. He decries as naïvely reductive the use of such postulates as the existence of the hot and the cold to explain the complexities of disease. Likewise, Huffman writes that "the author [of *Fleshes*] asserts that a common starting-point (*koinên archên*) must be postulated (*hupothesthai*), by which he means a starting-point common to the opinions of men. This sounds very much like the call for an indisputable initial premise which

32. The form *hupothesin* is the accusative case.
33. Xen. *Mem.* 4.6.14.
34. Xen. *Oec.* 21.1, *Cyr.* 5.5.13; Isoc. 2.7, 13.19.
35. Grg. 454c4; *Euthphr.* 11c5; *Hp. Ma.* 302e12; *Phd.* 92d6, 94b1, 101d2, 3, 7, 107b5; R. 510b5, 7, c6, 511a3, 5, d1, 533c1, 550c6 (twice); *Prm.* 127d7, 128d5, 136a1, 4, b2, 137b3, 142b1, 142c2, c9, 160b7, 161b8; *Tim.* 61d3; *Tht.* 183b3; *Sph.* 244c4; *Lg.* 743c5, 812a4. See also *Amat.* 134c3; *Def.* 415b10.
36. (1993) 78–92.

was seen [in *On Ancient Medicine, On the Art,* and *Diseases*]."[37] In these contexts, *hupothesis* evidently has the sense of "foundational principle."

No instance of *hupothesis* in a mathematical context predates *Meno*—even though the way in which Socrates introduces the method makes it clear that mathematicians used the word or at least the concept. Árpád Szabó proposes that Eudemus' discussion of Hippocrates of Chios' quadrature of lunes suggests that Greek mathematicians were already using *hupothesis* in the fifth century. The passage in question runs: "[Hippocrates] set down an *archên* and established as the first (*prôton etheto*) thing useful for his proof, that..."[38] And Szabó comments: "Although the word [*hupothesis*] does not occur in this sentence, the presence of such expressions as *archê, prôton* (first), and *etheto* (he established), which are either synonymous with it or related to it, seems to suggest that Eudemus is talking about a [*hupothesis*]..."[39]

The mathematical use of *hupothesis* most contemporaneous with *Meno* is a much discussed passage in *Republic* 6, where Socrates distinguishes the method of geometry and other mathematical sciences from that of dialectic. Socrates describes the mathematicians as *hupothemenoi,* that is, laying down as *hupotheseis* the odd and the even, the basic geometrical figures, the acute, right, and obtuse angles, and "other things akin to these according to each form of inquiry."[40] He then claims that the mathematicians have the following attitude toward these mathematical entities: "They treat these as things they know (*eidotes*) and as *hupotheseis*; they do not think it fit to give any explanation of them either to themselves or to others because they believe that they [the mathematicals] are evident to everyone."[41]

The *hupotheseis* here appear to be objectual rather than propositional. Possibly, as in case of the author of *On Ancient Medicine* who decries the uses of the hot and the cold to explain the complexities of disease, Socrates means that in laying down the odd and even and so forth, the mathematicians lay them down as fundamental beings, that is, fundamental to the given subdiscipline of mathematics that they study. But the main point is that the mathematicians' *hupotheseis* are not tentative or provisional. Rather, the existence, or nature, of the mathematical entities is taken to be obvious and beyond dispute: "evident to everyone." Consequently, the sense of *hupothesis* that here emerges is "a solid foundation."

Socrates proceeds to contrast the mathematicians' treatment of *hupotheseis* with that of dialecticians: "[Dialectic] treats the *hupotheseis* not as foundational principles (*archas*), but really (*tôi onti*) as under-lyings (*hupotheseis*), that is, as footholds (*epibaseis*) and springboards (*hormas*)..."[42] Here Plato is punning on

37. (1993) 82.
38. Simp. *in phys.* 9.61.5.
39. Szabó (1978) 245–46.
40. *R.* 510c5.
41. *R.* 510c6–d1.
42. *R.* 511b5–6.

the literal sense of the word *hupo-thesis*, under-lying. His idea is that putative *hupotheseis* are merely provisional anchors or bearings in the process of inquiry. On the one hand, Socrates' epistemological degradation of *hupotheseis* in *Republic* indicates an important methodological and epistemological moment in Plato's intellectual career. But on the other hand, the dialectician's rejection of mathematical *hupotheseis* as *archai* precisely confirms Huffman's claim that laying down a *hupothesis* (*hupotithesthai*) was understood in intellectual and more specifically methodological contexts as positing an *archê*.

In sum, the evidence presented strongly suggests that the introduction in *Meno* of the method *ex hupotheseôs*, which is explicitly said to derive from geometry, is not a *hypothetical* method, but rather a method of reasoning from a *postulate*.[43] The *Oxford English Dictionary* offers the following definition of "postulate": "something claimed...as a basis of reasoning, discussion, or belief; hence, a fundamental condition or principle." I will argue that the evidence from the *Meno* passage confirms this interpretation of *hupothesis*.

Finally, I would like to emphasize two complications. First, insofar as *hupothesis* in *Meno* is used to mean "postulate," rather than "hypothesis," there is a conflict between *Meno* and certain dialogues of Plato's middle period, specifically *Republic*, *Parmenides*, and arguably *Phaedo*. We have just seen that in *Republic* 6, Socrates contrasts the mathematician's and the dialectician's attitudes toward *hupotheseis*. Here the dialectician treats the mathematician's *hupotheseis* as hypotheses. Consequently, at least by the time *Republic* 6 was composed, reasoning from a *hupothesis* is no longer innocently shielded from the epistemological problem of foundations. For example, in *Parmenides*, *hupotheseis* indeed are hypotheses.

Second, when we turn to consider the specific *hupotheseis* employed in the *Meno* passage, we will find a puzzling mélange. In the geometrical illustration, we have a biconditional: If a given area possesses a given property, then the given area is triangularly inscribable in a circle; and if the given area lacks the given property, then it is not so inscribable. In the second of the two steps in the ethical inquiry, we appear to have an analytically true atomic proposition "excellence is good." Finally, in the first step of the ethical inquiry, the identity of the *hupothesis* is unclear. Most scholars take it to be the hypothesis "excellence is knowledge." Some scholars take it to be the conditional proposition "if excellence is knowledge, then it is teachable." And some scholars take it to be the analytically true atomic proposition "knowledge is teachable." In short, it is unclear whether the *hupothesis* here is explicitly, that is, linguistically, conditional; whether it is implicitly hypothetical; or whether it is neither explicitly nor implicitly hypothetical. I will maintain that the *hupothesis* is the analytically true atomic proposition "knowledge is teachable."

In short, the geometrical and ethical *hupotheseis* consist of a biconditional and two analytically true atomic propositions respectively. Thus, Socrates is willing to

---

43. Note that the word *ex* is a preposition meaning "out of" or "from."

Let us, therefore, dismiss the common reading. Instead, given that *hupothesis* here means "postulate," (d) must be interpreted as

> (d6) And it is clear, Socrates, according to the postulate [that knowledge is teachable], if indeed excellence is knowledge, that excellence is teachable.

The proposition whose status is expressed hypothetically here is "excellence is knowledge." And this is as it should be. Socrates has just argued that knowledge is the only psychological good. Thus, in expressing (2) in (d) Meno is acknowledging that the teachability of excellence depends upon the (uncontroversial) postulate (b) that knowledge is teachable and the controversial claim that excellence is knowledge.

3.3. The Geometrical Illustration

We come now to the postulate in the geometrical illustration. As I have said, the basic character of the geometrical problem is straightforward: to inscribe an area as a triangle within a circle. But Socrates' description is vague and ambiguous at several points:

> By "from a postulate" (*to ex hupotheseôs*) I mean the following—the way the geometers often inquire whenever someone puts a question to them; for example, concerning area (*chôrion*), whether this area (*tode to chôrion*) can be extended in this circle (*tonde ton kuklon*) as a triangle (*trigônon*). One of them would say, "I do not yet know if it [the area] is of that sort [that is can be so extended]; but I have, as it were, a certain postulate (*tina hupothesin*) useful for the task, the following one (*toiande*). If this area (*touto to chôrion*) is of such a kind that when one extends it along its given line (*para tên dotheisan autou grammên*), it can fall short by an area (*chôriôi*) that is of such a kind as (*toioutôi...hoion*) the extended [area] (*to paratetamenon*) itself, then one consequence follows; and on the other hand, if it is impossible for it to experience these things, then another consequence follows. Therefore, laying down a postulate (*hupothemenos*), I want to tell you what follows in the case of the extension of it [the area] (*tês entaseôs autou*) into a circle, whether it is impossible or possible."[48]

The passage involves a number of geometrical and philological difficulties. No interpretation is both compelling in itself and wholly free from problems. The so-called Cook Wilson interpretation is currently the most widely accepted, and it is the one I endorse. In order to clarify this interpretation, I will introduce a few of the exegetical problems of the passage.

Let us call the figure to be inscribed in the circle X, as shown in figure 4.1.

---

48. *Men.* 86e4–87b2.

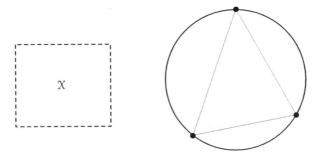

FIGURE 4.1. Basic problem

X, which is described as "this area" (*tode to chôrion* and *touto to chôrion*), can be conceived in terms of its area or its shape. We can assume that the shape of X is rectilinear, but it is unclear whether X is regular or how many sides X has. Typically these obscurities are taken to be insignificant, for, following Euclid 1.45, any rectilinear figure can be converted into a parallelogram in a given angle. Whether the necessity for such conversion is insignificant is questionable. In any event, let us refer to any such converted parallelogram as Y.

It is unclear whether X refers to a particular rectilinear figure that Socrates has drawn in the geometrical illustration that he conducted earlier in the dialogue (82b–c) or whether X refers to a rectilinear figure that he draws as he introduces the present problem. Likewise, it is unclear whether the circle to which he is referring relates to any particular figures that he has previously drawn or that he draws as he introduces the problem.

It is unclear whether Socrates has a specific kind of triangle in mind. He uses the word *trigônon* (triangle) once, but without qualification. Interpreters often assume that the triangle is isosceles. But there is no explicit evidence for this.

It is unclear whether in presenting the problem, Socrates is seeking an actual solution or rather the determination of the possibility of a solution. On this point, it is worth quoting Wilbur Knorr's comments at some length:

> A remarkable feature of the *Meno* passage is that it expresses the mathematical project not as the actual *solution* of a problem, but rather as the determination of the *possibility* of its solution. This has led many to view the passage as discussing a "diorism" [*diorismos*], that is, the statement of the necessary condition for the solvability of the problem. But in the mathematical literature diorisms have the form of explicit conditions on the givens of the problem. In the present case, this might be the statement that the given area must be less than [or equal to] the area of an equilateral triangle inscribed in the circle;[49] having verified this relation to hold for

---

49. The equilateral triangle is the triangle of maximum area that can be inscribed in a circle.

particular values of the givens, one would know that the problem is solvable in this case, even before one has begun the solution of the problem as such. Although it is often the case that the analysis of a problem reveals the appropriate form of diorism, nevertheless, the articulation of the diorism is quite different from the analysis or reduction of the corresponding problem. We thus have to explain why Plato here frames this example of problem reduction as if it were equivalent to the determination of possibility.[50]

X is said to be extended *para tên dotheisan autou grammên*, literally "along the given line *of it*." The pronoun *autou* (it) has variously been interpreted to refer to the circle, to X, or to Y. For example, according to one interpretation, the line in question is the diameter of the circle, whereas others have claimed that the given line is the base of X or of the converted parallelogram Y. Related to this problem is

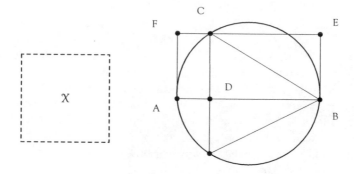

FIGURE 4.2. Cook Wilson 1

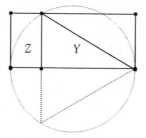

FIGURE 4.3. Cook Wilson 2

50. Knorr (1986) 73.

the question of the meaning of "given." For example, if the line (grammên) refers to the base of Y, then "given" means *resulting* from the conversion of X into Y. But if the line refers to the diameter of the circle, then "given" means *produced before* X is applied to the circle.

Furthermore, whatever figure is applied to the circle, the success of the inscription requires that it fall short by a figure Z of such a kind (*toioutôi . . . hoion*) as the figure applied. It is unclear whether the correlatives here mean that the area of Z is *equal* to the area of X or Y or whether the shape of Z is *similar* to that of X or Y.

According to the Cook Wilson interpretation, Socrates offers a reduction of the problem by means of geometrical analysis, rather than an actual solution to the problem (see figs. 4.2 and 4.3). Precisely, the problem reduces to the problem of applying X to the diameter of the circle (ΛB) such that the applied figure BDCE (= Y) falls short by a similar figure DAFC (= Z).

According to the Cook Wilson interpretation, the phrase *toioutôi . . . hoion* means that Y and Z are geometrically similar, not equal. Consequently, Socrates first uses the word *chôrion* to refer to equal areas of X and Y, but then to the similar shapes of Y and Z. The phrase *para tên dotheisan autou grammên* (along the given line of it) refers to the diameter of the circle. The pronoun *autou* (it), which is here in the genitive case, is possessive; thus, the more fluid translation "its given line," compared to "the given line of it." But possession may be variously conceived. I suggest that the sense here is equivalent to the sense that we have when, for example, with regard to driving on the highway, we criticize a driver for not sticking to *his* lane. Here we mean that the lane *belongs to him* in the sense that it is *for the driver to drive on*. Accordingly, X's given line is the line for X to be extended along, in other words, the line to which X is to be applied. In this case, this line is the diameter of the circle.

Note that in theory any area can be extended along any line segment such that it equals, exceeds, or falls short of that line. Accordingly, the application of a figure to a line on what we would call the X-axis requires a correlative line on the Y-axis. Compare Euclid 1.42, the first problem to employ techniques for the application of areas in *Elements*.[51] The problem is to construct a parallelogram (see fig. 4.4)—the result here is EFGC—equal to a given triangle ABC in a given rectilinear angle D. Note that in the diagram shown in figure 4.4 ∠CEF = ∠D.

Here the altitude of the triangle, specifically the vertex A, determines the correlative points that constitute a straight line parallel to the line to which the figure is applied. In the case of the Cook Wilson interpretation, X's application to the diameter of the circle is correlative to a point on the circumference of the circle, for example, point C in figure 4.2, Cook Wilson diagram 1.

The equilateral triangle is the triangle of maximum area that can be inscribed within a circle. In other words, this constitutes the limiting condition or diorism of

---

51. On the technique of application of areas, see Euclid, proposition 1.44, with discussion by Heath (1908) 343–45.

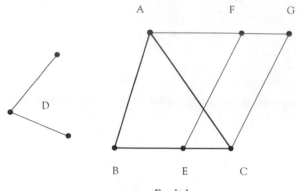

FIGURE 4.4. Euclid 1.42

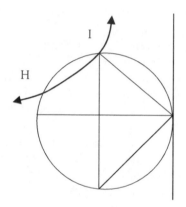

FIGURE 4.5. Hyperbola

the problem. Therefore, if the area of X is equal to the area of the equilateral triangle, there is only one solution to the problem. However, if the area of X is less than the area of the equilateral triangle, there will be two solutions. In that case, the problem is equivalent to that of finding two mean proportionals between two given lengths. The point or points (H and I in figure 4.5) on the circumference of the circle determining the length and height of the possible solutions will lie in a hyperbola whose asymptotes are the diameter of the circle and tangent at its endpoint.

The actual solution cannot be achieved by ruler and compass, but requires the use of conics. In the second half of the fifth century, Hippocrates of Chios had reduced the problem of cube duplication to the problem of finding two mean proportionals between two given lengths. And around 370, at the earliest, Menaechmus, a mathematician working within the Academy, had solved the problem of finding two mean proportionals through the use of conic sections. Menaechmus' solution, then, postdates the composition of *Meno*. Thus, Wilbur Knorr concludes that "Plato's emphasis on the possibility of the inscription might be taken to signify that geometers had then discovered the diorism, but not the actual solution of this problem."[52]

So much then for a basic account of the Cook Wilson interpretation. Let us now state the geometrical *hupothesis* that follows from this interpretation. First, recall Socrates' words:

> I have, as it were, a certain postulate (*hupothesin*) useful for the task, the following one. If this area is of such a kind that when one extends it along its given line, it can fall short by an area that is of such a kind as the extended [area] itself, then one consequence follows; and on the other hand, if it is impossible for it to experience these things, then another consequence follows.

In accordance with the Cook Wilson interpretation, this *hupothesis* is interpreted as

(e) If X can be applied to the diameter of the circle so that
   the application yields Y and Z, then X can be inscribed
   as the triangle; and if not, not.

Observe that (e), like (a) and (b), is true and regarded by Socrates as such. In other words, (e) is not a hypothetical proposition. I emphasize that this is so, even though (e) is a conditional proposition. As stated above, hypotheticality is an epistemic attitude; conditionality is a syntactic form. While a conditional sentence may also be hypothetical, it need not be. In short, (e) shares with (a) and (b) the characteristic of being *nonhypothetical*.

What is distinctive about (e) qua *hupothesis* relative to (a) and (b), then, is that (e) is a conditional, whereas (a) and (b) are atomic propositions. Evidently, for Socrates and so Plato *hupotheseis* may assume either form. It is not hard to see the reason for this. Let us call the property of being able to be applied to the diameter of a circle such that the resulting applied figure falls short of the diameter by a figure similar to the applied figure the *elliptic-property*; and let us call the property of being able to be inscribed as a triangle in a circle the *inscription-property*. Observe, then, that (e) depends upon the following atomic proposition: An area that has the elliptic-property has the inscription-property. From this it follows that if X has the elliptic-property, then X has the inscription-property. In other words, the *hupothesis* in the geometrical illustration simply involves the application of the principle to the given figure X. Conversely, turning to the ethical problem, it would have been reasonable for Socrates to have expressed the *hupotheseis* as the following conditionals: If excellence is knowledge, then excellence is teachable; and if knowledge is the only psychological good, then knowledge is excellence.

---

52. (1986) 73.

3.4. Geometrical Analysis

According to the Cook Wilson interpretation, elucidation of the geometrical illustration involves reference to the method of geometrical analysis. Indeed, it has been suggested that the method *ex hupotheseôs*, which Socrates says he is deriving from geometry, is specifically indebted to the method of geometrical analysis. Granted this, precisely how the method *ex hupotheseôs* is indebted to geometrical analysis requires clarification. To begin, it will be helpful to clarify the method of geometrical analysis itself.[53]

The twentieth century was shot through with debate over the nature of Greek geometrical analysis. Most of the debate concerns the *direction* of analysis.[54] Jaakko Hintikka and Unto Remes have suggested that unfortunately this is "one of the more superficial" aspects of analysis.[55] But contrast Ali Bebhoud's more recent assessment: "It makes a cognitive difference whether one is looking for premises of or deriving conclusions from given propositions... differences which have an effect on analysis as a heuristic method... Therefore, the directional aspect of geometrical analysis... is important and deserves detailed consideration."[56] The clarification of the direction of analysis *is* crucial to the understanding of the significance of the method for Plato. The horns of the basic dilemma pertain to whether analysis proceeds "upward" or "downward."

Analysis is a method of discovery. The analyst seeks to determine whether a theorem is true (theoretical analysis) or whether a construction is possible (problematic analysis). The theorem or construct is called the thing-sought (*to zêtoumenon*). The analysis begins by assuming the truth of the theorem or the existence of the construct. The nature of the next step in the procedure is at the heart of the controversy. Hintikka and Remes articulate the problem well:

> Does analysis consist of (1) drawing logical conclusions from the desired theorem, or (2) in looking for the premises from which such conclusions (ultimately leading to the theorem) can be drawn?[57]

Proposition (1) suggests that the analyst draws logical consequences from the assumed thing-sought. The drawing of consequences stops when the analyst hits upon something independently known to be true. Consider the definition given by

---

53. Beware hereafter of confusing geometrical analysis with the concept of analysis as it is commonly used in philosophy.

54. Throughout this section, it is useful to bear in mind the following distinctions: (1) *geometrical use* of analysis, in general or in a given case, individual, or historical period; (2) *geometers' descriptions* of analysis, in general or in a given case, individual, or period; (3) *philosophical use* of geometrical analysis, in general or in a given case, individual, or period; and (4) *philosophical description* of geometrical analysis, in general or in a given case, individual, or period. None of these needs to correspond to another—although we may hold out the hope that a philosopher's or mathematician's description will correspond to his or another's practice.

55. (1974) 11.

56. (1994) 56–57.

57. Hintikka and Remes (1974) 11; I have inserted numerals to facilitate discussion.

the scholiast on Euclid 13.1–5: "Analysis is the taking of what is sought, as if admitted, through the things that follow . . . to something admitted as true." In this case, the direction of analysis is conceived as "downward,"[58] that is, by deduction from the thing-sought to its consequences.

In contrast, (2) suggests that the analyst seeks the premises from which the thing-sought is deducible, the premises from which those premises are deducible, and so on, until one hits upon a first principle or proven theorem. Consider Pappus' account: "In analysis . . . we suppose the thing-sought to be done and look for that from which it follows, and again the antecedent of the latter, until, by so working backwards, we arrive at something that is already known or has the status of a first principle." In this case, the direction of analysis is conceived as being "upward," from the thing-sought through its antecedents. The idea is that axioms, definitions, first principles, or more fundamental theorems preside over, govern, or control the rest.

The principal datum upon which the debate has turned is Pappus' description at the beginning of book 6 of his *Collection* (composed ca. 340 CE), the most complete description of analysis to survive from antiquity. The problem is that Pappus appears to give two contradictory accounts, the first favoring the downward interpretation, the second favoring the upward interpretation. Most scholars favor the downward interpretation.

Adjudicating between the upward and downward interpretations involves consideration of the relation of analysis to the complementary method of synthesis. The basic question is what synthesis contributes to analysis. For instance, assume the downward interpretation of analysis where one begins with the assumption of the thing-sought and deduces to something independently known. In that case, synthesis reverses the procedure and reasons from the thing independently known to the thing-sought. For example, Heron (2nd–3rd c. CE) describes synthesis as follows: "We begin from a thing known; then we compose until the thing-sought is found." The problem here is the reversibility or convertibility of the deductions from the thing-sought to the thing independently known; P's implication of Q does not assure Q's implication of P. Successful analysis, therefore, requires convertible implications, in other words, equivalences. In contrast, according to the upward interpretation of analysis, where one reasons from the assumed thing-sought through premises from which the thing-sought can be deduced to more fundamental theorems or first principles, synthesis simply is the natural deduction of the thing-sought from premises. Consider Pappas: "In synthesis, on the other hand, reversing the procedure we posit as already done that which was last found in the analysis, and arranging in their natural order as consequents what were there antecedents and linking them one with one another, we arrive finally at the construction of the thing sought." Accordingly, here where analysis involves the logic of discovery, synthesis involves the logic of demonstration.

---

58. Despite the word "up" (*ana*), which occurs in the scholiast's definition.

In arguing that Plato was aware of analysis as a geometrical practice, Stephen Menn cites several passages from Aristotle that both name and describe analysis; among them, *Posterior Analytics* 1.12, 78a6–13, and *Sophistical Refutations* 16, 175a26–8. The passage from *Posterior Analytics* runs:

> If it were impossible to prove (*deixai*) truth from falsehood, it would be easy to analyze (*to analuein*), for then the propositions would necessarily convert (*antistrephein*). Let A be something that is the case; and if A is the case, then *these* things are the case (things which I know to be the case—call them B). From the latter, then, I will prove that the former is the case. (In mathematics conversion is more common because mathematicians assume nothing incidental, but only definitions—and in this too they differ from those who argue dialectically.)[59]

This passage indicates that Aristotle conceives of analysis according to the downward interpretation, and it is further supported by the passage from *Sophistical Refutations*: "Sometimes too it happens as with diagrams; for there we can sometimes analyze (*analusantes*) the figure, but not construct (*suntheinai*) it again."[60] As I have noted, according to the upward interpretation of analysis, the problem of conversion does not arise. So this passage supports the view that Aristotle understood geometrical analysis according to the downward interpretation.

Menn, who endorses the Cook Wilson interpretation of the geometrical problem in *Meno*, proposes the following analysis to explain Socrates' articulation of the geometrical *hupothesis*:

> So let BCG be an isosceles triangle, BC = BG, inscribed in the circle [see fig. 4.6]; the diameter BA perpendicularly bisects the chord CG at a point D. Connect AC. The angle ACB is inscribed in a semicircle, and is therefore a right angle. So the triangles ADC and CDB are similar, to each other and to the triangle ACB. So, completing the rectangles ADCF and CDBE, we see that these rectangles are similar, and therefore the rectangle CDBE falls short of the line AB by a figure similar to itself. Since the rectangle CDBE is double the triangle CDB, which is half the triangle BCG, it follows that CDBE = BCG; but BCG = X, so CDBE = X. So the given area X has been applied to a diameter of the given circle in the form of a rectangle, in such a way that it falls short of the diameter by a figure similar to the applied area.[61]

Recall that, according to the Cook Wilson interpretation, analysis is employed in Socrates' geometrical problem not to solve the problem, but to *reduce* one problem (the triangular inscription of an area into a circle) to another (the application of areas). Indeed, it has been suggested that the method of analysis was originally employed to reduce less tractable problems to more tractable ones.

---

59. The translation is influenced by Barnes (1993) 19.
60. The translation follows Pickard-Cambridge in Barnes (1984) 298.
61. (2002) 212.

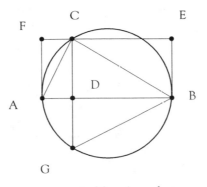

FIGURE 4.6. Menn's analysis

For example, I mentioned that Hippocrates of Chios reduced the problem of cube duplication to the problem of finding two mean proportionals. There is a remarkable passage in *Prior Analytics* where Aristotle illustrates reduction (*apagôgê*) by an example strongly reminiscent of the ethical section of our *Meno* passage:

> By reduction we mean an argument in which the first term clearly belongs to the middle, but the relation of the middle to the last term is uncertain, though equally or more convincing than the conclusion ... For example, let A stand for what can be taught, B for knowledge, and C for justice. Now it is clear that knowledge can be taught; but it is uncertain whether excellence is knowledge. Now if BC is equally or more convincing than AC, we have a reduction ... [62]

This passage lends support to the Cook Wilson interpretation of the geometrical passage in *Meno*, to the view that the *hupothesis* in the passage alludes to geometrical analysis, and to the view that the analysis alluded to was used to reduce one problem to another.

3.5. The Method of Reasoning from a Postulate

The results of the preceding discussion provoke several questions. If the geometrical problem that Socrates uses to illustrate reasoning *ex hupotheseôs* involves analysis, we would expect the ethical problem to do so as well. We have just seen independent evidence from Aristotle's *Prior Analytics* that suggests that the examination of the ethical problem relates to reduction. But it is unclear precisely how geometrical analysis relates to the ethical problem. Indeed, it is unclear precisely how geometrical analysis relates to the geometrical problem, or, more

---

62. 2.25.

specifically, how it relates to the *hupotheseis* employed in the examination of the geometrical and ethical problems. Finally, it is unclear what role the *hupotheseis* in both the geometrical and ethical problems play.

Let's begin with the geometrical problem. In this case, Socrates' examination does not actually deploy analysis to reduce the problem of triangularly inscribing X in a circle. Rather, the geometrical *hupothesis* depends upon reduction *yielded by prior analysis*. To be more precise, we should distinguish two aspects of the *hupothesis*, the principle itself, that which has the elliptic-property has the inscription-property, and the application of the principle to a given figure X. The principle is the result of analysis that has occurred prior to and independently of the geometrical illustration. The actual *hupothesis* involves the application of the given figure X to the principle. Accordingly, reasoning *ex hupotheseôs* here means using something cognitively secure—in this case achieved by the method of geometrical analysis—to advance inquiry into something unknown. In other words, one reasons *from* the postulate *toward* the goal of inquiry.

In the case of the first step of the ethical problem, it appears that analysis—or, if you will, a method analogous to analysis—occurs. Socrates reasons:

> (1) What sort of being pertaining to the soul would excellence be if it were to be teachable or not teachable? (2) Firstly, if it were different from or such as knowledge, then it would be teachable or not teachable ... (3) Or is this at least clear to everyone, that there is nothing else that a person learns except for knowledge? ... (4) Then if excellence is a sort of knowledge, it is clear that it is teachable.[63]

The question governing the inquiry is whether excellence is teachable. Strictly, then, we would expect the analysis to begin with the assumption that excellence is teachable and to proceed with deduction from the assumption. Indeed, Socrates begins in a comparable way; (1) is similar to the question, "If we were to assume that excellence were teachable, what would this imply about excellence?"

Step (2), then, begins the deduction from being teachable to being a sort of knowledge. This step in the argument is clearly based on the proposition that knowledge is teachable, whose cognitive security is independent of the argument. As such, the proposition is akin to a geometrical proposition that a mathematician would know independently of and prior to the analysis and thus one that he could confidently deploy in the analysis. The striking difference, of course, is that such propositions of geometry were not only already to some extent formalized and systematized, but, in comparison with the range of propositions that might be deployed in the analysis of an ethical problem, extremely limited in number. Consequently, in ethical analysis a great deal more would be demanded of intuition.

Step (3) adds important information to the deduction. As we emphasized in our brief account of analysis, the success of analysis depends upon deductions that

---

63. *Men.* 87b5–c6. I have inserted numerals to facilitate exegesis.

are convertible, in other words, equivalences. In the case of the geometrical illustration, the elliptic- and inscription-properties are equivalent. Here too in the first step of the ethical problem, specifically in (3), Socrates is careful to deduce not merely that being teachable implies being a kind of knowledge, but that since a person learns nothing except knowledge, the two are equivalent.

It is the convertibility of the deduction that explains what would otherwise be a puzzling conclusion to the first step of the ethical problem. Having used the postulate that knowledge alone is teachable to complete the deduction, Socrates now draws the inference in (4) that if excellence is knowledge, then it is teachable. If Socrates were analyzing the assumption that excellence is teachable, we would instead expect him to conclude with the inference that if excellence is teachable, then excellence is knowledge. Strictly speaking, then, what we have in (4) is not the conclusion of the analysis, but what would in fact be the first step in the synthesis of the problem. Observe that the *hupothesis* in the geometrical problem has the same form. The conditional is not "if X has the inscription-property, then X has the elliptic-property"; rather, it is "if X has the elliptic-property, then X has the inscription-property." Of course, in both cases, the conditional does not mark the actual first step in the synthesis of the problem. Instead, the conditional expresses the reduction of the problem as the result of analysis. In other words, the conditional states that if it were the case that X or excellence had the elliptic-property or were a sort of knowledge, then the problem would be solved. So, in short, the analysis in the first step of the ethical problem serves to reduce one problem, the teachability of excellence, to another, the epistemic character of excellence.

Finally, as in the case of the geometrical problem, here in the first step of the ethical problem the *hupothesis*, which is something cognitively secure, serves to advance inquiry into that which is unknown. More precisely, we can say that the *hupothesis* serves as such in the analysis of the problem, which results in the reduction of the original problem to a different problem. In contrast, in the geometrical problem, the *hupothesis*, which includes the principle as well its application to the given figure X under examination, does not serve in the analysis, but in the expression of the reduction itself resulting from the analysis.

As I noted previously, the second step of the ethical problem has two parts. The first (87c11–d8), akin to the first step of the ethical problem, involves the reduction of one problem to another. The second part (87d8–89c4) involves an argument that knowledge is the only psychological good.[64] It is the first part that concerns us. It runs:

> (1) After this, it seems, we ought to inquire whether excellence is knowledge or different from knowledge... (2) What then? Do we affirm that excellence is a good thing. And does this postulate stand firm for us?... (3) Then if there is something that is both good and separate from knowledge, perhaps excellence would not be a sort of knowledge. But if there is nothing

---

good that knowledge fails to encompass, then our suspicion that it is a sort of knowledge is a good suspicion.[65]

Having employed analysis to reduce the problem of the teachability of excellence to the problem of the epistemic nature of excellence, the second step of the ethical problem begins in (1) with the statement of this problem: to determine whether excellence is a sort of knowledge. Here too analysis of the problem follows. This is confirmed by comparison with the analysis in the first step of the ethical problem. However, here in the second step, the order of reasoning differs. If the reasoning in the (first part of the) second step paralleled that in the first step, we would begin with an expression of the assumption that excellence is a sort of knowledge. But we get no question such as "What sort of being would excellence be if it were to be a sort of knowledge?" Next, we would expect the claim that knowledge alone is good and the deduction that if excellence is good, then excellence is a kind of knowledge. The reason why Socrates does not proceed in this way is as follows. It is controversial whether knowledge is the only (psychological) good. In contrast, it is uncontroversial that excellence is (psychological) goodness, in other words, that excellence is the only (psychological) good. Indeed, this, like the proposition that knowledge is teachable, is cognitively secure. Accordingly, instead of seeking to identify excellence with a sort of knowledge, Socrates attempts to identify knowledge with excellence.

We must, then, assume that the second step in the ethical problem proceeds upon the implicit question, "What sort of thing would knowledge be, if it were excellence?" Accordingly, (2) states the cognitively secure *hupothesis* regarding excellence; and (3) deduces that if knowledge is the only (psychological) good, then excellence is a kind of knowledge.

There are two points to observe about the deduction in (3). First, Socrates clearly recognizes the significance of the distinction between equivalence and mere implication: "If there is something that is both good and separate from knowledge, perhaps (*tach'*) excellence would not be a sort of knowledge." That is, he recognizes that the identification of knowledge with excellence requires that knowledge be the only psychological good. In other words, successful analytic deduction requires an equivalence: "If there is nothing good that knowledge fails to encompass, then our suspicion that it is a sort of knowledge is a good suspicion."[66]

Second, as in the first step of the ethical problem, the conditional in (3) does not state the deduction we would expect from analysis. We would expect the following: If excellence is a sort of knowledge (= the assumption of the thing-sought), then knowledge is (the only psychological) good. Instead, in (3) we get what appears to be the first step in the synthesis of the problem. But here again, (3) does not actually serve as the first step in the synthesis; instead, it is a statement of the reduction resulting from analysis. That is, the problem of determining whether excellence is a

---

65. *Men.* 87c11–d8. I have inserted numerals to facilitate exegesis.
66. Incidentally, note that what *is* hypothetical here, the identification of knowledge with excellence, is described as a suspicion.

sort of knowledge has been reduced to the problem of determining whether knowledge is the only psychological good. And, finally, as in the first step in the ethical problem, the *hupothesis*, as something cognitively secure, serves in the analytic process to reduce one problem to another.

In sum, it emerges that Socrates' method of reasoning *ex hupotheseôs* at *Meno* 86e1–87d8 derives from the method of geometrical analysis. More precisely, it derives from the particular use of geometrical analysis to reduce one less tractable problem to another more tractable one. *Hupotheseis* themselves, which are employed in the process, are not hypotheses, but cognitively secure propositions useful for those employing the method for purposes of reduction. Generally speaking, Socrates' presentation of the method *ex hupotheseôs* suggests that when seeking whether x has a property P, something that we do not know, we attempt to identify another property Q possessed by all things that have P, something that is cognitively secure. In that case, instead of inquiring whether x has P, we can inquire whether x has Q. The procedure is valuable precisely insofar the question whether x has Q may be more tractable than the question whether x has P.

Finally, it is worth reiterating that at *Meno* 86e1–87d8 analysis is not used to solve a problem. Having reduced the problem of the epistemic character of excellence to the problem of the (psychological) goodness of knowledge, Socrates proceeds to argue (87d8–89c4), by nonanalytic means—indeed, by means familiar from elsewhere among the early dialogues—that knowledge is the only psychological good and thereby to solve the problem.[67]

4. *Elenchus* and *Hupothesis*

As we have seen, the method *ex hupotheseôs* does not, in the face of ignorance or uncertainty, crucially employ a hypothetical proposition in order to advance inquiry. On the contrary, in the face of ignorance or uncertainty, the method *ex hupotheseôs* crucially employs a cognitively secure proposition to advance inquiry.

The standard view is that the method *ex hupotheseôs* is a hypothetical method *and* that it supersedes the so-called elenctic method employed in pre-*Meno* early dialogues. Having rejected the first conjunct, it remains to consider the second. Strictly, the second depends upon the first; so the rejection of the first implies the rejection of the second: The hypothetical method does not supersede the elenctic method *because there is no hypothetical method.* Even so, an important question remains: How does the method of reasoning from a postulate relate to the so-called elenctic method?

It is helpful to distinguish four aspects of a given Socratic method. The first is Socrates' *intention* in inquiry. The "hypothetical" method is typically said to contrast with the elenctic method in that the former is constructive, while the latter is critical. For instance, as we have seen, Gregory Vlastos characterizes the elenchus

---

67. Recall that in the discussion of this argument in section 3 of chapter 3, I also discussed the similar argument for the goodness of knowledge in *Euthydemus.*

as "adversarial"; and Hugh H. Benson claims that Socrates' immediate intention is to expose his interlocutor's false conceit of knowledge.[68]

The second is the *result* of inquiry. This might naturally correspond to Socrates' intention. For example, the result of elenctic inquiry may be rejection of the interlocutor's theses, while the result of "hypothetical" inquiry may be affirmation, if only ultimately tentatively or hypothetically, of some positive thesis. However, a positive result need not follow from a positive intention, and a negative result need not follow from a critical intention. So the questions of Socrates' intentions and the results of inquiry are distinct.

Third, the method *ex hupotheseôs* is introduced to advance inquiry at a point in the discussion where the interlocutors find themselves unsure how to grapple with a particular problem at hand. The reduction of the question whether excellence is teachable to the question whether excellence is knowledge is intended to make the former question more tractable. I will speak of this as the *use* of the method. Accordingly, we may ask how the use of the method *ex hupotheseôs* relates to the use of the elenctic method.

Fourth and finally, we may ask about the *epistemological condition* of the method. As I have argued, the *hupotheseis* in the *Meno* passage, far from being hypotheses, are cognitively secure propositions. Accordingly, at least within the *Meno* passage, Socrates pursues knowledge on the basis of what he takes to be cognitively secure propositions. We may, then, ask how this compares with the epistemological condition of the elenctic method.

I begin consideration of the relation between the method of reasoning from a postulate and the so-called elenctic method with the question of Socrates' intentions. As we have seen, the standard conception of the elenchus is that it is an adversarial method. But I have also argued that this view is misguided. Socrates is typically portrayed as cooperatively engaged in the pursuit of ethical knowledge with his interlocutors. For instance, Socrates tests proposed definitions because he himself wants to determine whether they are true, and he rejects proposed definitions because he believes that there are good grounds for thinking that they are false. The refutations of his interlocutors' positions is a consequence of the interlocutors' unsatisfactory reasons for holding particular positions and Socrates' disclosure of these reasons; it is not a function of Socrates' desire to undermine his interlocutors. In short, Socrates' intentions in the so-called elenchus are not critical.

Regarding the results of the so-called elenctic method, I have also shown that a number of early dialogues and a number of arguments within early dialogues do not merely conclude with the rejection of some thesis proposed by Socrates' interlocutor or Socrates himself.[69] Among the early dialogues we find Socrates

---

68. Vlastos (1983), Benson (2000).
69. I emphasize that I am not claiming that on the basis of any of these positive arguments, Socrates believes that he has achieved ethical *knowledge*. However, these arguments do provide Socrates with reasons to believe the conclusions.

developing arguments for positive ethical theses. Consequently, his method in the early dialogues is not necessarily a negative method with respect to its results.

We come now to the *use* of the elenchus. But given the immediately preceding points as well as our discussion in section 2 of this chapter, we must conclude that there is no such thing as the elenchus or elenctic method, as it is commonly conceived. Thus, there is no use of *the* elenchus among the early dialogues. Granted this, we may still inquire into Socrates' method among the early dialogues, whatever that method is.

We have observed that the method of reasoning from a postulate is introduced to make a less tractable question more tractable. We may ask then whether such situations arise among the early dialogues, and if so how Socrates handles them. Moments of aporia in the course of investigations and thus moments of questioning how to proceed occur among the early dialogues, of course. However, in fact there is no case where Socrates proceeds by reducing a more difficult question to a less difficult one, as he does in the *Meno* passage. This is a genuine distinction of the *Meno* passage. Indeed, this is a feature that distinguishes the use of *hupotheseis* in the *Meno* passage from the use of *hupotheseis* in *Phaedo*, *Republic*, and *Parmenides* as well.[70]

In sum, the standard view is that the constructiveness of the method in *Meno* is its distinguishing feature. But this view is based on the false belief that Socrates' earlier method is elenctic in the sense of critical and adversarial. Accordingly, it is not the constructive use of *hupotheseis* that distinguishes the method *ex hupotheseôs*. Rather, it is the *reductive* use of *hupotheseis*. As such, the momentousness of the introduction of the method in *Meno* has certainly been misconceived and also overblown.

Finally, we have to consider the relation between the epistemological condition of the method of reasoning from a postulate in *Meno* and among the early dialogues. Epistemologically, the distinctiveness of the method in *Meno* concerns the cognitive status of the *hupotheseis*. As I have repeatedly emphasized, the *hupotheseis* are not hypothetical, but cognitively secure. Accordingly, we must question precisely what it means to speak of the *hupotheseis* in *Meno* as "cognitively secure."

Throughout the discussion of the *Meno* passage, I deliberately avoided stating that Socrates or his interlocutor *knows* the *hupotheseis*. The two descriptions might be equivalent. But in fact Socrates never claims to know the *hupotheseis* he uses. As we have seen, in the case of the *hupothesis* in the second ethical section, Socrates says that it stands firm, literally, it remains (*menei*). It is fair to assume that Socrates thinks the other two *hupotheseis* also stand firm. The question is what this amounts to.

---

70. We have seen, however, that sometimes among the early dialogues *reductio* is employed, the outstanding example of this being Socrates' critique of *akrasia* in *Protagoras*. *Reductio* is a form of analysis, a negative form. It is proven that the thing-sought is false or cannot be constructed, for reasoning from its assumption results in something false.

Given the focus of the early dialogues on the problem of ethical knowledge and Socrates' repeated emphasis on the problems of putative ethical knowledge, it may be argued that we should resist the inference that the postulates in the ethical sections of the *Meno* passage are known propositions. On the other hand, examining the *Meno* passage we could very well bracket the general epistemological concerns of the early dialogues and say that Plato here allows the postulates in the ethical sections to stand as known propositions. But this is not hermeneutically significant for the general question of Platonic epistemology in the early dialogues. Indeed, Socrates' real point in the *Meno* passage is not that there are *and he has* epistemologically foundational propositions on the basis of which to build ethical knowledge. Rather, his emphasis lies in the procedure of reducing one problem to another through the employment of *relatively* secure propositions. In that case, the postulates in the ethical sections qua known propositions should be conceived as dialectically expedient.

Perhaps this is the right way to handle the problem—but, then again, perhaps not. There are at least two substantive alternatives that ought to be weighed. First, let us assume that the *hupotheseis* indeed are known and that this knowledge is not to be insulated, as dialectically expedient, from the epistemology of the early dialogues more broadly. In this case, the geometrical *hupothesis* in particular presents no epistemological problem, for nowhere among the early dialogues does Socrates deny that mathematical knowledge is possible or that humans have attained it. In the case of the postulate in the first ethical section, the content of the postulate in fact is not ethical. It merely occurs within the examination of the ethical problem. We might prefer to say that it is epistemological, or rather minimally epistemological. But, indeed, although its central concepts are epistemological, it is hardly even that. Compare the postulate "a mother is a parent." Is this a biological postulate? It seems that this and the "epistemological" postulate are actually logical postulates, in which case I am taking "logical" in the sense in which philosophers speak of analytic relations between concepts as logical.

But if this is so, it raises the question of how Plato would have conceived of such propositions. To what *technê* do they belong? And if they do not belong to a *technê*, what justifies their entitlement to epistemic status? Clearly, among the early dialogues there is no logical *technê* per se. In other words, such propositions are not known because those who know them are privy to a specialized body of knowledge upon whose principles they depend. Rather, they seem to be self-evident; and as such, anyone would reasonably claim to know them.

I do not see that the early dialogues provide the conceptual resources on the basis of which to articulate an epistemological account of such known propositions. Consequently, we are bound to accept one of two claims. One, the epistemological status of such propositions qua known is underdetermined; they may be known, but how and why is not explained or explicable. Such knowledge is, naïvely, taken for granted. Two, indeed, Socrates never claims to know such propositions. He says, of one, that it remains; that is, it is secure. This can be taken to mean that it is true, or at least believed to be true. But then we must distinguish known from cognitively secure propositions.

Given the epistemological preoccupations of Meno it is hard to see that Plato would have been blind to the problem we are presently addressing. As such, I favor the view that Plato recognizes a distinction between known and cognitively secure propositions. Consequently, I submit that the Platonic view is that the postulates in the ethical sections are not known, but cognitively secure.[71]

A cognitively secure proposition appears to be a *kind* of true belief. In Meno Plato introduces the distinction between knowledge and true belief for the first time among the early dialogues: Socrates claims that knowledge differs from true belief in that the former is bound (*dêsêi*) with a reasoning (*logismos*) of the *aitia*.[72] Consequently, things known are stable (*monimoi*). In contrast, true beliefs, being untethered, are apt to be dislodged from the mind, for example, by specious reasons. In contrast, cognitively secure propositions, like things known, are firm.

Granted this, it is a question what makes cognitively secure propositions secure. Here again, it is unclear that the early dialogues have epistemological resources to answer such a question. The postulates in the ethical sections of in the Meno passage appear to be cognitively secure insofar as they are self-evident.

5. Knowledge and *Aitia*

When Socrates distinguishes knowledge and true belief in Meno, he is speaking of knowledge and belief of a single proposition p. Both the knower and the believer believe that p, and p is true. But the knower, unlike the mere true believer, comprehends the *aitia* of p. In other words, the knower has the capacity to explain why p is so.[73] The knower's comprehension of the *aitia* of p also suggests that the knower understands p. Thus, it is often said that Plato's conception of knowledge is akin to our conception of understanding.

But the concept of understanding and specifically the concept of knowing why p is so are obscure. For instance, compare the following questions: Why is fire hot? Why is Socrates sitting in prison? Why is the product of odd numbers odd? Why is this war unjust? It seems that the answers to these heterogeneous questions must themselves be heterogeneous. Consequently, it is a question for Platonic epistemology: What counts as an epistemic *aitia* or rather an adequate epistemic *aitia*, and why?

In answering these questions, it must first be emphasized that the early dialogues are concerned with ethical knowledge specifically, rather than knowledge generally. Thus, it is unclear to what extent the view of epistemic *aitia* the early dialogues offer may be generalized across all epistemic domains.

---

71. It is difficult to determine whether the same should be said of the geometrical postulate, for it is difficult to determine Plato's commitments regarding the philosophy of mathematics at this stage.
72. *Men.* 98a.
73. Thus, the role played by the reasoning-of-the-*aitia* component in Plato's conception of propositional knowledge is akin to the role played by justification in the standard twentieth-century account of propositional knowledge as justified true belief, itself influenced by Plato's accounts in Meno and *Theaetetus*. Indeed, Gail Fine (2004) has recently argued that the reasoning-of-the-*aitia* component in Plato's conception is equivalent to justification.

Second, in considering Platonic epistemology in section 3 of chapter 3, I emphasized that the early dialogues conceptualize ethical knowledge in terms of technê. Thus, it is a question how propositional knowledge relates to technê and indeed whether there is propositional knowledge independently of technê.

The early dialogues are silent on the question of the relation between propositional knowledge and technê. Indeed, even the concept of a proposition is theoretically undetermined in the early dialogues.[74] On the other hand, it is reasonable to assume that possession of a technê entails knowledge whose contents may be represented as sentences or linguistically structured entities, and which it is convenient to refer to as propositions.[75]

On whether there may be propositional knowledge independently of technê, it will be observed that many ordinary nonethical knowledge claims are made in the course of the early dialogues. For example, when in Protagoras Protagoras asks Socrates whether he knows Simonides' Scopas ode, Socrates replies that there is no need for Protagoras to recite it, for he knows the ode.[76] If Plato intends to convey that Socrates indeed has knowledge, then the early dialogues will contain two distinction conceptions of knowledge: ordinary knowledge and technê. In that case, presumably distinct kinds of epistemic aitia are required for ordinary knowledge and technê respectively. For instance, the aitia for Socrates' claim to know the Scopas ode may simply be Socrates' capacity to recite the ode and his awareness of this capacity.

However, in section 6 of chapter 3, I rejected the idea that ordinary ethical knowledge is Platonic; and, more generally, in section 3 of chapter 3, I suggested that the epistemology of the early dialogues is an epistemology of technê. Therefore,

---

74. The concept of a proposition itself is not subject to theorizing until Plato's late dialogues *Theaetetus*, *Sophist*, and *Philebus*. For instance, consider that in *Republic* 5 Socrates distinguishes knowledge from opinion on the basis of the distinct kinds of object to which these *dunameis* are related, things that are and things that neither are nor are not, respectively.

75. Recall that in discussing Socrates and Polus' argument regarding the power of orators in section 3 of chapter 2 of, I observed that in *Gorgias* Socrates says that a technê, unlike an empeiria, entails a grasp of a relevant *phusis* and aitia. Accordingly, in his discussion with Callicles, Socrates says, "I was saying that cooking does not seem to me to be a technê, but an empeiria, whereas medicine has considered the nature (*phusin*) of the patient it treats as well as the reason for or cause of (*aitian*) the things it does . . . " (*Grg.* 500e4–501a2) I also suggested that the distinction between the physiological and aetiological components of a technê correlates with the argument structure of *Gorgias*, for Socrates' first argument with Polus focuses on instrumental reasoning, whereas much of the remainder of the dialogue focuses on reasoning about ends. Consequently, the concept aitia plays distinct roles in the *Gorgias* and *Meno* passages. In *Gorgias*, Socrates is speaking of conditions of a technê, versus an empeiria; in *Meno* he is distinguishing knowledge (of a given proposition) from true belief. An empeiria is not an alethic competence; the ethical hedonism on which it depends is false.

Granted this, it is, nonetheless, reasonable to think that the uses of aitia in *Meno* and in *Gorgias* may be related insofar as knowledge of a technê entails propositional knowledge and propositional knowledge entails a reasoning of the aitia. On the other hand, this does not imply that grasp of the aitia that a technê entails is identical to the reasoning of the aitia entailed by knowledge of any particular proposition within the relevant domain.

76. *Prt.* 339b4–5.

I believe that inquiry into the *aitia* of ordinary knowledge is misguided. The early dialogues are not interested in developing a theory of ordinary knowledge.

In short, in seeking to clarify the nature of *aitia* in propositional knowledge, the interpreter should focus on ethical propositions and on ethical propositions understood as propositions that the possessor of an ethical *technê* would know or would have the capacity to know.

Granted these preliminary remarks, consider now a passage from *Euthyphro* in which Socrates emphasizes the difficulty of settling disputes in the domain of ethics:

> If you and I were to disagree about number, for instance, which of two numbers were greater, would the disagreement about these matters make us enemies and make us angry with each other, or should we not settle it by resorting to reasoning (*logismon*) about these things?... But about what would a disagreement be which we could not settle and which would cause us to be enemies and be angry at each other? Perhaps you cannot give an answer offhand, but let me suggest it. Is it not about the just and unjust and fine and base and good and bad?[77]

Socrates indicates that there are different procedures for the evaluation of claims in different domains. Furthermore, the examples in the passage indicate that in many cases evaluation procedures are uncontroversial. For this reason, among others, they do not preoccupy Plato—even though, with the hindsight of the history of epistemology, we can see how fruitful examination of them has proven to be. In other words, once again, the early dialogues have little interest in the broad epistemological question of how facts or things in general are known. Rather, as Socrates suggests in the *Euthyphro* passage, it is in the domain of ethics that the evaluation procedure is remarkably obscure. And given the supreme value that the early dialogues place on ethical knowledge, their interest lies in determining a solution to this problem.

I suggest that the appeal to definitions is the Platonic answer to the problem of evaluating (nondefinitional) ethical claims. These are precisely the sorts of claims over which there is dispute. For example, the discussion between Crito and Socrates is motivated by the question whether it is just for Socrates to escape from prison, not what justice is. Likewise, Euthyphro and his father contend over whether the father's treatment of the hired laborer was holy, not what holiness is.

In *Euthyphro* Socrates says that the Form (*eidos*)—which is the object of definition—serves as a standard (*paradigma*) on the basis of which to judge.[78] Thus, the early dialogues advance the principle of the epistemological priority of definitional knowledge (π). In other words, the relevant definition is the *aitia* required to ground nondefinitional ethical claims.

---

77. *Euthphr.* 7b7–d2.
78. *Euthphr.* 6d–e.

There seem to be two reasons for the Platonic appeal to definitional *aitiai* in the domain of ethical epistemology. First, the kind of *aitia* required for grounding ethical claims is relatively theoretical.[79] Contrast this with knowledge of, say, cobbling; presumably the cobbler's *technê* is not so theoretical and hence might not require definitional knowledge. But theoretical knowledge in other domains might, like ethical knowledge, require correspondingly theoretical explanations, perhaps specifically definitional explanations. For instance, we have seen that in *Protagoras* and *Gorgias* Socrates makes two claims akin to the principle that I symbolized as (b) in section 5 of chapter 3: If one lacks definitional knowledge of F, one cannot know whether F has property P. In these cases, the subjects are nonethical kinds:

> I would be surprised if you knew what a sophist is. But if you don't know this, then you don't know whether the person to whom you are giving your soul is good.

> I will not answer him whether I think rhetoric is fine or base until I answer first what it is, for it would not be right.

The second reason for Platonic appeal to definitional *aitiai* and so to (π) is metaphysical. In several early definitional dialogues Socrates expresses the following principle: All *f*s—where "*f*" is the adjective corresponding to the general term "F"—have some one character F, which is the same character in the case of all *f* things and where all things are *f* in virtue of having this character. For example, in *Hippias Major* Socrates claims that just men are just because of justice, wise men are wise because of wisdom, fine things are fine because of fineness, and good things are good because of goodness.[80] Likewise, in *Euthyphro* Socrates claims that holy things are holy because of holiness.[81] The significance of such claims for the epistemological priority of definitional knowledge is that the Form F is conceived as the *aitia* or thing responsible for other things being *f*. Thus, an account of the Form, which is a definition, serves to explain why *x* is *f*. For example, knowing whether Euthyphro's prosecution of his father is holy requires knowing what holiness is, for if Euthyphro's prosecution of his father is holy, then it is holy because of holiness.

This particularly illuminates the principle that in section 5 of chapter 3 I labeled (a): If one lacks definitional knowledge of F, one cannot know, for any *x*, whether *x* is an instance F. Presumably, the same sort of account should hold for (b). That is, the proper explanation of a knowledge claim such as that F has a certain property P involves the definition of F. One example occurs in *Euthyphro*, where Socrates claims that holiness is god-beloved because it is such as to be loved (*hoion phileisthai*).[82] Another example occurs in the *Meno* passage where the

---

79. Compare Prior (1998).
80. *Hp. Ma.* 287c2–6.
81. *Euthphr.* 5d1–5; compare *Men.* 72a6–73c8.
82. *Euthphr.* 11a4–5.

method of reasoning from a postulate is introduced. After Socrates agrees to investigate the question whether excellence is teachable before settling the question of what excellence is, he proceeds on the basis of the view that excellence is knowledge. In other words, Socrates suggests that excellence is teachable because it is knowledge.

The preceding remarks provide some clarification of the role of *aitia* in the knowledge of ethical propositions, at least nondefinitional ethical propositions. It remains to consider ethical definitions and the role of *aitia* in their knowledge. To begin, there is no reason to assume that the same sort of *aitia* should be required for definitional knowledge as for nondefinitional knowledge. Indeed, there are at least two reasons why the same sort of *aitia* cannot be required. On the one hand, if definitional knowledge were to be explained in terms of nondefinitional knowledge, explanation would be circular. This problem is akin to Geach's Socratic fallacy. On the other hand, if definitional knowledge were required to explain definitional knowledge, regress would ensue.[83]

It is noteworthy that the pursuits of definitional knowledge in the early definitional dialogues commit neither of these logical infractions. Even so, these two options seem to be exhaustive. Consequently, it is unclear whether the early dialogues have a viable method of pursuing definitional knowledge. At this point, at least in theory, the distinction between known and cognitively secure propositions might provide some assistance. Cognitively secure propositions might serve as *aitiai* for definitional knowledge. Because they are secure, they may ground knowledge; but because they are not known, they do not require *aitiai* of their own. With this possibility in mind, I turn to consider how the early dialogues pursue definitions and whether, as they do, they employ cognitively secure propositions.

6.1. *F*-conditions

In the discussion of the elenchus in section 2, I said that proposed definitions of *F* are rejected in view of a premise set Q inconsistent with the proposed definition. Two premises are crucial to Q. One claims that the *definiendum* has a particular property; the other claims that the *definiens* lacks that property. For example, as we have seen, in the argument against Charmides' first definition of sound-mindedness as restraint, Socrates claims that sound-mindedness is necessarily or always fine, whereas restraint is not always or necessarily fine. Consider the premise concerning the property of the *definiendum*. Within the immediate argument, this premise functions to distinguish the *definiendum* from the *definiens*. But conceived more broadly, namely from the perspective of an inquiry into the

---

83. Note also that if excellence is a unity, then in fact there is only one ethical *definiendum*, excellence. In that case, the regress problem can't get started. Of course, this difficulty never emerges in the dialogues since the unity of excellence is a result of the investigations, not a point of departure. Still, it is an inevitable consequence of the dialogues' commitments. (On related problems of regress and circularity regarding *aitia* and knowledge, consider Aristotle's *Meno*-inspired comments at *APo.* A.1.)

identity of the *definiendum*, this premise also functions, at least partially, to elucidate the identity of the *definiendum*. This is because the premise indicates a condition that a satisfactory definition must satisfy. I will speak of this as an F-condition.

Here is a list of the F-conditions in the texts as well as the corresponding definitions that fail to satisfy them.[84]

Text	Definition	F-Condition
R. 1	(1) Truth-telling and returning borrowed items	[Being] just[85]
	(2) Rendering each his due[86]	Useful,[87] just[88]
	(3) Aiding a good friend and harming a bad enemy	Not harmful[89]
	(4) The good for the stronger[90]	Beneficial to others[91]
Chrm.	(1) Restraint	Fine[92]

---

84. Note that I am ignoring *Lysis* here.

85. "But in speaking of this very thing, justice, are we to say that it is simply telling the truth and returning borrowed items, or do we sometimes do these things justly and sometimes unjustly?" (*R.* 1, 331c1–5).

86. See following note.

87. Socrates' response to this definition is complex. It begins with the reinterpretation of the definition itself as aiding friends and harming enemies (*R.* 1, 331e5–332d9). It is then questioned how the just man is able to aid friends and harm enemies. In other words, an attempt is made more precisely to determine the just man's particular expertise. It appears that the just man is rather useless since he is only good for guarding items when they are not in use (*R.* 1, 332d10–333e5): "Then, my friend, justice would not be a thing of much significance if it happens to be useful only for things that are out of use" (*R.* 1, 333e1–2). Subsequently, Socrates suggests that the ability to guard also entails possession of the polar opposite skill, the ability to steal. Accordingly, the just man appears to be a thief (*R.* 1, 333e6–334b6). At this point, Polemarchus concedes perplexity, yet reaffirms that justice is aiding friends and harming enemies: "By Zeus, I no longer know what I mean. And yet I still think that justice is aiding friends and harming enemies" (*R.* 1, 334b7–9).

88. Given the possibility of misjudging people, one might harm a good person, mistaking him for an enemy, and benefit a bad person, mistaking him for a friend. In response to this, it is granted that it is just to harm the unjust and benefit the just (*R.* 1, 334d9–11).

89. "Then it is not the work of the just man to harm, Polemarchus, neither friend nor anyone else, but the work of his opposite, the unjust" (*R.* 1, 335d11–12).

90. In the first movement of Socrates' response to this definition, it is clarified that the genuine ruler does not pursue policies that are harmful to himself, mistakenly believing them to be beneficial to himself (*R.* 1, 338d7–341a4).

91. "Then no knowledge considers the good of the stronger, but the good of the weaker over which it rules . . . Then, Thrasymachus, no one in any official position insofar as he is a ruler considers or enjoins his own good, but the good of that which is ruled and for whom he practices his craft—and it is by looking to what is good for and fitting for that that he says what he says and does what he does" (*R.* 1, 342c11–e11).

92. "So sound-mindedness cannot be a sort of quietness, nor can the sound-minded life be quiet, by this argument at least, since being sound-minded, it must be fine" (*Chrm.* 160b7–9).

	(2) Modesty	Good[93]
	(3) Doing one's own thing[94]	Entailing knowledge[95]
	(4) Self-knowledge[96]	Existing,[97] beneficial[98]
La.	(1) Paradigmatic hoplite conduct	A power (*dunamis*)
	(2) Toughness of the soul	Fine[99]
	(3) Knowledge of what is to be feared and dared[100]	A part of excellence[101]
Euthphr.	(1) Prosecuting sacrilege regardless of personal relation	Not a type of holiness[102]
	(2) That which is loved by some gods	Purely holy[103]
	(3) That which is loved by all the gods	A being (*ousia*)[104]
	(4) Attention to the gods[105]	A being[106]

93. "Then sound-mindedness would not be modesty, if it happens to be something good, whereas modesty is no more good than bad" (*Chrm.* 161a11–b2).

94. Reinterpreted as doing what is good.

95. " 'Then it would seem that in doing what is helpful, [the doctor] may sometimes act in a sound-minded manner and be sound-minded, yet be ignorant of his own sound-mindedness.' 'But that,' [Critias] said, 'could never be. And if you think this in any way necessary from my previous admissions, I would rather withdraw some of them . . . and not be ashamed to say my statements were wrong, than to concede at any time that a man who is ignorant of himself is sound-minded' " (*Chrm.* 164c5–d3).

96. Reinterpreted as knowledge of knowledge (and lack of knowledge and of all other knowledges).

97. "For my part, I distrust my own competence to determine these questions, and hence I am neither able to affirm whether it is possible that there should be a knowledge of knowledge . . ." (*Chrm.* 169a7–b1).

98. Insofar as Socrates believes himself incompetent to determine whether knowledge of knowledge exists, he concedes that even if it did exist, it would not be beneficial: " 'Then what benefit,' I asked, 'Critias, can we still look for from sound-mindedness, if it is like that?' " (*Chrm.* 171d1–2; see also 172c).

99. "Then you will not agree that such toughness [namely foolish toughness] is courage, since it is not fine, whereas courage is fine" (*La.* 192d7–8).

100. Reinterpreted as knowledge of good and bad.

101. "Hence what you now describe, Nicias, will be not a part but the whole of excellence . . . But, you know, we said that courage is one of the parts of excellence" (*La.* 199e3–7).

102. "Now call to mind that this is not what I asked you, to teach me one or two of the many holy acts, but the Form because of which all holy acts are holy" (*Euthphr.* 6d9–11).

103. "Then you did not answer my question, my friend, for I did not ask you what is at once holy and unholy" (*Euthphr.* 8a10–12).

104. "And, Euthyphro, it seems that when you were asked what holiness is, you were unwilling to make plain its being, rather you mentioned an affection, something that has happened to the holy" (*Euthphr.* 11a6–b9).

105. Reinterpreted as service to the gods.

106. On the assumption that holiness is service to the gods, Socrates questions what benefit it provides. Euthyphro's response implies that holiness is pleasing to the gods, and as such this definition falters on the same grounds as the preceding definition: "Or do you not see that our account has come round to the point from which it started? For you remember, I suppose, that a while ago we found that holiness and what is god-beloved were not the same . . ." (*Euthphr.* 15b10–c2).

Hp. Ma.	(1) A fine woman	Purely fine[107]
	(2) Gold	Purely fine[108]
	(3) To be rich, healthy, honored, live to old age, etc.	Purely fine[109]
	(4) Propriety	Making things fine[110]
	(5) Utility[111]	Not harmful[112]
	(6) Benefit	Not a type of goodness[113]
	(7) Aesthetic pleasure[114]	Not a type of goodness[115]
Meno	(1) Managing political affairs, domestic affairs, etc.	Not a type of excellence[116]
	(2) Ability to govern people	Not a type of excellence[117]
	(3) Desiring what is fine and being able to acquire it[118]	Not a type of excellence[119]

---

107. " 'Then,' he will say, 'when you were asked for the fine, do you give as your reply what is, as you yourself say, no more fine than foul?' " (*Hp. Ma.* 287c3–5).

108. "For by this reply, if I say that the fine is gold, it seems to me that gold will appear no more fine than fig-wood" (*Hp. Ma.* 291c6–8; see 290d).

109. " . . . so that the same thing has happened to this as to the things we mentioned before, the young woman and the [golden] pot, in a still more ridiculous way than to them: It is fine for some and not fine for others" (*Hp. Ma.* 293c2–5).

110. " . . . but if, on the other hand, the decorous makes things appear fine, it would not be the fine thing that we are seeking. For that [the *definiendum*] makes things actually fine, but the same thing could not make things both appear and actually be fine" (*Hp. Ma.* 294d9–e3).

111. Reinterpreted as power.

112. "Well, then, this power and these useful things, which are useful for accomplishing something bad—are we to say that they are fine, or far from it?" (*Hp. Ma.* 296c6–d1).

113. No single line encapsulates the F-condition upon which the refutation of the definition depends. This will be discussed further in section 2 of chapter 5.

114. Reinterpreted as beneficial pleasure.

115. The refutation of this definition depends upon the same complex point as that involved in the refutation of the previous definition. But consider Socrates' statement: " 'Well, then,' he will say, 'benefit is that which creates the good, but that which creates and that which is created were just now seen to be different; and our argument has come round to the earlier argument, has it not?' " (*Hp. Ma.* 303e11–13).

116. "And likewise also with the excellences, however many and various they may be, they all have one common Form because of which they are excellences and on which one would of course be wise to keep an eye when one is giving an answer to the question of what excellence really is" (*Men.* 72c6–d1).

117. Socrates elicits Meno's assent to the view that excellence implies governing people with justice. But he also gains Meno's assent to the view that there are multiple excellences. Therefore, excellence will imply governing people with justice, courage, wisdom, sound-mindedness, and high-mindedness. But, then, excellence is identified by a number of excellences: "Once more, Meno, we are in the same plight. Again, we have found a number of excellences when we were looking for just one" (*Men.* 74a7).

118. Reinterpreted as desire for what is good and ability to acquire it. But see the following note.

119. Socrates argues that all people desire the good (*Men.* 77b6–78b8). Accordingly, this aspect of the definition is dropped, and Socrates concentrates on the ability to attain the good. As in the second definition, Socrates suggests that such acquisition should entail the exercise of specific

With a few exceptions, the F-conditions fall into two categories: ethical and metaphysical. In most cases it is clear from the list which F-conditions fall into which category. However, there are several misleading or ambiguous cases. Being purely holy, being purely fine, and making things fine are introduced to advance metaphysical rather than ethical ideas; therefore, I categorize them as metaphysical F-conditions. Compare Socrates' refutation of Hippias' first definition with his refutation of Charmides' first definition. Hippias' first definition of the fine is a fine young woman, and Socrates argues that in relation to a goddess a fine young woman is no more fine than foul.[120] As we have seen, in concluding the refutation of Charmides' first definition Socrates makes a similar statement: "In our argument we assumed that sound-mindedness is a fine thing, and it has appeared that vigorous actions are no less fine than restrained actions."[121] However, the contexts in which the statements occur indicate that Socrates is emphasizing distinct points. The argument in *Charmides* encourages Charmides to draw an ethical conclusion: The *definiens* must be fine in the case of all activities. In contrast, the investigation in *Hippias Major* begins with Hippias' failure to appreciate the distinction between the questions "What is the fine (*to kalon*)?" and "What is fine (*kalon*)?"[122] In other words, Hippias fails to appreciate the distinction between the Form fineness and fine instances or participants in the Form.[123] When Socrates notes that a fine young woman is not fine in comparison to a goddess, he is trying to indicate that fineness is not to be identified with some fine participant. This point can be profitably compared with Socrates' response to Euthyphro's first definition: "Now call to mind that this is not what I asked you, to teach me one or two of the many holy things, but the Form because of which all holy things are holy."[124]

In response to Euthyphro's second definition, that which is god-beloved (that is, loved by some god), Socrates introduces the F-condition being purely holy. As in *Hippias Major*, in *Euthyphro* the F-condition being purely *f* is introduced to help clarify the distinction between F qua Form and *f* participants, for unlike *f* participants, F is purely *f*; in other words, only the Form F satisfies the condition of being purely *f*.[125] In short, what distinguishes the F-condition being purely *f* from the ethical F-condition being *f* is the emphasis in the metaphysical F-condition on the purity of being *f* rather than the ethical or axiological character of being *f*.

---

excellences such as justice, whereupon the same problem arises: "And were we saying a little while ago that each of these things was a part of excellence—justice, sound-mindedness, and the rest of them?" (*Men.* 79a3–5).

120. *Hp. Ma.* 289c7–8.
121. *Chrm.* 160d1–3.
122. *Hp. Ma.* 287d2–9.
123. Here and throughout I use the word "participant" to refer to any entity that participates in a Form. Recall that the word "participant," rather than "particular," is useful since participants themselves may be universals.
124. *Euthphr.* 6d9–11.
125. Recall that the symbol *f* stands for the adjective corresponding to the general term "F."

Granted this, the two categories of F-conditions, ethical and metaphysical, can be summarized as follows. The ethical F-conditions include being just, being useful, not being harmful, benefiting others, and being fine, good, and beneficial; the metaphysical F-conditions include existing, not being an instance of holiness, being purely holy, being a being, being purely fine, making things fine, not being an instance of goodness, and not being an instance of excellence.

The exceptional cases include entailing knowledge, being a power, and being a part of excellence. Entailing knowledge obviously is an epistemic or cognitive psychological condition, and ostensibly not an ethical one. Being a power appears to be a metaphysical property. However, in the context in which it is used Socrates intends to convey the more specific idea that F is a psychological power. Therefore, being a power may more accurately be categorized as psychological, but not ethical.[126] Being a part of excellence is a meta-ethical condition. Beyond the apparent dissimilarities of these F-conditions, their functions within the contexts of the investigations pertain to the Platonic interest in considering the unity of excellence, the identification of excellence with knowledge of a kind, and the conception of knowledge as a psychological power. Accordingly, this miscellaneous set of three F-conditions may conveniently be subsumed under the rubric "intellectualist."

The basic division of F-conditions into ethical and metaphysical categories almost precisely corresponds with the division of two sets of dialogues. The investigations in Republic 1, Charmides, and Laches are almost wholly concerned with ethical and more broadly psychological and intellectualist aspects of F. The investigations in Euthyphro, Meno, and Hippias Major are also almost wholly concerned with metaphysical aspects of F. Specifically, only in Euthyphro, Meno, and Hippias Major are the concept of Form, including the suggestion that F is a Form, and the distinction between F and f participants introduced and developed.[127]

It is also noteworthy that while existing—introduced as an F-condition in examining the knowledge of knowledge and all other knowledges and lack of knowledge in Charmides—is an ontological and so metaphysical property, its function differs from all the other metaphysical F-conditions introduced in Euthyphro, Hippias Major, and Meno. All of these are employed to convey the idea that F is a Form and so distinct from f participants. In Charmides, Socrates' principal objective in examining whether the knowledge of knowledge and all other knowledges and lack of knowledge exists is not to develop a metaphysical idea, but to determine whether, on the assumption that sound-mindedness exists, knowledge of knowledge and all other knowledges and lack of knowledge does.

---

126. This point is developed in Wolfsorf (2005c).
127. In response to Laches' first definition, Socrates says that courage is the same in all cases; however, he does not speak of courage as a Form; rather, he emphasizes that it is a power that all courageous men share. In particular, the analogy with quickness Socrates draws to assist Laches in conceptualizing the *definiendum* emphasizes that courage is a power, not a universal. Contrast this with the analogies Socrates draws with bees and shapes to assist Meno; their purpose is to clarify that excellence is a Form and universal. On this, see Wolfsdorf (2005c).

In short, the investigations in *Republic* 1, *Charmides*, and *Laches* are distinct from those in *Euthyphro*, *Hippias Major*, and *Meno* in that the latter set involve the identification of F as a Form, whereas the former do not. The significance of this point may be underscored by comparing aspects of the investigations in a few dialogues. Consider the first definition in *Republic* 1, telling the truth and returning borrowed items. As a definition of justice, this could be criticized as being too narrow. Instead, Socrates criticizes the definition on ethical grounds. Charmides' first two definitions of sound-mindedness, restraint and modesty, arguably could also be criticized as inadequately general. But Socrates criticizes them on ethical grounds. In contrast, Euthyphro's and Meno's first definitions could be criticized on ethical grounds, but Socrates criticizes them on metaphysical grounds. This is especially noteworthy in the case of *Euthyphro*, for at no point in the investigation does Socrates criticize a definition on ethical grounds. Yet as the discussion in *Protagoras* makes clear, holiness, like courage, sound-mindedness, and justice, was conventionally recognized as a principal constituent of excellence. In short, Plato was not compelled to have Socrates criticize these particular definitions on exclusively either ethical or metaphysical grounds; rather, Plato choose to compose the investigations in certain definitional dialogues and not others to introduce the metaphysics of Forms. In other words, Plato could have introduced metaphysical F-conditions into the investigations in *Charmides*, *Laches*, or *Republic* 1, or only included ethical and intellectualist F-conditions in *Euthyphro*, *Hippias Major*, and *Meno*. Given the prominence, indeed almost exclusivity, of metaphysical F-conditions in the latter set of texts as well as the character of their employment and interrelations, it is clear that they are employed for pedagogical reasons, specifically to introduce and explain the metaphysics of Forms.

Generally speaking, the investigations advance in such a way that once a definition has been reached that satisfies an F-condition, a new F-condition is introduced that the definition does not satisfy. Insofar as this is the case, the investigations proceed in a linear fashion by satisfying a series of F-conditions— although in some instances it takes more than one try for the interlocutor to satisfy the F-condition originally introduced. As such, the investigations exhibit a consistent developmental form: A set of properties that Socrates believes are constitutive of the identity of F is incrementally clarified. (Of course, no indication is given that by the end of the investigation all properties necessary for a satisfactory definition have been introduced.) In the nonmetaphysical dialogues, this development coincides with the progress of the investigation toward unconventional Platonic conceptions of F, for what makes a definition Platonic is precisely its incremental satisfaction of the ethical and intellectualist F-conditions that Socrates introduces.[128] This is not quite the case with the metaphysical definitional dialogues insofar as their principal concern is to foster understanding of the

---

128. One exception to this is Thrasymachus' definition in *Republic* 1. In that case, Thrasymachus' aim is to radically undermine the ethical perspective that Socrates has developed in the course of the conversation with Cephalus and Polemarchus.

metaphysics of Forms. In that case, the ethical and intellectualist dimensions of F simply do not come under scrutiny, or do so only to a limited extent. In this case, then, it may be said that insofar as definitions incrementally satisfy metaphysical F- conditions they progress toward a Platonic conception of F qua Form.[129]

6.2. Cognitive Security

Socrates introduces the F-conditions in the early definitional dialogues; he introduces them because he is committed to them; and he introduces them in order to examine whether the proposed definitions are true. In *Republic* 1 the arguments Socrates develops for the views that it is not the function of justice to do harm and that justice is beneficial to others obviously reflect his own views. Consider his shock at Thrasymachus' suggestion that justice is not an excellence and therefore not good, as well as his expressed intent to try to persuade Thrasymachus otherwise.[130] In *Charmides* Socrates says, "I divine that sound-mindedness is something beneficial and good."[131] And at the end of the investigation, he says, "I think sound-mindedness is a great good."[132] Outside the response in which he introduces the condition that sound-mindedness entails knowledge, Socrates does not suggest that this is so. However, as we saw in chapter 3, Socrates' identification of excellence and some form of wisdom or knowledge is based on a wide range of evidence. For example, in *Laches* Nicias attributes to Socrates the view, and Socrates accepts the attribution, that a man is good insofar as he is wise.[133] Later in *Laches* Socrates suggests that a person who possessed the knowledge of good and bad would lack nothing so far as excellence is concerned.[134] Of course, Plato need not characterize Socrates as committed to the same propositions in all of the early definitional dialogues, but there is no good reason to assume that he is not committed to these views in *Charmides*.[135] In *Laches* Socrates says that courage

---

129. However, in the metaphysical dialogues there is rather limited progress in this direction. For example, Meno's three definitions all fail for the same reason—as do Hippias' first three definitions.
130. *R.* 1, 347e. With regard to the F-condition in *Republic* 1 that justice is just, compare Socrates' introduction of this premise in his argument for the identity of justice and holiness in *Protagoras*: "I would say that [justice] is just" (*Prt.* 330c5–6).
131. *Chrm.* 169b4–5.
132. *Chrm.* 175e6–7.
133. *La.* 194d1–3.
134. *La.* 199d4–e1.
135. Consider that early on in their discussion Socrates suggests to Charmides that sound-mindedness is a psychological entity, that is, an entity of the soul. He describes his alleged Thracian charm: "He said, my friend, that the soul is treated by means of certain charms, and that these charms are beautiful words. From such words sound-mindedness is engendered; and when sound-mindedness is engendered and present, then health comes more easily to both the head and the rest of the body" (*Chrm.* 157a3–b1). Shortly after, he says, "Now it is clear that if sound-mindedness is present in you, you are able to form some opinion about it. For it is necessary, I suppose, that if it is in you, it provides a sense of its presence, from which you would be able to form an opinion both of what it is and of what sort of thing sound-mindedness is . . . So, then, in order to guess whether or not it is in you, tell me what in your opinion sound-mindedness is" (158e7–159a3).

is a power (*dunamis*).[136] In *Laches*, outside of the argument where he introduces the condition, Socrates does not explicitly state his belief that courage is fine (*kalon*). But from a wide range of evidence in and out of this dialogue, it seems beyond dispute that he does. For instance, early in the discussion, he says that he and the others are "consulting about making the souls of Lysimachus' and Mele-sias' sons as good as possible (*hoti aristas*)."[137] Given his belief that courage is a part of excellence, it is reasonable to infer that he believes that courage is fine.[138] In *Euthyphro* Socrates suggests that the holy is a Form (*eidos*), the same in all instances and that because of which all holy things are holy.[139] He also says that the holy is not in any way unholy[140] and that the *definiens* must describe the being (*ousia*), rather than the affection (*pathos*) of the holy.[141] In *Hippias Major*, Socrates, rather his alter ego, insists that the fine is not in any way not-fine and that it makes entities fine.[142] In *Meno* Socrates explains that excellence is the same in all instances and that because of which all instances of excellence are such instances.[143] In short, it is clear that the propositions expressing the F-conditions Socrates introduces in examining proposed definitions are propositions to which he himself is committed.

The question is whether Socrates regards the F-conditions as cognitively secure and whether the Platonic view is that they are cognitively secure. Let us first consider the metaphysical F-conditions. Most of these depend on a concep-tion of F as a Form. Not being an instance of holiness, not being an instance of goodness, and not being an instance of excellence are species of the more general F-condition, not being an instance of F. Thus, this F-condition distinguishes F from its participants. Being purely holy and being purely fine are instances of the more general F-condition, being purely f. Observe that the F-condition, being purely f, is equivalent to the principle of the self-predication of Forms. Making things fine is a species of the more general F-condition, making things f. And we have seen several examples of the principle that all f things are f because of F. Being a being (*ousia*), in contrast to an affection or, for that matter, an action, is also closely connected to the Platonic conception of Form since Forms are preeminently real things. The same may be said for the F-condition, being in

---

136. *La.* 192a10–b3.
137. See also *La.* 186a3–6.
138. For evidence of Socrates' identification of what is *kalon* with what is *agathon*, consider his claim in *Charmides*: " 'Well, now, I asked, did you not admit a moment ago that sound-mindedness is *kalon*?' 'Certainly I did,' he said. 'And sound-minded men are also *agathoi*' " (160e6–10); and his claim in *Protagoras*: " 'Is going to war a *kalon* thing, I asked, or an *aischron* thing?' '*Kalon*,' he replied. 'Then, if it is *kalon*, we have admitted, by our former argument, that it is also *agathon*; for we agreed that all *kala* actions are *agatha*.' 'True and I abide by that decision.' 'You are right to do so, I said' " (359e4–8).
139. *Euthphr.* 6d9–e1; see also 5c8–d5.
140. *Euthphr.* 8a10–b6; see also 5c8–d5.
141. *Euthphr.* 11a6–b1.
142. For example, *Hp. Ma.* 292c9–d6.
143. *Men.* 72a6–d1.

existence—although, as we have mentioned, when this condition is introduced in *Charmides*, it is not related to F qua Form, but simply to the peculiar hypothetical entity, knowledge of knowledge and all other knowledges and lack of knowledge.

The question whether the metaphysical F-conditions are cognitively secure can, thus, be seen to reduce to the question whether the Platonic conception of Form is cognitively secure. Observe that the metaphysical F-conditions are never defended or challenged among the early dialogues; nor is the concept of Form itself. It is, of course, noteworthy that in *Phaedo* Socrates treats the existence of Forms and the principle that *f* things are *f* because of F as *hupotheseis*. Moreover, the standard interpretation of *hupothesis* in *Phaedo*, which I do not wish to challenge here, is "hypothesis," not "postulate" or "cognitively" secure proposition. Still, as I have already mentioned, the concept of *hupothesis* in *Meno* may well differ from that in *Phaedo* and other middle dialogues. Perhaps, then, the Platonic position is that the metaphysical F-conditions among the early dialogues are cognitively secure.[144]

It is unlikely that any of the intellectualist F-conditions are cognitively secure. In light of the discussion of the unity of excellence in chapter 3, being a part of excellence clearly is not. Entailing-knowledge also is not cognitively secure. This is because Socrates argues for it; he deploys the example of the lucky doctor who accidentally heals his patient to suggest to Critias that sound-mindedness is not identifiable with doing good. Moreover, on Callicles' admittedly unconventional view of sound-mindedness, the sound-minded person is stupid. Being a power is most likely also not cognitively secure. As we have mentioned, when Socrates poses his WF question, almost all of his interlocutors initially respond with types of action.

The ethical F-conditions may be divided into three kinds: valuable for the agent, valuable for others, and being *f*. Being useful, being good, and being beneficial all belong to the class of F-conditions that are valuable for the agent. But it is by no means uncontroversial whether any of the putative parts of excellence is valuable for its possessor. Callicles argues that sound-mindedness is not good for oneself. Callicles, Polus, and Thrasymachus argue that justice is not good for oneself. In *Laches*, Laches is reduced to aporia in the face of Socrates' example of a soldier who arguably demonstrates courage by maintaining his weak position against a more powerful enemy. The problem here is that the soldier's putative courage is harmful to himself.[145] F's being fine is not obviously valuable for oneself precisely because it is unclear whether something that is fine is good for oneself. In section 7 of chapter 2, we saw that Polus argues that suffering injustice is finer than doing injustice, but that suffering injustice is worse than doing injustice.

Not being harmful to others and benefiting others belong to the class of F-conditions that are valuable for others. Here too these F-conditions are not cognitively secure. We have noted that the conventional conception of justice

---

144. It is unfortunate that the dialogues do not license a stronger positive or negative conclusion.
145. Note that there is no direct consideration among the early dialogues of whether holiness is good for oneself.

entails harming enemies. And clearly, the exercise of courage, conventionally conceived, may harm others.

Being just is a peculiar case. It is a species of the more general F-condition, being f. Thus, it appears to be equivalent to the metaphysical F-condition, being purely f; and in that case, it may be cognitively secure. However, in *Republic* 1, it is indeed used as an ethical condition, not a metaphysical one. Observe the distinction between pre- and postdefinitional conceptions of F. For example, Socrates asks Cephalus what justice is. Cephalus responds that it is truth-telling and returning borrowed items. Postdefinitionally, being f implies precisely that, truth-telling and returning borrowed items. But then the proposed definition necessarily and trivially satisfies the condition of being f. Instead, being f is deployed to evoke an intuitive, predefinitional conception of F. So Socrates asks: If one borrows a weapon from a man who subsequently goes crazy, is it *just* to return that item? The implicit conception here is something such as that it is unjust to harm friends. Granted this, being f, where F is understood predefinitionally, is not cognitively secure precisely because it is controversial what F is.

In short, many of the F-conditions Socrates deploys among the definitional dialogues are not cognitively secure; and we can only suggest that perhaps the metaphysical F-conditions are. To this extent, Socrates' pursuits of definitional knowledge, certainly in the nonmetaphysical early dialogues, are epistemologically insecure. Moreover, while the pursuits of definitional knowledge in the metaphysical early dialogues may be relatively cognitively secure, clearly the investigations in those dialogues do not progress to the point where much of ethical substantive is secured regarding F.[146]

---

146. This suggests that the passage in which Socrates introduces the method *ex hupotheseôs* in *Meno* is distinctive insofar as it includes a number of cognitively secure propositions. Yet this fact should not mislead us. Although many of the F-conditions deployed in the definitional dialogues are not cognitively secure, arguably a number of cognitively secure propositions are introduced in arguments elsewhere among the early dialogues. A full-scale discussion of these is beyond the scope of this study. But consideration of a few examples will illustrate the point. Arguably, a few cognitively secure propositions occur among a couple of arguments in *Protagoras*. In the course of the argument for the identity of justice and holiness (330b–332a), Socrates elicits Protagoras' assent to the propositions justice is just and holiness is holy. As I suggested in section 2 of chapter 3, it has been a matter of considerable debate how to interpret these propositions. I interpret them to mean that the psychological conditions of justice and holiness are responsible for producing just and holy actions and states of affairs respectively. Moreover, these propositions are similar in content, although not form, to a set of propositions that Socrates employs in his subsequent arguments concerning the identity of sound-mindedness and intelligence (332a–333b) that we also considered in chapter 3: Stupid behavior is caused by stupidity; sound-minded behavior is caused by sound-mindedness; strong action is caused by strength, weak action is caused by weakness; swift action is caused by swiftness; and slow action is caused by slowness. Furthermore, in the course of this argument Socrates also elicits Protagoras' assent to the claims that goodness and badness, beauty and ugliness, highness and lowness of voice are contraries. None of these propositions is ever questioned in *Protagoras*; nor is any one explicitly or implicitly questioned elsewhere among the early dialogues. They appear to be accepted as truisms. And I presume that their acceptance as such depends upon their self-evidence. In short, the use of cognitively secure propositions is not confined to the *Meno* passage.

Recall that this chapter began where the previous chapter ended, with the epistemological priority of definitional knowledge. Given that (π) is Platonic, the pursuit of ethical definitions should preoccupy the early dialogues—and indeed it does. The question, then, is how Socrates and his interlocutors pursue definitions. This question broaches the subject of philosophy as a form of inquiry; in other words, it broaches the subject of method.

By considering how Socrates and his interlocutors pursue definitions, I have shown that there is no such thing as the elenchus, as standardly conceived. Furthermore, I have shown that the method *ex hupotheseôs*, introduced in *Meno*, neither is a hypothetical method nor supplants some earlier method of inquiry. Although the method of reasoning *ex hupotheseôs* is, in one important respect, distinct from the way Socrates reasons elsewhere, for the most part Socrates' manner of inquiry among the early dialogues is consistent; it is consistently cooperative and constructive.

The examination of reasoning *ex hupotheseôs* did, however, ironically, bring to light the notion of cognitively secure propositions. Consequently, I appealed to such propositions in an effort to answer Geach's charge of the Socratic fallacy. Given the *aitia*-requirement on propositional knowledge and (π), ethical definitions serve as *aitiai* for relevant nondefinitional propositions. Indeed, I offered a metaphysical as well as an epistemological explanation for this. Nevertheless, it remains unclear how definitional knowledge itself can reasonably be pursued. On pain of regress, definitions cannot serve as *aitiai* for definitions. Consequently, nondefinitional propositions, if anything, must serve as *aitiai* for definitions. But, on pain of circularity, the nondefinitional propositions that serve as such *aitiai* cannot be known.

Cognitively secure (nondefinitional) propositions offer a possible solution, since these are cognitively secure, yet also unknown. In pursuing this possibility, I considered the *F*-conditions that Socrates actually employs in his pursuit of definitions. The aim was to determine to what extent these *F*-conditions could be conceived as cognitively secure propositions. Unfortunately, I found that few if any *F*-conditions could be so conceived. Thus, there has in fact appeared no good reason to believe that the set of cognitively secure propositions, actually or even possibly available to Socrates and his interlocutors, may serve as adequate *aitiai* for definitional knowledge. In short, although definitional knowledge has epistemological priority among the early dialogues, it is doubtful that these texts offer a cogent method by which definitional knowledge can be pursued.

5

APORIA

1. Forms of Aporia

The early dialogues do not provide an adequate response to Geach's charge of the Socratic fallacy. The Platonic epistemological project is incomplete; the object that philosophy seeks remains obscure. Philosophy itself is a work in progress.

It is often thought that the condition of aporia, ubiquitous among the early dialogues, is to be explained by some such epistemological problems. Precisely, all of the early dialogues are aporetic in the sense that in none of these texts do the discussions or investigations conclude with Socrates affirming knowledge of the answer to the questions that govern them. Insofar as this view depends on a view of Platonic epistemology, I will call this form of aporia epistemological aporia. This type of aporia is a general feature of Plato's early dialogues.

Another kind of aporia characterizes some, but not all, of the early dialogues. At the end of *Gorgias* Socrates strongly affirms that the philosophical life is of greater value than the sort of political life that Callicles advocates, and his affirmation of this conclusion depends upon his affirmation of the conclusion to the argument that it is better to suffer than to do injustice. At the end of *Crito*, Socrates concludes that it is just for him to remain in prison and suffer the punishment for impiety and corruption of the youth, rather than to escape. At the end of *Ion* he concludes that Ion does not possess knowledge. *Apology* concludes with Socrates' statement that the nature of death and the afterlife are unclear to all but the divine. However, this is not the question that governs the text. The central issue is whether Socrates is impious and has corrupted the youth. Despite the verdict, the conclusion of the text is clear: He is not impious or a corrupter of the youth. Moreover, Socrates does not conclude his speech to the jury by admitting that he is unsure whether he is. The conclusion of *Euthydemus* is slightly, but only slightly more oblique. It is clear by the end of the dialogue that Euthydemus and Dionysodorus do not possess the knowledge of how to make others excellent and that they belong to the class of pseudophilosophers that Socrates characterizes as charlatans. Granted, none of these five dialogues concludes with Socrates affirming knowledge of the pertinent subject. However, Socrates affirms, or Plato clearly conveys through the drama, reasonable grounds for the relevant conclusion.

In contrast, all of the early definitional dialogues conclude without Socrates affirming a reasoned belief in the answer to the WF question. The case of *Protagoras* is somewhat more complex. At the conclusion of this dialogue Socrates says that he began the discussion believing that excellence could not be taught, but that insofar as it appears to be wholly knowledge, it is teachable. In contrast, whereas Protagoras began believing that excellence could be taught, insofar as he believes that it is not knowledge, he must believe that it is not teachable. Socrates' final remarks on the state of the investigation are, "Seeing how completely topsy-turvy (*anô katô*) all these things have become jumbled up, Protagoras, I have my mind wholly set on clearing them up. And I would like us to go through these things together and determine what excellence is and then, once again, consider whether it is teachable."[1]

In contrast to epistemological aporia, I will speak of the form of aporia in which the early definitional dialogues and *Protagoras* end as dramatic aporia. Dramatic aporia is, then, the failure at the conclusion of a given early dialogue to satisfy the following condition: A positive Platonic thesis regarding the central problem of the drama clearly emerges from the text. In some, but not all, cases, this condition is satisfied by Socrates endorsing a positive thesis, albeit without avowing knowledge, regarding the answer to the question that governs the investigation. Granted this, dramatic aporia is not a feature of *Gorgias*, *Crito*, *Apology*, *Ion*, or *Euthydemus*.

The question why Plato composed the early definitional dialogues and *Protagoras* to end in dramatic aporia is difficult. Prima facie, it might seem explicable by the fact that these texts are variously preoccupied with the WF question. Accordingly, Plato would be emphasizing the deep epistemological problem of definitional knowledge of excellence. However, one other early dialogue, *Hippias Minor*, ends in dramatic aporia, and this dialogue does not broach the WF question.

The argument between Socrates and Hippias compels the conclusion that it is in the nature of the good man to do injustice willingly. At the same time, both Hippias and Socrates admit to the intuition that this cannot be so. Socrates says that he cannot agree with himself, but that according to their argument this conclusion necessarily follows. He concludes that "regarding these matters, I go astray topsy-turvy (*anô kai katô*) and never hold the same opinions."[2] It is noteworthy that the same phrase, "topsy-turvy," occurs in the *Protagoras* and *Hippias Minor* passages. Contrast this in particular with Socrates' statement in *Gorgias* that he has always arrived at the same opinion of the topic under discussion: "No one I've encountered before as now has been able to claim

---

1. *Prt.* 361c2–6.
2. *Hp. Mi.* 376c2–3.

otherwise without becoming ridiculous. And so once more I say that it is so."[3] Socrates' statement in *Gorgias* underscores the relative stability of his belief and its grounds, whereas the phrase "topsy-turvy" emphasizes the instability of his belief.

Dramatic aporia in some of the early dialogues is not, then, explicable in view of the epistemological problem of definitional knowledge. Collectively, the early dialogues convey as clearly as anything else that excellence is a kind of knowledge. Accordingly, Plato could have composed the early definitional dialogues and *Protagoras* to end with Socrates affirming, although without claiming to know, that excellence or a putative part of it is knowledge of some kind. Similarly, in the case of *Hippias Minor*, the good person has the capacity to do what is bad in a way that no other sort of person does. This is because the good person possesses knowledge of goodness and knowledge of a given subject entails knowledge of its contrary. For example, a doctor has knowledge of health and so also of sickness. Thus, the doctor, in contrast to all others, is best able to cause sickness. *Hippias Minor* does not, however, introduce the principle of eudaimonism, that everyone pursues well-being, the subjectivist conception of desire, according to which everyone desires what he or she regards as good, or the rejection of the popular conception of *akrasia*. Given these psychological principles, although the good person is most capable of doing what is bad, the good person would never in fact do what is bad, since he would never desire to do what is bad and since he would never fail to do what he desires. As I have noted, there is an important disanalogy between the *technê* of excellence and all other *technai*. In short, Plato could have had Socrates introduce these psychological principles in *Hippias Minor* and, as a result, affirm, albeit without claiming knowledge, that although the good person, on account of his knowledge, is most capable of doing what is bad, the good person would never in fact willingly do what is bad.

Instead, the fact that the definitional dialogues, *Protagoras*, and *Hippias Minor* end in dramatic aporia, whereas *Gorgias*, *Crito*, *Euthydemus*, *Ion*, and *Apology* do not, is explicable on the basis of a distinction between ethical action and ethical theory. Consider that in *Gorgias*, *Crito*, *Euthydemus*, and *Apology*, the discussions are closely tied to practical problems. Broadly speaking, *Gorgias* dramatizes an engagement between rhetoric and philosophy and between the distinct modes of political life to which adherence to each of these disciplines relates. Socrates concludes by strongly advocating philosophy and by condemning rhetoric as conventionally conceived and employed. It is often hypothesized that *Gorgias* is a kind of advertisement for Plato's Academy in competition with Isocrates' rhetorical school.[4] This hypothesis at least conforms well to the notion that the dialogue dramatizes an evaluation of the two disciplines. And insofar as the dialogue aspires to encourage the pursuit of philosophy over rhetoric, that is, to encourage a particular practical decision, a dramatically aporetic conclusion would undermine this objective.

---

3. *Grg.* 509a6–b1.
4. Isocrates had been a student of Gorgias.

The drama of *Euthydemus* is similar to *Gorgias*. The difference is that a form of pseudophilosophy plays the role in *Euthydemus* that rhetoric plays in *Gorgias*. Again, *Euthydemus* encourages the pursuit of philosophy. This dialogue is widely regarded as Plato's protreptic dialogue. Accordingly, if the discussion concluded in dramatic aporia, unable to determine whether to advocate the philosophy Socrates practices or the eristic dialectic of Euthydemus and Dionysodorus, it would fail to encourage a particular practical decision.

The question governing *Crito*, whether Socrates should escape from prison or suffer captial punishment, is obviously a practical one; and it would be absurd for Socrates to conclude his discussion with Crito unable to affirm one of the disjuncts. Likewise, the problem facing Socrates in *Apology* is practical. Socrates is compelled to defend his philosophical activity against the charge of impiety and corruption of the youth. The practical problems in *Crito* and *Apology*, of course, differ from those in *Gorgias* and *Euthydemus*, for in the latter two dialogues it is the reader whose decision to pursue philosophy versus rhetoric or sophistry is at stake, whereas in the former two Socrates' life is at stake. For the reader, the questions of Socrates' guilt or innocence and of Socrates' obedience or disobedience may be relatively theoretical. However, the way in which Socrates is portrayed as responding to these challenges is surely also intended to have practical significance for the reader—even if Socrates' conduct and the rationality upon which that conduct is based serve as a regulative ideal.

The question that governs *Ion* is ostensibly theoretical, not practical. Of course, it may have practical ramifications. For example, the fact that this or that poet or rhapsode lacks knowledge may have consequences for the way in which individuals or communities appeal to or utilize these figures as authorities. Even so, the explanation for the fact that *Ion* ends in epistemological, not dramatic, aporia falls outside of the present paradigm—not because it contradicts the conditions of the paradigm, but because the governing question of the dialogue is ostensibly epistemological, not ethical. Evidently, then, Plato did not regard as deeply puzzling, or rather did not think it important to convey as deeply puzzling, understanding of an alleged authority figure's lack of knowledge.

In contrast, the investigations in the definitional dialogues, *Protagoras*, and *Hippias Minor* are ethical, but predominantly theoretical. Granted, in a number of these texts, the theoretical questions are embedded in practical problems; and, indeed, all of the theoretical questions, which are metaethical questions, have practical significance. However, again, the dialogues place emphasis on theoretical problems whose answers are necessary for the answers to the practical problems. For instance, in *Protagoras*, the basic practical problem is whether Hippocrates should commit his soul to Protagoras' tutelage. The dialogue clearly conveys a negative answer to this question. First, in the atrium of his house, Socrates, using the unflattering analogy of the indiscriminate huckster, explicitly warns Hippocrates of the dangers. Second, Protagoras' inability to provide a satisfactory account of excellence is intended to serve as evidence that he is not fit to educate youths. This important issue frames the dialogue. However, the principal philosophical work of the dialogue is the examination of excellence and the identity of its parts, which is a theoretical question, albeit, again, within the domain of ethics.

Similarly, the investigation of the identity of courage in Laches is framed by an immediate practical consideration, whether Stesilaus is a fitting instructor for Lysimachus' and Melesias' sons, insofar as the fathers aspire to engender excellence in their sons. In one respect, this question is not answered. At least, when they are first presented the question, Laches and Nicias express divided opinions. Ultimately, however, it becomes clear that insofar as the solution to the problem depends upon the answer to the WF question, the question whether the fathers should send their sons to Stesilaus must be deferred.

Again, the investigation in Euthyphro is embedded within a clearly practical context. Socrates explicitly says that he wants to learn from Euthyphro what holiness is so that he can defend himself against Meletus' accusation. But as in the cases of Protagoras and Laches, the question whose answer is regarded as necessary for the practical solution is the theoretical WF question.

In Lysis too, the investigation into the nature of friendship emerges in the context of a practical problem: how to treat a beloved, specifically how Hippothales should treat his beloved. In contrast, in Charmides, Meno, Republic, Hippias Major, and Hippias Minor, relatively little dramaturgical energy is expended on defining practical problems to which the WF questions pertain. Clearly, this does not indicate that the theoretical questions have comparatively little practical significance. Rather, it suggests that in these texts, as in the others, the theoretical questions are focal because they are epistemologically primary. Consequently, the dramatic aporiai in all these cases underscore the importance of pursuing the theoretical questions. More generally, the contrast between the dialogues that end only in epistemological aporia and those that end in dramatic aporia shows two things. In the former case, the failure to achieve ethical knowledge does not and should not paralyze agents; rather, we should deliberate over and provide well-reasoned grounds for our ethically significant decisions. In the latter case, the failure to achieve stable ethical or metaethical beliefs indicates the depth of the theoretical problems pertinent to the practical problems. There is, indeed, a tension here between the theoretical and the practical, but not a contradiction. Practical solutions are theoretically, but not practically, dependent upon theoretical solutions. One obvious consequence of this is that since the reasons upon which one acts are unlikely to be wholly adequately justified relative to the demands of ethical knowledge, even though they are relatively well reasoned, they may result in bad conduct. That is a hard but inevitable fact of the weakness and limitations of humanity. Another consequence or potential consequence, inferred and developed in Republic, is a social distribution of cognitive labor. Since ethical knowledge is extremely difficult to achieve, there may have to be those trained to prescribe codes of ethical conduct and those who merely obey them.

2. Dramatic Aporia

In the early definitional dialogues, Protagoras, and Hippias Minor, dramatic aporiai correspond to an emphasis on the theoretical difficulties of ethical problems. In these cases, we can observe a distinction between the reasons within the conceptual horizons of the dramatic actors and those of the author. In other words, we can observe that the reasons why, from the perspective of the dramatic actors, the investigations of the particular theoretical problems end in aporia do not represent Platonic reasons. To understand this point we need to look more closely at the forms of the aporiai in the dialogues. In the previous section I discussed the problem in the case of *Hippias Minor*; here I will focus on several salient examples from the definitional dialogues and *Protagoras*.

Given the structure of the definitional dialogues as defined in accordance with the F-conditions in the investigations, it is conceivable that the investigations would end in something like the following way. Socrates would emphasize that, whatever F is, a satisfactory definition ought to satisfy the set of F-conditions that emerged in the course of the investigation. Furthermore, Socrates might propose a definition that does satisfy those conditions and then suggest that, at this stage of investigation, that definition is the most promising alternative, even though further F-conditions might subsequently be disclosed that undermined the proposed solution. For example, consider the set of F-conditions in *Charmides*: being fine, being good, entailing knowledge, existing, and being beneficial. In view of these, at the end of the investigation, Socrates could suggest that sound-mindedness is a kind of beneficial knowledge, specifically knowledge of the good, or he could at least suggest that this conception should be a point of departure for further investigation. But none of the definitional dialogues or *Protagoras* ends in this way.

The investigation in *Euthyphro* is arguably divisible into two movements, although Socrates only engages one interlocutor. The first is devoted to Euthyphro's first three definitions. As I discussed in section 6.1 of chapter 4, Socrates' criticisms of these focus on various metaphysical aspects of F—its unity, purity, and *aetiological* capacity—whose collective aim is the clarification of F qua Form. By the unity of F is meant that all f participants are f in virtue of *one* thing, namely F. By the purity of F is meant that F itself is f and does not admit a compresence of the contrary of F. For example, holiness is holy and not in any way unholy. By the *aetiological* capacity of F is meant that F is responsible for, that is, is the *aitia* of, f things being f.

Euthyphro's first response to the WF question suggests that he is unclear about the distinction between a Form and its participants. Socrates accepts Euthyphro's second definition, being loved by some god, as being of the right kind. In other words, it can plausibly be considered to identify the Form holiness. The definition is rejected, however, because if the gods have opposing attitudes toward the same entity, that entity will be both god-beloved and god-hated. As such, the definition fails to satisfy the purity condition. Consequently, the definition is amended to the condition of being loved by all the gods. But this third definition is criticized on the grounds that it refers to the attitude of the gods, as opposed to holiness itself, toward which the gods are well disposed. Socrates argues that holy things are god-beloved because they are holy; they are not holy because they are god-beloved. In short, holiness, not god-belovedness, is responsible for holy participants being holy; and so an adequate definition must define this, the being (*ousia*) of that which is holy, in other words, holiness, not something that happens to, that is, is an affection of (*pathos*) that which is holy, namely that it is god-beloved.

Following Socrates' response to his third definition, Euthyphro is perplexed. Consequently, Socrates assumes greater responsibility in the formulation of the fourth definition. He suggests that holiness is a part of justice. In the legalistic context of the discussion this is intended to mean that acts that are fitting with respect to the divine form a subset of just acts. Euthyphro is thereby encouraged to consider the distinctive character of holy acts. He suggests that holiness is a kind of care (*therapeia*) for the gods. This is rejected on the grounds that caring typically benefits the object of care; however, the gods qua perfect cannot be benefited. Care for the gods is, therefore, reinterpreted as service to the gods. But when Socrates questions the nature of this service, Euthyphro's response implies that doing what is god-beloved benefits humanity. The notion of doing what is god-beloved casts the investigation back to the concept of god-belovedness, which was previously rejected. At that point Euthyphro runs off, claiming he has an appointment.

In *Protagoras*, holiness, like justice, courage, and sound-mindedness, is treated as one of the constituents of human excellence; moreover, all of these constituents are identified with a kind of knowledge. In view of this as well as the investigations in *Charmides*, *Laches*, and *Republic* 1, the structure of the investigation in *Euthyphro* is especially remarkable. No definition is criticized on ethical grounds, and no definition explicitly entails an epistemic component. This is to be explained as a deliberate decision on Plato's part to focus on the metaphysics of F. Thus, once the principal metaphysical aspects of F have been introduced through criticism of the first three definitions, the investigation proceeds, in a sense, from the point at which the investigations in *Charmides*, *Laches*, and *Republic* 1 begin, that is, with a conventional conception of F as a type of action, care for the gods, which is then reinterpreted as service to the gods. But since clarification of the nature of service to the gods involves a regress to the difficulty upon which the third definition falters, the ethical and epistemic aspects of F are never broached. In short, from Plato's perspective, the pedagogical work of the dialogue is essentially complete with the clarification of the metaphysical aspects of F. But if this is the case and the Platonic conception of holiness is epistemic, then the dramatic aporia in which Socrates and Euthyphro cease their investigation in *Euthyphro* is wholly distinct from the Platonic view of the nature of holiness as the knowledge of good and bad.

The investigation in *Hippias Major* is divisible into at least two movements. The first runs through Hippias' three definitions. Following criticism of the third definition, Socrates himself offers the remaining definitions. Arguably, the final definition, aesthetic pleasure, constitutes a distinct movement in the investigation. However, I will not develop this point here. Instead, I emphasize the continuity between the sixth and seventh definitions in view of the manner in which they are criticized.

The first movement is preoccupied with achieving two points. One is clarification of fineness qua universal. This is advanced through repeated emphasis on the satisfaction of the purity condition. The other, related, point, is clarification of the range of valences of fineness, from physical attractiveness or aesthetic value to functional utility to ethicality. In short, on the assumption that all fine things are fine because of fineness, the first movement clarifies the range of kinds of entities considered to be fine and in view of which fineness itself must be identified. Socrates criticizes the kinds of definitions Hippias offers as simple-minded. Their simple-mindedness relates precisely to their failure to satisfy the purity condition and thus to capture the common element among the wide range of fine entities.

In the second movement of the dialogue Socrates proposes definitions. These involve so-called incomplete predicates,[5] the decorous, the useful, and the beneficial. Since the fine or fineness is also an incomplete predicate, Socrates' definitions stand a better chance of satisfying the purity condition. Plato also uses these definitions to further clarify the metaphysics of F and in particular to clarify the distinction between F and f participants. This is achieved through emphasis on the *aetiological* condition. In response to the fourth definition, it is stressed that F makes f participants f. Socrates' response to the fifth definition is the one ethical criticism introduced. But even this is made to advance understanding of the *aetiological* condition, for it emphasizes that F is not responsible for entities being not-f; in other words, F is not harmful. The sixth definition concerns the same point, F's responsibility for entities being f.

Dramatic aporia in *Hippias Major* occurs once the seventh definition, pleasure through sight and hearing, is reinterpreted as beneficial pleasure. This itself results from the idea that pleasure through sight and pleasure through hearing, in contrast to the other senses, share the property of being beneficial. Insofar as beneficial pleasure entails the concept of benefit, this definition falters for the same reason as the previous one. We need, then, to consider the criticism of the sixth definition more closely.

The criticism of the sixth definition, benefit, depends upon a fallacy of ambiguity involving the confusion of the phrase *to agathon* (the good). This phrase-type is common in Plato, and the ancient Greek language itself commonly forms general terms using the singular definite article *to* (the) and a corresponding adjective. Indeed, in *Republic* 1, *Euthyphro*, and *Hippias Major*, Socrates and his interlocutors use general terms and *to* phrases interchangeably for F: *to dikaion* and *dikaiosunê* for justice, *to hosion* and *hosiotês* for holiness, and *to kalon* and *kallos* for fineness.

In contexts of metaphysical discourse, Plato often appends to the *to* phrase the emphatic pronoun *auto* (itself) or the prepositional phrase *kath' hauto* (by itself) in order to clarify that the referent is a Form. However, such an appendage is unnecessary, and there are occasions, specifically in *Euthyphro* and *Hippias Major*, where the *to* phrase is employed without an appendage to designate a

---

5. Linguists now more commonly refer to these as subsective adjectives. For example, "small" is a subsective adjective. "Small" does not have an independent referent; its reference depends upon the noun that it modifies; for example, "small elephant" versus "small mouse." In these cases, the referent is a *subset* of elephants or mice, respectively. See Chierchia and McConnell-Ginet (1990) 263–65.

Form. This is significant because *to* phrases in fact are semantically ambiguous. Aside from their Platonic use as Form-designators, or rather more generally as referring expressions, in conventional discourse *to* phrases can also function as quantifier-phrases.[6] Consider the following two interpretations of the sentence *to kalon estin agathon*: "fineness is good," and "that which fine is good." According to the second interpretation, the subject is nonreferring; it functions as a quantifier phrase ranging over the domain of fine instances.

The dual use of *to* phrases, referential and quantificational, is remarkable insofar as these uses correspond to the distinction of Forms and participants, respectively. As such, the semantic ambiguity of the *to* phrase could obscure the very metaphysical distinction that the investigations introduce and develop. Remarkably, in *Hippias Major*, this ambiguity is exploited in Socrates' response to the sixth definition. Consider first the confusion that the *to* phrase provokes in Hippias when Socrates initially poses the WF question:

SOCRATES   What is this thing, *to kalon*?

HIPPIAS   Well, Socrates, does he who asks this want to find out anything else than what is *kalon*?

SOCRATES   I do not think that is what he wants to find out, but what *to kalon* is, Hippias.

HIPPIAS   And what difference is there between them?

SOCRATES   Does it not seem to you that there is a difference between them?

HIPPIAS   No difference at all.

SOCRATES   Well, surely you know better than I. But still consider closely, my friend, for he is not asking what is *kalon*, but what is *to kalon*.[7]

In this passage Hippias interprets the *to* phrase quantificationally. That is, he interprets Socrates to be asking him "What is that which is fine?"—in other words, "What is something fine?" Hippias fails to appreciate the semantic distinction between sentences of the form G is *f* and G is F. And accordingly, Hippias fails to appreciate the distinction between identifying something that is fine (a participant) and the fineness (a Form) in virtue of which fine things are fine. In short, Plato has Socrates draw attention at the beginning of the investigation to the semantic ambiguity of the *to* phrase.

In response to the sixth definition, benefit (or the beneficial), Socrates develops the following argument:

---

6. Quantifiers are expressions denoting quantity, for example, "one," "some," "all." Quantifier phrases are noun phrases in which the nouns are modified by quantifiers, for example, "one hat," "some shoes." In Greek, *to* phrases, such as *to agathon* (the good) and *to kalon* (the fine) can function as quantifier phrases, where the definite article *to* functions as a universal quantifier, equivalent to the words "all" or "every."

7. *Hp. Ma.* 287d4–e1. Note that the ambiguity is compounded here by the fact that the English distinction in word order that we encounter in the clauses "what fineness is" and "what is fine" is irrelevant in Greek.

To ôphelimon (the beneficial) is *to poioun agathon* (that which makes good). *To poioun* (that which makes) is nothing other than *to aition* (the cause).

(a)   *To kalon* (the fine) is *aition tou agathou* (responsible for the good). But the cause and that of which the cause is the cause are different.

(b)   But if *to kalon* is *aition agathou* (responsible for good), then *to agathon* (the good) would come into being from *to kalon*. Then neither is *to kalon agathon* (good), nor is *to agathon* (the good) *kalon*. But this is absurd; therefore, *to ôphelimon* is not *to kalon*.

The fundamental problem with the argument is its failure to distinguish between the Forms fineness and goodness, on the one hand, and fine and good participants, on the other. Premise (a) is reasonable *if* the grammatical object of *aition* (cause or thing responsible for), namely the *to* phrase *tou agathou* (the good), is interpreted not as a Form-designator referring to the Form goodness, but as a quantifier phrase ranging over good instances: Fineness is responsible for that which is good. However, in the dialogue *tou agathou* is mistakenly interpreted as a Form-designator.

Observe also that in the phrase *aition agathou* (cause of good) in (b) the definite article *tou* (the) is lacking. Perhaps Plato omitted it to playfully hint at the confusion between *ti agathon* (something good) and *to agathon* (the good), where the latter phrase may be interpreted as Form-designator or a quantifier phrase. Again, the apodosis in (b) would make sense *if* the phrase *to agathon* were interpreted as a quantifier phrase rather than a Form-designator. In sum, the problems of the argument directly relate to the ambiguities of the *to* phrase that were adumbrated at the beginning of the investigation.

Finally, the rejection of the seventh definition, beneficial pleasure, on the grounds that the sixth definition, benefit, is rejected again depends upon the confusion of the *to* phrase and the corresponding failure to recognize the metaphysical distinction between Forms and participants. Clearly, however, confusion over the two interpretations of the *to* phrase is not Platonic. Nor is confusion over the distinction between Forms and participants, at least not in this respect.

Finally, we have seen that Socrates concludes the investigation of the parts of excellence in *Protagoras* with an account of the division between his and Protagoras' positions. He says that he would like to go through the investigation of excellence again and then consider whether it is teachable. He does claim that insofar as excellence appears to be knowledge, it is teachable; and in this respect, Socrates' view is Platonic. However, Socrates also acknowledges that he began the investigation with the assumption that excellence was not teachable.

The Platonic position differs from Socrates' at this point in *Protagoras*. Surely, it is not the Platonic view that excellence is teachable in a conventional sense. But, more importantly, the Platonic position is not that excellence is unteachable on the grounds that Socrates offers early on in his discussion with Protagoras. There, Socrates presents the following argument. The Athenians are sensible people. In their political assemblies, when technical matters are under discussion, they heed only specialists. In contrast, when matters pertaining to excellence, which is to say political *technê*, are under discussion, they yield the floor to anyone who chooses to speak. On the basis of the form of Athenian government, excellence must not be teachable.[8]

The preceding accounts indicate that it is naïve to conceive of the dramatic *aporiai* in which Socrates' discussions with his interlocutors end as reflecting the honest perplexity that Plato himself experienced as he wrestled with the problems in these texts. This is the case even if Plato was in some state of perplexity regarding the problems that govern the discussions in the dialogues, for Plato's perplexity would not have had the form that Socrates' and his interlocutors' have. The fact that Plato could have composed the dialogues that end in dramatic aporia to conclude otherwise, precisely with Socrates endorsing, as he does in *Gorgias* and *Crito*, the most well-reasoned belief to derive from the investigation, reemphasizes a central thesis of this study: Socrates is not simply Plato's mouthpiece; the relationship between Plato and his favored character is complex. In the case of dramatic *aporiai*, Plato manipulates Socrates for philosophical-pedagogical purposes.

The dramatic aporia in which the early definitional dialogues, *Protagoras*, and *Hippias Minor* end can also be understood as variously related to the general theme of the conflict between philosophy and antiphilosophy that pervades the early dialogues. As I emphasized in chapter 1, the discussions in the texts are not wholly situated within the sphere of philosophical discourse. Rather, the pursuits of ethical knowledge emerge out of broader, more conventional cultural milieus. This is consonant with the propaedeutic function of the texts; and the dramaturgical characteristics of *a*-structure and the common doxastic base conform to this function.

In the course of the dialogues, philosophical inquiry is pursued dialogically. Socrates always engages a set of interlocutors. Broadly speaking, Socrates and his interlocutors are participants in a common culture; however, the dialogues emphasize differences of value and opinion among the actors. Plato portrays the enterprise of philosophy as a trial (*agôn*). The conflict it engages may be conceived abstractly, as between forms of discourse, such as reasoned argumentation, rhetoric, sophistry, and poetry, or concretely as between individuals. Accordingly, dramatic *aporiai* can be seen to result from the conflict, and the parties to the conflict can be subsumed under the categories of philosophy and antiphilosophy.

Socrates' trial well encapsulates the idea. The champion of philosophy is forced into the people's court to be evaluated according to conventional criteria. Socrates begs the jurors' pardon for his manner of speech, unaccustomed as he is to the setting and its particular habits. From the perspective of philosophical values,

---

8. *Prt.* 319b–c.

Socrates' condemnation is a travesty; in any case, for all their ignorance, the Athenians cannot harm his soul. But from the conventional perspective of the polis and its citizens, Socrates and his philosophical enterprise are tested, deemed intolerable, confined, and finally destroyed. The subculture of philosophy with its ambitions to social and political reform thus remains under the control of the dominant antiphilosophical culture.

Dramatic aporiai among the early dialogues variously reflect the ordeals of philosophy in a manner akin to Socrates' trial before the Athenians. For instance, as I discussed in section 6 of chapter 3, the investigations in *Laches* and *Lysis* end as a result of a conflict between two conceptions of F. In the case of *Laches*, the conception of courage that results from the investigation, the knowledge of good and bad—which is Platonic—conflicts with the pretheoretical conventional conception of courage as a part of excellence with which the investigation began. In *Lysis*, the conventional conception of friendship based on likeness, which is actually rejected in the course of the investigation, continues to influence Lysis and Menexenus at the end of the investigation. For when Socrates ultimately suggests to the boys a cogent conception of friendship dependent upon the distinction between belonging and likeness, the boys claim that things that are good, bad, and neither-good-nor-bad belong to one another and thus fail to uphold the distinction. In both *Laches* and *Lysis*, then, conventional conceptions conflict with Platonic conceptions, and aporiai follow failure to liberate the mind from the conventional conceptions.

The conclusion in *Euthyphro* resembles that in *Lysis* in the following sense. The fourth and final definition, service to the gods, ultimately fails on the same grounds as the preceding definition. In explaining how service to the gods is beneficial, Euthyphro claims that doing what is dear to the gods yields goods for humanity. The implication that service to the gods is dear to the gods suggests that Euthyphro remains committed to a conception of holiness as god-belovedness, even though this view was previously rejected. Similarly, in *Hippias Major*, the final definition, beneficial pleasure, fails on the same grounds as the preceding definition, benefit. And both definitions fail on account of confusion of two interpretations of the *to* phrase, the fine (*to kalon*), whose disambiguation in turn requires a grasp of the distinction between Form and participants. In these respects, the texts dramatize the limitations of the investigation; they emphasize the way that conventional or commonsensical ideas tether thought and impede philosophical satisfaction.

The final passage of *Lysis* further exposes the social and psychological conditions responsible for dramatic aporia. When the group's powers of investigation reach exhaustion, Lysis' and Menexenus' pedagogues emerge to take the boys home:

> Having thus spoken, I was minded to stir up somebody else among the older people there, when like otherworldly spirits (*daimones*), there came upon us the pedagogues of Lysis and Menexenus. They were bringing the boys' brothers and called out to them the order to go home, for it was quite late. At first we tried with the help of the group around us to drive them off, but

they took no notice of us and went on angrily calling, as before, in their foreign accents (*hupobarbarizontes*). We decided that they had taken a drop too much at the festival and would prove awkward people to deal with. So we gave in an broke up our party.[9]

By referring to the slaves as "otherworldly spirits" and as speaking in "barbarian accents," Socrates characterizes the boys' pedagogues as foreign to the discussion group. Since pedagogues were slaves, Lysis' and Menexenus' pedagogues would literally have been foreigners. The conclusion of *Lysis* shows the boys returning to their familiar roles under the care of their customary pedagogues. But Socrates' emphasis on the foreignness of the pedagogues, immediately following an investigation that has developed a theory of friendship based on belonging, intimates that these pedagogues are foreign to the boys in a philosophical sense too.

Socrates, the boys, and the other attending youth are reluctant to break off the discussion when the slaves come to fetch Lysis and Menexenus to take them home. It is remarked that the slaves have been drinking wine during the rites of the Hermaia, the day on which the discussion at Miccus' palaestra occurs; and Socrates says that it seemed on this account that the slaves would be intractable. The word Socrates uses to describe the slaves' demeanor is *aporoi*.[10] This image of the drunken intractable slaves serving as Lysis' and Menexenus' pedagogues contrasts with the image of Socrates as Lysis' and Menexenus' temporary pedagogue. At the beginning of *Lysis*, Socrates describes himself as making his way from the Academy to the Lyceum. The word Socrates uses to describe his walk, the first word of the dialogue, is *eporeumên* (I was making my way).[11] The aporia or intractability of the slaves at the end of the dialogue contrasts with Socrates' passage (*poros*) at the beginning of the dialogue. While Socrates is engaged in philosophy, the drunken slaves literally disband Socrates', Lysis', and Menexenus' convivium (*sunousian*).

The drunkenness of the slaves also recalls Hippothales' drunkenness and suggests that the slaves, like Hippothales, may have a detrimental influence on the boys. In this particular case, as they hinder the boys from philosophical inquiry, they are perhaps intended to appear as doing so. To this extent the slaves are, like Hippothales, also inauthentic friends, with whom Lysis and Menexenus do not belong. The harmfulness of the drunken slaves and Hippothales may be contrasted with that beneficial drunkenness from which Socrates describes himself and the boys as suffering as a result of the tortuous investigation: "Since it is as if we were drunk (*methuomen*) from the discussion."[12]

As Lysis and Menexenus leave Socrates' company, they leave the site of beneficial extrinsic friendship and risk the dangers of the inauthentic friendships

---

9. *Ly.* 223a1–b2.
10. *Ly.* 223b2. The adjective *aporos* literally means "without passage." The "*a*" is privative, and *poros* is a noun meaning "a means of passage."
11. *Ly.* 203a1.
12. *Ly.* 222c2.

surrounding them. The final scene of the dialogue, with the entrance of the slaves and the disbanding of the group, indicates that the philosophical investigation has occurred within a space governed by the antiphilosophical conventions of the polis. The dramatic aporia of the investigation may be seen to result from this condition of the investigation as well. While Socrates' communion with the boys has sought to provoke philosophical inquiry and develop understanding beyond received views, the boys remain deeply entrenched in the familiar practices of their daily lives.

3.1. The Example of *Charmides*

The investigation and aporia in *Charmides* similarly dramatize the vulnerability of philosophy to antiphilosophical social and psychological forces. I will conclude my discussion of aporia with a close examination of this dialogue. In addition, the discussion of *Charmides* is intended to recall the various strands of thought developed over the preceding chapters and to draw them together in a concrete and graphic manner by identifying their operation within a single text. In partic- ular, we will show how Plato integrates argumentative, dramatic, and historical elements in dramatizing the conflict of philosophy and antiphilosophy. *Charmides* is particularly well suited to this end because of its literary and philosophical richness and because we are particularly well informed about the historicity of its elements. As will also become clear, *Charmides* is the most autobiographical of Plato's early dialogues. The political-philosophical concerns it engages were clearly formative in his life. Thus, the dialogue can be read as a sort of manifesto for Plato's early philosophical enterprise.

It will be helpful to have in mind an outline of the dialogue's contents. It opens with Socrates having returned from battle in Potidaia to Athens. He arrives at Taureas' wrestling-school and inquires into the state of philosophy and the condition of the youths in Athens. He learns that Charmides is especially promising and in particular most sound-minded. Charmides then enters the wrestling-school, and he is called over to have a discussion with Socrates. The remainder of the dialogue is devoted to an inquiry into the nature of sound- mindedness (*sôphrosunê*). First, Charmides offers two successive definitions of sound-mindedness, restraint and modesty. Each is criticized for failing to satisfy the F-conditions of being fine and being good in all instances, respectively. Subsequently, Critias, Charmides' guardian, assumes the role of Socrates' principal interlocutor in the inquiry. He defines sound-mindedness as doing one's own thing. This is explained to as doing good things, but then is criticized on the grounds that one may do good things by accident. Critias offers self-knowledge as his second definition of sound-mindedness. Socrates attempts to clarify the nature of self-knowledge by analogy with other types of *technê*. First he asks after the product of self-knowledge, as medicine and architecture produce health and building. Then he asks after the object of self-knowledge, as numeration is concerned with the odd and the even. Critias rejects Socrates' attempts to identify the product or object of self-knowledge, and in the course of this discus- sion the conception of sound-mindedness as self-knowledge is transformed into the knowledge of knowledge and all other knowledges as well as lack of knowledge (K). K is then criticized with respect to two F-conditions. It is unclear whether such a thing as K exists; and even if it existed, it would not be beneficial. The investigation ends in failure to provide a satisfactory definition of sound-mindedness.

3.2. *Charmides* as Autobiography

Critias' first statements in *Charmides* are superlative praise of Charmides: Charmides is considered the most attractive youth in Athens; the quality of his soul is fine; he is philosophical and poetic;[13] he excels his peers not only in appearance, but in sound-mindedness.[14] In sum, "he is considered to be by far the most sound-minded person around and in all other respects, for a person of his age, second to none."[15]

Socrates relates the praise of Charmides to his family and ancestry: "It is, I think, fitting [that his soul is well constituted,] Critias, since he is of your family";[16] and more elaborately in response to Critias' statement immediately above:

It is right, Charmides, that you should excel [your peers] in [all respects], for I do not suppose there is anyone else here who could readily point to a case of any two Athenian families uniting together that would be likely to produce handsomer or finer offspring than those from which you are sprung. Your father's family, which comes from Critias son of Dropides, has been celebrated by Anacreon and Solon and many other poets, so that it is famed by tradition among us as preeminent in beauty and excellence and all else that is considered well-being. And then your mother's family is famous in the same way, for it is said of Pyrilampes, your uncle, that no one in all the continent was considered to be his superior in appearance or stature, whenever he served as envoy to the Great King or to anyone else in Asia. Sprung from such people, it is to be expected that you would be first in all things.[17]

The connection between Charmides' excellence and his family is deliberate; its significance is complex. On the one hand, Plato's incorporation into the text of the praise of Charmides' family is self-aggrandizing, for the historical Charmides was a member of Plato's own family. Charmides was Plato's uncle, the brother of Plato's mother Perictione. Pyrilampes, also praised in the passage, was Plato's stepfather. He married Perictione some time after the death of Plato's biological father Ariston, and with her he fathered Plato's half-brother Antiphon.

---

13. *Chrm.* 154a4–155a1.
14. *Chrm.* 157d1–3.
15. *Chrm.* 157d6–8.
16. *Chrm.* 154e1–3.
17. *Chrm.* 157d9–158a7.

At the same time, the praise of Charmides' excellence in relation to his family is dramatically ironic. The historical Critias was also a member of the family. He was Charmides' first cousin, the son of Callaeschrus, the brother of Charmides' father Glaucon. Both Charmides and Critias brought ignominy upon their family through their participation in the oligarchic regime that briefly replaced the democracy at the end of the Peloponnesian War. Following the demise of this regime and the restoration of the democracy, the oligarchs came to be demonized as tyrants.

Plato was intimately involved with the regime. In the *Seventh Letter* he famously describes his experience as a young man encouraged by Critias and Charmides to participate:

> In the government then existing, reviled as it was by many, a revolution took place; and the revolution was headed by fifty-one leaders, of whom eleven were in the city, ten in the Piraeus ... and thirty were established as irresponsible rulers of all. Now some of these were actually connections and acquaintances of mine. And indeed, they invited me at once to join their administration, thinking it would be congenial. The feelings I then experienced, owing to my youth, were in no way surprising, for I imagined that they would administer the state by leading it out of an unjust into a just way of life, and consequently I gave my mind to them very diligently to see what they would do. And indeed, I saw how in a short time these men caused others to look back on the former government as a golden age ... So when I beheld all these actions and others of a similar kind, I was indignant, and I withdrew myself from the bad practices then going on.[18]

At least psychologically, Plato ultimately distanced himself from the oligarchy. Following the restoration of the democracy, a general amnesty for those involved was decreed. But Plato's relationship to the oligarchs certainly placed him in an awkward relation to the majority of his fellow citizens. Consider Socrates' own relation to the oligarchs. In *Apology* and *Seventh Letter*, Plato notes that Socrates refused to heed the order of the oligarchs to seize for execution the general Leon of Salamis. Plato includes the detail to distance Socrates from the regime. But the fact that Socrates remained in Athens during their government indicates complicity. Only three thousand citizens were allowed to live in the city,[19] and these were selected on account of their perceived ideological sympathies. With the democracy restored, animosity toward Socrates arose on account of his relationship to Critias and others, such as Alcibiades, who in the course of the Peloponnesian War had been disloyal to Athens. In his study of the political psychology of Athens in the wake of the oligarchy, Andrew Wolpert writes:

---

18. *Ep. VII* 324c2–325a5; the translation follows Bury (1929).
19. "The excluded (those outside the 3,000) were banned from living in the city." (Krentz, 1982, 65)

But did the jury consider Socrates an oligarchic sympathizer? The answer must be yes. In spite of the amnesty, litigants often recalled what their opponents did during the civil war, and defendants were often accused of having remained in the city...The prosecutors needed only mention that [Socrates] had stayed in Athens in order to put him on the defensive. And it certainly did not help his cause that they could also remind the jurors that he had been an intimate friend of Critias, along with other young men who had overthrown the democracy. What better proof that Socrates had in fact corrupted the youth? What better reason to fear that a new generation under his influence might follow in the path of Alcibiades and Critias?[20]

Polycrates' lost *Accusation of Socrates* (composed around 393) attacked Socrates for this very thing, and Xenophon's *Memorabilia* opens with a rejoinder to absolve Socrates of corrupting Critias and Alcibiades. Likewise a fragment from a Socratic dialogue by Aeschines of Sphettus: "I wonder how one ought to deal with the fact that Alcibiades and Critias were associates of Socrates, against whom the many and the upper classes made such strong accusations."[21] As late as 345, the orator Aeschines (not Aeschines the Socratic) could ask a jury: "Did you kill Socrates the sophist, men of Athens, because he was shown to have taught Critias, one of the Thirty who overthrew the democracy?"[22] In composing an investiga-tion of sound-mindedness with Socrates, Critias, and Charmides, Plato enters into this complex of associations.

3.3. The Politics of *Sôphrosunê*

The beginning and conclusion of *Charmides* allude to events that frame the Peloponnesian War. The dialogue opens with Socrates narrating to an anonymous acquaintance his return from battle in Potidaia. Potidaia was a city in Chalcidice at the southern base of Macedonia, a Corinthian colony and tributary ally of Athens until 432. At that time it broke with Athens and was subsequently besieged by Athenian forces, beginning in the spring of 432 and lasting until the city capitulated in the winter of 430/29. Thucydides describes the siege of Potidaia as marking the outbreak of the Peloponnesian War.

At the conclusion of the dialogue, Charmides expresses doubt that he pos-sesses sound-mindedness, since Critias and Socrates have been unable to deter-mine its identity, and Charmides says that he wishes to engage in discussion with Socrates every day as long Socrates deems it fitting.[23] At this point, Critias and Charmides talk among themselves about Charmides' future involvement with Socrates. When Socrates engages their discussion, he asks, as though they have

---

20. Wolpert (2002) 64.
21. Fr. 1 K, translation from Brickhouse and Smith (2002) 112.
22. Aesch. 1.173.
23. *Chrm.* 176a6–b4.

been plotting behind his back, what they are planning to do. Charmides plays along with the mock conspiratorial innuendo and refuses to tell him; Charmides says only that Critias and he have made their plan. The mock conspiracy continues. Socrates presumes that the plan implicates him and that Charmides, having excluded him from his and Critias' deliberation, will force him to comply without a preliminary hearing (*anakrisis*). Charmides says that Socrates will indeed be forced, since Critias commands it, and Charmides tells Socrates to deliberate on what he will do. Socrates responds that the threat of force precludes deliberation and that no one could resist Charmides if he used force. Charmides commands Socrates not to resist, and Socrates concedes that he will not resist.[24] The mock conspiracy and specifically Socrates' mock dismay that Critias and Charmides will not grant him a preliminary hearing allude to the oligarchy's abuse of power, for many were not granted due process, but, like Leon of Salamis, forcibly detained and executed.

By opening and closing the dialogue with allusions to events that began and ended the Peloponnesian War, Plato frames the dialogue in relation to the sociopolitical events of that period. *Sôphrosunê*, the term I am translating as "sound-mindedness," had antidemocratic connotations in late-fifth-century Athens that underwent transformation in the fourth century in the wake of the Peloponnesian War and specifically the oligarchic regime. Noburu Notomi writes that

> *sôphrosunê* was highly praised by the Spartans as their leading excellence. The oligarchs in Athens [supported by Sparta] regarded this excellence as their ideal;[25] they called their ideal government *aristokratia sôphrôn* [sound-minded aristocracy]...and indeed [as Thucydides writes] the oligarchic government of the Four Hundred [that replaced the democracy in 411/10] was introduced as "*sôphronesteron*" [especially sound-minded].[26]

Victor Ehrenberg discusses the antonyms "meddlesomeness" (*polupragmosunê*) and "inactivity" (*apragmosunê*) in terms of fifth-century Athenian foreign policy. In this context, sound-mindedness was conceived as an aspect of political inactivity, in the sense of not acting on behalf of democratic policies. Ehrenberg suggests that to "Thucydides being sound-minded (*sôphronein*) was almost identical with being a conservative and an enemy of radical democrats."[27] Moreover, he speaks of the contrast between meddlesomeness and inactivity as reflecting "the two opposing groups in post-Periclean Athens...the peace party and the war party."[28] The conception of Athenian politics operating according to a party system is now regarded as anachronistic. But the point remains that since in the fifth century sound-mindedness was predominantly associated with oligarchy—or,

---

24. *Chrm.* 176b5–d5.
25. See DK 88B6 (Critias' *Elegeia*).
26. Notomi (2000) 245.
27. Ehrenberg (1947) 50; see Thuc. 1.84.3; 8.24.4, 48.6, 53.3, 64.5.
28. Ibid.

as the oligarchs viewed their government, aristocracy—sound-mindedness as a form of political inactivity corresponds to antidemocratic protest. Consider the following verse from a lost tragedy by Euripides, which became famous in antiquity: "The man of reserve (*apragmôn*) denounces the ignorance of the mob (*ochlos*)."[29]

In this regard, the sociopolitical significance of the Delphic oracle and its relation to the antagonism between democratic and oligarchic factions may also be significant. In 432, when Sparta inquired of the oracle whether they should go to war with Athens, they allegedly received the answer, "If you go to war with all your might, you will have victory and I, Apollo, will help you, both when you call for my aid and when you do not."[30] Soon after the war began, the plague that afflicted Athens and killed perhaps a third of its population was viewed as an act of Apollo. The plague itself involved the infringement of another oracle: "The Pelargicon is better unused." The Pelargicon was an open space on the Acropolis employed for ritual purposes, and piety required that it remain uninhabited; however, the flood of war refugees from the country necessitated its use as a residence.[31]

Also noteworthy is a story about the oracle and the Sicilian expedition—whose "tragic conclusion naturally suggested divine vengeance on Athens for her imperial presumption":[32]

> It was said that when the Athenians consulted the Pythia concerning the expedition they received a response to "bring the priestess of Athena from Erythrae." They carried out this injunction literally by fetching the woman who was named Hêsuchia [Restraint]. But the oracle was also susceptible of a second interpretation, for "bring Hêsuchia" might also mean ["exercise restraint"]. Hence Plutarch, who tells the story, suggests that the Delphic oracle really was advising the Athenians to abstain from the expedition.[33]

The likelihood that this story did in fact emerge in the wake of the expedition is at least strengthened by the circulation of the concept of restraint (*hêsuchia*) in connection with pro-Spartan, anti-imperialist sentiment in Athens.

In domestic politics, Helen North suggests,

> the identification of *sôphrosunê* with the democratic spirit, rather than with the oligarchic or aristocratic—with which it was most often linked in the fifth century—is clearly a sign of Athenian revulsion from the tyranny of the Thirty...the return of democracy after the expulsion of the Thirty is described in so many words as the restoration of a *sôphrôn politeia* [sound-minded constitution]. So violent was the reaction against the oligarchs

---

29. B29 = fr. 2004N; cited by Ehrenberg (1947) 53.
30. Thuc. 1.28.2; cited from Parke and Wormell (1956) 188.
31. "The great shortage of sites for dwellings caused the Pelargicon to be occupied in spite of prohibitions. It was only to be expected that the pious would attribute any such disasters as the plague which followed to the sacrilegious disregard of the warning" (ibid., 190).
32. Ibid., 198–9.
33. Ibid., 199.

that...the antithesis between the *sôphrôn* democrat and the disloyal oligarch persists as a rhetorical topic in the speeches of Demosthenes and Aeschines.[34]

In short, the democrats ultimately appropriated the term to their ideology.

While the first two definitions in the investigation in *Charmides*, restraint (*hêsuchiotês*) and modesty (*aidôs*), were conventionally associated with the ethical conduct of, in particular, aristocratic youths such as Charmides, these as well as Critias' first definition, doing one's own thing or minding one's own business (*to ta heautou prattein*), also had distinctly antidemocratic connotations. "Minding one's own business" was conventionally used as a synonym for "inactivity," whose antonym, we noted, was "meddlesomeness." In *The Quiet Athenian*, L. B. Carter argues that in fifth century Athens the political quietists were the antidemocratic, anti-imperialist citizens who remained aloof from the affairs (*pragmata*) of the people (*dêmos*).[35] In short, Plato's introduction and refutation of these three definitions of sound-mindedness in the mouths of notorious oligarchs would have had powerful political connotations.

The problem Plato faced as a young man and an Athenian citizen in the fourth century that he engages in *Charmides* is anchored in the remarks with which he begins the passage from the *Seventh Letter* cited above: "When I was a young man, my experience was the same as many. I thought that as soon as I came of age, I would immediately enter into public affairs."[36] To have been born into a family of the Athenian leisure class with the prominent political achievements Socrates describes and with which, however misguided, Critias' and Charmides' roles in the oligarchy were connected, Plato's civic function—which at this time and place in history was largely constitutive of his personal identity—was, as he says, to go into politics. Initially he pursued this path through involvement with the oligarchs. But the failure of the oligarchy seriously undermined Plato's personal credentials as a politically ambitious citizen of Athenian society as well as his practical ability to galvanize a substantial cohort. As he writes,

> In considering these things [that is, what was transpiring in Athens in the early fourth century] and the kind of people that were involved in political affairs, their laws and characters, the more I deliberated on these matters and the older I myself became, the more difficult it seemed to me to conduct political affairs rightly. For it is impossible to act without good men and trustworthy comrades—and it was not easy to find such men, for our city-state was no longer managed in accordance with the customs and in the manner of our forefathers, and to build a new cohort of men with any facility was impossible.[37]

---

34. North (1966) 135, 136, 139, 141, who refers to Aeschin. 2.176, 3.168; Dem. 24.75, *Ep.* 3.18.
35. Carter (1977), especially 19, 58, 71–75.
36. *Ep.* VII 324b8–c1.
37. *Ep.* VII 325c5–d5.

As an Athenian citizen of the early fourth century, Plato's political interests were essentially paralyzed. Beyond the sort of impotence, just described, to which he viewed himself as subject, he had seen in the trial and death of Socrates what the *dêmos* could do to those it considered subversive and influential. As Josiah Ober writes, the *Seventh Letter* "makes Platonic philosophy into an alternative politics," and the "dialogues may be read as installments in Plato's grand project of establishing secure foundations for a respectable alternative to active engagement in the politics of the polis-as-it-is."[38]

As we know from Plato's involvement in Syracuse, he did attempt to exercise his political ambition in a concrete fashion outside of Athens. However, in Athens he was compelled to content himself with the development of a theoretical vision and ethical-metaphysical justification for a new aristocratic republic.

3.4. Critias' *Philotimia*

One of the striking features of *Charmides* is the characterization of Critias. As I have noted, the relationship between the historical Critias' political career and the character Critias' involvement in an investigation of sound-mindedness is dramatically ironic. But Critias' contributions to the investigation themselves are not sound-minded. Gerasimos Santas summarizes this point well:

> [Critias] is hardly able to explain what he means by the various phrases he uses, and is reduced to making dubious and fruitless appeals to Hesiod and epigrams at Delphi—sayings that are themselves in need of explanation. And when it comes to Socrates' objections, he is like a windmill that is not in gear: on meeting the least resistance he changes direction... Critias, it seems, will say *anything* to get out of trouble...[39]

The notion that Critias is portrayed as lacking sound-mindedness has generally been recognized. On the other hand, commentators have not adequately appreciated the relationship between the portrayal of Critias' character and his contributions to the investigation. Santas also provides a case in point; immediately after accurately summarizing Critias' defects of character, he writes: "But of course we can hardly suppose that we can explain everything that goes on in the dialogue by reference to the personalities of Charmides and Critias—far from it. We need to consider the definitions themselves, the difficulties in them, and the outcome."[40] It is true that one's character and ability to make substantive contributions to philosophical investigation may in certain respects be independent. However, Plato in fact portrays Critias' character and contributions to the investigation of sound-mindedness as intimately related.

---

38. (1998) 165.
39. (1973) 107–8.
40. (1973) 108.

The portion of the investigation in which Critias is Socrates' principal interlocutor, especially 165–75, has provoked more discussion than any other section of the dialogue. In part, this relates to the complexity of the argumentation it involves. More precisely, it is due to the definitions of self-knowledge and knowledge of knowledge. First, these seem to be philosophically pregnant. So, for example, this section of *Charmides* has been mined for evidence of early Platonic epistemology. Second, it is frequently noted that these conceptions of sound-mindedness pertain to the way Socrates describes his human wisdom and conception of philosophy in *Apology*. Such associations with Critias' definitions are tantalizing. However, the contexts in which they occur and their significance for Plato's broader dramaturgical strategy and objectives in the dialogue must not be overlooked.

Critias' character is best understood in terms of *philotimia* (love of esteem); his principal motivation is the desire to maintain or enhance his reputation. Throughout the dialogue, Critias' *philotimia* consistently contrasts with Socrates' *philosophia*. Critias would rather appear intelligent than admit confusion or error. He would rather that Socrates simply agree with his opinions than engage in an examination of them to determine the truth. As such, Critias enters the investigation reluctantly, and throughout he remains anxious. He views the investigation antagonistically rather than as a cooperative effort to achieve a mutually beneficial result. The discussion, set among the company of upper class citizens and their sons at Taureas' wrestling school, threatens his honor and reputation. To a large extent, Critias' conceptions of sound-mindedness are consonant with traditional aristocratic beliefs, and to support himself he appeals to traditional authorities such as Hesiod and the Delphic oracle. Yet Critias' grasp of these proves specious, and when Socrates attempts to examine the views, Critias becomes defensive; he assumes that Socrates' principal objective is to refute him.

In contrast to Critias, as we have seen, the dialogue begins by conveying an estimable portrait of Charmides in conventional aristocratic terms. Moreover, although by the end of the dialogue Charmides concedes that he may not have sound-mindedness, he expresses a desire to continue conversations with Socrates in order to achieve it. He demonstrates a genuinely philosophical attitude.

There is no evidence of a negative characterization of Charmides in the text, and it would be odd to find Plato directing serious criticism at a teenager. The Greeks generally regarded youth as unformed or imperfectly formed adults, and as such, they did not expect a great deal of them beyond obedience. Consider Socrates' remark to Critias, in Charmides' presence, when Charmides misinterprets Critias' conception of sound-mindedness: " 'But, excellent Critias,' I said, 'it is no wonder that Charmides is ignorant, given his age, whereas it is fitting in view of your age and experience that you should know. So if you agree that sound-mindedness is as Charmides says and you accept the claim, I would be much more pleased to investigate with you whether the statement is true.' "[41]

---

41. *Chrm.* 162d7–e5.

The dialogue describes Critias as Charmides' legal guardian.[42] This implies that Charmides' father, Glaucon, is dead, and that Charmides has not reached his maturity. Socrates' return from Potidaia indicates a dramatic date of approximately 432. Accordingly, some scholars have assumed that Glaucon died before 432 and that Charmides was born shortly after 450. But as John Davies notes, "The fact that Critias has taken over the responsibility and not his father Callaeschrus ought to indicate that Callaeschrus had died before 432, but why Pyrilampes was not considered is mysterious."[43] According to the Athenian conventions of guardianship, if a father died before his son had reached maturity, his nearest male relative typically adopted the boy and served as his guardian. Charmides' father Glaucon had two brothers, Callaeschrus and Pyrilampes. Both would have been eligible for this position before Critias. Since Callaeschrus was not chosen, Davies assumes that he was dead at the time of Glaucon's death. However, Pyrilampes was still alive; at least, Plutarch mentions that Pyrilampes was wounded at the battle of Delium, which occurred in 424.[44]

Since Plato is writing about his own family, it may seem surprising that he confuses their history. But puzzlement over Plato's misrepresentation of this history may be dispelled in view of the prevalence of anachronism among the early dialogues and Plato's predilection for historical pastiche. A further historical inaccuracy in *Charmides* corroborates this point. Plato makes Socrates, in praising Charmides' ancestry, speak of Pyrilampes as though he were dead: "For of Pyrilampes, your uncle, it is said that no one in all the continent was considered (*doxai*) to be his superior in beauty or stature, whenever he came as envoy to the Great King... And, indeed, in regard to your visible form, dear son of Glaucon, I consider that nowhere have you fallen behind any of your predecessors (*tôn pro sou*)."[45] This suggests that historians should resist the assumptions that since Plato portrays Critias as Charmides' guardian, Glaucon had died by 432, his brother Callaeschrus had died by 432, Charmides had not reached his maturity by 432, and Pyrilampes was for some reason unfit to become his guardian. Compare the fact that the battle from which Socrates describes himself as having just returned actually occurred at the beginning of the siege of Potidaia. Plato evidently transposed it to the end of the siege in order to connect it more closely with Socrates' return.

Plato has a dramatic reason for portraying Critias as Charmides' guardian. As the event narrated in the dialogue is depicted as occurring at the beginning of the Peloponnesian War, and Socrates' principal interlocutors were associated in the popular imagination primarily with their activities during the oligarchy, the text throughout implies a correlation between the conditions of these interlocutors at the dramatic date of the narrated event and the histories, decades later, of the

---

42. *Chrm.* 155a6, 176c1.
43. Davies (1971).
44. Plut. *Mor.* 581d.
45. *Chrm.* 158a1–b2.

people they represent. As Socrates becomes curious about the condition of Charmides' soul and engages him in discussion concerning sound-mindedness in order to determine whether, as Critias claims, Charmides possesses it, dramatic tension is established between Socrates' and Critias' pedagogical influence on Charmides. As Charles Kahn remarks, "The capacity for virtue may be inborn, as the aristocratic tradition believed, but how it develops will depend upon moral education, and in this case upon the baneful influence of Charmides' *epitropos* [guardian]."[46]

In the fourth century and later, Critias was demonized in the Athenian and more broadly Greek popular imagination. For instance, Xenophon describes him as "the greediest, most violent, and most murderous of them all [the Thirty]."[47] Similarly, Aeschines the Socratic writes, "It is hard to imagine a more pernicious person than Critias, who stood out among the Thirty, the worst of the Greeks."[48] This characterization of Critias became orthodox in Greek history. Six centuries later, for example, Flavius Philostratus speaks of Critias as "the worst of all those who are notorious for badness."[49]

Plato's characterization of Critias is negative, but not demonic. Thrasyma-chus and Callicles receive more unfavorable treatment. Still, the unflattering portrayal of Critias begins early in the dialogue. When Charmides attributes to Critias the conception of sound-mindedness as doing one's own thing, Critias denies that the view is his. Socrates later indicates that in fact this view is Critias'.[50] Why should Critias be unwilling to admit his beliefs? His initial reluctance is due to fear of having his views and therefore his reputation under-mined through engagement with Socrates before the company.

As we have seen, Critias initially extols Charmides' virtues and talents. But insofar as Critias is Charmides' guardian, Critias intends his praise to reflect the influence of his own excellence. In other words, by praising Charmides, Critias in fact is propping himself up. This view is supported by Critias' contributions in the ensuing dialogue. As Charmides is unable to give a satisfactory account of sound-mindedness, Critias' estimation of Charmides is indirectly undermined, and thus Critias himself falls within the ambit of the criticism. In the course of Socrates and Charmides' exchange, Critias grows increasingly agitated. When Socrates' first attempt to explain the conception of sound-mindedness that Charmides heard from Critias renders this conception idiotic, Critias is, again, implied to be incompetent. Charmides provocatively responds to Socrates' initial ridiculous interpretation of Critias' conception with the suggestion that "it may be that not even he who said it knew in the least what he meant."[51] Moreover, Socrates

46. (1996) 187, n.7.
47. *Mem.* 1.2.12.
48. Fr. 1 K, translated from Brickhouse and Smith (2002) 112.
49. *Vit. Soph.* 1.16 (501) = DK 88A1 (cited from Notomi, 2000, 237). On the reception of Critias see ibid., 237–42.
50. *Chrm.* 161c2 with 162c4–6.
51. *Chrm.* 162b9–10.

narrates that as Charmides says this, he "gave a sly laugh and glanced at Critias."[52]
At this point, Socrates narrates a description of Critias:

> Critias had clearly for some time been struggling (agôniôn), wanting to
> distinguish himself (philotimôs) in front of Charmides and the others present,
> and having barely restrained himself up to this point, he was now no longer
> able. For it seems that what I had suspected was entirely true, that Char-
> mides had heard this answer about sound-mindedness from Critias. And
> Charmides, not wanting to continue discussion of the answer himself, but to
> have Critias do so, subtly pushed him by showing that he had been refuted.
> But Critias did not take to this. Rather, it seems to me that he became angry
> with Charmides, as a poet does with an actor who mishandles his verses.[53]

The passage suggests that Critias is concerned to maintain a certain elevated
impression of himself. As the adverb philotimôs suggests, Critias is a lover of esteem.
His praise of Charmides and Charmides' ability to sustain that praise serve to buttress
his own reputation. As such, Critias perceives Charmides as an extension of himself.
Charmides' failure to provide an adequate account of sound-mindedness and
specifically his failure to support Critias' account of sound-mindedness, therefore,
provoke Critias' anger. Critias perceives Charmides' weakness and incompetence as
undermining his own image. Thus, although Critias is initially unwilling to contribute
to the discussion, eventually he is drawn into it in order to save face.

In seeking to clarify Critias' definition, Socrates wonders whether doing
(prattein) one's own thing can be a correct conception of sound-mindedness
insofar as craftsmen who make (poiein) things for others and, as such, do not do
their own thing, act in a sound-minded manner. In other words, Socrates urges
Critias to clarify what he means by doing one's own thing. One possible and
seemingly natural response is that "doing one's own thing" does not mean
"making one's own possessions," for any complex society requires a specialization
of labor. Rather, "doing one's own thing" means "fulfilling the social role in which
one is appropriately situated and for which one has the requisite knowledge."

Critias' explanation differs; he claims that there is a distinction between
doing (prattein), making (poiein), and working (ergazesthai). He appeals to Hesiod's
verse "work is no disgrace" to legitimate the idea that work has value, and he
explains that things made (poioumena) finely and usefully are works. In other
words, working is a kind of making. However, Critias then identifies works
(ergasiai) and things done (praxeis).[54] Thus, Critias initially claims that working
and doing are distinct, but then identifies the two. Moreover, the distinction is
irrelevant to his main point, which is to distinguish doing and making. Doing is a
kind of making; precisely, a thing made is base if it lacks fineness,[55] and things

---

52. Chrm. 162b10–11.
53. Chrm. 162c1–d3.
54. "And works (ergasias) and things made (praxeis) are such doings (poiêseis)" (Chrm. 163c3–4).
55. "And a thing done (poiêma) sometimes is disgraceful, whenever it does not have fineness" (Chrm. 163c1–2).

done are fine and useful things made. But this implies that "doing one's own thing" means "making fine things that are one's own." As such, the phrase in need of explanation, *ta heautou* (one's own things), receives none.

Socrates does not make anything of Critias' failure to explain the crucial phrase, and he does not press Critias too hard. Throughout the investigation Socrates conducts himself toward Critias rather gingerly. He appears to be sensitive to Critias' volatility. Accordingly, here he charitably interprets Critias' response to mean that "doing one's own thing" means "doing good things." Furthermore, it is clear from his immediately subsequent remarks that Socrates does not take Critias' distinction between doing and making to be significant: "I have heard Prodicus make countless distinctions between terms. And I will allow you any application of a term that you please. Only, make clear to what thing you attach a given term. So now begin over again and define more plainly. Do you say that this doing or making—or whatever you call it—of good things is sound-mindedness?"[56]

Furthermore, Critias' unqualified assent to Socrates here—" 'I do,' he replied"[57]—indicates that he himself has no genuine investment in the distinction he has just described. This is remarkable, and it is indicative of Critias' attempts to convey an appearance of intellectual sophistication. In this instance, Critias quickly drops his initial distinctions and, in order to avoid exposing their defects, grants Socrates' interpretation of doing one's own thing as doing good things.

Beyond the specious linguistic distinctions, Critias' point is that some occupations are fine and others base. Critias specifically cites being a leathersmith, grocer, and cook as base occupations.[58] As such, his remarks have sociopolitical significance, for these were lower-class occupations. In contrast, by citing from Hesiod's *Works and Days*, Critias alludes to the value of the labor of the traditional farmer and so to the value of the political structure of traditional, nondemocratic Greek society.

Throughout the fifth century, antidemocratic sentiment in Athens was often coupled with *lacônismos* (sympathy toward the Spartan way of life). Critias himself is known to have composed two works on Spartan politics and customs; the Spartans helped install the Thirty, who attempted to remodel Athenian society in accordance with the Spartan constitution. The Thirty themselves were analogous to the *gerousia*, Sparta's principal governing body, which consisted of thirty members. The three thousand whom the Thirty selected to reside within the city walls were analogous to the Spartan *homoioi*, members of the Spartan citizen-body, who in the late fifth century also numbered about three thousand. And the remainder of the former democratic citizenry was banned from living in the city. With the Athenian navy demolished and the long walls to the harbor dismantled,

---

56. *Chrm.* 163d3–e1.
57. *Chrm.* 163e3.
58. *Chrm.* 163b7.

the Thirty sought a return to traditional agrarian society where military and political power resided among the landed wealthy.

In his *Accusation*, Polycrates had apparently criticized Socrates for making reference to or appropriating traditional poetic verses in his antidemocratic teachings, for Xenophon alludes to this in an attempted rebuttal:

> His accuser alleged that he selected from the most famous poets the most depraved material and that he used this as evidence to teach his companions to be malfeasant and tyrannical (*turannikous*). He is supposed to have explained Hesiod's line "work is no disgrace; idleness is a disgrace" as meaning that the poet bids us shrink from no kinds of work, not even such as are unjust and base, but to do even these for the sake of gain.[59]

Xenophon's passage, thus, indicates that Plato himself is alluding to the charge in Polycrates' *Accusation*. But in *Charmides* it is the future tyrant Critias who employs the Hesiodic verse in formulating his antidemocratic account of sound-mindedness.[60]

In relation to Charmides' first two definitions, doing good things is a powerful definition, since it is not susceptible to the same criticisms as restraint and modesty. Doing good things satisfies the conditions of being fine and good. Socrates, however, suggests a difficulty with the definition by using the example of a physician who accidentally heals a patient. In healing the patient, the physician does something good; however, he does not know what he is doing. Socrates encourages Critias to consider whether such a person should be considered sound-minded.[61] In other words, he employs the example to shift conceptualization of sound-mindedness as a type of action to a psychological state responsible for the appropriate action, and more specifically to draw attention to the epistemic nature of sound-mindedness.

Socrates' appeal to the epistemic nature of sound-mindedness is compelling; Critias concedes that knowledge is necessary for sound-mindedness. Yet Critias' reply again reveals defects of character: " 'But, Socrates,' he said, 'that could never be the case. If you think this in any way necessary from my previous admissions, I would rather withdraw some of them and not be ashamed (*aischuntheien*) to say that my statements were wrong than to admit at any time that a man who is ignorant of himself is sound-minded.' "[62] Why should Critias mention shame he might feel by admitting a mistake? I suggest that since he feels compelled to accept Socrates' criticism, Critias also feels compelled to comment on the fact that he is admitting error. He actually does feel ashamed. He believes that being mistaken, having his error exposed, and having to admit his error are shameful and that the

---

59. *Mem.* 1.2.56.
60. It is noteworthy that Xenophon himself proceeds to explain that in fact Socrates understood Hesiod's line to mean that being a worker meant doing good work.
61. *Chrm.* 164a9–c6.
62. *Chrm.* 164c7–d3.

company at the wrestling-school share his perception. By admitting error and claiming that there is no shame in that admission Critias is attempting to manage the company's perception of him.

Contrast this with Socrates' reaction later in the investigation, when Critias criticizes him for analogizing self-knowledge with forms of productive knowledge such as architecture. Critias claims that some forms of specialized knowledge lack products. In this case, Socrates simply concedes Critias' point and proceeds to pose a different question. Socrates' willingness to accept criticism and to acknowledge the limitations of his understanding provide a clear and dramaturgically deliberate contrast to Critias.

While Critias claims that he is not ashamed to admit that his previous definition was mistaken, clearly he does believe that in having to retract his previous definition his image suffers a blow. Critias proceeds to give a speech about sound-mindedness as self-knowledge. The speech is rather specious, as was his previous explanation of doing one's own thing. Moreover, the principal function of this response is to obscure the inadequacy of his first definition by overshadowing it with a semblance of sophistication.

Critias claims that sound-mindedness is self-knowledge. He explains himself by reference to the famous inscription on the shrine at Delphi. Critias suggests that the inscription was originally established to serve as a form of salutation from Apollo. Rather than addressing suppliants with the conventional human saluta-tion "Be joyful (to chairein)." the god salutes humans with "Be sound-minded." Yet, Critias explains, in the god's customary cryptic fashion, the salutation is expressed indirectly as "Know yourself."[63]

The interpretation of the inscription as a salutation rather than an injunction is absurd. Moreover, it is not germane. The association of sound-mindedness with the injunction and with Apollo and the oracle is more reasonable. The traditional interpretation of the inscription was that humanity ought to recognize its subordi-nation to the divine, specifically its inferior knowledge and power. As such, the oracle was conventionally associated with human limitations and the sense that one ought not to attempt to transcend these.

Critias concludes his speech by remarking, "I am saying all this, Socrates, for the following reason. I dismiss all that was said before. Perhaps there was some-thing more correct in what you were saying, or perhaps in what I was saying. Still, nothing that we said was clear. But now I want to offer you this account—if you agree that sound-mindedness is knowing oneself."[64] Critias does not simply concede that his previous account was mistaken and then offer another in its place. He attempts to obscure the fact that he was mistaken by suggesting that it might just as well have been Socrates who was wrong. Given the content of the Delphic motto, this maneuver is, of course, also comic. Note, furthermore, Socrates' response to Critias' final clause: " 'But, Critias,' I said, 'you are treating

---

63. Chrm. 164d–165a.
64. Chrm. 165a7–b4.

me as though in speaking about the matters into which I am inquiring I had knowledge and as though if I would merely desire it, I could agree with you.'"[65] Socrates' response suggests that Critias does not want to investigate the truth of his account; he simply seeks Socrates' agreement. Critias does not want to engage in inquiry because, again, he is fearful that doing so will expose his intellectual limitations and damage his reputation. In contrast, Socrates clarifies his own position: "But that is not how things stand. Rather, I am always investigating with you into the statement proposed because I myself do not have knowledge. And therefore, I want to consider whether or not I should agree."[66] Socrates' statement indicates a philosophical disposition, a sense of ignorance, and a genuine desire for knowledge.

3.5. Self-Knowledge and the Knowledge of Knowledge

Socrates' example of the lucky physician draws attention to the epistemic character of sound-mindedness. But the self-knowledge that the lucky physician lacks is of a limited kind: The physician does not know that his treatment will heal his patient; he is ignorant of how his action is related to his goal. The self-knowledge implied here is not equivalent to the traditional conception of the Delphic injunction concerning the general limitations of human capabilities. Thus, the conception of self-knowledge introduced in Critias' second definition is unclear. Socrates, therefore, attempts to clarify the epistemic state that constitutes sound-mindedness. Indeed, the remainder of the investigation is devoted to clarifying this epistemic state.

It is noteworthy that the investigation ends immediately after Critias suggests that the knowledge of good and bad is beneficial for society. The knowledge of good and bad itself is not proposed as a definition of sound-mindedness; rather, Critias suggests that it is an aspect of the knowledge of knowledge and all other knowledges and lack of knowledge. On the other hand, the knowledge of good and bad is the only concept introduced in the investigation that clearly satisfies the F-conditions for the identity of sound-mindedness that Socrates introduces in the course of the investigation, specifically being good, fine, beneficial, and an epistemic state. Furthermore, these conditions have all been introduced by the time Critias offers his second definition. There is, then, a clear conceptual link between Critias' first definition, reinterpreted as doing good things and including its refutation, and the concept of the knowledge of good and bad. Doing good things satisfies Socrates' conditions for the identity of sound-mindedness. Its defect is that it is a type of action rather than the psychological state responsible for that action. But clearly the knowledge of the good should be responsible for doing what is good. Moreover, as we have discussed, evidence from other early dialogues suggests that the view of excellence and its putative components as

---

65. *Chrm.* 165b5–b7.
66. *Chrm.* 165b7–c2.

knowledge of good and bad is Platonic. It is a question, then, why, when there is a clear conceptual link between doing the good and knowing it, such a long section of *Charmides* (165–174) is devoted to clarifying the epistemic state of sound-mindedness.

The question is a long-standing one. Hermann Bonitz, distinguished Aristotelian scholar of the nineteenth century, claimed that "the section dealing with [the knowledge of knowledge] is self-contained and irrelevant to the main purpose of the dialogue." Wilamowitz wrote, "The theme of sound-mindedness is truly left behind as soon as Critias enters the discussion." More recently, Chun-Hwan Chen has argued that "both scholars are . . . correct in understanding that the passage can be studied separately from the rest of the dialogue."[67] In contrast, I suggest that the section of the investigation that explores the epistemic dimension of sound-mindedness is not only integral to the dialogue as a whole, but that its correct interpretation requires understanding the relevance of the preceding text to it.

I have suggested that the appropriate conceptual step from Critias' first definition should be the knowledge of the good. I have also emphasized the antiphilosophical, specifically *philotimic* nature of Critias' character, his anxiety and specious suggestions. It is questionable how well Critias understands the conception of sound-mindedness as self-knowledge that he proposes. The introduction of the concept of self-knowledge and its association with Delphi arguably is important for understanding sound-mindedness. Again, the inscription was understood to emphasize humanity's limitations and proper place in the cosmos, specifically in relation to the divine. The idea also correlates with the three preceding definitions, restraint, modesty, and doing one's own thing interpreted as doing good things. Still, it makes sense that Socrates targets the concept of self-knowledge as vague, for it is questionable what humanity's limitations are and what the place of individuals within society is. These questions are particularly important in view of Plato's critical attitude toward both the Athenian democracy and the oligarchy of the Thirty.

Accordingly, Socrates proceeds to clarify the nature of self-knowledge. He does so by analogy with other forms of knowledge. First, he inquires after the product (*ergon*) of self-knowledge. Critias, however, objects that self-knowledge, unlike architecture and medicine, lacks a product. Socrates concedes the objection and inquires after the distinct object of self-knowledge, that is, the *relatum*. Critias again objects: Self-knowledge, unlike numeration, lacks a distinct object. Critias now claims that Socrates in fact is aware that self-knowledge differs from all other forms of knowledge; he accuses Socrates of posing his questions deliberately to refute him: "You are far from being unaware of this [that sound-mindedness qua self-knowledge is distinct from all other forms of knowledge]. Rather, I believe you are doing the very thing that you denied you were doing just now; for you are attempting to refute me without bothering to follow the subject of our

---

67. (1978) 13. The preceding quotations from Bonitz and Wilamowitz are cited from Chen.

discussion."[68] Critias' anxiety here again surfaces and manifests itself in a false accusation of Socrates. He perceives his interaction with Socrates as a zero-sum contest and therefore believes that he must fight to preserve his reputation. In response Socrates clarifies his intentions and the value of a cooperative philosophical investigation:

> "How can you think," I said, "that if I am refuting you, I am doing so with any other motive than that which would impel me to investigate what I myself say, from a fear of carelessly supposing that at any moment I knew something when I did not know it? And so it is now; that is what I am doing, I tell you. I am examining the argument—mainly for my own sake, but also perhaps for that of my peers. Or do you not think it is for the common good almost of all people that the truth about everything should be discovered?"[69]

Socrates' questions concerning the product and object of self-knowledge are sincere and legitimate. Again, it is unclear what self-knowledge is. Moreover, even if the analogies could not be strictly maintained, Socrates would still be justified in inquiring after the product and object of self-knowledge. After all, the products of architecture and medicine, buildings and health, are themselves unlike one another in certain fundamental respects. Furthermore, Socrates explicitly identifies the product of a form of knowledge with the benefit that it yields;[70] and since self-knowledge is assumed to be beneficial, it is reasonable to clarify the benefit it yields. Similarly, self-knowledge, at least conceived literally, seems to have an obvious object, the soul. In the dialogue *Alcibiades I*, the soul is identified as the object of self-knowledge.[71] In short, it is not obvious that self-knowledge lacks a product or object; and therefore, it is reasonable to inquire after these things in an effort to clarify self-knowledge.

Some commentators have accepted as compelling Critias' resistance to Socrates' analogies insofar as sound-mindedness qua ethical knowledge or wisdom is sui generis. Yet that is not inconsistent with ethical knowledge having a distinct product and object. In any case, at this point Socrates is attempting to clarify the nature of sound-mindedness qua self-knowledge. Commentators have also found Critias' account of sound-mindedness here compelling insofar as it relates to Socrates' own emphasis on self-knowledge, most notably in *Apology*. It must be stressed, however, that the recognition of one's ignorance, specifically one's lack of wisdom, which Socrates emphasizes in *Apology*, is merely the first, albeit crucial, step in the enterprise of philosophy. Recognition of one's ignorance is not the attainment of the excellence that is the objective of philosophy. Ethical knowledge—if it is attainable by humans at all—will be attained as a result of philosophical investigation that follows the recognition of ignorance. Thus,

---

68. *Chrm.* 166c3–6.
69. *Chrm.* 166c7–d6.
70. *Chrm.* 165c9–d2.
71. *Alc. I* 129a.

self-knowledge qua recognition of one's ignorance is not sound-mindedness qua excellence.

If Critias were correct and self-knowledge lacked a distinct product and object, then analysis of self-knowledge would have to proceed by means other than those that Socrates has employed. In principle, there is nothing odd in this. However, the manner in which the investigation does proceed is odd, for Critias does not simply deny Socrates' analogies by saying, for instance, that self-knowledge does not have a distinct product or object. After Critias accuses Socrates of deliberately trying to refute him and Socrates explains and defends his motivation, Socrates asks him again what he means by sound-mindedness. Socrates is, then, asking for clarification of self-knowledge on terms that Critias finds more congenial. In response, Critias claims: "I mean that [sound-mindedness] alone of all forms of knowledge is a knowledge of itself (hautês) and of all other knowledges (tôn allôn epistêmôn)."[72]

Critias' response clearly relates to his objections to Socrates' previous analogies, for he explicitly articulates his re-conception of self-knowledge by distinguishing sound-mindedness qua knowledge from all other forms of knowledge. On the other hand, beyond the conceptual link of reflexivity that the two share, knowledge of knowledge and all other knowledges seems to be a peculiar and discontinuous interpretation of self-knowledge. It is, therefore, a question how Critias understands knowledge of knowledge and all other knowledges and why he offers this as an account of self-knowledge.

It is difficult to be sure what Critias understands himself to mean; arguably he does not clearly understand what he is saying. Since he at least assents to Socrates' subsequent interpretation of the phrase, it is useful to consider Socrates' interpretation of "knowledge of knowledge and all other knowledges." He first infers that the phrase also implies knowledge of lack of knowledge, for the ability to identify an object as of a given kind entails the ability to identify an object as not being of that kind. Observe here the implicit principle that a given epistemic capacity to realize a given end entails the capacity to realize the contrary end. Consequently, Critias' definition is refined to the knowledge of knowledge and all other knowledges and lack of knowledge (K). Socrates then interprets K: "Then the sound-minded man alone will know himself and be able to determine what he happens to know and not know, and he will be able to evaluate others similarly, to determine what they know and [what they do not know]...And this will be...sound-mindedness and knowing oneself: knowing what one knows and does not know."[73] This account of K is complex, and it will be helpful to distinguish two interpretations. One interpretation of K is the knowledge of whether something, say, a body of beliefs or information, is knowledge. I will refer to this as K_K. Another interpretation of K is the knowledge of what kind of knowledge a body of knowledge is, for example, medical or architectural. I will call this K_C.

72. Chrm. 166e5–6.
73. Chrm. 167a1–7.

At 167b–172c, Socrates makes two criticisms of K: It does not seem possible for K to exist; and even if it did exist, it would not be particularly beneficial: "Let us consider first if it is possible for such as thing [as K] to exist . . . And then if it is entirely possible, let us consider what benefit we would get by knowing it."[74] In making these two criticisms, Socrates interprets K as K_K. That is, Socrates argues that it does not seem possible for K_K to exist; and even if K_K did exist, it would not be particularly beneficial.

Socrates argues against the existence of K_K. He examines K_K by analogy with a range of other types of entity: forms of sense perception (seeing and hearing), motivational states (desiring and wishing), emotions (loving and fearing), another cognitive state (opining), and relational quantities (for example, the exceeding and the double). He then argues that "whatever has the capacity to affect (*dunamis*) an object, which is itself, will not have the being (*ousia*) upon which this effect can work."[75] The gist of his argument is that the impossibility or unlikelihood of reflexivity in the various cases considered suggests that K_K is unlikely to exist. In short, Socrates offers a thoughtful response; he earnestly engages K_K as a conception of sound-mindedness and presents Critias with a problem that he frankly admits he is incompetent to solve, but that he regards as important for the inquiry.

It is significant that Socrates explicitly leaves unresolved the question whether K_K can exist: "My friend, we need some great man who will adequately determine whether anything is naturally so constituted that it can have its own power applied to itself . . . I myself distrust my competence to resolve these matters."[76] Several authors have seen in this criticism of the nonexistence of K_K a criticism of Socrates' manner of examining his fellow citizens as he describes this in *Apology*. For example, how can Socrates know that an alleged expert in theological matters lacks knowledge of holiness if Socrates himself lacks that knowledge? For instance, Charles Kahn claims that in *Charmides* Plato is explicitly criticizing the Socrates of the *Apology* because he has come to recognize that this Socrates must have the appropriate first order knowledge, say, of holiness in order to know whether, say, Euthyphro does. But consider the way Socrates evaluates answers to the WF question. Without knowing the definition of F, Socrates can determine whether his interlocutor has the definitional knowledge he claims. As long as his interlocutor cannot maintain a consistent set of beliefs about F, this enables Socrates to determine that his interlocutor lacks the relevant knowledge.

On the other hand, while Socrates may determine that his interlocutor lacks knowledge, it is less clear how he could determine that his interlocutor has knowledge. In the case of ethical knowledge, his interlocutor would have a consistent set of beliefs about F, but not merely so. His interlocutor would have to be able to define F. Still, it is not clear from the contents of the early dialogues

---

74. *Chrm.* 167b1–4.
75. *Chrm.* 168d1–3.
76. *Chrm.* 169a1–8.

how Socrates could determine that a putative definition of F, which entailed a consistent set of beliefs about F, constituted knowledge of the definition of F. As we have discussed, the *aitia*-requirement on propositional knowledge, which apparently applies to definitional knowledge, remains unresolved.

Thus, there seems to be an asymmetry between determining that someone lacks ethical knowledge and determining that someone possesses ethical knowledge. But this asymmetry is problematic, for it is characteristic of *technai* to have the capacity for contrary ends. Thus, the possessor of K_K should be able to determine both the possession of and lack of knowledge.

One consequence of this consideration may be that Socrates' capacity to expose false claims to knowledge is not a *technê*. Indeed, he never speaks of it as such. For example, in *Apology* Socrates describes himself as having a kind of wisdom, namely human wisdom. But there is no reason to believe the Platonic view is that this as a *technê*. Evidently, in *Charmides* Plato did not intend to determine the possibility of K_K. Rather, again, Socrates' first criticism of K_K presents one legitimate and sophisticated critique of K_K.

It is also noteworthy that, unlike in the previous movement of the discussion, Critias does not object here to Socrates' use of an analogical argument. I presume this is because Critias is quite overwhelmed by the sophistication of Socrates' response:

> Now when Critias heard this and saw me in a state of confusion, he seemed to me—just as the sight of someone yawning provokes people to suffer the same—to be compelled by my confusion and become seized by confusion himself. But since he always attempted to preserve his good reputation (*eudokimôn*), he was ashamed (*êischuneto*) in front of the others present, and although he was unable to confirm what I was submitting to him, he was also unwilling to agree with me. And so he said nothing clearly and concealed his confusion.[77]

This passage provides further evidence of Critias' *philotimia*. Socrates' response to Critias here is once again gentle and charitable. "In order to advance the discussion," as he says, he permits that K_K might exist, and he proceeds on that assumption. But Socrates' concession to Critias proves to be problematic. Since neither Critias nor he well understands what K_K is, the subsequent inquiry into its benefit lacks control. As we will see, at the end of the investigation Socrates criticizes himself as well as Critias for faults, such as this, in their inquiry.

Presently, granted K_K's existence, Socrates proceeds to his second criticism, the benefit of K_K. He claims that if K_K existed, it would not be particularly beneficial. Specifically, K_K would not enable one to know the contents of a body of knowledge, but only whether something, again, say, a body of information, constituted knowledge. For example, confronted with a physician, the possessor of

77. *Chrm.* 169c3–d1.

K_K would be able to determine that that individual possessed knowledge, but not that that individual possessed medical knowledge specifically.[78] Consequently, K_K would not be particularly beneficial, for it would not enable a lay person or private individual to determine whether he possessed the right kinds of knowledge to achieve particular objectives; nor would it enable a statesman to appoint specialists to the appropriate offices.[79]

Following the conclusion that K_K is of limited benefit, Socrates laments that the inquiry has been worthless.[80] The inquiry does not, however, end at this point. Rather, Socrates now expresses an afterthought, which he describes as coming to him as though in a dream. He suggests that even on an interpretation of K as K_C, K would not be beneficial. Specifically, although a statesman who possessed K_C would be able to organize his society in such a way that knowledgeable people occupied the appropriate positions, that itself would not result in the citizens living and doing well (*eu prattoimen kai eudaimonoimen*).[81]

The same sort of maneuver occurs in a late stage of the investigation in *Laches*. There it is claimed that a seer who was omniscient insofar as he possessed knowledge of the past, present, and future, would lack knowledge of how individuals should govern their lives; for although such a person would know the course of events, he would not know whether it was good or bad for a given event to occur.[82] In having Socrates offer his dream in *Charmides*, Plato adumbrates a distinction between ethical *technê* and nonethical *technai*. In contrast to nonethical *technai*, ethical *technê* is valuable both in ensuring that possessors of nonethical *technai* fulfill their responsibilities and in determining whether, in any given case, the end of a given nonethical *technê* should be realized. Precisely this is the function of ethical *technê*, and as such, when possessed by a political leader, ethical *technê* conduces to well-being in the polis.

At this point it may be wondered whether K, understood as K_C, would be beneficial precisely because it would include ethical knowledge. Indeed, this suggestion is made in the ensuing exchange. Following the articulation of his dream, Socrates asks Critias to clarify the type of knowledge that enables individuals to do well (*eu prattein*) and be well (*eudaimonein*). A number of absurd suggestions are rejected, for instance, knowledge of draught-playing. Finally, Critias suggests the knowledge of good and bad. Socrates naturally accepts this claim: Ethical knowledge is conducive to well-being. Moreover, he emphasizes that ungoverned by ethical knowledge, none of the nonethical *technai* will conduce to well-being.

The problem now emerges that if ethical knowledge is the only truly beneficial *technê*, sound-mindedness itself is rendered useless. In view of this, Socrates

---

78. *Chrm.* 169d–171c.
79. *Chrm.* 171e–172a.
80. *Chrm.* 172c4–5.
81. *Chrm.* 173a7–d5.
82. *La.* 195e8–196a3. In *Charmides* precisely the same point is made at 173e10–174a12.

despairs that the investigation is to blame: "I cannot believe that what is agreed to be the finest of things would have appeared useless to us, if I were of any use in making a fine investigation."[83] To combat this counterintuitive result, Critias insists that K will be beneficial, for K, interpreted as K_C, will include ethical knowledge: "If sound-mindedness is a knowledge of knowledge and it presides over the other knowledges, then I would think it rules over the knowledge of goodness and benefits us."[84] Socrates responds: "And will this knowledge [K] also produce health?... Or is it not medicine that will produce this? And will this knowledge [K] also produce the other things of the *technai*? And will not each of them produce their own *ergon*? Did we not long ago testify that it is only the knowledge of knowledge and lack of knowledge and of nothing else?"[85]

The final aporia in which the investigation here ends can be seen to result from the following line of argumentation. Sound-mindedness is beneficial. Sound-mindedness is a kind of knowledge (*epistêmê* = *technê*). Sound-mindedness is K. But interpreted as K_K, K is not beneficial. Rather, ethical knowledge is beneficial. If K can be interpreted to include ethical knowledge, then it will be beneficial. K_C seems to satisfy this condition. But, in fact, K cannot be interpreted as K_C, for K_C is omniscience. But omniscience is not a *technê*, for a *technê* has a determinate subject matter. Rather, K_C is simply the set of all *technai*. But only one *technê* is beneficial, again, ethical knowledge.

Ethical knowledge satisfies the F-conditions, being fine, being good, entailing knowledge, existing, and being beneficial, that Socrates introduces in the course of the investigation. Ethical knowledge is the Platonic candidate for sound-mindedness. Moreover, although the concept of ethical knowledge ultimately enters their investigation, the interlocutors in *Charmides* fail to reach the conclusion that sound-mindedness is ethical knowledge. Their chances for success might have looked good when it was agreed that sound-mindedness was a kind of knowledge, but the attempt to specify the kind of knowledge (165–74) was plagued by irrationality. Socrates had noted that "if sound-mindedness is knowing something, then clearly it is an *epistêmê* of something."[86] At that point he inquired into the product and object of the knowledge. But in both cases Critias rebuffed him, claiming that sound-mindedness could not be analogized with other forms of knowledge. Indeed, ethical knowledge is not analogous to other *technai* in that it is invariably beneficial. However, it is analogous to the other *technai* in that it has a distinct object and a distinct product. At least, the object of ethical knowledge is goodness, and the product is well-being. Granted, goodness and well-being are not like other sorts of objects and products; but neither is the odd or the even like health; and producing health is not like producing a house.

83. *Chrm.* 175a11–b1.
84. *Chrm.* 174d8–e2.
85. *Chrm.* 174e3–7.
86. *Chrm.* 165c4–6.

At the conclusion of the investigation, Socrates holds himself as well as Critias responsible for the failure of the investigation:

> So, do you see, Critias, that it is reasonable and just that I hold myself responsible for the fact that the inquiry into sound-mindedness was entirely useless?... You see, we granted many things that did not accord with the argument. For we granted that a knowledge of knowledge existed, when the argument did not permit it. And in order to claim that the sound-minded person knew what he knew and didn't know, we granted that this knowledge [K] could know the *erga* of the other knowledges. And we granted this in an entirely extravagant way, for we did not consider the impossibility of a person knowing what he does not know. For we agreed that a person could know that he does not know. But nothing seems to me more irrational than this.[87]

The aporia in *Charmides* is, thus, a function of the contributions of all the discussants. Critias' anxiety and desire to maintain a reputation for intelligence and sophistication play a fundamental role in misguiding the investigation of sound-mindedness as a kind of knowledge. But in certain respects Socrates is also too docile and concessive. Socrates is the more rational of the two, and for this reason he should not have allowed Critias to mislead the investigation as he did.

Of course, there is a danger in demanding too much of one's interlocutors. They may fall silent and refuse to participate. We have seen that Critias at once point does fall silent. But interlocutors may do worse; they may become hostile and hold grudges. Indeed, this is precisely how Socrates in *Apology* describes the genesis of the public's animosity toward him. If the historical Socrates had angered Critias as he angered other Athenian citizens, the Thirty might have preempted the jury of 399 in silencing Socrates more severely than by mere prohibition of the teaching of the *technê* of words. Thus, the dramatic aporia in which the investigation in *Charmides* concludes is symptomatic of the conflict between philosophy and antiphilosophy.

3.6. Knowledge of Knowledge and the Form of the Good

In closing the discussion of *Charmides* one further point deserves mention. We have seen that knowledge of the good, rather than knowledge of knowledge, satisfies Socrates' F-conditions and thus is the most reasonable candidate for sound-mindedness to emerge from the dialogue. There is, however, an important connection between knowledge of the good and K, which is revealed by our identification of goodness and *eidos* (Form and order) in section 4 of chapter 3

---

87. *Chrm.* 175b4–c8.

and which lends further, albeit oblique, support to the thesis that the Platonic view is that goodness is order and Form.

In section 4 of chapter 3, I introduced the following problem. The identification of wisdom as excellence is equivalent to the identification of wisdom with the human good. Granted that wisdom is the good, wisdom itself is knowledge of the good. Therefore, knowledge of the good is the human good. Thus, the identification of excellence with wisdom seems to be circular. I also cited a passage from *Republic* where Socrates himself explicitly states the difficulty. So clearly Plato was aware of the problem. The identification of goodness as order and Form suggests a possible solution. In that case, the human good is knowledge of order. Yet, now, it is questionable how the Form of the good itself should be construed. In other words, we are asking how the Form of Form is to be construed. Observe the parallel between the knowledge of knowledge.

One possibility is that the Form of the good is the principle of Form, that in virtue of which all Forms are Forms. Observe that this is akin to K_K. Another possibility is that the Form of the good is the ideal order of the cosmos as an entirety and a unity. In other words, the Form of the good is the form, order, or structure of all Forms. Observe that this is akin to K_C.

From this perspective, the long, misguided investigation of K can be seen to relate to problems in the conceptualization of the Form of the good with which Plato himself arguably wrestled. Furthermore, insofar as K is Critias' confused response to Socrates' questions regarding the identity of self-knowledge, the Platonic identification of goodness and Form perhaps suggests a Platonic revision of the traditional conception of self-knowledge as knowledge of one's place within the cosmic order. As such, Plato might have claimed that the Delphic motto "Know yourself" enjoins human beings to pursue philosophy.

4.   Philosophy and the Polis

The most explicit and sustained attack on philosophy among the early dialogues occurs in *Gorgias* shortly after Callicles enters the discussion. Callicles is incensed at Socrates' handling of Gorgias and Polus. He expresses his view of natural justice and then says that Socrates would accept it if he "put philosophy aside and turned to greater things."[88] Callicles argues that philosophy is agreeable when confined to the young: "Philosophy is, I grant you, a pleasant thing if one engages in it in moderation in one's youth."[89] "It is a fine thing to partake of philosophy for the sake of one's education (*paideia*), and there is no shame when a teenager practices philosophy."[90] The problem arises when one persists into adulthood. "Philosophy corrupts those who continue to engage in it beyond the appropriate time."[91]

---

88. *Grg.* 484c4–5.
89. *Grg.* 484c5–7.
90. *Grg.* 485a4–5. See also 485c3–6 and the verb *neanieuesthai* (to behave in a dissolute manner like a youth) at 482c4.
91. *Grg.* 484c7–8. See also 486a5–7.

"When I see an older man still philosophizing and not getting rid of it, I think such a man is overdue for a whipping."[92]

Philosophizing beyond one's youth is despicable because it coincides with failure to participate in the conventional fora of adult life. "However well endowed he may be by nature, if a man pursues philosophy beyond his youth, he will necessarily end up incompetent (*apeiron*) in all things in which a man must be competent (*empeiron*)."[93] "[Such people] become incompetent (*apeiroi*) in the customs (*tôn nomôn*) of their city-states and in the forms of discourse (*tôn logôn*) in which people negotiate their private and public affairs."[94] "They become incompetent in human pleasures (*hêdonôn*) and desires (*epithumiôn*); and, in a word, they become utterly incompetent in human characters (*êthôn*)."[95] "Consequently, when they undertake a private or public enterprise, they become laughable."[96] An adult who pursues philosophy becomes "unmanly (*anandrôi*) because he avoids the centers of the city-state (*ta mesa tês poleôs*) and the marketplaces."[97] Instead, "he spends his life huddled in a corner whispering with three or four teenagers."[98]

The philosopher is a person out of place. He fails to integrate with the world of men, and his life is a protracted childhood. It is in civic arenas and institutions of the state that men strive to become "noble and good (*kalon kagathon*) and to gain renown (*eudokimon esesthai*)."[99] The centers of the polis are where, as Homer says, "men achieve glory (*ariprepeis*)."[100] The life to be pursued is the life of "repute (*doxa*)."[101] But the philosopher risks "spending his life utterly without honor (*atimon*)."[102] In fact, he risks being wholly undone; for "anyone who wished, however trivial (*paulou*) or depraved (*moxthrou*)," could "drag him into court, prosecute him for an injustice he did not commit," and succeed in bringing "the death penalty upon him."[103] In short, a philosopher might wind up "unable to save himself from the greatest dangers and stripped by his enemies of all his *ousian* (property)."[104]

At the beginning of chapter 3, I said that the implicit ethical question in the early dialogues is "What sort of character ought one to cultivate?" Given the chauvinism of Athenian culture and the early dialogues, the question is ultimately

---

92. Grg. 485d1–3.
93. Grg. 484c8–d1.
94. Grg. 484d2–5.
95. Grg. 484d5–7.
96. Grg. 484d7–e1.
97. Grg. 485d4–5.
98. Grg. 485d6–e1.
99. Grg. 484d1–2. The phrase *kalon kagathon* refers to the paradigm of traditional excellence.
100. Grg. 485d5–6.
101. Grg. 486d1.
102. Grg. 486c1–2.
103. Grg. 486a7–b4.
104. Grg. 486b6–c1. The word *ousian* is in the accusative case.

indistinguishable from the question, "What sort of man ought one to be?" Callicles' answer is clear. The good is *timê*; therefore, a man should be *philotimos*. As Callicles characterizes it here, and as I said at the end of chapter 2, the quest for honor is a competitive one, a zero-sum game. But in this case competition entails conformity as the contestants orient around a common goal. Thus, Callicles is exhorting Socrates to conform to conventional aristocratic values, to educate himself in the desires, discourses, and characters of his fellows, and thereby to outgrow the puerile games of logic-chopping and become a man.

Callicles' speech is riddled with dramatic irony. The philosopher is not characterized in terms of ignorance and knowledge, but incompetence (*empeiros*) and competence (*apeiros*). These words echo Socrates' distinction earlier in *Gorgias* between *technê* and *empeiria*. Socrates criticizes the *empeiriai* of the city-state. The discourse with which Callicles encourages Socrates to familiarize himself is rhetoric, and conventional human pleasures are pseudogoods. Critias' criticism of philosophers as children, thus, contrasts with the Platonic view, which I discussed in section 7 of chapter 2, that the ethical hedonism of rhetoric, as commonly practiced, and other forms of flattery befits children.

The chief dramatic irony is the allusion to Socrates' trial and execution. Callicles claims that the philosopher will be unable to save himself from the greatest dangers. But, as Socrates had previously argued with Polus, Callicles' view of danger is based on a misconception of goodness. Human value resides in the soul, not the body. Therefore, no harm can come to a good man. Callicles' claim that the philosopher will be stripped of his *ousia* is also ironic. By *ousia* Callicles means "property." Recall that the ability to confiscate property is one of the emblems of despotic power that Polus admired. But the word *ousia* is also a metaphysical concept associated with ontology and Forms. Accordingly, one can imagine Socrates responding that nobody could strip him of his *ousia*.

Callicles appears to identify philosophy with eristic dialectic, the practice of using sophistical arguments to compel one's interlocutor to contradict himself. Callicles believes that Socrates' success in refuting Polus lay in a fallacy of ambiguity and that Socrates deliberately used the word *kalon* inconsistently, now with respect to convention, now with respect to nature:

> Yet these things, nature and convention, are for the most part contrary to one another; and if someone is ashamed and doesn't dare to say what he thinks, he is forced to contradict himself. And this is the wisdom (*to sophon*) you've acquired to undo us in discussion. If one speaks according to convention (*nomon*), you insert according to nature (*phusin*); and if one speaks according to nature, you insert according to convention.[105]

Yet "how is this wisdom (*sophon*) . . . if it does not enable a man to save himself from the greatest dangers?"[106]

---

105. *Grg.* 482e5–483a4.
106. *Grg.* 486b4–7.

Callicles' denigrating view of philosophy is blind to the real significance of the *nomos/phusis* debate in Socratic circles. In clarifying this point, it is convenient to refer to a pertinent debate among scholars today. A controversy currently exists regarding Socrates' heirs Aristippus and the Cyrenaics, on the one hand, and Antisthenes and the Cynics, on the other. These two parties maintain contrary views of pleasure. Aristippus and the Cyrenaics are hedonists, while Antisthenes was celebrated for having proclaimed that he would rather go mad than experience pleasure. Scholars question how these individuals and schools could have stemmed from the same Socratic source. Commonly, reconciliation is achieved by diminishing Antisthenes' antihedonism and Aristippus' hedonism in favor of a conception of pleasure as an attitude of appreciation of the good. But consider another solution. Assuming that the historical Socrates was engaged in the *nomos/phusis* debate with his intellectual contemporaries, Socrates' ethical project can be seen as the pursuit of the true nature of humanity. On this view, Aristippus and Antisthenes are Socratics insofar as their hedonism and antihedonism respectively constitute two opposed, but genuine, answers to a common question, "What is a human being, and what is the human good?"

This suggestion gains credibility precisely from the way Plato juxtaposes Socrates and Callicles. The problem of the nature of humanity is implicit throughout Callicles' critique of philosophy, following, as it does, Callicles' introduction of the *nomos/phusis* distinction and preceding his defense of ethical hedonism. As I suggested in section 4 of chapter 3, the Platonic view is that Callicles' position in fact is conventional; it is merely expressed starkly because Callicles dispenses with a sense of shame.

For Callicles, the philosopher's detachment from conventional political life renders him ignorant of human character. But Callicles does not appreciate that philosophy, as Socrates practices it, is a quest for the truth, not for the sort of trivial victories in debating games that puerile pseudophilosophers such as Euthydemus and Dionysodorus seek.

Socrates begins his discussion with Callicles by characterizing the two of them as distinct sorts of lovers. Socrates is a lover of *sophia*; Callicles a lover of *dêmos*. Socrates is punning here; *dêmos* refers to a particular youth as well as to the Athenian populus. Socrates emphasizes that in the Assembly Callicles says whatever the people desire. In other words, Callicles' speech conforms to the whims of the many. In contrast, Socrates says whatever seems most reasonable on the basis of his examinations.

For Callicles—and, no doubt, for many of Plato's fellow citizens—the philosophical question of the nature of humanity simply fails to impress itself with any force. The appearance of reality is taken for reality itself. Pleasures and pains, honor and shame, life and death obviously possess the values widely associated with them. One does not question such things. Rather, one attempts to conduct oneself in accordance with them. For people with such commitments, there is little confidence, indeed there is little cognizance, that reason is capable of disclosing the Form of excellence. Thus, Callicles' critique of philosophy emphatically reveals, as the early dialogues variously do in their dramatizations, the trials to which reason is subject.

More than once I have said that the dramas are not wholly situated within the sphere of philosophical discourse. Rather, one of the basic functions of the texts is to craft philosophy. As the dialogues unfold, philosophical discourse emerges out of the various discourses of the polis. In the process, Plato works to establish why philosophical discourse must be the authoritative political discourse. These facts generate interpretive challenges alien to the genre of the monologic treatise and relatively unique among canonical Western philosophical literature. I began the study with this problem, and I have attempted to chart a course between the poles of doctrinal and skeptical interpretation, wedding the argumentative and dramatic dimensions of the texts.

The conflict of philosophy and antiphilosophy is the dominant theme of the texts. In this final chapter, I have suggested that dramatic aporia reflects this conflict. Consequently, the question arises of the practicability of philosophy as a collaborative and specifically political enterprise. Philosophy is a project of inquiry; human cognition is limited; and so, as Socrates says to Protagoras, two heads are better than one. Yet, as a figure such as Callicles in *Gorgias* or Critias in *Charmides* demonstrates, antiphilosophical motivations such as the love of pleasure or the love of esteem corrupt life in general and in particular tarnish the pursuit of wisdom.

Dramatic aporia, thus, intimates that the historical Socrates' project of social and political reform in the particular public manner in which it was enacted was perhaps too bold. It suggests the desirability of building a distinctly philosophical community. But if philosophy must, in a sense, remove itself from the polis in order to be effective, this efficacy will merely be of a theoretical nature. Philosophy may succeed in clarifying the order of things, but the actual state of political life will remain deeply disjoint from goodness thus disclosed. If the conditions of political life in Athens were good, philosophy would not have arisen. Consequently, if philosophy is to remain true to its original inspiration, it will ultimately have to find a way of engaging and prevailing over the Callicleses and Critiases of the polis.

The means of engagement and success are a practical problem for philosophy, one to which Plato is deeply sensitive. In *Gorgias* Socrates is relatively successful in arguing that it is better to suffer than to do injustice. But in the course of the argument, Callicles ceases to participate. Socrates is eventually compelled to employ himself as his own interlocutor.[107] Socrates claims that it is the love of *dêmos* in Callicles' soul that makes him inflexible. Admittedly, Socrates also claims that if he and he were to examine the subject matter more than once and in a better way, Callicles would be persuaded.[108] But if this suggests grounds for hope, recall also the problem Socrates recognizes in his defense speech in *Apology*: It is difficult to disabuse the public, in the short allotted time, of long-standing

---

107. *Grg.* 505c–e.
108. *Grg.* 513c–d.

prejudices.[109] In the hustle and bustle of life, leisure is available only to select citizens. Time is short. Before long Socrates is condemned and executed.

Philosophy, thus, emerges as an ideal. Indeed, as my discussions of Platonic epistemology and methodology have shown, philosophy is a theoretical as well as a practical ideal. At the same time, if the neoplatonic conception of desire in *Lysis* is also Platonic, then it is the nature of human beings to become philosophers. Plato's practical problem is, therefore, to enable his fellow Athenians to realize themselves. The early dialogues are Plato's answer to this problem.

---

109. *Ap.* 19a.

APPENDIX I

COMMONLY USED GREEK WORDS

Note that since the Greek language is highly inflected, forms of adjectives and nouns may appear in the main text with slightly different endings. For example, *agathon* indicates neuter gender, whereas *agathos* is masculine.

agathon	(ἀγαθόν)	good	(noun, *to agathon*)
agôn	(ἀγών)	trial, contest	(plural, *agônes*)
aischron	(αἰσχρόν)	base, shameful, ugly, foul	
aitia	(αἰτία)	cause, reason	(plural, *aitiai*)
aition	(αἴτιον)	cause, reason	
akrasia	(ἀκρασία)	weakness (of will)	
andreia	(ἀνδρεία)	courage	(adjective, *andreion*)
aporia	(ἀπορία)	perplexity, no-passage	(plural, *aporiai*)
archê	(ἀρχή)	beginning, principle, rule	(plural, *archai*)
aretê	(ἀρετή)	excellence, virtue	(adjective, *ariston*)
boulêsis	(βούλησις)	desire	(plural, *boulêseis*)
dêmos	(δῆμος)	populus	
dikaiosunê	(δικαιοσύνη)	justice	(adjective, *dikaion*)
dunamis	(δύναμις)	power, capacity	(plural, *dunameis*)
eidôlon	(εἴδωλον)	image, phantom	
eidos	(εἶδος)	order, organized form, Form	(plural, *eidê*)
eirôneia	(εἰρωνεία)	dissembling, "irony"	(adjective, *eirôn*)
empeiria	(ἐμπειρία)	competence, knack	(plural, *empeiriai*)
epistêmê	(ἐπιστήμη)	knowledge	(plural, *epistêmai*)
epithumia	(ἐπιθυμία)	desire	(plural, *epithumiai*)
ergon	(ἔργον)	work, product, function	(plural, *erga*)
eudaimonia	(εὐδαιμονία)	well-being, happiness	(adjective, *eudaimon*)

hêdonê	(ἡδονή)	pleasure	(plural, hêdonai)
hosiotês	(ὁσιότης)	holiness, piety	(adjective, hosion)
homoiotês	(ὁμοιότης)	likeness	(adjective, homoion)
hupothesis	(ὑπόθεσις)	postulate, foundation	(plural, hupotheseis)
kakon	(κακόν)	bad	
kalon	(καλόν)	beautiful, fine, admirable	(noun, kallos, to kalon)
nomos	(νόμος)	convention, custom, law	
oikeiotês	(οἰκειότης)	belonging	(adjective, oikeion)
ousia	(οὐσία)	being, essence, property	
paideia	(παιδεία)	education	
pathos	(πάθος)	affection	
philia	(φιλία)	friendship	(adjective, philon)
philhêdonia	(φιληδονία)	love of pleasure	(adjective, philhêdonos)
philonikia	(φιλονικία)	love of winning, ambition	(adjective, philonikos)
philosophia	(φιλοσοφία)	philosophy, love of wisdom	(adjective, philosophon)
philotimia	(φιλοτιμία)	love of esteem	(adjective, philotimon)
phronêsis	(φρόνησις)	wisdom, intelligence	(adjective, phronimon)
phusis	(φύσις)	nature	
poiêma	(ποίημα)	action	
psychê	(ψυχή)	soul	
sophia	(σοφία)	wisdom, knowledge	(adjective, sophon)
sôphrosunê	(σωφροσύνη)	sound-mindedness	(adjective, sôphron)
technê	(τέχνη)	craft, expertise, knowledge	(plural, technai)
timê	(τιμή)	esteem, honor, repute	

APPENDIX 2

THE IRONY OF SOCRATES

Irony has variously been conceived as central to the character of Socrates. This is significant for my treatment of Socrates in two respects. On the one hand, appeals to Socratic irony may be made in order to preserve the mouthpiece principle. Rather than distinguishing Platonic and Socratic beliefs and intentions, it may be proposed that Socrates himself does not literally or sincerely intend certain utterances, specifically utterances that figure in apparently inconsistent sets. Of course, such appeals may be problematic. Iakovos Vasiliou well expresses the concern: "Socratic irony is potentially fertile ground for exegetical abuse. It can seem to offer an interpreter the chance to dismiss any claim [that] conflicts with his account...merely by crying 'irony.' If abused in this way, Socratic irony can quickly become a convenient receptacle for everything inimical to an interpretation."[1]

On the other hand, irrespective of the mouthpiece principle, the possibility that irony, disingenuousness, or the like is characteristic of Socrates complicates the interpretation of the dialogues. All interpretations engage the utterances of Socrates. But if it is disputable whether in any given instance Socrates is being sincere, the hermeneutic enterprise will fundamentally be hamstrung. For both reasons, then, it is desirable to assess criteria for determining whether in any given instance Socrates is being ironic.

It is useful to begin with the basic terminology, the word "irony" and its Greek ancestor *eirôneia*. The standard view is that *eirôneia* means "dissembling." I believe

---

The argument in this appendix will strike many as extreme. Whether or not the argument succeeds, my hope is that the discussion will be found valuable insofar as it attempts to draw the problems of this topic into sharper focus.

1. (1998) 456.

that this is not adequately precise, at least for the earliest usage, which includes Plato's early dialogues.

The earliest surviving instances of the word *eirôneia* and its cognates occur in Aristophanic comedies of the late fifth century. In *Clouds*, produced in 423, Strepsiades, plagued by debt and intent upon acquiring rhetorical training to elude his creditors in the law courts, envisions that he will be subject to a salvo of insults if he submits himself to the sophists' teachings. The insults he rattles off are loosely organized into the following semantic clusters: boldness, linguistic facility, familiarity with the legal system, and deception. The word *eirôn* occurs in this last cluster. Unfortunately, it is unclear from the context how or whether the meaning of *eirôn* differs from the other associated terms. Little more can be derived from the passage than that *eirôneia* involves duplicity and is undesirable.

More clarification comes from Aristophanes' *Peace*, produced in 422. Hermes describes how some tributary allies, disgruntled with Athens, succeeded in persuading Spartan leaders to break the peace. Peace, here personified, was then victimized by the notorious Spartan habit of expulsion of foreigners. The Spartans are described by the Aristophanic coinage *dieirônexenoi*, that is, *eirôn* toward foreigners (*xenoi*). Liddell and Scott's Greek–English dictionary provides "treacherous under the mask of hospitality" as a gloss on this adjective. Their interpretation is supported by the other instances of cognates of *eirôneia* in Aristophanes.

In *Wasps*, produced in 421, Philocleon, imprisoned in his own house, fails to trick the house-slave Xanthias and his own son Bdelycleon into letting him out. Noting the failure of his father's ploy, Bdelycleon remarks, "he caught nothing by this means."[2] The expression is drawn from angling. The idea that Philocleon has attempted to lure the others with bait is also suggested by Xanthias' preceding remark (which I translate rather literally to convey the point): "He has laid down the pretense, in such an *eirôn* manner, so that you let him out."[3]

Finally, in *Birds*, produced in 418, Peisthetairos catches the goddess Iris flying over the city. He suspects that she has infiltrated through one of the gates. When he asks her how she entered, she replies, honestly, that she has no idea. Her interrogator thinks she is prevaricating and accuses her of withholding information: "You've heard her, how she *eirônizes*."[4] Peisthetairos thinks that Iris is playing naïve and also that her denial conceals knowledge that threatens the city.

There are many reasons for dissembling: to conceal one's ignorance or incompetence, to spare the feelings of others, to illustrate a point that could not be illustrated otherwise, or because frankness would be dangerous. A culture concerned with any particular form of dissembling might generate a word for that particular form. In the case of the Aristophanic usages, at least the last three—but given the temporal and generic proximity of *Clouds*, most likely here too—*eirôneia* and its cognates appear to mean something more specific than

2. *Vesp.* 174–75.
3. *hoian prophasin kathêken . . .*
4. I will be using this coinage to allow the sense of the word to emerge through context.

"dissembling." These examples suggest that *eirôneia* is a sly, crafty dissembling by which the *eirôn* presents himself in a positive manner, as beneficent, amiable, or modest, when in fact he is self-seeking and harmful.

In a fragment of a lost drama of the Middle Comic poet Philemon, the fox is characterized as *eirôn*;[5] compare our expression "sly as a fox." In discussing cunning intelligence among the Greeks, Marcel Detienne and Jean Pierre Vernant cite a description of the fox from Oppian's treatise *On Hunting*. When he sees a flock of wilds birds, the fox crouches low to the ground and pretends to be asleep so that when his unsuspecting prey approach him, he can effectively spring upon them.[6] The fox's hunting tactics well illustrate the concept of *eirôneia*. *Eirôneia* is the use of deception to profit at the expense of another by presenting oneself as benign in an effort to disarm the intended victim. Let us call this the vulpine sense of *eirôneia*.

Outside of Aristophanes' comedies, *eirôneia* and its cognates first occur in Plato's dialogues, and assuming that the dialogues classed as early are in fact early, they first occur in these. I suggest that in these cases the vulpine sense of *eirôneia* is operative.

In *Apology* Socrates explains why he cannot stop philosophizing; he notes that the jury are unlikely to regard him as sincere: "If I say that it is impossible for me to keep quiet because that means disobeying the divine, you will not believe me and think that I am *eirônizing*."[7] Socrates does view his philosophical activity as obedient to the divine. However, the jurors are bound to think that this man, who is on trial for impiety, is presenting his philosophical activity as pious precisely to exculpate himself and to conceal from them its seditious dimensions.

In *Euthydemus*, Dionysodorus attempts to defeat Socrates with one of his sophisms. Having elicited Socrates' commitment to a set of premises, Dionysodorus prepares to draw the fatal conclusion: "Then he, pausing in a wholly *eirôn* manner as though he were considering some weighty matter, said..."[8] Dionysodorus here gives the impression of being deep in thought; he pretends to be treating the discussion in an earnest fashion. Of course, the opposite is the case, and Socrates' subsequent remark makes this clear: "I tried to escape by some futile turn and twisted around as though I were caught in a net."[9] As in the *Wasps* passage, the hunting or angling metaphor occurs here. Compare the passage in Plato's *Sophist* where the Eleatic stranger's attempt to define the sophist begins with an account of the angler, ostensibly to demonstrate the diairetic method. The model chosen is loaded, for the sophist is subsequently defined, among other ways, as a kind of hunter who preys on wealthy youth. Comparable also is Socrates' description in *Protagoras* of the sophist as dangerous precisely because, like a

---

5. *ouk est' alôpêx hê men eirôn têi phusei, ê d' authekastos...* (fr. 3.6 K)
6. Detienne and Vernant (1978) 35; Oppian, 2.107–18.
7. *Ap.* 37e5–38a1.
8. *Euthd.* 302b3–4.
9. *Euthd.* 302b6–7.

merchant, he extols his wares without genuine concern for their benefit to the naïve young customer.

In *Republic* 1, Thrasymachus accuses Socrates of *eirôneia*: "By Heracles . . . there it is, Socrates' accustomed *eirôneia*. I knew it all along, and I told these people in advance that you'd be unwilling to answer, that you'd *eirônize* and do anything except given an answer if someone were to ask you a question."[10] Thrasymachus believes that Socrates is concealing his views under the pretense of ignorance; by falsely disavowing competence, Socrates can criticize the views of others and avoid exposure to criticism himself. In fact, Socrates' profession of ignorance is honest and frank, but Thrasymachus interprets it as an offensive strategy.

At *Gorgias* 489e Callicles accuses Socrates of *eirôneia*, and Socrates accuses Callicles of *eirôneia* in turn:

CALLICLES   You are *eirônizing*, Socrates.

SOCRATES   No, by Zethos, Callicles, whom you used just now in *eirônizing* with me.[11]

Immediately before this, Socrates says that he had guessed some time ago that Callicles, in saying that the stronger are better, didn't mean that the many are better because physically stronger. Therefore, Callicles is annoyed with Socrates for deliberately misinterpreting him in order to make him appear foolish. In other words, Callicles accuses Socrates of pretending to be simple-minded by offering an extremely literal interpretation of Callicles' account precisely in order to criticize that simple-minded account and thereby Callicles. Socrates' accusation of *eirôneia*, in turn, refers to Callicles' earlier remarks in which Callicles, in criticizing Socrates' involvement in philosophy, claimed that he was sympathetic to Socrates and looking out for his best interests. Socrates now appears to think that Callicles actually believes that Socrates' involvement in philosophy is despicable, yet that Callicles previously articulated himself in a disingenuous way to give the impression that he was concerned with Socrates' well-being. In short, Callicles' principal aim was to attack philosophy, not to support Socrates.

In sum, the vulpine sense of *eirôneia* and its cognates is manifest in or is at least compatible with all of the instances of these terms in the late fifth century and in Plato's early dialogues.

Eirôneia (in the vulpine sense) and "irony" have distinct meanings. There are two basic kinds of irony, verbal and situational. Verbal irony occurs when a speaker deliberates highlights the literal falsity of his utterance, typically for the sake of humor. For example, a squash player mocks a lousy shot with "brilliant!" A crucial distinction between verbal irony and *eirôneia*, then, is the absence, in the former case, of intended deception. Verbal irony succeeds when the intended audience grasps that the speaker is highlighting the literal falsity of the utterance, whereas

10. *R.* 1, 337a4–7.
11. *Grg.* 489e1–3.

if the audience were to grasp the speaker's sincere belief, *eirôneia* would fail. Furthermore, the intent of the verbal ironist is benign, whereas the *eirôn* is malevolent.

Situational irony entails a certain incongruity between what a person says, believes, or does and how, unbeknownst to that person, things actually are. Oedipus vows to discover Laius' murderer, unaware that Laius was his father and that he himself is guilty of patricide. Whatever the precise nature of the incongruity involved in situational irony, verbal and situational irony loosely share a conceptual core of incongruity, often tending toward polar opposition, between two elements, such as a semblance of things and reality.

Dramatic irony may be further distinguished as a type of situational irony; it is simply when situational irony occurs in a drama. The incongruity is between what a dramatic character says, believes, or does and how unbeknownst to that character, the dramatic reality is. The example in the preceding paragraph is, then, specifically of dramatic irony.

Given these distinctions, the question whether Socrates is ironic is ambiguous. It could be interpreted as inquiring whether Socrates exhibits *eirôneia* or verbal or situational irony. Situational irony is irrelevant to the interpretive problem at issue. The question, then, is whether Socrates is verbally ironic or an *eirôn*. To be more precise, since there is no good reason to assume that Socrates is a strictly transtextually identical character, the question is whether in any particular instance he is being verbally ironic or *eirôn*.

It is quite clear that Plato never or, at most, very rarely portrays Socrates as an *eirôn* and that doing so would undermine the philosophical interest of the dialogues. Socrates' interlocutors may occasionally think that he is deliberately trying to refute them and thereby to present himself in a more compelling light than his victims. However, as I discussed in chapter 4, sections 2 and 4, Socrates is principally portrayed as pursuing truth not victory in debate.

It remains to consider to what extent Socrates is verbally ironic. In addressing this question, I will focus on a passage in *Euthyphro*. The passage has limited philosophical significance in its own right; however, it is valuable for broaching and examining a set of fundamental interpretive problems to which, as we will see, the question of Socratic verbal irony relates.

The preceding definition of verbal irony provides a clear criterion for determining whether a speaker is being ironic. Since the ironist, unlike the *eirôn*, does not intend to deceive, but to highlight the falsity of the literal meaning of his utterance, typically for the sake of humor, the reaction of his interlocutor should give some indication of whether the utterance is ironic. Granted, attempted irony may fail because a speaker is too subtle or an interlocutor too obtuse. But even if that occurs, the speaker's response to the interlocutor's response should correct misunderstanding—save in the exceptional case where the ironist allows the point to die.

Armed with this criterion, I turn to a passage that is widely recognized as exemplifying the trope. The passage occurs at the beginning of *Euthyphro*, where Socrates is recounting to Euthyphro the nature of his suit and prosecutor:

> What sort [of case is Meletus prosecuting]? No mean one, it seems to me, for the fact that, young as he is, he has apprehended so important a matter

reflects no small credit upon him. For he says he knows how the youth are corrupted and who those are who corrupt them. He must be a wise man, who, seeing my lack of wisdom and that I am corrupting his fellows, comes to the state, as a boy runs to its mother, to accuse me. And he seems to me to be the only one of the politicians who begins in the right way, for the right way is to take care of the young men first, to make them as good as possible, just as a good husbandman will naturally take care of the young plants, as he says. Then, after this, when he has turned his attention to the older men, he will bring countless most precious blessings upon the state—at least that is the natural outcome of the beginning he has made.[12]

Consider a representative response to this passage and to Socrates' treatment of Euthyphro in general. Alexander Nehamas refers to the "incredibly heavy-handed irony with which Socrates treats [Euthyphro] throughout the dialogue," and he claims that "Socrates' irony is so extreme that it soon ceases to be humorous."[13]

In view of the definition given, if Socrates' remarks are verbally ironic, then he is intending to highlight their falsity for humorous effect. Accordingly, it is to be expected that Euthyphro would laugh at or comment on the absurdity of Socrates' praise of Meletus. But Euthyphro responds as though Socrates has spoken in earnest: "I hope it may be so, Socrates, but I fear the opposite may result, for it seems to me that he begins by injuring the state at its very heart when he undertakes to harm you. Now, tell me, what does he say you do that corrupts the youth?"[14] Moreover, Socrates does not correct Euthyphro's interpretation of his remarks; he proceeds to answer Euthyphro's question. Thus, Euthyphro's response and Socrates' reaction to it indicate that Socrates' initial remarks are not verbally ironic.

This argument is unlikely to receive warm welcome. It will be vigorously objected that one of the dialogue's basic features is Euthyphro's obtuseness; therefore, it is natural that Euthyphro fails to appreciate Socrates' irony. Again, Nehamas claims that "Plato's Euthyphro...is unusually stupid" and "remains totally impervious to [Socrates' irony]."[15] Consequently, the reaction may come that to interpret Socrates' remarks as earnest is as dim-witted as Euthyphro himself and as Meletus for prosecuting Socrates in the first place.

Since a clear criterion for verbal irony has been given and the passage has been shown to fail to satisfy it, it is necessary to consider why readers so readily attribute verbal irony to Socrates in a case such as this. One reason is supplied by a recent scholarly discussion of so-called conditional irony. Conditional irony is said to occur when the speaker asserts a proposition to which he is sincerely

---

12. *Euthphr.* 2c2–3a5. The translation follows Fowler (1914).
13. (1998) 37.
14. *Euthphr.* 3a6–9.
15. (1998) 37–38.

committed, but which is explicitly or implicitly embedded as the consequent in a conditional, the antecedent to which the speaker does not sincerely believe. For example, Vasiliou suggests that Socrates' remarks in *Euthyphro* contain an example of conditional irony. Socrates claims that "(1) Meletus charges Socrates with a charge that is not ignoble, for it is no base thing for a young man to have knowledge of such a subject."[16] But the irony here depends upon the assumption that Meletus possesses knowledge of excellence, so that "in (1) the implied conditional is: *If* Meletus has knowledge of [excellence], it is surely no base thing and the charge he has raised against Socrates is not ignoble. Socrates literally means this, but *we know* that Socrates does not believe the antecedent. Given *this*, however, Meletus' false pretence to knowledge and his charge against Socrates based on that pretence *are* base and ignoble."[17]

But let us press Vasiliou here. How do "we know" that Socrates does not believe Meletus has knowledge of excellence? Vasiliou writes that "we know from [Socrates'] treatment of Meletus in the *Apology* (esp. 24b–28b), as well as from the other dialogues, that Socrates does not believe that Meletus truly fits [(1)]."[18] Consider the matter now from the perspective interior to the texts' fictional worlds. Regardless of when Plato composed *Euthyphro* and *Apology*, Socrates' chance meeting with Euthyphro at the Basileic Stoa precedes Socrates' trial. Accordingly, Socrates' discussion with Meletus at *Apology* 24b–28b provides no evidence that Socrates knows that Meletus lacks knowledge of excellence. Furthermore, in *Euthyphro* Socrates explicitly says that he hardly knows Meletus: "I don't know the man very well myself, Euthyphro, for he seems to be a young and unknown person. I believe, however, that his name is 'Meletus' and that he is of the deme Pitthus—if you recall any Meletus of Pitthus with long hair, a short beard, and a hooked nose."[19] Socrates gives the impression that he has seen Meletus, but had little if any personal contact with the man. How, then, could Socrates know that Meletus lacks knowledge of excellence? I emphasize that Plato, obviously, believes that Meletus lacks knowledge of excellence and so that Socrates' praise of Meletus is dramatically ironic. But dramatic irony is beside the point—except, we might say, insofar as the interpreter is confusing Socrates' assumed verbal irony with Plato's genuine dramatic irony.

Granted, then, from the fictional perspective interior to the texts Socrates cannot know that Meletus lacks knowledge of excellence insofar as Socrates has never met him. But let us now consider a second objection to my claim that Socrates is not verbally ironic in the *Euthyphro* passage. On my interpretation, Socrates' sincerity would be intertextually inconsistent. In other words, to interpret Socrates' praise of Meletus as earnest would yield inconsistency with other of Socrates' experiences and utterances in other dialogues. For example, in *Gorgias* Socrates emphasizes that if he is ever brought to court on a capital charge "it will

---

16. I have inserted the numeral to facilitate exegesis.
17. Vasiliou (1998) 468–69, with my italics.
18. Ibid., 468.
19. *Euthphr.* 2b7–11.

be some villain who brings me there, for no honest man would prosecute a person who had done no wrong."[20] Furthermore, Socrates' praise of Meletus occurs at the end of his life, which has been devoted to examining excellence with his contemporaries. In all the ethical investigations that Plato portrays in the early dialogues, Socrates' interlocutors are revealed to be ignorant of excellence; and in *Apology* Socrates emphasizes his fellow citizens' ignorance of their ignorance. Regardless of whether Socrates has so interrogated Meletus himself, such experience with so many others should provide strong grounds upon which to assume that Meletus does not have knowledge of excellence.

Further specific confirmation of this view comes from the beginning of *Meno*, where Socrates claims, "I have never come upon anyone who, in my opinion, knew [what excellence is]."[21] The dramatic date of *Meno* surely precedes that of *Euthyphro*. And so—the argument may run—it is unbelievable that in *Euthyphro* Socrates would sincerely assume that Meletus possessed such knowledge.

My response to this objection will proceed in two steps. First I want to dwell on Socrates' specific claim in *Meno*. Subsequently, I will address inconsistency among Socrates' utterances as a general hermeneutic problem.

First, then, consider that Socrates' remark in *Meno* is also inconsistent with a passage at the beginning of the investigation of courage in *Laches*, which was discussed in section 6 of chapter 3:

SOCRATES   Then it is necessary that we begin by knowing what excellence is, for, surely, if we had no idea at all what excellence is, we could not possibly consult with anyone regarding how he might best acquire it.

LACHES   I certainly think not, Socrates.

SOCRATES   Then we agree, Laches, that *we know what it is.*

LACHES   We do.

SOCRATES   And what we know we can, I suppose, describe.

LACHES   Of course.

SOCRATES   Then, my good man, let's not at once examine the whole of excellence, for that may be too much work. Rather, let's first look at a part of it to see if we have sufficient knowledge of that. And, most likely, this will make our inquiry easier ... So, then, which part of excellence should we choose? Or isn't it clear that it is the part that *is believed* (*dokei*) to pertain to the study of fighting in arms? And, I believe, this *is thought by many* (*dokei tois pollois*) to be courage.[22]

---

20. *Grg.* 521d1–3.
21. *Men.* 71c3–4.
22. *La.* 190b7–d5, with my italics.

As I have noted, this passage is remarkable in a number of respects. It is the only passage in the early dialogues where Socrates presumes to know what excellence is. Also, Socrates explicitly bases his conception of courage and the relation between courage and excellence on conventional views.

Terry Penner, who maintains that Socrates regards excellence as a unity, appeals here to Socrates' disingenuousness, a trait frequently conflated with irony: "Since the primary way in which Socrates identifies the parts of [excellence] he wants to narrow the inquiry down to, is as the part that has to do with fighting in heavy armor, he must be *wickedly trying to lure* Laches into giving the account of courage he knows Laches is itching to give anyway."[23] Likewise, Terry Irwin, who maintains that Socrates is committed to the unity of excellence, claims that the "assumption that bravery is a proper part of [excellence is] introduced to make the inquiry easier, because bravery [seems] to be the [part of excellence] most closely connected with training in armed combat."[24]

In short, Penner and Irwin appeal to Socratic "irony" in order to explain away a Socratic claim, which, if accepted as sincere, would jeopardize their thesis that Socrates (and therefore Plato) is committed to the unity of excellence. In contrast, Thomas Brickhouse and Nicholas Smith use this passage in their argument that Socrates is committed to the disunity of excellence. Accordingly, they criticize Penner's appeal to "irony": "One dubious consequence of [Penner's position] is that Socrates feels free to exempt himself from the requirement he so often places on his interlocutors, that when developing an argument about a moral matter that they always 'say what they believe.' "[25]

This scholarly dispute suggests that the attempt *locally* to resolve problematic passages such as that in *Laches* is unlikely to succeed. Likewise, the appeal to the *Meno* passage as evidence that in the *Euthyphro* passage Socrates is conditionally ironic is also problematic. Satisfactory treatment of these local problems is going to require plumbing deeper, more general assumptions that govern the interpretation of the dialogues. The general problem, which I have reiterated throughout this study, is that to some extent Socrates' statements among as well as within individual early dialogues are inconsistent.

As I discussed in chapter 1 and in section 6 of chapter 3, scholars tend to treat Socrates' intertextual and intratextual inconsistencies as though they were merely apparent. There are various ways in which this is done; but the variety may be conceived as ranging between two poles. At one end, apparent inconsistency is resolved by appeal to so-called irony and various forms of disingenuousness, from polite concession to ad hominem argumentation to jesting to pedagogical savvy. Let us call this style of interpretation and its accompanying conceptualization of Socrates as characteristically insincere "the complex view." At the other end of the spectrum, Socrates' claims are accepted as sincere, and their apparent

---

23. (1992) 16, with my italics.
24. (1995) 43.
25. (1997) 318, n. 20.

inconsistency is resolved by appeal to developmentalism or to deeper, subtler unifying principles. Let us call this style of interpretation "literalist."

Interpretations of Socrates' epistemological commitments provide a good and, as we will see, topically relevant example of this range of responses. According to the complex view, Socrates' denials of knowledge are insincere. As such, they tend to be interpreted as serving some pedagogical function. According to the literalist view, Socrates' disavowals of knowledge are accepted as genuine, yet it is observed that Socrates also occasionally sincerely avows knowledge. The inconsistency is resolved by appeal to explanations such as that Socrates uses words for knowledge in two different senses or that Socrates avows knowledge of certain propositions, but disavows knowledge of how such propositions are true or that Socrates disavows expertise, but avows nonexpert knowledge.

But the very conceptualization of Socrates' apparent or genuine inconsistencies as an interpretive problem itself rests on a deeper assumption about the nature of intertextual interpretation. A remark Socrates makes in one text that is inconsistent with a remark he makes in another text need not be conceived as a hermeneutic problem unless it is already assumed that intertextual interpretation involving the assembly and distillation of all of Socrates' utterances is itself a legitimate, indeed, *the* legitimate interpretive procedure. But on what grounds can that assumption be justified?

Typically, the kind of justification given is post hoc; the interpreter's success in demonstrating a consistent set of Socratic philosophical principles is taken to confirm what begins as a methodological presupposition. In the case of many philosophical texts, that kind of approach may be perfectly warranted. However, as we have seen, in the particular case of Plato's early dialogues good reasons can be marshaled against this sort of intertextual interpretation.

Even granting the possibility of revisions and overlapping or relatively simultaneous composition, Plato must have written the dialogues in some chronological order. Accordingly, some dialogue—or, if one insists, some small set of dialogues—was composed first. Consequently, Plato's first dialogue could not have been interpreted intertextually and could not have been intended to be interpreted intertextually. What if *Euthyphro* were the first Platonic dialogue? In fact, in the traditional organization of the corpus transmitted since Diogenes Laertius, *Euthyphro* is the first dialogue. How, then, would a reader be situated to recognize the verbal irony in Socrates' remarks when Euthyphro himself does not?

But this suggestion is, admittedly, weak insofar as it is speculative. The corpus of Thrasyllus, which Diogenes adopted, may not reflect Plato's intended order. Moreover, although Plato composed the early dialogues in some chronological order, he need not have disseminated them in that order, but as a whole set or in subsets.

There are more concrete reasons against the sort of intertextual interpretation of the dialogues in question. The most important and fundamental reason is that each text shares what I have called a common doxastic base, and related to the early dialogues' common doxastic base is the prevalence of α-structure. Recall that α- structure serves a linear pedagogical function: to lead the intended audience from a conventional conception of the topic treated in the text to a Platonic conception of that topic. The fact that α-structure and a common doxastic base are basic features of the early dialogues strongly encourages the view that Plato conceived the reading of each of the early dialogues individually in the sense proposed. In view of this—to return to the *Euthyphro* passage—it is difficult to see how a reader could be expected to appreciate the verbal irony in Socrates' remarks to Euthyphro about Meletus.

Appeal to the operation of α-structure can be made precisely to support the view that Socrates is being sincere in his praise of Meletus. The dialogue begins by suggesting an analogy between Meletus and Euthyphro as individuals who are allegedly knowledgeable about affairs of importance to the state. In contrast, Socrates initially appears to be relatively ignorant and their intellectual inferior. However, in the course of the investigation, Euthyphro and, by analogy and implication, Meletus are gradually revealed to be ignorant and ignorant of their ignorance, while Socrates' humility emerges as well founded and enlightened. In short, the propaedeutic function of α-structure explains why Socrates so confidently claims that Meletus is praiseworthy and that Euthyphro has expertise in theological matters.

Granted this, the appeal to the propaedeutic function of α-structure does not adequately explain why, from a realistic historical and psychological perspective, Socrates so confidently claims that Meletus is praiseworthy and that Euthyphro has expertise in theological matters. With this point we come to a further question pertaining to the sort of intertextual interpretation under scrutiny and to the interpretation of the early dialogues still more broadly. Given the admission that the texts were intended to be read individually in the sense proposed, what significance does this have for our conceptualization of the character Socrates? Specifically, what grounds remain to support the view that Plato conceptualized and composed the character Socrates as having a strict transtextual identity among the early dialogues? Furthermore—and the following question remains alive even if, as I argued in chapter 1, strict transtextual identity is denied to Socrates—to what extent did Plato intend to portray Socrates in any given dialogue as historically and psychologically realistic?

Let me reiterate here the relevance of the question to the *Euthyphro* passage. An objection to my view that Socrates is sincere in praising Meletus is that Socrates, consequently, emerges as historically and psychologically implausible, in other words, unreal. Let us, therefore, examine the parameters of realism in the early dialogues.

In section 5 of chapter 1, I said that realism, the prevailing dramatic mode of the early dialogues, is achieved through three complicit dimensions: the discursive style in which the characters engage, the portrayal of the psychological profiles of the dramatic characters through their speech and nonverbal action, and the historicity of the settings and characters. To this may be added the following two salient features of these texts: the language of prose versus poetry and the unities of time and place. The events portrayed in the early dialogues largely occur in real time,[26]

---

26. *Apology* is slightly exceptional since there are time lapses between the conclusion of Socrates' defense, his suggestion of a fine, and his concluding comments.

and the discussions are set in a single location. Note that the latter is true even for dialogues such as *Protagoras*, for Socrates recounts to the anonymous aristocrat the events that transpired at his and then Callias' house. Likewise, in *Republic* 1 Socrates narrates from a single unspecified location his and Glaucon's meeting with Polemarchus and company somewhere between Athens and Piraeus and their subsequent visit at Cephalus' house.

As I have noted, in comparison with almost all preceding Greek literature, the realism of Plato's dialogues is extraordinary. On the other hand, I also claimed that Plato's intentions were ultimately not to represent historical events that actually occurred, nor, to the extent that Plato employed history instrumentally, to represent events with precise and accurate historical details. Furthermore, Plato's intentions were *ultimately* not to portray the uniqueness of subjective experiences, the historically conditioned individuality of personal psychologies, or, more generally, the actual character of human psychology, including Socrates'. Of course, Plato was concerned to portray human psychology, as he conceived it, insofar as this was instrumental to the achievement of particular ethical-pedagogical objectives. But—and this is the fundamental point—Plato's dramaturgical objectives principally were philosophical, and realism, to the extent that it is employed, is done so in the service of philosophical objectives. Consequently, however psychologically fascinating certain modern scholars find the character Socrates, it should be appreciated that Plato was not *principally* concerned to portray a psychologically fascinating individual. Likewise, however much certain modern scholars seek to infer about the identity of the historical Socrates from Plato's characters named "Socrates," it should be appreciated that Plato's principal objective was not to portray the historical Socrates as he actually was, nor to represent the precise details of episodes in Socrates' life.

Indeed, as is often the case in literature, realism in character portrayal serves or, more strongly, is compromised to serve other dramaturgical objectives. This subject has received little treatment in Greek literary scholarship. I emphasize that I am not dealing here with the topic of the representation of personhood or individuality in Greek literature, a subject that has received a good deal of attention. Rather, my interest is in the fact that although Plato generally tends to portray his characters in a relatively realistic manner, such realism may be compromised in the service of other dramaturgical objectives.

Of course, all literature, even the most realistic, is selective in the aspects of the fictional world it portrays. One could spend pages detailing all that occurs when a person turns his head. It is a matter of relative degree of detail. More importantly, it is a matter of the manner of handling the details selected. In developing and clarifying the point, it will be helpful to refer to Michael Silk's discussion of character portrayal in Aristophanes, specifically through his attention to inconsistencies in style of speech:

> For stylistic idiom to be compatible with realism, it must involve a range of expression which is *consistently* related to a vernacular language, a language of experience, a language of life. Either the idiom is felt to amount to a "selection of the language really spoken by men," as Wordsworth called it; or alternatively it involves a broadly consistent stylization, like (for

instance) the stylization of Greek tragic language, which does not constitute anything like a language of life, but is, nevertheless, fixed and conventionalized at a set, comprehensible distance from some hypothetical and more naturalistic idiom, which *would* pass for a language of life *à la* Wordsworth... In Aristophanes, the inconsistency within a given speaker's range of idiom points the opposite way. The style in which his people are made to express themselves is incompatible with any kind of realism; and more fundamentally, as this consideration of style serves to suggest, the people of Aristophanes per se are not strictly containable within any realist understanding of human character at all.[27]

In describing realism in characterization, Silk emphasizes internal consistency, however stylized, unnaturalistic, and unrepresentative of the language of life a character's manner of discourse is. He calls the dramaturgical deployment of discontinuous stylistic idiom and, by extension, character *imagistic*, in contrast to realistic:

Words used in images—that is, words used tropically, and especially words used metaphorically—disrupt the terminological continuity of their context. Like words used literally, they evoke some reality. Unlike words used literally, they evoke their reality through discontinuity... Aristophanes' characters, similarly, have their realist elements, or moments, or sequences, disrupted by [imagistic] elements, or moments, or sequences.[28]

Perhaps we might replace the word "imagistic" by "poetic" or "tropical" precisely insofar as such discontinuities are hallmarks of literary and especially poetic composition in general and because, as Silk observes, they operate not only in tropical constructions at the level of the phrase or clause, but, as in Aristophanes, analogously in characterization more generally. In fact, it can be seen that such discontinuity often operates at the level of the entire drama or story. Consider a play such as *Waiting for Godot* or, to take more commonplace examples from ancient literature, the fables attributed to Aesop or the sort of parables we find in the New Testament. In these cases, the drama, story, or episode is in its entirety to be understood as metaphorical.

Whatever we choose to name this discontinuous mode of literary or linguistic form, it is also convenient to retain the more commonsensical notion of nonrealism or antirealism that we associate with unnatural idiom, as most saliently in versification, distortion and deformation of character, as often in comedy, as well as the impossible events and elements of, say, fantasy and science fiction. In short, this general literary mode, which we may call nonrepresentationalism, unlike imagism, involves, as Silk describes it, a relatively internally consistent departure from reality.

27. Silk (1990) 154.
28. Silk (1990) 159.

While Plato's early dialogues, and specifically his characterization of Socrates, are to a great extent realistic in the sense of representational, they also involve some admixture of imagism. It will be helpful to consider some striking un-realistic and specifically imagistic moments in the portrayal of Socrates. Note that the following two are complicated by the fact that they turn on a literary distinction introduced by Gérard Genette between narrated time and narrative time.[29] Narrative time is the chronological sequence of the fictional events; narrated time is the sequence in which fictional events, however chronologically ordered, are ordered in the literary work. Clearly, the two sequences may be inconsistent; for instance, when a narrative begins at the end of events and proceeds to recount how things came to pass.

Accordingly, the first movement of Protagoras consists of Socrates encountering an anonymous aristocrat in an unidentified location in Athens. The aristocrat questions Socrates about his relationship with Alcibiades, and Socrates responds that at Callias' house, from which he has just come, he ignored Alcibiades and was far more impressed by the wisdom of Protagoras. Socrates proceeds to recount the earlier events of the day when Hippocrates awoke him at home and then urged him to go to Callias' house to meet with Protagoras. This constitutes the second movement of the dialogue. The events and discussion at Callias' constitute the third and main movement of the dialogue. In narrated time Socrates' discussion with the anonymous aristocrat precedes the third movement, but in narrative time it occurs after the third movemen, in which Protagoras' claims to wisdom are undermined. Therefore, when Socrates meets the anonymous aristocrat in the first movement of the dialogue and praises Protagoras' wisdom, Socrates has already undermined Protagoras' claim to wisdom.

A similar inconsistency occurs in Euthydemus. According to the chronological order of fictional events, the first movement of the dialogue in which Socrates is talking with Crito is temporally posterior to Socrates' discussion with Euthydemus and Dionysodorus, which, according to the narrated order, follows the first movement. In the first movement, Socrates praises the brothers' wisdom. The final movement of the dialogue returns to Socrates' conversation with Crito. The first and final movements are temporally contiguous; no event has intervened except the story of the meeting with Euthydemus and Dionysodorus that Socrates recounts and which constitutes the main body of the dialogue. However, in concluding his discussion with Crito, Socrates suggests that, as in all fields, there are also pseudopractitioners of philosophy who must be avoided. Socrates does not explicitly cite the brothers as examples, but this clearly is the Platonic point.

In these passages from Euthydemus and Protagoras Socrates is psychologically inconsistent or implausible. Yet both examples are explicable as serving a dramaturgical function in accordance with α-structure. Both texts begin with Socrates praising the wisdom of individuals who will become his principal interlocutors.

---

29. (1980).

Thus, the reader begins with the conventional notion that these celebrated indivi-duals will demonstrate their intellectual capabilities. Naturally, these expectations are subverted as the ensuing discussion reveals that they cannot satisfactorily answer Socrates' questions.

This pervasive feature of the early dialogues does not depend upon the complication of inconsistency between narrative and narrated time. Generally speaking, when Socrates begins a discussion with an alleged expert or authority figure, he praises that individual, and, as in the *Euthyphro* passage, there is no indication in these instances that he is being verbally ironic. The traditional tendency, of course, is to interpret Socrates' praise as disingenuous. But, again, I submit that in such instances Socrates is used, in accordance with the function of a-structure, to introduce a conventional conception that the ensuing dialogue proceeds to undermine. According to this interpretation, Socrates sometimes does emerge as a remarkably naïve individual, indeed, as an unrealistically naïve individual relative to his hypothetical fictional history and to the discursive sophistication he demonstrates in the ensuing discussions. Likewise, his praise of Meletus is remarkably naïve. However, I submit that this is one strategy within Plato's multifarious dramaturgical arsenal, an arsenal not beholden to realist injunctions.

Other notable examples of imagistic treatment of Socrates' character in the early dialogues include Socrates' interpretation of Simonides' ode in *Protagoras*, his argument in response to Polemarchus' definition of justice in *Republic* 1 to the effect that the just man is a thief, and, perhaps most remarkably, his disguised self-reference through much of his discussion with Hippias in *Hippias Major*. It is perhaps especially noteworthy that all of these characterologically unrealistic and imagistic moments, passages, or aspects of the texts have a comic dimension. Indeed, I venture that imagism may be particularly suited to comedy insofar as it is one species of a common and general comic maneuver, the amusing distortion or, more radically, subversion of reality.

With this, we come to one further objection that is likely to be made to my thesis that, given Euthyphro's response and Socrates' response to Euthyphro's response, Socrates' remarks are in earnest. The objection is that Socrates is being verbally ironic, but that this irony is not intended for Euthyphro who indeed is a dullard. Rather, the target audience of Socrates' verbal irony is the intended reader of the dialogue. It is the reader who appreciates Socrates' sense of humor at the expense of and, in fact, compounded by Euthyphro's obtuseness.

This sort of consideration is particularly appropriate in the context of a discussion of the limits of realism in character portrayal. For Socrates to be verbally ironic and for this irony to be directed over the head of his fictional interlocutor and at the flesh-and-blood intended reader, he would have to be portrayed as conscious of himself as within a fiction and of the reader as privy to this fiction. Moreover, this is precisely the sort of nonrealism in which literature may indulge, a salient example of this kind being the aside in drama.

But while this is the kind of dramaturgical move that can occur, as a matter of fact there is no compelling evidence that it does occur in *Euthyphro*. Generally speaking, there isn't a single instance in the early dialogues where Plato makes

Socrates say or do something that indicates Socrates' awareness of himself as within a fiction and of the reader as existing in a world beyond the fiction. Moreover, while there is some precedent for a related dramaturgical technique within Greek literature, namely the *parabasis* in Aristophanic comedy, that device operates in a most conspicuous fashion. Were Plato to have adapted and applied such a device to the early dialogues, it would presumably bear more striking resemblance to the original. Consequently, there would be no doubt whether it actually was occurring. I suggest, then, that the claim that Socrates' irony is directed at the intended reader is another case of the misidentification of Plato's genuinely dramatic, situational irony as Socratic verbal irony.[30]

In sum, if Socrates is, in any instance, being verbally ironic, given that the intended audience of his irony is his interlocutor and not Plato's intended reader, the response of his interlocutor should, for the most part, confirm that verbal irony is occurring. Accordingly, as a matter of fact, Socrates seldom is verbally ironic. Instances occur here and there, as do instances of sarcasm, both of which are to be expected in some measure among a set of dramatic dialogues that employ natural language. But verbal irony is not a dominant trait of Socrates. Consequently, since I introduced the problem of Socratic (verbal) irony as a potential hermeneutic problem, we can conclude that in fact Socratic verbal irony does not present a problem for the interpretation of Socrates' utterances. Indeed, at no point in the preceding study have I cited a case of Socratic verbal irony, let alone appealed to it in order to explain away a textual problem. I add this point as evidence in support of my argument.

Generally speaking, it should be emphasized that in those instances where Plato thought it important to register Socrates' psychological states, but not transparently through Socrates' directly corresponding utterances, he employed other means to do so. For example, in *Charmides*, when Charmides proposes a definition of sound-mindedness and Critias denies that he is its source, Socrates at that moment grants that the identity of its author is unimportant. However, shortly afterward, he notes—in the narrative, but not aloud to the interlocutors—that he had thought Critias was responsible for the definition.[31] Later in *Charmides*, when he has shown that the knowledge of knowledge and all other knowledges and lack of knowledge is unlikely even to exist, and Critias cannot bring himself to admit his confusion and ignorance, Socrates narrates, but does not say to the interlocutors, that he conceded the possibility of its existence "to

---

30. Another problem for the objection has to do with the background conditions of the culture or, more accurately, subculture in which the intended reader of *Euthyphro* is embedded. The objector must assume that the intended reader's situation would enable him to appreciate Socrates' statement as verbally ironic. But what evidence is there that the intended reader would be situated in such a subculture? If, indeed, the function of the early dialogues is to win adherents to philosophy, then presumably the reader would not already be sympathetic to Socrates' mission. Thus, it also falls to the objector to show that the subculture in which the intended reader would have been embedded would have enabled him to appreciate Socrates' utterance as verbally ironic.

31. *Chrm.* 161c, 162c.

advance the discussion."[32] In other words, he reveals that he acted tactfully so as not to humiliate Critias. In *Lysis*, once Socrates has humbled Lysis through an ad hominem argument whose conclusion is that Lysis' parents will not love Lysis to the extent that he lacks knowledge, he casts a look at Hippothales to indicate that this is how one should treat one's beloved.[33] Thus, Socrates confirms his intentions in the argument with Lysis without actually vocalizing them to the interlocutors. Still further, in *Protagoras*, following Protagoras' account of the relativity of goodness, Socrates claims that his memory is poor and, therefore, that he is unable to hold a conversation with Protagoras unless Protagoras refrains from speechifying. Shortly afterward, Alcibiades remarks that Socrates was not seriously claiming to have a weak memory.[34] Thus, Socrates is tactfully self-depreciating to avoid upsetting Protagoras for failing to adhere to the discursive mode of succinct question and answer. In short, to a large extent, when Socrates does not mean what he says or does not say what he believes, Plato has dramaturgical means by which the interlocutors or Socrates himself are made to acknowledge this.

In sum, the general literalizing interpretation of Socrates' utterances that I am advocating yields a character who sometimes is less psychologically complex and unified than is often conceived, while at the same time more dramaturgically complex as well as psychologically unrealistic, specifically imagistic and discontinuous. If this is correct, then we present-day interpreters of Plato's early dialogues find ourselves in an awkward position. It would seem that rather deep and unconscious realist assumptions inform seemingly natural readings of the texts. Yet perhaps especially in view of intertextual inconsistencies that are the inevitable consequence of those realist assumptions studiously applied, we may find reason to question those very assumptions.

Misinterpretation of Socratic irony is, then, to be fully explained by tracing scholarship back through the much broader context of the history of realism as well as its cousin historicism. At the other end of Western literary history, the ideas advanced here invite more thorough consideration of the conventions of characterization in the genre of *sokratikoi logoi* (Socratic discussions) specifically. If more examples of this relatively widely practiced literary form had survived, our preconceptions in reading Plato's Socrates would surely be altered. And while relatively little does survive, it still seems that among Xenophon's work and the pseudo-Platonic dialogues there is enough to say considerably more than what has been said.

In closing, let us turn to consider from a more limited perspective how misunderstanding of Socratic irony arose. The topics of Socratic verbal irony and situational irony share a conceptual ground, Socrates' attitude toward knowledge, specifically his tendency to disavow knowledge. On the one occasion where

---

32. *Chrm.* 168c–d.
33. *Ly.* 210e.
34. *Prt.* 335b–c, 336c–d.

an interlocutor speaks of Socrates' "customary" *eirôneia*,[35] it is because that interlocutor, Thrasymachus, thinks that Socrates is concealing beliefs and shielding himself from the sort of scrutiny to which he allegedly subjects others. Why Thrasymachus should suspect this is not hard to understand. Socrates is portrayed as spending most of his time engaged in philosophical discussions, and in doing so he displays remarkable facility in argumentation, particularly in criticizing conventional beliefs. It is reasonable to suppose that such an individual would have achieved a sophisticated grasp of the topics with which he is so preoccupied, indeed a far more sophisticated grasp than those with whom he holds these discussions. In this light, it is reasonable for Thrasymachus to challenge Socrates to articulate his views and for Thrasymachus to suspect that Socrates' resistance bespeaks a sort of insincerity.

Generally speaking, I suspect that such a perception of Plato's Socrates, especially Socrates' ease in criticizing his interlocutors' beliefs, is responsible for the tendency to regard his disavowals of knowledge as disingenuous. But this is an impressionistic conception. As we saw in sections 5 and 6 of chapter 3, more careful examination of Socrates' avowals and disavowals of knowledge throughout the early dialogues yields a different conclusion.

Among the early dialogues Socrates does not consistently disavow all knowledge. Socrates is not a Cartesian skeptic preoccupied with the grounds of ordinary knowledge claims. Moreover, while Socrates does disavow eschatological and theological knowledge on a few occasions, such disavowals are relatively marginal to his interests and investigations. It is Socrates' frequent disavowals of ethical knowledge that distinguish him from his interlocutors and which must have distinguished the historical Socrates from his contemporaries—if, that is, the historical Socrates did disavow ethical knowledge. Xenophon, for instance, does not portray Socrates as characteristically disavowing ethical knowledge. Furthermore, it is not that Plato portrays Socrates as a noncognitivist; Socrates is an ethical realist, and he believes that some ethical propositions are true. It is just that Socrates is emphatic about the difficulty for humans of achieving ethical knowledge.

To the extent that Socrates' sensitivity to the difficulty of attaining ethical knowledge was extraordinary—and it was—it is not difficult to see why those insensitive to the problem would have presumed that he must secretly harbor such knowledge. In addition, the Platonic epistemology of the early dialogues entails requirements for ethical knowledge that are wholly unconventional relative to Socrates' interlocutors and Plato's contemporaries.

Interpretation of Plato's early dialogues is haunted by the specter of Socrates, specifically by the deeply embedded idea that beyond or at least within the texts there is a strange and remarkable individual driving the philosophical enterprise. Whether we identify this individual with the historical Socrates, with Plato's conception of the historical Socrates, or, finally, with Plato's construction of a literary figure, in all cases it is assumed that this figure is a unity and so a unified source. In contrast, I emphasize that the character Socrates is not only a literary construction—whatever its debt or causal relation to the historical Socrates—but that in accordance with certain dramaturgical objectives, Plato took liberties in his treatment of this character that transgress realism. Socrates' unrealistically naïve, sincere praise of Meletus at the beginning of *Euthyphro* is one such instance. In the face of such passages, the quick appeal to Socratic "irony" blocks our appreciation of the strange complexity of Plato's dramaturgy and the various uses to which he put his favored character.

BIBLIOGRAPHY

There is far too much secondary literature on Plato's early dialogues for one person to compass. I hope to have covered the most important contributions to the particular questions and problems discussed in the study, as well as all of the relevant contributions of the last thirty years up to 2005 in the major ancient philosophy journals.

Generally speaking, in the main body of the study, I have tried to avoid as much direct engagement with secondary literature as possible. Given my penchant for journal articles heavy with such discussions, this has been rather unsatisfying. However, my aim in writing the book has been accessibility. I would like to reach a relatively broad audience. Those who seek more engagement with the secondary literature and who would like to know where my particular contributions stand relative to the *status quaestionum* should consider, for chapter 1, Wolfsdorf (1998), (1999), (2004a); for chapter 2, Wolfsdorf (2006a), (2006b), (2006d), (2008b); for chapter 3, Wolfsdorf (2002), (2004b), (2004c), (2005c), (2006b), (2006c); for chapter 4, Wolfsdorf (2003a), (2003b), (2003c), (2008c); for chapter 5, Wolfsdorf (1997), (2005a), (2006c), (2008a); and for appendix 2, Wolfsdorf (2007). Let me also note two points in respect to which the present study differs from certain of my other publications. In Wolfsdorf (2006a) I make an appeal to Socratic irony to justify an interpretation of the final step in Socrates' argument. In section 2 of chapter 2, I avoid that misguided maneuver. Also, section 6 of chapter 2 supersedes Wolfsdorf (2008a). In fact, Wolfsdorf (2008a) was actually written in 2002 and is an immature effort.

Adam, J. *Platonis Protagoras*. Cambridge: Cambridge University Press, 1928.
Adams, Don. "Elenchos and Evidence." *Ancient Philosophy* 18 (1998): 287–307.
Adkins, A. W. H. *Merit and Responsibility*. Oxford: Clarendon Press, 1960.
———. *Moral Values and Political Behavior in Ancient Greece*. London: Chatto and Windus, 1972.

Adkins, A. W. H. "*Polugramosune* and 'Minding One's Own Business': A Study in Greek Political and Social Values." *Classical Philology* 71 (1976): 301–27.

Algra, Keimpe, et al., eds. *The Cambridge History of Hellenistic Philosophy*. Cambridge: Cambridge University Press, 1999.

Allen., F., et al., eds. *Scholia Platonica*. Haverford: American Philological Society, 1938.

Allen, R. E., ed. *Studies in Plato's Metaphysics*. New York: Routledge and Kegan Paul, 1965.

———. *Plato's Euthyphro and the Earlier Theory of Forms*. New York: Humanities Press, 1970.

Anderson, Albert. "Socratic Reasoning in the *Euthyphro*." *Review of Metaphysics* 22 (1969): 461–81.

Annas, Julia. "Plato and Aristotle on Friendship and Altruism." *Mind* 86 (1977): 532–44.

———. *An Introduction to Plato's Republic*. Oxford: Oxford University Press, 1981.

———. "Aristotle on Inefficient Causes." *Philosophical Quarterly* 32 (1982): 311–26.

———. "Virtue as the Use of Other Goods." *Apeiron* 26 (1993): 53–66.

Arieti, J. A. *Interpreting Plato: The Dialogues as Drama*. Lanham, Md.: Rowman and Littlefield, 1991.

August, E. F. *Zur Kenntniss der geometrischen Methode der Alten in besonderer Beziehung auf die platonische Stelle im Meno*. Berlin, 1829.

Ausland, Hayden W. "Forensic Characteristics of Socratic Argumentation." In Scott (2002): 36–60.

Barnes, J., ed. *The Complete Works of Aristotle*. Vol. 1. Princeton, N.J.: Princeton University Press, 1984.

———, ed. *Aristotle: Posterior Analytics*. Oxford: Oxford University Press, 1993.

Beals, K. "A Linguistic Analysis of Verbal Irony." Ph.D. diss., University of Chicago, 1995.

Bedu-Addo, J. T. "Recollection and the Argument 'from a Hypothesis' in Plato's *Meno*." *Journal of Hellenic Studies* 54 (1984): 1–14.

Bebhoud, Ali. "Greek Geometrical Analysis." *Centaurus* 37 (1994): 52–89.

Belnap, Nuel, Jr., and Thomas Steel, Jr. *The Logic of Questions and Answers*. New Haven, Conn.: Yale University Press, 1976.

Benecke, A. *Über die geometrische Hypothesis in Platons Meno*. Elbing, 1867.

Benson, Hugh H. "The Problem of the Elenchus Reconsidered." *Ancient Philosophy* 7 (1987): 67–85.

———. "The Priority of Definition and the Socratic Elenchus." *Oxford Studies in Ancient Philosophy* 8 (1990): 19–65.

———. "Misunderstanding the 'What-is-F-ness?' Question." In Benson (1992): 123–36.

———, ed. *Essays on the Philosophy of Socrates*. New York: Oxford University Press, 1992.

———. "The Dissolution of the Problem of the Elenchus." *Oxford Studies in Ancient Philosophy* 13 (1995): 45–112.

———. "Socratic Dynamic Theory: A Sketch." *Apeiron* 30 (1997): 79–94.

———. *Socratic Wisdom*. New York: Oxford University Press, 2000.

———. "Problems with the Socratic Method." In Scott (2002): 101–13.

———. "The Method of Hypothesis in the *Meno*." *Proceedings of the Boston Area Colloquium in Ancient Philosophy* 18 (2002): 95–126.

Benardete, José. "Real Definitions: Quine and Aristotle." *Philosophical Studies* 72 (1993): 265–82.

Beversluis, John. "Does Socrates Commit the Socratic Fallacy?" *American Philosophical Quarterly* 24 (1987): 211–23.

———. *Cross-Examining Socrates*. New York: Cambridge University Press, 2000.

Blackson, Thomas A. "Cause and Definition in Plato's *Hippias Major*." *Philosophical Inquiry* 14 (1992): 1–12.

Blass, C. *De Platone mathematico*. Bonn, 1861.

Bluck, R. S. *Plato's Meno*. Cambridge: Cambridge University Press, 1961.

———. "Logos and Forms in Plato: A Reply to Professor Cross." In Allen (1965): 31–44.

Boder, Werner. *Die sokratische Ironie in den platonischen Frühdialogen*. Amsterdam: Grüner, 1973.

Bolinger, Dwight. "Adjectives in English: Attribution and Predication." *Lingua* 18 (1967): 1–34.

Bolotin, David. *Plato's Dialogue on Friendship*. Ithaca, N.Y.: Cornell University Press, 1979.

Bolton, Robert. "Aristotle's Account of Socratic Elenchus." *Oxford Studies in Ancient Philosophy* 11 (1993): 121–52.

———. "Plato's Discovery of Metaphysics." In Gentzler (1998): 91–111.

Bonitz, Hermann. *Platonische Studien*. Berlin, 1858.

Bostock, David. *Plato's Phaedo*. Oxford: Oxford University Press, 1986.

Bouchard, Denis. "The Distribution and Interpretation of Adjectives in French: A Consequence of Bare Phrase Structure." *Probus* 10 (1998): 139–83.

Brandwood, Leonard. *The Chronology of Plato's Dialogues*. Cambridge: Cambridge University Press, 1990.

Brentlinger, John. "Incomplete Predicates and the Two-World Theory of the *Phaedo*." *Phronesis* 17 (1972): 61–79.

Brickhouse, Thomas C., and Nicholas D. Smith. "Vlastos on the Elenchus." *Oxford Studies in Ancient Philosophy* 2 (1984): 185–95.

———. "Socrates' Elenctic Mission." *Oxford Studies in Ancient Philosophy* 9 (1991): 131–60.

———. *Plato's Socrates*. New York: Oxford University Press, 1994.

———. "Socrates and the Unity of the Virtues." *Ethics* 1 (1997): 311–24.

———. *The Trial and Execution of Socrates*. New York: Oxford University Press, 2002.

Brown, John H. "The Logic of *Euthyphro* 10A–11B." *Philosophical Quarterly* 14 (1964): 1–14.

Burford, Alison. *Craftsmen in Greek and Roman Society*. Ithaca, N.Y.: Cornell University Press, 1972.

Burge, Evan L. "The Ideas as *Aitiai* in the *Phaedo*." *Phronesis* 16 (1971): 1–26.

Burger, R. "Socrates εἰρωνεία" *Interpretation* 13 (1985): 143–9.

Burnet, John, ed. *Platonis Opera*. 5 vols. Oxford: Oxford University Press, 1900–1907.

Burnyeat, M. F. "Examples in Epistemology: Socrates, Theaetetus, and G. E. Moore." *Philosophy* 52 (1977): 381–98.

———. *The Theaetetus of Plato*. Indianapolis: Hackett, 1990.

Bury, R. G. "Δύναμις"and"Φύσις" in Plato." *Classical Review* 8 (1894): 394–96.

———. *Plato IX*. Cambridge, Mass.: Harvard University Press, 1929.

Butcher, S. H. "The Geometrical Problem of the *Meno* (p. 86E–87A)." *Journal of Philology* 17 (1888): 219–25.

Carpenter, Michelle, and Ronald M. Polansky. "Variety of Socratic Elenchoi." In Scott (2002): 89–100.

Carrithers, M., et al., eds. *The Category of the Person*. Cambridge: Cambridge University Press, 1985.

Carter, L. B. *The Quiet Athenian*. New York: Oxford University Press, 1977.

Chappell, T. D. J. "The Virtues of Thrasymachus." *Phronesis* 38 (1993): 1–17.

———. "Thrasymachus and Definition." *Oxford Studies in Ancient Philosophy* 18 (2000): 101–7.

Chen, Chun-Hwan. "On Plato's *Charmides* 165c4–175d5." *Apeiron* 12 (1978): 13–28.

Cherniss, Harold. "Plato as Mathematician." *Review of Metaphysics* 4 (1951): 395–425.

Chierchia, Gennaro, and Sally McConnell-Ginet. *Meaning and Grammar.* Cambridge, Mass.: MIT Press, 1990.

Clay, Diskin. "The Origins of the Socratic Dialogue." In *The Socratic Movement,* ed. Vander Waerdt, 23–47. Ithaca, N.Y.: Cornell University Press, 1994.

Coby, Patrick. *Socrates and the Sophistic Enlightenment.* Lewiston, Pa.: Bucknell University Press, 1987.

Cohen, Mark. "The Aporias in Plato's Early Dialogues." *Journal of the History of Ideas* 23 (1962): 163–74.

Cohen, S. Marc. "Socrates on the Definition of Piety: *Euthyphro* 10A–11B." *Journal of the History of Philosophy* 9 (1971): 1–13.

Cook Wilson, J. "On the Geometrical Problem in Plato's *Meno.*" *Journal of Philology* 28 (1903): 222–40.

Cooper, John. *Plato: Complete Works.* Indianapolis: Hackett, 1997.

Cornford, F. M. "Mathematics and Dialectic in *Republic* VI–VII." *Mind* 41 (1930): 43–7, 173–90.

———. *Plato's Theory of Knowledge.* London: Routledge, 1935.

Crane, Tim, ed. *Dispositions: A Debate.* New York: Routledge, 1996.

Creswell, M. J. "Plato's Theory of Causality: *Phaedo* 95–106." *Australasian Journal of Philosophy* 9 (1971): 244–9.

Dancy, R. M. *Plato's Introduction of Forms.* New York: Cambridge University Press, 2004.

Davies, John K. *Athenian Propertied Families, 600–300 B.C.* Oxford: Oxford University Press, 1971.

———. *Wealth and the Power of Wealth in Democratic Athens.* New York: Arno Press, 1981.

Denyer, Nicholas. *Alcibiades I.* Cambridge: Cambridge University Press, 2001.

Detienne, Marcel, and Jean-Pierre Vernant. *Cunning Intelligence in Greek Culture and Society.* Atlantic Highlands. N.J.: Humanities Press, 1978.

Devereux, Daniel T. "Protagoras on Courage and Knowledge." *Apeiron* 9 (1975): 37–39.

———. "Pauline Predication in Plato." *Apeiron* 11 (1977): 1–4.

———. "Courage and Wisdom in Plato's *Laches.*" *Journal of the History of Philosophy* 15 (1977): 129–41.

———. "The Unity of the Virtues in Plato's *Protagoras* and *Laches.*" *Philosophical Review* 101 (1992): 765–89.

Dillon, John. *The Middle Platonists.* Ithaca, N.Y.: Cornell University Press, 1977.

Dimas, Panos. "Happiness in the *Euthydemus.*" *Phronesis* 47 (2003): 1–27.

Donlan, Walter. "Social Vocabulary and Its Relationship to Political Propaganda in Fifth-Century Athens." *Quaderni Urbanati* 27 (1977): 95–111.

———. *The Aristocratic Ideal in Ancient Greece.* Lawrence, Kans.: Coronado Press, 1980.

Dover, K. J. *Aristophanic Comedy.* London: Batsford, 1972.

———. "Classical Greek Attitudes to Sexual Behavior." *Arethusa* 6 (1973): 69–73.

———. "The Freedom of the Intellectual in Greek Society." *Talanta* 7 (1975): 24–56.

———. *Greek Popular Morality in the Time of Plato and Aristotle.* Oxford: Oxford University Press, 1974.

———. *Greek Homosexuality.* Cambridge, Mass.: Harvard University Press, 1978.

Dye, James Wayne. "Plato's Concept of Causal Explanation." *Tulane Studies in Philosophy* 27 (1978): 37–56.

Dyson, M. "Some Problems Concerning Knowledge in Plato's *Charmides.*" *Phronesis* 19 (1974): 102–11.

Ehrenberg, Victor. *The People of Aristophanes:* Oxford: Oxford University Press, 1950.

———. "Polypragmosyne." *Journal of Hellenic Studies* 67 (1947): 46–67.

Erler, Michael. *Der Sinn der Aporien in den früheren Dialogen Platons.* Berlin, 1987.

Everson, Stephen. "The Incoherence of Thrasymachus." *Oxford Studies in Ancient Philosophy* 16 (1998): 99–131.

Faller, Mark Andrew. "Plato's Philosophical Use of Mathematical Analysis." Ph.D. diss., University of Georgia, 2000.

———. "Plato's Philosophical Adaptation of Geometrical Analysis." Unpublished.

Farness, Jay. *Missing Socrates.* University Park: Pennsylvania State University Press, 1991.

Farquharson, A. S. L. "Socrates' Diagram in the *Meno* of Plato, pp. 86E–87A." *Classical Quarterly* 17 (1923): 21–6.

Ferejohn, Michael. "The Unity of Virtue and the Objects of Socratic Inquiry." *Journal of the History of Philosophy* 20 (1982): 1–21.

———. "Socratic Thought-Experiments and the Unity of Virtue Paradox." *Phronesis* 29 (1984): 105–22.

———. "Socratic Virtue and the Parts of Itself." *Philosophy and Phenomenological Research* 44 (1984): 377–88.

Finamore, John F. "The Role of $\Delta\acute{v}\nu\alpha\mu\iota\varsigma$" in Plato's *Protagoras* 329c2–332a2." *Elenchos* 9 (1988): 311–27.

Findlay, John. *Plato: The Written and Unwritten Doctrines.* London: Routledge and Kegan Paul, 1974.

Fine, Gail. "Knowledge and *Logos* in the *Theaetetus*." *Philosophical Review* 88 (1979): 366–97.

———. *On Ideas.* New York: Oxford University Press, 1995.

———. "Knowledge and True Belief in the *Meno*." *Oxford Studies in Ancient Philosophy* 27 (2004): 41–81.

Fodor, Jerry, and Ernest LePore. *Holism: A Shopper's Guide.* New York: Oxford University Press, 1992.

Føllesdal, Dagfinn. "Quantification into Causal Contexts." In *Reference and Modality*, ed. Linsky, 52–62. London: London University Press, 1971.

Fowler, H. N. *Plato I.* Cambridge, Mass.: Harvard University Press, 1914.

———. *Plato VIII.* Cambridge, Mass.: Harvard University Press, 1925.

———. *Plato IV.* Cambridge, Mass.: Harvard University Press, 1926.

Frede, Michael. "The Original Notion of Cause." In *Doubt and Dogmatism*, ed. Barnes et al., 217–49. Cambridge: Cambridge University Press, 1980.

———. "Plato's Arguments and the Dialogue Form." In Klagge and Smith (1992): 201–19.

Friedländer, Paul. *Platon.* Berlin, 1930.

Friedman, Joel I. "Plato's *Euthyphro* and Leibniz's Law." *Philosophia* 12 (1982): 1–20.

von Fritz, K. "Die *APXAI* in der griechischen Mathematik." *Archiv für Begriffsgeschichte* 1 (1955): 12–103.

Gadamer, Hans-Georg. *Dialogue and Dialectic: Eight Hermeneutical Studies on Plato.* New Haven: Yale University Press, 1980.

Gaiser, K. "Platons *Menon* und die Akademie." *Archiv für Geschichte der Philosophie* 46 (1964): 241–92.

Gallop, David. "The Socratic Paradox in the *Protagoras*." *Phronesis* 9 (1964): 117–29.

———. *Plato's Phaedo.* Oxford: Clarendon Press, 1965.

Geach, P. T. "Good and Evil." *Analysis* 17 (1956): 33–42.

———. "Plato's *Euthyphro*: Analysis and Commentary." *Monist* 50 (1966): 369–82.

Genette, G. *Narrative Discourse.* Ithaca, N.Y.: Cornell University Press, 1980.

Gentzler, Jyl. "Recollection and 'The Problem of the Socratic Elenchus.'" *Proceedings of the Boston Area Colloquium in Ancient Philosophy* 10 (1994): 257–95.

———, ed. *Method in Ancient Philosophy.* Oxford: Oxford University Press, 1998.

Gersch, Stephen. *Middle Platonism and Neoplatonism*. Notre Dame, Ind.: University of Notre Dame, 1986.

Gersch, Stephen, and J. F. M. Hoenen. *The Platonic Tradition in the Middle Ages*. New York: de Gruyter, 2002.

Gerson, Lloyd. *Aristotle and Other Platonists*. Ithaca, N.Y.: Cornell University Press, 2005.

Giannantoni, G. *Socratis et Socraticorum Reliquiae*. Vol. 2. Naples: Bibliopolis, 1990.

Gifford, Mark. "Dramatic Dialectic in *Republic* Book I." *Oxford Studies in Ancient Philosophy* 20 (2001): 35–106.

Gilardi, Roberto. "Teoria linguistica e semantica delle proposizioni valuative." *Rivista di Filosofia Neoscolastica* 74 (1982): 285–320.

Gill, Christopher. "The Character-Personality Distinction." In Pelling (1990): 1–31.

———. *Personality in Greek Epic, Tragedy, and Philosophy*. Oxford: Oxford University Press, 1996.

Goldberg, Larry. *A Commentary on Plato's Protagoras*. New York: P. Lang, 1983.

Gonzalez, Francisco J. "Plato's *Lysis*: An Enactment of Philosophical Kinship." *Ancient Philosophy* 15 (1995): 69–90.

Gooch, P. "Socratic Irony and Aristotle's *Eiron*: Some Puzzles." *Phoenix* 41 (1987): 95–104.

Gordon, Jill. "Against Vlastos on Complex Irony." *Classical Quarterly* 46 (1996): 131–7.

———. *Turning toward Philosophy*. University Park: Pennsylvania State University Press, 1999.

Gottlieb, Dale V., and Lawrence H. Davis. "Extensionality and Singular Causal Sentences." *Philosophical Studies* 25 (1974): 69–72.

Gottlieb, Paula. "The Complexity of Socratic Irony: A Note on Professor Vlastos' Account." *Classical Quarterly* 42 (1992): 278–79.

Gouldner, Alvin. *Enter Plato*. New York: Basic Books, 1965.

Griswold, Charles, Jr., ed. *Platonic Writings, Platonic Readings*. New York: Routledge, 1988.

———. "Irony in the Platonic Dialogues." *Philosophy and Literature* 26 (2002): 84–106.

Grote, George. *Plato and the Other Companions of Sokrates*. London, 1865.

Gutglueck, John. "πλεονεξία to πολυπραγμοσύνη A Conflation of Possession and Action in Plato's *Republic*." *American Journal of Philology* 109 (1988): 20–39.

Gulley, Norman. "Greek Geometrical Analysis." *Phronesis* 3 (1958): 1–14.

———. *The Philosophy of Socrates*. New York: St. Martin's Press, 1968.

———. "Socrates' Thesis at *Protagoras* 358b–c." *Phoenix* 25 (1971): 118–23.

Guthrie, W. K. C. *A History of Greek Philosophy*. Vol. 4. Cambridge: Cambridge University Press, 1975.

Haden, James. "Friendship in Plato's *Lysis*." *Review of Metaphysics* 37 (1983): 327–56.

Hadgopoulos, Demetrius J. "Thrasymachus and Legalism." *Phronesis* 18 (1973): 204–8.

Hall, John C. "Plato: *Euthyphro* 10a1–11a10." *Philosophical Quarterly* 18 (1968): 1–11.

Haliwell, Stephen. "Traditional Greek Conceptions of Character." In Pelling (1990): 32–59.

Hankel, H. *Zur Geschichte der Mathematik im Altertum und Mittelalter*. Leipzig, 1874.

Hankins, James. *Plato in the Italian Renaissance*. New York: Brill, 1990.

Hankinson, R. J. *Cause and Explanation in Ancient Greek Thought*. New York: Oxford University Press, 1998.

Hansen, Mogens Herman. *The Athenian Assembly in the Age of Demosthenes*. Oxford: Blackwell, 1987.

Hare, R. M. "Geach: Good and Evil." *Analysis* 17 (1957): 103–11.

Heath, T. L. *The Thirteen Books of Euclid's Elements*. Vol. 1. Cambridge: Cambridge University Press, 1908.

———. *A History of Greek Mathematics*. Vol. 1. Oxford: Clarendon Press, 1921.

Heijboer, A. "Plato Meno 86E–87A." Mnemosyne, 4th series, 8 (1955): 89–122.

Hemmenway, Scott R. "Sophistry Exposed: Socrates on the Unity of Virtue in the Protagoras." Ancient Philosophy 16 (1996): 1–23.

Henderson, T. Y. "In Defense of Thrasymachus." American Philosophical Quarterly 7 (1970): 218–28.

Herman, V. Dramatic Discourse. New York: Routledge, 1995.

Hermann, Karl Friederich. Die Geschichte und System der platonischen Philosophie. Leipzig, 1839.

Hintikka, Jaakko. "Knowledge and Its Objects in Plato." Ajatus 33 (1971): 168–200.

Hintikka, Jaakko, and Unto Remes. The Method of Analysis. Boston: D. Reidel, 1974.

Hoerber, Robert. "Plato's Euthyphro." Phronesis 3 (1958): 95–107.

Hopper, R. J. Trade and Industry in Classical Greece. London: Thames and Hudson, 1979.

Hourani, George F. "Thrasymachus' Definition of Justice in Plato's Republic." Phronesis 7 (1962): 110–20.

Huffman, Carl. Philolaus of Croton. Cambridge: Cambridge University Press, 1993.

Hyland, Drew A. The Virtue of Philosophy. Columbus: Ohio State University Press, 1981.

Inwood, Brad. The Poem of Empedocles. Toronto: University of Toronto Press, 2001.

Irwin, Terence. Plato's Moral Theory. Oxford: Clarendon Press, 1977.

———. Plato: Gorgias. Oxford: Clarendon Press, 1979.

———. "Socrates and the Tragic Hero." In Language and the Tragic Hero, ed. Pucci, 55–83. Atlanta: Scholars Press, 1988.

———. "Socratic Puzzles." Oxford Studies in Ancient Philosophy 10 (1992): 241–66.

———. Plato's Ethics. New York: Oxford University Press, 1995.

Jaeger, Werner. Paideia. Vol. 2. New York: Blackwell, 1943.

Jones, Alexander, ed. Pappus of Alexandria: Book VII of the Collection. New York: Springer, 1986.

Kahn, Charles H. "The Greek Verb 'To Be' and the Concept of Being." Foundations of Language 2 (1966): 245–65.

———. "Did Plato Write Socratic Dialogues?" Classical Quarterly 31 (1981): 305–20.

———. "The Beautiful and the Genuine." Oxford Studies in Ancient Philosophy 3 (1985): 261–87.

———. "Vlastos's Socrates." Phronesis 37 (1992): 233–58.

———. Plato and the Socratic Dialogue. New York: Cambridge University Press, 1996.

Kerferd, G. B. "The Doctrine of Thrasymachus in Plato's 'Republic.'" Durham University Journal 9 (1947): 19–27.

———. The Sophistic Movement. Cambridge: Cambridge University Press, 1981.

Kirchner, L. Prosopographia Attica. Berlin, 1901.

Klagge, J., and Nicholas Smith, eds. Methods of Interpreting Plato and His Dialogues. Oxford: Oxford University Press, 1992.

Klibansky, Raymond. The Continuity of the Platonic Tradition in the Middle Ages. London: The Warburg Institue, 1939.

Klosko, George. "On the Analysis of Protagoras 351b–360e." Phoenix 34 (1980): 307–22.

———. "Socrates on Goods and Happiness." History of Philosophy Quarterly 4 (1987): 251–64.

Knapp, J. Literary Character. Lanham, Md.: University Press of America, 1993.

Kneale, William, and Martha Kneale. The Development of Logic. Oxford: Clarendon Press, 1962.

Knorr, Wilbur. The Ancient Tradition of Geometric Problems. Boston: Brikhäuser, 1986.

Knox, D. Ironia: Medieval and Renaissance Ideas on Irony. New York: Brill, 1989.

Knox, N. *The Word "Irony" and Its Context, 1500–1755.* Durham, N.C.: Duke University Press, 1961.

Korsgaard, Christine. "Two Distinctions in Goodness." *Philosophical Review* 92 (1983): 27–49.

Kraut, Richard. "Two Conceptions of Happiness." *Philosophical Review* 88 (1979): 167–97.

———. "Comments on Gregory Vlastos, 'The Socratic Elenchus.' " *Oxford Studies in Ancient Philosophy* 1 (1983): 59–70.

———. *Socrates and the State.* Princeton, N.J.: Princeton University Press, 1984.

———, ed. *The Cambridge Companion to Plato.* New York: Cambridge University Press, 1992.

Krentz, Peter. *The Thirty at Athens.* Ithaca, N.Y.: Cornell University Press, 1982.

Kunsemüller, Otto. *Die Herkunft der platonischen Kardinaltugenden.* Erlangen: Reinhold & Limmert, 1935.

Lamb, W. R. M. *Plato II.* Cambridge, Mass.: Harvard University Press, 1924.

———. *Plato III.* Cambridge, Mass.: Harvard University Press, 1925.

———. *Plato XII.* Cambridge, Mass.: Harvard University Press, 1927.

Ledbetter, Grace M. "Reasons and Causes in Plato: The Distinction between αἰτία and αἴτιον." *Ancient Philosophy* 19 (1999): 255–65.

Ledger, Gerard. *Re-Counting Plato: A Computer Analysis of Plato's Style.* New York: Oxford University Press, 1989.

Lesher, J. H. "Socrates' Disavowal of Knowledge." *Journal of the History of Philosophy* 25 (1987): 275–88.

———. "Parmenidean *Elenchos.*" In Scott (2002): 19–35.

Lévystone, David. "La figure d'Ulysse chez les Socratiques: Socrate polutropos." *Phronesis* 50 (2005): 181–214.

Lloyd, A. C. "The Principle That the Cause is Greater Than the Effect." *Phronesis* 21 (1976): 146–56.

Lloyd, G. E. R. "The *Meno* and the Mysteries of Mathematics." *Phronesis* 37 (1992): 166–83.

Long, A. A., and D. Sedley. *The Hellenistic Philosophers.* Cambridge: Cambridge University Press, 1987.

Luhmann, Niklas. *The Differentiation of Society.* New York: Columbia University Press, 1982.

Maguire, Joseph. "Thrasymachus ... or Plato?" *Phronesis* 16 (1971): 142–63.

Mahoney, M. S. "Another Look at Greek Geometrical Analysis." *Archive for the History of the Exact Sciences* 5 (1968/9): 318–47.

Makin, Stephen. "An Ancient Principle about Causation." *Proceedings of the Aristotelian Society* 91 (1990–1991): 135–52.

Malcolm, John. "On the Place of the *Hippias Major* in the Development of Plato's Thought." *Archiv für Geschichte der Philosophie* 50 (1968): 189–95.

———. "Vlastos on Pauline Predication." *Phronesis* 30 (1985): 79–91.

Mann, Wolfgang-Rainer. *The Discovery of Things.* Princeton, N.J.: Princeton University Press, 2000.

Manuwald, Bernd. "Lust und Tapferkeit: Zum gedanklichen Verhaltnis zweier Abschnitte in Plato's 'Protagoras.' " *Phronesis* 20 (1975): 22–50.

———. *Platon Protagoras.* Göttingen: Vandenhoeck & Ruprecht, 1999.

Marrou, H. I. A. *A History of Education in Antiquity.* Madison: University of Wisconsin Press, 1982.

McCoy, Marina Berzins. "Protagoras on Human Nature, Wisdom, and the Good: The Great Speech and the Hedonism of Plato's *Protagoras.*" *Ancient Philosophy* 18 (1998): 21–39.

McKay, Thomas, and Michael Nelson. "Propositional Attitude Reports." In *The Stanford Encyclopedia of Philosophy*. Online. Available: http://plato.stanford.edu/archives/win2005/entries/prop-attitudes-reports. 2005.

McKirahan, Richard D., Jr. "Socrates and Protagoras on Σωφροσύνη and Justice: *Protagoras* 333–334." *Apeiron* 18 (1984): 20–26.

———. "Socrates and Protagoras on Holiness and Justice (*Protagoras* 330c–332a)." *Phoenix* 39 (1985): 342–54.

McPherran, Mark. "Elenctic Interpretation and the Delphic Oracle." In Scott (2002): 114–44.

McTighe, Kevin. "Socrates on the Desire for Good and the Involuntariness of Wrongdoing: *Gorgias* 466a–468e." *Phronesis* 29 (1984): 193–236.

Menn, Stephen. "Plato and the Method of Analysis." *Phronesis* 47 (2002): 194–223.

Méron, Evelyn. *Les idées morales des interlocuteurs de Socrate dans les dialogues platoniciens de jeunesse*. Paris: J. Vrin, 1979.

Meyers, J. I. "Plato's Geometric Hypothesis: *Meno* 86e–87b." *Apeiron* 21 (1988): 173–80.

Miller, Harold W. "*Dynamis* and *Physis* in *On Ancient Medicine*." *Transactions and Proceedings of the American Philological Association* 83 (1952): 184–97.

Moline, John. *Plato's Theory of Understanding*. Madison: University of Wisconsin Press, 1981.

Momigliano, A. *The Development of Greek Biography*. Cambridge, Mass.: Harvard University Press, 1993.

Montuori, M. *De Socrate Iuste Damnato*. Amsterdam: Grieben, 1981.

———. *Socrates: Physiology of a Myth*. Amsterdam: Grieben, 1981.

———. *Socrates: An Approach*. Amsterdam: Grieben, 1988.

Morgan, Michael L. "The Continuity Theory of Reality in Plato's *Hippias Major*." *Journal of the History of Philosophy* 21 (1983): 133–58.

Moravcsik, J. M. E. "Understanding and Knowledge in Plato's Philosophy." *Neue Hefte für Philosophie* 15–16 (1978): 53–69.

Morris, T. F. "Plato's *Lysis*." *Philosophical Research Archives* 11 (1986): 269–79.

———. "Knowledge of Knowledge and Lack of Knowledge in *Charmides*." *International Studies in Philosophy* 21 (1989): 49–61.

Muecke, D. *Irony and the Ironic*. New York: Methuen, 1982.

Mueller, Ian. "Platonism and the Study of Nature (*Phaedo* 95eff.)." In Gentzler (1998): 67–89.

———. "On the Notion of a Mathematical Starting Point in Plato, Aristotle, and Euclid." In *Science and Philosophy in Classical Greece*, ed. Bowen, 59–97. New York: Garland Publishing, 1991.

Nails, Debra. *Agora, Academy, and the Conduct of Philosophy*. Boston: Dordrecht, 1995.

———. *The People of Plato*. Indianapolis: Hackett, 2002.

Nehamas, Alexander. "Confusing Universals and Particulars in Plato's Early Dialogues." *Review of Metaphysics* 29 (1975): 287–306.

———. "Voices of Silence: On Gregory Vlastos' Socrates." *Arion* 2 (1992): 157–86.

———. *The Art of Living*. Berkeley: University of California Press, 1998.

Nicholson, P. P. "Unravelling Thrasymachus in 'The Republic.' " *Phronesis* 19 (1974): 210–32.

Nightingale, Andrea. *Genres in Dialogue*. New York: Cambridge University Press, 1995.

North, Helen. *Sophrosyne*. Ithaca, N.Y.: Cornell University Press, 1966.

Notomi, Noburu. "Critias and the Origins of Plato's Political Philosophy." In *Plato: Euthydemus, Lysis, Charmides*, Proceedings of the V Symposium Platonicum, ed. Brisson et al., 237–50. Sankt Augustin: Academia, 2000.

Novotny, F. *The Posthumous Life of Plato*. The Hague: M. Nijhoff, 1977.

Nozick, Robert. "Socratic Puzzles." *Phronesis* 40 (1995): 143–45.

Nussbaum, Martha. *The Fragility of Goodness*. New York: Cambridge University Press, 1986.

O'Brien, Denis. *Empedocles' Cosmic Cycle*. Cambridge: Cambridge University Press, 1969.

———. "Socrates and Protagoras on Virtue." *Oxford Studies in Ancient Philosophy* 24 (2003): 59–131.

O'Brien, Michael. "The 'Fallacy' in *Protagoras* 349D–350C." *Transactions of the American Philological Association* 92 (1961): 408–17.

Ober, Josiah. *Mass and Elite in Democratic Athens*. Princeton, N.J.: Princeton University Press, 1989.

———. *Political Dissent in Democratic Athens*. Princeton, N.J.: Princeton University Press, 1998.

Owen, G. E. L. "A Proof in the Peri Ideon." In *Studies in Plato's Metaphysics*, ed. Allen, 293–312. New York: Humanities Press, 1965.

Palmer, John A. *Plato's Reception of Parmenides*. New York: Oxford University Press, 1999.

Parke, H. W., and D. E. W. Wormell. *The Delphic Oracle*. Oxford: Blackwell, 1956.

Patze, A. *Commentatio de loco mathemathico in Platonis Menone*. Susati, 1832.

Paxson, Thomas D., Jr. "Plato's *Euthyphro* 10A–11B." *Phronesis* 17 (1972): 171–90.

Pelling, Christopher, ed. *Individuality and Characterization in Greek Literature*. Oxford: Oxford University Press, 1990.

Penner, Terry. "The Unity of Virtue." *Philosophical Review* 82 (1973): 35–68.

———. "Desire and Power in Socrates." *Apeiron* 24 (1991): 147–202.

———. "What Laches and Nicias Miss—and Whether Socrates Thinks Courage is Merely a Part of Virtue." *Ancient Philosophy* 12 (1992): 1–27.

———. "Knowledge versus True Belief in the Socratic Psychology of Action." *Apeiron* 29 (1996): 199–230.

———. "Socrates on the Strength of Knowledge: *Protagoras* 351B–357E." *Archiv für Geschichte der Philosophie* 79 (1997): 117–49.

Penner, Terry, and Christopher J. Rowe. "The Desire for Good: Is the *Meno* Inconsistent with the *Gorgias?*" *Phronesis* 39 (1994): 1–25.

Platts, Mark. *Ways of Meaning*. Cambridge, Mass.: MIT Press, 1997.

Polansky, Ronald M. "Professor Vlastos' Analysis of Socratic Elenchus." *Oxford Studies in Ancient Philosophy* 3 (1985): 247–59.

Press, Gerald. *Plato's Dialogues: New Studies and Interpretations*. Lanham, Md.: Rowman and Littlefield, 1993.

———. "The State of the Question in the Study of Plato's *Dialogues*." *Southern Journal of Philosophy* 34 (1996): 507–32.

Prior, William. "Plato and the 'Socratic Fallacy.' " *Phronesis* 43 (1998): 97–113.

———. "Socrates Metaphysician." *Oxford Studies in Ancient Philosophy* 27 (2004): 1–14.

Puster, Rolf F. *Zur Argumentationsstruktur platonischer Dialoge*. Freiburg: K. Alber, 1983.

Quine, W. O. *Word and Object*. Cambridge, Mass.: MIT Press, 1960.

Reeve, C. D. C. *Socrates in the Apology*. Indianapolis: Hackett, 1989.

Rescher, N. "Reductio ad absurdum." *The Internet Encyclopedia of Philosophy*. Online. Available: http://www.iep.utm.edu/r/reductio/htm. 2006.

Reshotko, Naomi. "The Socratic Theory of Motivation." *Apeiron* 25 (1993): 145–70.

———. "Plato's *Lysis*: A Socratic Treatise on Desire and Attraction." *Apeiron* 30 (1997): 1–18.

———. "The Good, the Bad, and the Neither Good nor Bad in Plato's *Lysis*." *Southern Journal of Philosophy* 38 (2000): 251–62.

Reshotko, Naomi. "Virtue as the Only Unconditional—But Not Intrinsic—Good: Plato's *Euthydemus* 278e3–281e5." *Ancient Philosophy* 21 (2001): 325–34.

Ribbeck, Otto. "Über den Begriff des Eiron." *Rheinisches Museum* 31 (1876): 381–400.

Richardson, Henry. "Measurement, Pleasure, and Practical Science in Plato's *Protagoras*." *Journal of the History of Philosophy* 28 (1990): 7–32.

Richardson, N. J. "Homeric Professors in the Age of the Sophists." *Proceedings of the Cambridge Philological Society* 201 (1975): 65–81.

Roberts, Jennifer. "Aristocratic Democracy: The Perseverance of Timocratic Principles in Athenian Government." *Athenaeum* 64 (1986): 355–69.

Robinson, David B. "Plato's *Lysis*: The Structural Problem." *Illinois Classical Studies* 11 (1986): 63–86.

Robinson, Richard. "Analysis in Greek Geometry." *Mind* 46 (1935): 464–73.

———. *Plato's Earlier Dialectic*. Oxford: Clarendon Press, 1941.

Roochnik, David. "Plato's Use of the Techne-Analogy." *Journal of the History of Philosophy* 24 (1986): 295–310.

———. *Of Art and Wisdom*. University Park: Pennsylvania State University Press, 1996.

Rose, Lynn E. "A Note on the *Euthyphro* 10–11." *Phronesis* 10 (1965): 149–50.

———. "Plato's *Meno* 86–89." *Journal of the History of Philosophy* 8 (1970): 1–8.

Ross, Sir David. *Plato's Theory of Ideas*. Oxford: Clarendon Press, 1951.

Roth, Michael D. "Did Plato Nod? Some Conjectures on Egoism and Friendship in the *Lysis*." *Archiv für Geschichte der Philosophie* 77 (1995): 1–20.

Rowe, Christopher. "Explanation in *Phaedo* 99c6–102a8." *Oxford Studies in Ancient Philosophy* 11 (1993): 49–69.

Rudebusch, George. "The Righteous Are Happy." *History of Philosophy Quarterly* 15 (1998): 143–60.

———. *Socrates, Pleasure, and Value*. New York: Oxford University Press, 1999.

Russell, Daniel C. "Protagoras and Socrates on Courage and Pleasure: *Protagoras* 349d *ad finem*." *Ancient Philosophy* 20 (2000): 311–38.

Rutherford, R. B. *The Art of Plato*. London: Duckworth, 1995.

Ryle, Gilbert. *Plato's Progress*. Cambridge: Cambridge University Press, 1966.

Salkever, Stephen G. "Plato on Practices: The *Technai* and the Socratic Question in *Republic* 1." *Proceedings of the Boston Area Colloquium in Ancient Philosophy* 8 (1992): 243–67.

Santas, Gerasimos Xenophon. "The Socratic Paradoxes." *Philosophical Review* 73 (1964): 147–64.

———. "Plato's *Protagoras* and Explanations of Weakness." *Philosophical Review* 75 (1966): 3–33; reprinted in Santas (1979): 195–217; 318–23.

———. "The Socratic Fallacy." *Journal of the History of Philosophy* 10 (1972): 124–41.

———. "Socrates at Work on Virtue and Knowledge in Plato's *Charmides*." In *Exegesis and Argument*, eds. Lee et al., 105–32. Assen: van Gorcum, 1973.

———. *Socrates: Philosophy in Plato's Early Dialogues*. New York: Routledge and Kegan Paul, 1979.

———. "Socratic Goods and Socratic Happiness." *Apeiron* 26 (1993): 37–52.

———. *Goodness and Justice*. New York: Blackwell, 2001.

Saunders, Trevor J. *Early Socratic Dialogues*. London: Penguin, 1987.

Sauppe, H. *Platons ausgewählte Dialoge*. Bd. 2. Berlin, 1884.

Savan, David. "Self-Predication in *Protagoras* 330–331." *Phronesis* 9 (1964): 130–35.

Sayers, Kenneth. *Plato's Literary Garden*. Notre Dame, Ind.: University of Notre Dame Press, 1995.

Scaltsas, Theodore. "Socratic Moral Realism: An Alternative Justification." *Oxford Studies in Ancient Philosophy* 7 (1989): 129–50.

Schanz, M. *Platonis opera quae feruntur omnia.* Bd. 7. Leipzig, 1873.

Schleiermacher, F. D. *Platons Werke.* Bd. 1. Berlin, 1804.

Schmid, W. Thomas. *Plato's Charmides and the Socratic Ideal of Rationality.* Albany, N.Y.: SUNY Press, 1998.

Schofield, Malcolm. "Ariston of Chios and the Unity of Virtue." *Ancient Philosophy* 4 (1984): 83–96.

Scott, Gary Alan, ed. *Does Socrates Have a Method?* University Park: Pennsylvania State University Press, 2002.

Sedley, David. "Is the *Lysis* a Dialogue of Definition?" *Phronesis* 34 (1989): 211–4.

———. "Platonic Causes." *Phronesis* 43 (1998): 114–32.

Segvic, Heda. "No One Errs Willingly: The Meaning of Socratic Intellectualism." *Oxford Studies in Ancient Philosophy* 19 (2000): 1–45.

Sellars, Wilfred. "Vlastos and the 'Third Man.'" *Philosophical Review* 64 (1955): 405–37.

Senn, Scott. "Virtue as the Sole Intrinsic Good in Plato's Early Dialogues." *Oxford Studies in Ancient Philosophy* 28 (2005): 1–21.

Sesonske, A. "Hedonism in the *Protagoras.*" *Journal of the History of Philosophy* 1 (1963): 73–9.

Sharples, R. W. *Plato: Meno.* London: Aris and Phillips, 1985.

Sharvy, Richard. "Euthyphro 9d–11b: Analysis and Definition in Plato and Others." *Nous* 6 (1972): 119–37.

Shorey, Paul. *The Unity of Plato's Thought.* Chicago: University of Chicago Press, 1903.

———. *Plato: Republic 1.* Cambridge, Mass.: Harvard University Press, 1930.

———. *What Plato Said.* Chicago: University of Chicago Press, 1933.

Silk, Michael. *Interaction in Poetic Imagery.* Cambridge: Cambridge University Press, 1974.

———. "The People of Aristophanes." In Pelling (1990): 150–73.

Slezáck, Thomas. *Platon und die Schriftlichkeit der Philosophie.* Berlin: de Gruyter, 1985.

Smith, Angela M. "Knowledge and Expertise in the Early Platonic Dialogues." *Archiv für Geschichte der Philosophie* 80 (1998): 129–61.

Smith Pangle, Lorraine. "Friendship and Human Neediness in Plato's *Lysis.*" *Ancient Philosophy* 21 (2001): 305–23.

Socher, Josef. *Über Platons Schriften.* Münich, 1820.

Souilhé, Joseph. *Étude sur le terme δύναμις dans les dialogues de platon.* Paris: F. Alcan, 1919; reprinted in *Greek and Roman Philosophy: A Fifty-Two Volume Reprint Set*, ed. Táran. Vol. 36. New York: Garland, 1987.

Sparshott, F. E. "Socrates and Thrasymachus." *Monist* 50 (1966): 421–59.

Stenzel, Julius. *Platon der Erzieher.*Leipzig: F. Meiner, 1928.

Stern, Cindy. "On the Alleged Extensionality of 'Causal Explanatory Contexts.'" *Philosophy of Science* 45 (1978): 614–25.

Stern, J. *On Realism.* London: Routledge and Kegan Paul, 1973.

Sternfeld, R., and Zyskind, H. "Plato's *Meno* 89c: 'Virtue is Knowledge' A Hypothesis?" *Phronesis* 21 (1976): 130–4.

———. "Plato's *Meno*: 86E–87A: Geometrical Illustration of the Argument by Hypothesis." *Phronesis* 22 (1977): 206–11.

Stokes, Michael. *Plato's Socratic Conversations.* Baltimore, Md.: Johns Hopkins University Press, 1986.

Stokes, J. L. "The Argument of Plato, *Protagoras* 351b–356c." *Classical Quarterly* 7 (1913): 100–104.

Stough, Charlotte. "Forms and Explanation in the *Phaedo.*" *Phronesis* 21 (1976): 1–30.

Strauss, Barry. *Fathers and Sons in Athens*. Princeton, N.J.: Princeton University Press, 1993.

Strauss, Leo. *Persecution and the Art of Writing*. Chicago: University of Chicago Press, 1953.

Sullivan, J. P. "The Hedonism in Plato's *Protagoras*." *Phronesis* 6 (1961): 10–28.

Szabó, Árpád. *The Beginnings of Greek Mathematics*. Boston: D. Reidel, 1978.

Tarrant, Dorothy. *The Hippias Major*. Cambridge: Cambridge University Press, 1928.

———. "The Pseudo-Platonic Socrates." *Classical Quarterly* 32 (1938): 167–73.

Tarrant, Harold. "*Elenchos* and *Exetasis*: Capturing the Purpose of Socratic Interrogation." In Scott (2002): 61–77.

Taylor, C. C. W. *Plato: Protagoras*. Oxford: Clarendon Press, 1976; revised 1990.

———. "Forms as Causes in the *Phaedo*." *Mind* 78 (1969): 45–59.

Taylor, Kenneth. *Truth and Meaning*. New York: Oxford University Press, 1998.

Teloh, Henry. "Self-Predication or Anaxagorean Causation in Plato." *Apeiron* 9 (1975): 15–23.

———. *The Development of Plato's Metaphysics*. University Park: Pennsylvania State University Press, 1981.

Tenneman, G. W. *Geschichte und System der platonischen Philosophie*. Leipzig, 1792–94.

Tessitore, Aristide. "Plato's *Lysis*: An Introduction to Philosophical Friendship." *Southern Journal of Philosophy* 28 (1990): 115–32.

Thesleff, Holger. *Studies in Platonic Chronology*. Helsinki: Societas Scientarum Fennica, 1982.

———. "Platonic Chronology." *Phronesis* 34 (1989): 1–26.

Thom, Paul. "*Euthyphro* 9D–11B." *Philosophical Inquiry* 1 (1978): 65–70.

Thomas, John E. *Musings on the Meno*. Boston: Martinus Nijhoff, 1980.

Tigerstedt, Eugene Napoleon. *The Decline and Fall of the Neoplatonic Interpretation of Plato*. Helsinki: Societas Scientarum Fennica, 1974.

———. *Interpreting Plato*. Stockholm: Almqvist & Wiksell International, 1977.

Tindale, Christopher W. "Plato's *Lysis*: A Reconsideration." *Apeiron* 17 (1984): 102–9.

Tuckey, Richard. *Plato's Charmides*. Cambridge: Cambridge University Press, 1951.

van der Ben, N. *The Charmides of Plato: Problems and Interpretations*. Amsterdam: Grüner, 1985.

Vasiliou, Iakovos. "Conditional Irony in the Socratic Dialogues." *Classical Quarterly* 49 (1998): 456–72.

———. "Socrates' Reverse Irony." *Classical Quarterly* 52 (2002): 220–30.

Vendler, Zeno. "The Grammar of Goodness." *Philosophical Review* 72 (1963): 446–65.

Versenyi, Laszlo. "Plato's *Lysis*." *Phronesis* 20 (1975): 185–98.

Vlastos, Gregory. "The Third Man Argument in the *Parmenides*." *Philosophical Review* 63 (1954): 319–49.

———. "Socrates on Acrasia." *Phoenix* 23 (1969): 71–88.

———. "Reasons and Causes in the *Phaedo*." *Philosophical Review* 78 (1969): 291–35; reprinted in Vlastos (1981): 76–110.

———. "The Unity of the Virtues in the *Protagoras*." *Review of Metaphysics* 25 (1972): 415–48; reprinted with notes and appendix in Vlastos (1981): 221–65, 266–69, 427–45.

———. *Platonic Studies*. Princeton, N.J.: Princeton University Press, 1981.

———. "The Socratic Elenchus." *Oxford Studies in Ancient Philosophy* 1 (1983): 27–58.

———. *Socrates: Ironist and Moral Philosopher*. Ithaca, N.Y.: Cornell University Press, 1991.

———. *Socratic Studies*. Cambridge: Cambridge University Press, 1994.

Wakefield, Jerome C. "Why Justice and Holiness are Similar: *Protagoras* 330–331." *Phronesis* 32 (1987): 267–76.

———. "Vlastos on the Unity of Virtue: Why Pauline Predication Will Not Save the Biconditionality Thesis." *Ancient Philosophy* 11 (1991): 47–65.

Weiss, Roslyn. "'Ο Ἀγαθός as 'Ο Δυνατός in the *Hippias Minor*." *Classical Quarterly* 31 (1981): 287–304.

———. "Courage, Confidence, and Wisdom in the *Protagoras*." *Ancient Philosophy* 5 (1985): 11–39.

Weiss, Roslyn. "Hedonism in the *Protagoras* and the Sophist's Guarantee." *Ancient Philosophy* 10 (1990): 17–39.

———. *Virtue in the Cave*. New York: Oxford University Press, 2001.

Welleck, R. "The Concept of Realism in Literary Scholarship." *Neophilologus* 45 (1961): 1–20.

White, Nicholas. *Individual and Conflict in Greek Ethics*. Oxford: Oxford University Press, 2002.

Whitehead, D. "Competitive Outlay and Community Profit: Φιλοτιμία in Democratic Athens." *Classica et Mediaevalia* 34 (1983): 55–74.

Wolfsdorf, David. "Aporia in Plato's *Charmides*, *Laches*, and *Lysis*." Ph.D. diss., University of Chicago, 1997.

———. "The Dramatic Date of Plato's *Protagoras*." *Rheinisches Museum für Philologie* 140 (1997): 223–30.

———. "The Historical Reader of Plato's *Protagoras*." *Classical Quarterly* 48 (1998): 126–33.

———. "Plato and the Mouthpiece Theory." *Ancient Philosophy* 19 (1999): 13–24.

———. "Δικαιοσύνη and Ὁσιότης at *Protagoras* 330–1." *Apeiron* 35 (2002): 181–210.

———. "Socrates' Pursuit of Definitions." *Phronesis* 48 (2003a): 271–312.

———. "Understanding the 'What-is-F?' Question." *Apeiron* 36 (2003b): 175–88.

———. "Comments on Benson: 'Socrates' Method of Hypothesis in *Meno*.'" *Proceedings of the Boston Area Colloquium in Ancient Philosophy* 18 (2003c): 127–43.

———. "Interpreting Plato's Early Dialogues." *Oxford Studies in Ancient Philosophy* 27 (2004a): 15–41.

———. "Socrates' Avowals of Knowledge." *Phronesis* 49 (2004b): 74–142.

———. "The Socratic Fallacy and the Epistemological Priority of Definitional Knowledge." *Apeiron* 37 (2004c): 35–67.

———. "*Euthyphro* 10a2–11b1: A Study in Platonic Metaphysics and its Reception Since 1960." *Apeiron* 38 (2005a): 1–72.

———. "Αἴτιον and Αἰτία in Plato." *Ancient Philosophy* 25 (2005b): 341–9.

———. "Δύναμις in *Laches*." *Phoenix* 59 (2005c): 324–47.

———. "Desire for Good in *Meno* 77B2–78B6." *Classical Quarterly* 56 (2006a): 77–92.

———. "Daniel C. Russell, *Plato on Pleasure and the Good Life*, Oxford University Press, 2005." *Notre Dame Philosophical Reviews*. Online. Available: http://ndpr.nd.edu. 2006.

———. "*Hippias Major* 301b2–c2: Plato's Critique of a Corporeal Conception of Forms and the Form-Participant Relation." *Apeiron* 39 (2006c): 221–56.

———. "The Ridiculousness of Being Overcome by Pleasure: *Protagoras* 352b1–358d4." *Oxford Studies in Ancient Philosophy* 31 (2006d): 113–36.

———. "Courage and Knowledge at *Protagoras* 349E1–351B2." *Classical Quarterly* 56 (2006e): 436–44.

———. "The Irony of Socrates:." *Journal of Aesthetics and Art Criticism* 65 (2007): 175–87.

———. "Φιλία in Plato's *Lysis*." *Harvard Studies in Classical Philology*, forthcoming, 2008a.

———. "Rhetoric's Inadequate Means: *Gorgias* 466a4–468e5." *Classical Philology*, forthcoming, 2008b.

———. "The Method ἐξ ὑποθέσεως at *Meno* 86e1–87d8." *Phronesis*, forthcoming, 2008c.

———. "Hesiod, Prodicus, and the Socratics on Work and Pleasure." *Oxford Studies in Ancient Philosophy*, forthcoming, 2008d.

Wolpert, Andrew. *Remembering Defeat*. Baltimore, Md.: Johns Hopkins University Press, 2002.

Wolz, H. G. "Hedonism in the *Protagoras*." *Journal of the History of Philosophy* 5 (1967): 205–17.

Woodruff, Paul. "Socrates on the Parts of Virtue." *Canadian Journal of Philosophy* (1976): 101–16.

———. "The Socratic Approach to Semantic Incompleteness." *Philosophy and Phenomenological Research* 38 (1978): 453–68.

———. "Socrates and Ontology: The Evidence of the *Hippias Major*." *Phronesis* 23 (1978): 101–17.

———. "Plato's Early Theory of Knowledge." In *Ancient Greek Epistemology*, ed. Everson, 60–84. Cambridge: Cambridge University Press, 1990.

———. *Plato's Hippias Major*. Indianapolis: Hackett, 1982.

Woolf, Raphael. "Consistency and *Akrasia* in Plato's *Protagoras*." *Phronesis* 47 (2002): 224–52.

Young, C. "Plato and Computer Dating." *Oxford Studies in Ancient Philosophy* 12 (1994): 227–50.

Zeller, Eduard. *Die Philosophie der Griechen*. Bd. 2. Berlin, 1839.

Zeyl, Donald J. "Socrates and Hedonism: *Protagoras* 351b–358d." *Phronesis* 25 (1980): 250–69.

———. "Socratic Virtue and Happiness." *Archiv für Geschichte der Philosophie* 64 (1982): 225–38.

Ziff, Paul. *Semantic Analysis*. Ithaca, N.Y.: Cornell University Press, 1960.

INDEX OF PASSAGES CITED

GENERAL INDEX

Academica, Cicero's, 5
aetiology
    causation of like to like, 62
    dunamis-ergon, 111
    epistemological, 147–8, 181–5, 196
    versus *physiology*, 42–3, 182, n.75
aitia. See *aetiology*
akrasia, 51–9, 90–2, 113–4
anachronism, 17, 219
Antiochus of Ascalon, 5
antiphilosophy, 13, 14, 20, 234–9
    See also *philosophia*
application of areas, 167–8
aporia
    dramatic, 198, 201–10, 238
    epistemological, 197
aretê
    definition of, 9
    conventional and traditional conceptions of, 74–5, 82
a-structure, 15, 16, 21, 30, 143, 207,
    251–2, 255
Arcesilaus, 5
belonging (*oikeion*), 66–8
    natural, 70, 72, n.131
boulêsis, versus *epithumia*, 32
Benson, Hugh H., 111, n.68, 135–6,
    178, n.68

Beversluis, J., 136–7
Brickhouse, Thomas, and Smith, Nicholas,
    9, 20, 95, 213, n.21, 220, n.48, 250
Brucker, Jacob, 5
causation. See *aetiology*
Carneades, 5
Carter, L. B., 216
Chen, Chun-Hwan, 226
cognitive security, 179–81, 192–6
Contra Academicos, Augustine's, 5
Cook Wilson, interpretation of geometrical
    problem in *Meno*, 164–9, 172
Cornford, F. M., 102
Dancy, R. M., 4
desire
    de dicto, 34, n.20
    deficiency conception of, 65, 72
    de re, 34, n.20
    Empedocles' conception of, 65, 66
    extrinsic, 46
    instrumental, 46
    intrinsic, 46
    irrational, 49–51
    neoplatonic, 31, 239
    object-oriented, 63, 72
    rational, 49–51
    subjectivist, 32, 72
    terminal, 46